Learning to Care

Learning to Care

Elementary Kindness in an Age of Indifference

ROBERT WUTHNOW

New York   Oxford
OXFORD UNIVERSITY PRESS
1995

Oxford University Press

Oxford   New York
Athens   Auckland   Bangkok
Calcutta   Cape Town   Dar es Salaam   Delhi
Florence   Hong Kong   Istanbul   Karachi
Kuala Lumpur   Madras   Madrid   Melbourne
Mexico City   Nairobi   Paris   Singapore
Taipei   Tokyo   Toronto
and associated companies in
Berlin   Ibadan

Copyright © 1995 by Robert Wuthnow

Published by Oxford University Press, Inc.
198 Madison Avenue, New York, New York 10016

Oxford is a registered trademark of Oxford University Press, Inc.

Library of Congress Cataloging-in-Publication Data
Wuthnow, Robert.
Learning to care :
elementary kindness in an age of indifference /
Robert Wuthnow.
p.   cm.   Includes index.
ISBN 0-19-509881-1
1. Voluntarism—United States.
2. Teenage volunteers in social service—United States.
3. Moral development—United States.
4. Caring.
5. Helping behavior.
I. Title.
HN90.V64W89   1996   649'.7—dc20   94-46878

1 3 5 7 9 8 6 4 2

Printed in the United States of America
on acid-free paper

Preface

When I was eight years old, something happened to me that would forever shape my view of kindness. It was customary in those days, especially in small towns in the Midwest, for children to be sent to Vacation Bible School at the end of the regular school year. In that way parents could enjoy one more quiet week before we hellions were released to the neighborhood for the summer. Not growing up in, but near, one of these small towns, I was thus sitting in the basement of the Baptist church, coloring my picture of Noah's ark, when Mrs. Pulliam strode in.

The Pulliam children were younger than I was: two girls and a boy, all in the little kids' class on the other side of the divider, and a baby still at home. I could tell by the way Mrs. Pulliam stormed in that she was mad about something. She called out before she was even down the stairs, demanding to see the preacher.

He had tried hard to be nice to her, inviting the kids to church and visiting her husband every week in jail that whole long winter. She was sort of his community project. I knew how bad it was for her.

We were poor, too. My father had come home from the war with next to nothing. He hadn't been able to save anything during the Depression, not even enough to get married on. Only the threat of being shipped overseas had finally forced him to the altar. Five years later, with a wife and child to support, he had taken the little that was left when they buried his father and bought a farm. It was mostly bindweed; the soil too hard to grow much else. My father put indoor plumbing and electricity in the house himself. It stood there on the prairie, unpainted, only one room with heat, and oilcloth tacked over the windows, waiting for some tamarack to grow up and keep the wind from blowing it away.

But Mrs. Pulliam was *really* poor. That time we went over from the church to sing Christmas carols, I'd seen it. Boards were rotted clear through on the front porch. Inside there was one big room kept barely above freezing by an old potbellied wood-burning stove. Several of the windows had rags and newspapers stuffed in where the panes used to be. Large sections of plaster had given way, exposing the laths beneath, and one part of the ceiling had caved in completely.

There'd never been any indoor plumbing, and judging from the smell, the privy out back was too far for the children to make it through the snow. They slept on two badly stained mattresses at the edge of the room.

I'd never heard anybody swear in church before, but that's what Mrs. Pulliam did, right to the preacher's face, and so loud we all could hear. I wished I could see his face. It was a good thing the partition was there, though, because we all were scared of what she might do next. We weren't used to mothers who used naughty words and didn't have their hair combed just right when they went out in public.

The preacher had just been trying to help, and it wasn't even his fault. It must have been one of the church ladies that morning who decided it was time to do something about the lice. I guess she was afraid the lice would get on the rest of us, and then there'd be hell to pay. And of course there was, but it was because Susie had run home crying when the soap got in her eyes and told her mother what had happened.

I'm sure Pastor Chuck was as surprised as anyone when Mrs. Pulliam came rushing in. He was barely out of high school, preaching only so that he could have a place to live while he went to college. In a community like that, everyone just expected you'd help out. For instance, we all got together, even us kids, one Saturday and painted the baptistry to keep it from rusting out. My dad used to drive around the township, pulling into neighbors' muddy driveways, waiting until they called off the dogs, to raise money for poor relief. One night, after he got sick again, a neighbor came over after dark and finished plowing his field. Helping out was just the thing to do.

So I felt sorry for Pastor Chuck standing there, trying to remember to turn the other cheek while Mrs. Pulliam yelled indignities in his ear. And I was glad when she took Susie by the hand, and said we'd never see her face in this place again.

But somehow, deeper down, I also thought maybe we had done something wrong. I'm not sure why I felt that way. Maybe it was because I'd seen the sadness in my father's eyes that night when the neighbor plowed his field. I don't think it was pride or some noble desire for self-sufficiency that made him sad. Neighbors helped one another all the time, chasing cows back to pasture when a fence broke and coming over to pull out a pickup that got stuck in the mud. Instead, I think the sadness came from knowing that this particular neighbor had risen above all that. Buying land dirt cheap at foreclosure auctions during the Depression and now, finding oil on some of it, had made him a wealthy man. Generous as he was and kindhearted to his neighbors, he no longer needed them, and so there was no way for them to pay him back. Kindness was now somehow different, depending more on what you had than on who you were. Our neighbor could perform random acts of kindness, sending out some of his machinery and hired men, without these acts reflecting on his character. He was no longer part of a community that could determine whether he was a person of virtue.

I think this—more than the soap in Susie's eyes—was why we were wrong in what we did for Mrs. Pulliam, too. In her mind, I'm sure, we were a community that didn't need her help at all. She was as far below us on the social scale as my father was below his wealthy neighbor. Mrs. Pulliam would always be an outsider, a person without virtue who was impossible for us to understand or appreciate. For us, living in the taken-for-granted world of our families and our faith, good behavior was easy to define. We would never have dreamed of coming to church dirty, and to us, it was an act of kindness to make sure that nobody else did either. As that community began to break up—pressured by the forces that made some very rich and others very poor—it became harder to know what helping meant. In the future, we would have to think more deeply about who we were and about who we wanted to be.

Every one of us in that church basement had learned to recite by memory the verse that counseled, "Be ye kind one to another." We knew it was our Christian duty to help the Pulliams. If we'd thought about it, we'd probably have said that helping her was a way to please God, just as it was to receive the little gold stars each week for memorizing our verses. What we didn't realize is that kindness involves a lot more than just doing good deeds.

Only much later, indeed, in the last few years, as I have pondered again what it means to care—listening to teenagers tell their experiences—has it again occurred to me how significant that event with Mrs. Pulliam was. Caring was something we all cherished, a value instilled in us so deeply that we took it for granted, even as eight-year-olds. But it was also something that needed to mature as we faced new situations. Learning to care was not so much a matter of learning it from scratch but of reconfiguring it to be of value in the more complex worlds we would inhabit as adults.

Most of us, I think, do learn about caring and kindness while we are children. We learn what it means to care by being cared for. Our mothers and fathers, our grandparents, and our aunts and uncles or older siblings—perhaps our Sunday school teachers—all show us the meaning of kindness. It feels good and makes us want to help others, too. Then, however, we begin to feel the pressures of growing up and playing roles in our institutions, and the warmth and understanding of our families start to be replaced by impersonal and specialized expectations. We long to go back, to rediscover ways to be cared for and to care, and we find small ways to be kind in our families and among our friends, but it is harder for us to carry this behavior into our work, our communities, and our thinking about economic, political, and social issues.

This difficult transition is why late adolescence and early adulthood are the crucial years. Developing a mature understanding of kindness is not so much a matter of accomplishing some psychological task as it is of bridging the gap between the primordial experiences of our families and the roles we must learn to play in our social institutions. Many of us fail to make that transition successfully. We still think of ourselves as caring people but wake up years later with the realization that there is very little evidence of caring in the work we do, in how we vote, in how we spend our money, or in our relationships with our communities.

Volunteering is one of the best ways in which to make the transition from primary caring to institutional kindness. It can preserve the personal touch that makes caring an emotionally enriching experience while communicating the value of working with others, of being trained, and of doing small deeds that add up to significant contributions. But volunteer work must be properly guided in order for it to serve these purposes. People must have role models to help them make the transition from one kind of caring to another. They must have frameworks and motives that help them make sense of what they are doing. And they must be encouraged to think about the relationships between their volunteering and their careers, their futures, and the society in which they live.

By volunteering, young people are given a way of examining the process by which learning to care takes place. And by listening to them talk about their experiences, we can discover what is helpful and where the potential dangers may lie. Young people are now widely encouraged to do some kind of community service, as it can alleviate not only some of the specific problems in our society but also the need to communicate the nature of elementary kindness. My hope is that this book will contribute to that process.

My profound appreciation goes to the scores of teenagers and adults who gave freely of their time, not only to be interviewed, but also to be of service to their communities, to show compassion to their neighbors, and thereby to learn at first hand the meaning of caring. I wish it were possible for me to identify them all by name both here and in the text. As is customary in social research, however, my agreement with them was that they would remain anonymous. In that way they would feel more at liberty to speak candidly, and many of them did indeed talk with exceptional candor. They will, of course, recognize themselves from the descriptions I have given of their activities and from my quotations from their interviews.

It would not have been possible for me to conduct this research without the generous assistance provided through grants from the W. K. Kellogg Foundation and the Lilly Endowment. Virginia Hodgkinson and Brian O'Connell graciously permitted me to use the resources of Independent Sector, Inc., in Washington,

D.C., for administrative purposes and made available the data from two national surveys concerned with volunteering, giving, and the various values and attitudes surrounding these activities. I am especially grateful to Virginia Hodgkinson for inviting me to serve on the national advisory committee that oversaw these surveys and for giving me the opportunity to include a number of questions of my own design and from my previous research on compassion. I owe special thanks to Elizabeth T. Boris, Emmett D. Carson, E. Gil Clary, Harry Cotugno, Robert O'Connor, Paul G. Shervish, Ervin Staub, Nathan Weber, and Julian Wolpert for their service on the advisory committee and to Murray S. Weitzman, Stephen M. Noga, and Heather A. Gorski for their work on the surveys.

My own analysis of these surveys and several other national surveys that form the basis for the quantitative conclusions presented in the book was facilitated by the programming assistance provided by Timothy Clydesdale and John Schmalzbauer. The field research on and interviews with the teen volunteers was conducted by Natalie Searl. I also benefited from interviews with adults conducted by Heather Behn, Elaine Friedman, Roberta Rusciano, John Schmalzbauer, Tracy Scott, Natalie Searl, and Yvonne Veugelers.

Many guidance counselors, members of the clergy, and heads of national and local community service agencies also contributed immeasurably by providing comments, reports, newspaper clippings, and suggestions of people to talk to. John Sutton served as the chief adviser and evaluator for the Kellogg component of the project. The students in my senior seminar on individualism and altruism contributed many insights that helped formulate my research. I appreciate the assistance of Sue Ann Steffy Morrow of Princeton University's Office of the Chapel for her participation in the seminar and her cooperation in arranging field opportunities through Princeton's Student Volunteer Council and the support of the University Center for Human Values, headed by Amy Gutmann, for its sponsorship of the course. I also appreciate the opportunity offered to me by Sam Hill to lecture to and interact with students at the University of Florida on some of the topics of the book. Finally, I owe special thanks to my wife Sally and my children Robyn, Brooke, and Joel for their interest in caring and for the caring and love that I have received from them.

Princeton, N.J.   R. W.
June 1995

Contents

Learning to Care

1

Pearl's Kitchen

Jason McKendrick crawled wearily into the back of the van. He wanted just a moment to be alone with his thoughts. It had been such a long evening, though not so different from the others. The sounds and the smells and the faces still crowded in front of his eyes.

That old man with the purple pillow case. Mary, poor Mary, hmmm, always a smile. The new guy (or had he been there before?), shy at first. But yeah, he brightened up. So many tonight, probably more than a hundred. Well, but it's cold. Freezing out here. That always brings them in. Liquor. Keeps you warm. The stench. Never will get used to it. Megan. Glad she came along. She's cute, smart, could be a model.

Eyes shut, head resting at an awkward angle against the vinyl seatback, Jason sat there for another minute. It felt good just musing like this. It was like having a butterscotch lifesaver. You could pop two or three in your mouth at once and swish them around with your tongue until they were all gone.

"Helper high?"

"What?" It was Freddie, climbing in beside him. "Oh yes, I guess so," Jason responded. Freddie was only a junior, but he was one of the faithfuls. Usually he was the most talkative one of the group, but right now he seemed subdued.

Helper high. Funny phrase. Who came up with that, anyway? Don't remember anymore. But yeah, that's what it is. You just feel really good afterward, at least for a few moments. We've all talked about it. You come out after a long evening. You're exhausted, but the adrenaline is still pumping. You're all sitting here in the van. Freddie, me, Susie, Roger, sometimes Nikki. You just sit there. You don't say anything. You're all just savoring how you feel at that moment. Was that why he did it? Jason wondered.

They were moving now, still on the old cobblestone paving that followed Franklin out from center city to Pine. Then they would take the bypass and fifteen minutes later arrive safely back in the suburbs. What a contrast it always was. The comfortable houses with their well-manicured lawns, some of them right out of *Better Homes and Gardens*. Oh, yes—Where was it?—down the street a few blocks. Some camera crew had just been out taking pictures the other day. Light snow still covered the lawns and bushes. Inside, fireplaces were ablaze. Families were turning up their electric blankets and getting ready for bed.

It was different at Pearl's Kitchen. No warm couches to lounge on. No hummingbirds in the spring. Jason could not remember exactly why they called it that. Pearl, he thought, had started it back in the 1970s. She and a friend just started going around collecting food and handing it out. There never had been an actual kitchen; it was just a place to pick up the food. Next door there was a shelter for the women and children. The men still lived on the street. Every evening there would be casseroles. Drinks, too. Some came from restaurants and hotels. Some came from churches and synagogues. People like Jason came to Pearl's Kitchen and picked up the food. Their first stop would be the park a few blocks away. Then city hall. Then another park. At each location people would already be lined up waiting. Afterward, the van returned to Pearl's. The helpers then became pot scrubbers, getting everything ready for the next day.

This was Jason's fourth year. He started coming to Pearl's Kitchen as a freshman. A senior girl in his high school, a real "mover and shaker," had gotten him involved. After she graduated, Jason took over the leadership. Usually there are at least seven volunteers, sometimes as many as ten. They come every Thursday evening, leave at six, and get home after ten. Jason spends at least two more hours each week making arrangements and soliciting volunteers.

He always looks forward to the lively conversations driving back and forth in the van. Each year the group is different. But he gets to know them well. It kind of makes him feel warm. He guesses that is it. Or maybe he's just not out in the cold. More connected. He enjoys meeting the helpers that come from other places, too. Like Megan. He wanted to know her better.

Megan Wyse comes to Pearl's Kitchen from another part of the city. Her neighborhood is comfortable, but the houses are much more modest than in Jason's community. Generally she comes on Monday nights, but sometimes she comes on other nights just to meet other volunteers. This is her second year. When she moved to the East Coast three years ago, she felt it was time to learn about the real world. Growing up in a midwestern suburb, she had never seen people sleeping in the streets. Now they seemed to be everywhere. It bothers her that she can do so little. Many of these homeless people are Vietnam veterans who are still recovering emotionally from the war. Some of them had lost their jobs because of the recession. Some are drug addicts or alcoholics. Megan knows there is little she can do to help the men sober up or find them jobs, but she feels she can still make a small difference in their lives. "We really are there just to make them feel good," she explains, "to give them hope, to make them a good dinner. We bake them fresh cookies. It's a really nice experience."

Megan, too, became involved through her school, a private academy called Hebrew Day School, which encourages students to do some kind of community service. Megan makes good grades, enjoys biology and history, listens to music, has a boyfriend, babysits for one of the neighbors, and still has time to be involved in several of the clubs at school. Last year the Social Action Club organized a committee to address the needs of the homeless. None of the students had done this kind of thing before, and in retrospect, they say they were probably a little naive. Megan recalls that they just went walking through back alleys, found homeless people, and tried to help them with whatever problems they might have, for example, with tracking down Social Security checks, getting a shower, or just having somebody to talk to. But it soon became clear that wandering in back alleys was dangerous. So the club eventually called the Salvation Army—for want of a better source—which put them in touch with Pearl's Kitchen. The club now sends several volunteers at least one night a week to help prepare casseroles, wash dishes, and help clean the shelter next door.

Helping at Pearl's has been a rewarding experience for Megan. She tells about one encounter that was particularly meaningful: "There was this one man—his name was Sam—who lived there last year, an elderly man. He always told me stories about the Bible and from other things he'd read, like *War and Peace* and Shakespeare. We would just talk. We talked about colleges. This is when I was trying to explore my different college options. We had this big musical that I was in last year. So we invited him and his sister, who lives at a different shelter, to come to the play. It was so nice. We went to pick them up. He got all dressed, he was all excited. He came to this musical and loved it. Afterward he was in the hospital. He got really sick. He had pneumonia. So a friend and I went to the hospital to visit him. He really appreciated it, because he didn't have family that would come visit him. He told us he understands that we don't have to be doing what we're doing, and he really appreciates the fact that people are there to care for him. He just gave us a lot of knowledge. It really showed me the fact that you can be very knowledgeable and you can be very smart, but life runs its course, and you can end up on the streets. That was one experience that I really learned a lot from."

The helpers who come to Pearl's Kitchen are trying to make a small difference in a small corner of the world: a few meals, some conversation, now and then a smile. Somewhere in the past, they learned the importance of caring for others; as volunteers, they are developing new ideas about kindness. Sometimes they are unsure whether what they are doing makes any difference, as they are doing little more than planting a few seeds of hope. And were they the only ones, they might wonder whether their efforts were being wasted. But they are not alone: Elsewhere, others are also bending over their hoes, seed packets in hand.

The National Debate

Every newspaper and telecast is filled with accounts of violence, much of it committed by teenagers. Commentators insist that Generation X (the very name is revealing) has no morality and no purpose. Reared by the baby boomers of the 1960s, Generation X has allegedly not been exposed to proper moral guidance but has been allowed to be seduced by advertising, rock music, and drugs. The result is a generation at sea, struggling to find themselves, and offering little promise for America's future.

Other than crime statistics, however, the media have paid little attention to what Generation X really is doing. It should be clear, therefore, to any thoughtful person that the picture of rampant violence, drug use, and selfishness is distorted, but how much so is difficult to determine. Statistics on declining test scores, reports of violence and decay in the nation's schools, evidence of defection from religious organizations, and debates about public morality do not present an encouraging view of the future. Against these images, the volunteers at Pearl's Kitchen provide a stark contrast.

Community service requirements are being instituted in schools across the nation, and the federal government has launched a modest but innovative national service program. With the jails overflowing, judges are turning increasingly to community service as a means of rehabilitating juvenile offenders. Churches and synagogues are recruiting teenagers to work in soup kitchens. In fact, nationally, two-thirds of American teenagers now report having done some kind of volunteer work within the past twelve months.

The hope is that these community service programs can somehow combat the malaise in our society. Generation X can learn in these programs what their parents failed to teach them at home: that caring for others can be personally rewarding as well as contribute to the solution of social ills. It is hoped that when they are exposed to the needy, young people will find an altruistic impulse within themselves that will make them better people.

But is this hope justified? Can we assume that simply encouraging young people to become involved in community service will improve our society morally? Indeed, isn't it likely that the very meaning of altruism will be altered—perhaps even undermined—by these programs?

This book is an attempt to paint a better picture of kindness in American life, both as it currently exists among American young people and as it may exist in the future if properly nurtured. I am less interested in the fact that some people are helping the needy than in questions about the *quality* of their kindness. What motivates it? How does it differ from the caring they experience in their own families? Have we become cynical about our reasons for kindness? Does kindness compel us to think harder about the larger problems facing our world?

I am especially concerned with the reasons that people become involved in activities such as visiting the sick, sheltering the homeless, and caring for the needy. These reasons are important because they provide clues to how we can motivate other people to become involved in caring. They also are important because they tell us about the culture in which we live and the ways in which kindness is being manipulated and in which it succumbs to self-interested assumptions in American culture, thereby becoming less genuine and less clearly a manifestation of virtue. By examining these reasons, we can decide whether behavior that on the surface is quite good can nonetheless be misunderstood and manipulated. If it is, we need to find ways to make it better, so that good deeds can become better deeds.

Kindness is not an entity, like a tree, that simply exists or does not exist. Rather, kindness exists as we interpret it and absorb it in our sense of who we are, not simply as a deed we perform. It is a value, an impression, a perception that is nudged, shaped, and defined by the cultural forces that surround us. These forces invariably leave their imprint on it, often manipulating it and sometimes abusing it, especially in a society like ours in which so much of life is governed by norms of acquisition and self-interest. These abuses need to be recognized if kindness is to be nurtured toward higher levels of quality.

My aim is not, however, to chronicle the abuse of kindness, focusing on egregious misuses of charitable funds and the like, for the sheer purpose of arousing public consternation about these abuses. Rather, my hope is to sensitize the reader to the more subtle and pervasive ways in which our society manipulates and abuses kindness. In short, kindness is often treated too casually, is misunderstood, and, if it is expressed at all, is engaged in for the wrong reasons. I want readers to ask themselves what kindness is, whether the good deeds they see around them are really the best they can be or whether there may be ways to rethink them and to improve their understanding of them.

The central argument of this book is that kindness needs to be reconceived if it is to contribute to the public good in our society. The problem is not that Americans—even Generation Xers—are lacking in kindness. Contrary to what many social critics have argued, we are not so controlled by selfishness that we must teach people from scratch what it means to care. Virtually all of us already know what it means to care and to be cared for, because we have learned this elementary kindness in our families. We have witnessed parents, siblings, and other role models showing kindness to friends and relatives. We even have a primordial understanding of why caring is a good thing. The problem is that this elementary understanding of kindness has remained idealistic, naive, private. What we often have *not* done is to learn how to translate these caring impulses into behavior that makes a difference in the ordinary lives we lead as adults. In order to be responsible citizens, we need to relearn the caring impulses of our childhoods and to understand what kindness means in an adult world.

When young people who have been actively involved in community service and who have reflected deeply on their experiences talk about their involvement, it quickly becomes evident that what they did is often less important than how they understand what they did. That is, their caring is not simply an ideal, an instinct, or an empathic response; it was nurtured by their families, teachers, and mentors. These young people have developed a sophisticated view of kindness that has permitted them to grow and to contribute more effectively. It is this understanding, more than anything else, that has given them a sense of personal virtue that can be carried into the roles they will need to play as adults.

The reality of American life at the end of the twentieth century is that complex social institutions have been established to do much of the business that our society requires. Despite their obvious shortcomings, these institutions actually work quite well most of the time. And because they do, each of us can get along in our personal lives by treating these institutions with relative indifference. Indeed, they are designed to minimize the degree of planning and attention that must be devoted to them at any given moment by the average person. Institutions depend on the fact that most people most of the time are relatively indifferent to them. But this indifference seems to contradict the ideal of being devoted, caring, and concerned about the common good. Thus, we live a kind of schizophrenic existence, having a primordial impulse to be caring but knowing that we are indifferent much of the time.

The solution to this dilemma is not to replace all our indifference with valorous deeds of kindness but, rather, to find a new understanding of kindness that is effective in the institutional reality in which we live. We do not need to learn from scratch what it means to be kind, but we do need to relearn how to put our caring impulses into practice in effective ways. We need to bridge the gap between the idealistic images of caring that we learn as children and the more nuanced understanding of kindness that we must have as adults. This is not an easy transition to make, as it involves a painful process of becoming aware of our own limitations, narrowing our horizons, and also realizing that small contributions are still part of a larger picture.

One of the best ways of making this transition is by becoming involved in community service and other volunteer activities. Such activities permit caring impulses to be put into practice and, in the process, to be reshaped. People learn that kindness outside the home is not entirely different from caring within the family—but that it is not exactly the same, either. They are exposed to new scripts that give them a language for describing their caring activities, thus linking these actvities with a basic part of their self-identity. Women and men, it turns out, forge these links in quite different ways, and each can learn from the other. In addition, community service activities must spark the imagination, providing insights into careers, public policy, and the future rather than focusing only on the tasks at hand.

It is fortunate that many schools, churches and synagogues, and other community agencies are encouraging people to become involved in community service. Young people especially can benefit from these opportunities. But community service must not be advocated simply as a means of recruiting free labor. Nor should it be assumed that simply exposing young people to community service is enough. Its leaders must also be concerned about the messages that volunteers receive as a result of their involvement. Occasions must be provided for reflection on their experience. Guidance must be offered to help volunteers see the connection between the caring they learned as children, on the one hand, and the institutions governing our society, on the other hand. Above all, *virtue*—the habitual practice of courage and compassion—must be an explicit element of community service programs. People need to understand themselves as persons of strength who can make a difference in their worlds. They must do so not in the heroic terms of the past but in the realistic terms of the present, gaining power by learning specific skills and by coming to grips with the roles they must play in complex social institutions.

These are tasks with which educators, community leaders, clergy, and scholars must be concerned. Schools and community agencies have been in the forefront of efforts to enlist young people in service activities, and churches and synagogues remain the primary place where instruction is given about the spiritual dimension of caring.[1] Already there has been a major shift among scholars (especially in the study of moral philosophy) toward a rediscovery of virtue and of character.[2] There has been some movement in this direction in social theory as well, but scarcely any attention has yet been given to these matters in the empirical sciences and perhaps even less in many of the settings in which our young people are being educated.[3]

So much of the public debate about national service, community service, and volunteering has centered on the economic value of these activities, their real and implied costs and benefits to the society, and the needs to which they can be directed that hardly any consideration has been given to the ways in which these activities might actually build strong character and better citizenship. To be sure, these are often recognized as possible by-products. Little thought has been given, however, to the ways in which these by-products might be achieved or, for that matter, to the possibility that they might actually be undermined by these very activities. In the absence of ways to think about such matters, learning to care has become a matter of generating specific activities, of putting young people in caregiving contexts for a few weeks, for example, and simply hoping that good character will be the eventual result. Moral education, however, has always meant more than this. It has always been predicated on the hope that young people could learn not only to make right choices but also to be good people.

There is, of course, a long tradition of scholarship that has sought to clarify and nurture the ways in which we individually and collectively can contribute to the common good of our society. In recent years, the debate about the moral fabric of America has been rekindled. As chaos, fragmentation, and crime have increased, social observers have recognized the need not simply to crank out statistics and abstract theories but also to speak candidly about the quality of social life. Discussions of virtue have become central to this recent debate. Among others, William J. Bennett's *Book of Virtues*, Michael Lerner's "politics of meaning," Amitai Etzioni's "communitarianism," and Robert N. Bellah and his colleagues' *The Good Society* are prominent examples.[4]

This book is intended as a contribution to the present discussion of virtue in American life. It seeks to build on and add specificity to each of the works just mentioned. With Bennett, I argue that there is an urgent need to rediscover ways to instill virtue in ourselves and in our young people. The retelling of moral tales from the past is one way of doing this. My research also underscores the value of storytelling. But the stories that young people learn while engaged in community service are a special kind: They add realism to youthful idealism, showing that virtue need not be heroic but involves character that makes use of the institutional resources at hand. With Michael Lerner, I believe that politics—indeed, service careers of many kinds—must be inscribed with meaning. Community service is an effective way of shifting this idea from platitude to practice. With Etzioni, I argue that kindness must ultimately be directed toward the betterment of our communities. But a communitarian spirit depends not only on good deeds; it also requires instruction and reflection. Otherwise, young people become cynical and self-serving—even in the midst of community-oriented activities. And with Bellah and his associates, I contend that institutions are of such vital importance in our society that learning to be responsible role players in (and monitors of) our institutions is an effective way of contributing to the common good. But we must also recognize that institutions themselves encourage indifference and that being attentive to institutional responsibilities is quite different from the ways in which caring is often conceived.

This book is about the young. It is especially concerned with the challenge we face in training the next generation of Americans to lead lives of virtue. It comes at a time when many public leaders seem to have given up hope. Faced with daily evidence in the news media that teenagers are killing other teenagers, that gang violence is rampant, and that drug use, unsafe sex, and teen pregnancies are widespread, many leaders are convinced that only huge investments in law enforcement can make a difference. Others place their hope in a return to public prayers and Bible reading in the schools as a way of instilling lessons in morality. Still others look to national service programs to inspire young people but recognize that advertising may be inhibiting any generous impulses that may exist among young people.

My research also convinces me that nurturing the common good requires us to pay special attention to young people. The pressures to behave selfishly and permissively are powerful, but there also are reasons to be hopeful. In record numbers, young people are being drawn into community service programs through their schools, churches, and synagogues. National campaigns have been mounted to encourage youthful volunteerism. None of these programs is entirely effective; indeed, many young people feel their time is being wasted, that they are being coerced, and that they would rather be doing something else. But young people are learning a deeper understanding of kindness in some of these programs, and it is not simply the comfortable, white, middle-class youngsters from the suburbs who are benefiting. Homeless teenagers, runaways, youths who have been on drugs, victims of sexual abuse, and members of gangs are among those who have benefited as well. There is much to be learned from their stories.

A Look Ahead

The evidence that forms the basis for my discussion comes largely from interviews with teenagers who have become involved in volunteer activities and from a national survey of teenagers. Young people are a strategic population to be concerned with, for several reasons. First, they are the future. If kindness is to be a continuing feature of our world, it must come from people who have learned how to care while they were young. This is not to say that people cannot learn new habits as they grow older, although studies of caregiving among adults hint strongly at the importance of habits that are cultivated before adulthood.[5] By focusing on young people, we can learn what factors encourage some of them to become caring persons. Second, young people are exposed to all the social influences that I have been discussing. They are subject to the pressures that schools and parents place on them to learn marketable skills and play specialized roles. They are exposed to the influences of the mass media and of popular culture. They are at a stage of identity formation in which many of their uncertainties about self in our culture come rushing to the surface. Young people are, in fact, more exposed to the influences of contemporary culture than many adults are because they have yet to acquire the resources to resist these pressures. Most adults, for example, have been able to choose which career suits them best, but young people are still in settings where much of their life is orchestrated by institutional requirements. And third, much less is known about caring and kindness among young people than is the case among adults. Although earlier research shows that many adults appear to have learned kindness when they were young, little effort has been devoted to studying young people directly. We do not know, for example, whether young people engage in caring for essentially the same reasons that adults do, whether their caring activities may be subject to different kinds of abuses, or whether there may be special obstacles that we should take into account because of young people's stage of life-cycle development.

The questions I have raised suggest the importance of utilizing qualitative evidence. To understand kindness, we must talk to people, paying close attention to the language they use to describe their activities, their motives, and the ways in which their caring behavior fits into their world. Much of the evidence discussed in the following chapters comes from in-depth, qualitative interviews with young people between the ages of thirteen and eighteen. These interviews lasted for a minimum of two hours, some ranging up to five hours. They consisted of a standard set of open-ended questions that encouraged the respondents to tell stories about themselves and to discuss their backgrounds, their families, their interests, and their values. (These questions are reproduced at the end of this book. Some of the questions varied, of course, depending on respondents' answers to other questions.)

All the young people we interviewed were involved in some type of caring or community service activity. Some were quite extensively involved, and others were involved only to a small degree. Their activities also were quite diverse. For example, some were participating in programs to help the homeless; others were working with fellow students who were in need; still others were concerned with environmental problems; and so on. In all, we conducted sixty such interviews. All the respondents were in high school at the time they were interviewed. They ranged from rich to poor and included many racial, ethnic, and religious backgrounds. Even the areas in which they lived were quite diverse, ranging from the inner city, to large suburban developments, to small towns and farms and spanning sixteen states. The reason for selecting young people who were participating in caring activities was that some involvement in such activities was necessary in order for us to ask questions about why they had become involved, how they understood kindness, and what place it played in their lives. The reason for choosing young people who were otherwise quite diverse was to minimize the possibility that our findings might pertain to only one segment of American society.

These qualitative interviews provide rich evidence from which to consider the ways in which young people in our contemporary culture regard kindness. We also are able to look at whether some of these understandings and attitudes are indeed common to the American people as a whole. To make inferences of this kind, I drew on several recent national surveys. One is a national survey of teenagers that I helped design. Another was a national survey of adults that included many of the same questions that the teenage survey did. I also used two other national surveys that I recently conducted for other purposes. The 1992 teen survey was of a nationally representative sample of 1,404 young people between the ages of twelve and seventeen. The 1992 adult survey was of a nationally representative sample of 2,671 persons aged eighteen or older. The other two surveys to which I occasionally referred were conducted among a nationally representative sample of 2,110 adults in 1989 and among a nationally representative sample of 2,013 employed adults in 1992.

In Chapter 2 I introduce several of the young people we interviewed and examine the extent of volunteering in the United States. I develop my arguments about the uses and abuses of kindness and suggest that we need to reconsider what kindness now means in our society. In Chapter 3 I examine the family backgrounds of the young people who became actively involved in volunteer work. Drawing on interviews and evidence from surveys, I show that young people almost universally base their understanding of caring on their having been cared for themselves by loving parents or by other adults to whom they have been close. Contrary to popular psychological theories, I suggest that being cared for is more commonly the basis for caring than is some instinctive tendency to empathize with pain. The caring that one experiences as a child, however, is personal and unspecialized. The valuable lessons that young people learn from volunteer work, I suggest, are therefore a step toward learning a new meaning of caring—one that fits more easily with the impersonal, specialized roles that adults play in social institutions.

Chapter 4 discusses the frameworks and motives that help volunteers understand what they are doing. I show that frameworks emphasizing humanitarianism, happiness, reciprocity, and self-realization are readily available in American culture and that all these frameworks give us ways in which to make sense of caring activities. Motives are more specific understandings consisting of stories that help us account for becoming involved in particular kinds of activities. I believe that leaders of volunteer organizations need to pay more attention to cultural frameworks and motives, or otherwise services may be performed but volunteers may lose sight of the ways in which their activities reflect kindness and caring. I also extend these observations in Chapter 5 by considering the special ways in which religious language influences contemporary understandings of caring.

I then turn in Chapter 6 to the social contexts in which volunteering takes place. For young people in the process of learning how to serve others, the most relevant contexts are their schools, community agencies, and churches or synagogues. It is significant that these are formal organizations and that the volunteer work that takes place in them is institutionalized—following formal rules, involving specialized activities, and being subject to norms of efficiency and effectiveness. In such settings, volunteer activity is thus a way of bridging the gap between the caring that one already knows as a child and the roles that one will play in social institutions as an adult. The volunteer experience provides a way of relearning the meaning of caring so that it can be retained in complex institutional settings. By paying close attention to what young people say about their experiences in schools, community agencies, and religious organizations, I show the pressures they feel and the ways in which their understandings of caring are changed.

The process of relearning what it means to care is greatly influenced by role models and by storytelling. This, as I describe in Chapter 7, is the drama of volunteering. I show that the stories young people tell about their volunteer experiences, the stories they hear from other volunteers, and the examples they see modeled in the behavior of people they admire reflect—and resolve—the tensions they face in learning new meanings of kindness. Much of what young people experience is also deeply influenced by their understanding of gender. I discuss this in Chapter 8.

Chapter 9 takes up the important question of how volunteering builds character. I argue that service should in fact aim to build character, rather than simply to perform specific tasks, and that character involves virtue. It is, however, difficult to build character, because our institutions do so much for us that we often feel weak, rather than strong, and do not have a clear sense of identity. I demonstrate that volunteer work not only can strengthen self-identity but also can create a kind of identity that fits well with the demands and responsibilities of our society.

Chapters 10 and 11 are concerned with the broader implications of volunteering—for the individual futures of young people and for the future of our society. I contend that volunteering broadens the horizons of young people and helps them imagine ways in which they can show kindness to people around them both in other volunteer roles and through their work. I also believe that volunteers are realistic—yet hopeful—about the future. They recognize the need to enlist government, schools, and corporations in compassionate social efforts and, above all, to have faith that their own efforts can make at least a small difference toward making the world a better place.

2

Kindness as a Social Problem

The very least you can do in your life is to figure out what you hope for. And the most you can do is live inside that hope. Not admire it from a distance but live right in it, under its roof. What I want is so simple I almost can't say it: elementary kindness. Enough to eat, enough to go around. The possibility that kids might one day grow up to be neither the destroyers nor the destroyed. That's about it. Right now I'm living in that hope, running down its hallway and touching the walls on both sides.

Barbara Kingsolver, *Animal Dreams*

Let's use our minds," says Tanika Lane. "Drugs cause brothers to kill brothers, sisters to hate their mothers, and drugs steal our minds." She is on her way, she hopes, to becoming the next Oprah Winfrey. It all started last summer, after her freshman year in high school. As part of Literacy Education and Direction (LEAD), a job-training program for inner-city youth, Tanika learned word processing, basic research and writing skills, and even a bit of journalism. The director, Miss Gillis, noticed that she had talent. Not only was Tanika willing to learn, she also was a leader and showed promise as a writer. Throughout the summer, Tanika wrote. She wrote about what she knew: her sister's drill team, sports, problems in the neighborhood, racial tension, drugs. She learned how to do interviews. LEAD put out a free newspaper, and Tanika wrote for it. She gained confidence in herself and in her ability to work with people.

"The first time they took me somewhere," she recalls, "I didn't know my potential. But Miss Gillis, she said, 'Okay, Tanika, I know you can do this. Go over there and talk to that man.' And I said, 'I can't do that.' She told me to. I was eating an orange and everything, and I just went over to him, and I began to talk to him. He was somebody big. So many people were around him, and they couldn't hold his attention, but when I went to talk to him, other people began to gather around to listen to what I was saying. He asked me about my writing abilities because of the editorial I wrote. He asked me, where did I learn how to write? It was so profound to me. That really made a mark on me because

I was proud of myself. So I never knew that I had that ability. I knew I could talk, because everybody always [would] say, Tanika, you need to shut up because you talk too much, but nobody ever really gave me a chance to really interview. I never really knew I wanted to do that until I got the chance."

At the end of the summer, Tanika, Miss Gillis, and everyone else was sad because the program was ending. So they made a promise with one another to stay involved and to keep the free newspaper coming out during the year. Tanika spends three of her study halls on the newspaper each week. She also puts time into it after school, probably about twenty hours a month. Her articles, interviews, and editorials have become regular features.

Tanika feels good about the newspaper because it helps teenagers express themselves and addresses important issues in the community. "The purpose is really to let people know how we feel inside," she explains. "To express ourselves, to empower other teenagers, to give them inspiration to write or to deal with the problems that they have. A lot of people in our newspaper—they really tell their business. One boy, he told about his father being on drugs. That helped a lot of other people in our class who have family on drugs. 'Well, yeah, my mom is on drugs, and my dad is on drugs, also.' That sort of thing. A lot of people come to our school now. Our newspaper draws a lot of people to our school. We had an all-female assembly recently. These women came. A lot of them were alumni. They told us their trials and tribulations and what they had to go through."

Recent issues of the newspaper have been filled with stories about drugs. One article, entitled "Hugs Not Drugs," tells about a man who had become homeless and paralyzed from the waist down because of cocaine. Eventually the man found help from an older woman in the community who just reached out and hugged him. Another article describes antidrug workshops sponsored by a local community agency. The following page is filled with addresses and hot lines for drug and alcohol abuse counseling. In her editorial, Tanika wrote: "Let's look into our hearts, minds and souls to find our pride; loosen the chains."

The newspaper, as Tanika says, also provides a forum for teens to express themselves. One freshman wrote that "drugs is one of the main reasons a lot of our race is dying." A senior counseled her peers to have "self-respect, self-confidence, a lot of will power and a goal to pursue." A "profiles" section printed short résumés of students who were looking for part-time jobs. Younger children write for the paper as well. A third grader, for example, wrote this about her family:

It means caring to me.
It means sharing to me.
It means people to me.

Tanika says the same thing about her family. Although it was LEAD that taught her to write, it was her family that taught her to care, despite the fact that neither parent has much energy left by the end of the day. Her father works for the sanitation department. Her mother—who had a better-paying job at an auto assembly plant until it closed—now works at a day care center. Both parents, however, have always tried to care for people outside their own family. Not long ago, for instance, there was an elderly couple across the street: She had Alzheimer's disease and he was unable to feed himself. So Tanika's mother went over every day and fed him. And when another neighbor had surgery, Tanika recalls, "we were her only family." These experiences have made a huge difference in Tanika's outlook on life. Caring seems only natural to her. "I guess that's the way I was raised," she says.

The Man with AIDS

Several hundred miles away, Amy Stone was reflecting on her day at school. The man who came had AIDS and then he had gotten cancer, which had destroyed most of his nose. His illness was plainly visible. He spoke with brutal frankness about how he had contracted the virus, of what the sickness felt like inside his stomach. The bleeding. What it was like to be dying before his thirtieth birthday. He warned the students about sex and drugs and cautioned them to take responsibility for themselves. More than four hundred stayed after school to hear him speak.

Amy Stone had organized the rally. A beautiful young woman, tall with shoulder-length hair, she was both homecoming queen and student body president of a southern high school with more than a thousand students. Two of her classmates had already died of AIDS, and Amy knew it would be only a matter of time before more died. Nearly everyone was sexually active, but very few of them practiced safe sex. The school had an approved curriculum that included sex education, one course in the seventh grade and another in the tenth grade. But in the seventh grade, Amy was too embarrassed to listen, and in the tenth grade, she remembers nothing being said at all about AIDS. So the rally was her way of trying to make a difference.

Amy had hoped to have an AIDS awareness assembly during the school day, but the school board turned her down. They also refused to let her put up posters but changed their minds when the principal appealed their decision. Nor had the county health department been willing to provide pamphlets, as it feared the event would become political. That was also the newspaper's excuse for refusing to cover the rally. Amy was, however, able to secure cooperation from a number of local restaurants, donating food that she hoped would help draw an audience. With the help of a few volunteers, she worked every day for four months during study halls and after school, making banners, printing slogans on T-shirts (such as "Don't get AIDS, get the facts" and "Wear a Condom"), and distributing red ribbons to symbolize support for AIDS victims. Amy got the health department in an adjacent county to contribute pamphlets, made daily announcements on the school's closed-circuit television network, staffed awareness tables during the lunch hour, and brought in an AIDS task force from the state capital to make an educational film.

By the time that John, the man with AIDS, finished speaking, virtually the entire audience was in tears. Students wrote down questions they wanted him to answer but were too embarrassed to ask in person. They passed them forward, and he responded without either hesitation or reserve. When it was over, people shook his hand, thanked him for coming, and told him that he would be in their prayers. The response was overwhelmingly positive. A local television station phoned to ask for a follow-up interview. Teachers who had been opposed to the rally complimented Amy on its success. The message she hoped the students had heard was that no form of sex can be considered entirely safe. In her view, abstinence is the best policy of all, and short of that, her goal is to promote safer sex.

What prompted Amy to take action was seeing the Names Project quilt. She and a friend drove forty-five miles to see it. "We stayed for about two hours and looked at it. It's huge. I've never seen anything like that. The panels are about as big as sleeping bags. Some of them have pictures sewn on them, jewels, pieces of clothing, poems, names of books, authors, shoes. One whole panel was made out of ties. The thing that touched me most was that the panels were made by the people who were still living and who had lost somebody to AIDS.

"Before, it was like if you have AIDS, then you're different and you've done something bad so we don't need to feel sorry for you anyway. But when you see the quilt, you see that these people were loved by their families and friends and that somebody must have really loved them a whole lot to make a panel that big and that detailed. It's so big now, the whole thing would cover the entire mall in Washington, and then some.

"If you could have just been there. Everybody was crying. The whole time we were there they had a microphone. They had a list of every person that has died of AIDS. They were reading them off, a different name every second, and you're looking at these panels. That's a pretty big shock, especially to high school students who think they're invincible. That was what got us started."

But for Amy, it had actually started well before that. She herself was not a victim of AIDS, nor was anyone in her immediate family. She had, however, lived an unusual life, and this was the reason, rather than the Names Quilt, that she was moved to be of service to her school. Indeed, her life holds a valuable key to understanding the nature of true kindness in American society—and the forces that make this virtue so unusual.

Amy Stone grew up in a sheltered middle-class environment. Her father held a managerial position, and her mother, a college graduate, had a full-time job. Amy had two siblings, one older and one younger. Like many others of her background, she attended church regularly at one of the more prestigious congregations in town, took piano lessons, went to summer camp, and never lacked the material comforts of middle-class life. She describes her family as close. Her parents cared for her, and she was loyally devoted to them. She did have, however, one big problem.

Whenever Amy tried to eat food, her throat swelled shut, and she would get sick to her stomach. Indeed, she suffered from such severe allergic reactions that she was seldom able to digest her food and was constantly malnourished. Because she had been adopted, she had no way of knowing whether the problem was in her family history or her environment. She spent much of her childhood in hospitals and doctors' offices. Her parents tried to keep her on a strict diet, for example, allowing her to eat only the beef patty when they went to McDonalds or feeding her spinach for breakfast to cleanse her system, and eventually they installed a padlock on the pantry to keep her from cheating and winding up in the hospital again.

Amy remembers being in the hospital for two months when she was six, in a totally sterilized environmental health unit. The sheets were sterilized. The toilet water was sterilized. If someone brought a present, it had to be sterilized. Amy was the only child to be admitted to the unit. Her friends were garbage collectors and crop dusters and teachers. One day a woman in the unit had a severe seizure, and Amy went into shock. "When you see stuff like that," she says, "you remember it, and it makes you realize how lucky you are. Even though you can be so sick, I was so glad that I didn't have to go through what she went through, because it looked so awful." But the greatest effect of her illness was, as she explains, that "I grew up very fast. I had to." In fact, by the time she was six, she was giving herself her shots. It was a big responsibility for a six-year-old, especially when she had to have eleven shots a day.

Another four years passed before Amy got better. When she was invited to friends' birthday parties, she couldn't eat birthday cake. She couldn't eat regular meals at the school cafeteria or at friends' houses. She was ten before she had her first pizza, and then it was without cheese. Even now she takes her shots every day and follows a fairly rigid diet. She knows what it is like to be nauseated and unable to eat. So when John talked about being sick to his stomach because of AIDS, she could empathize with him.

It's Pretty Neat

"Just call me a fun-loving guy. I like to have a good time. Very outgoing, you know? I get along with most everybody. I don't want anybody not to like me." This is Rafe Ramirez, a high school senior who lives in rural Indiana. He dresses casually—blue jeans and tie-dyed T-shirts—and his dark hair is long. He lives with his mom and dad in a two-bedroom trailer house. They get along, but they are dirt poor. The place is seedy and run down. Out back there are several rusted automobiles. A couple of horses graze in a nearby field, but they look like they have not been ridden for a while. Several dogs lie in the yard. Rafe's favorite type of music is grunge rock, and somehow it seems to fit.

He is an average student in many respects, making mostly Bs, a few As, and some Cs. Rafe does fairly well in math and science without really trying, but he does not do as well in social studies and history, no matter how hard he tries. Next year he plans to attend a local college, so he can still live at home. Some of his friends got scholarships for being in sports; Rafe's best sport was ice hockey. He played from the time he was six until he was ten, and then he had to quit because it was too expensive. After that he mostly just skated on frozen ponds in the winter for fun.

Rafe enjoys being by himself. He is an only child. As he says, he likes to get along with everybody, but that often means keeping things at a superficial level. He does not want to offend anyone or be a burden to them. He is the kind of guy who could spend a lot of time in his room or just hanging out with one or two of his buddies. He could be that way, except for Pete.

Rafe met Pete when he was eleven, shortly after having to drop out of ice hockey. Pete was the soccer coach, or rather, he was someone who coached the soccer team because his sons played soccer. He had never played himself. But he was the coach when Rafe joined the team. He taught Rafe how to play the game, mostly by just encouraging him to do what the other boys did. Rafe liked it, and soon he was on the traveling team that took the more advanced players to compete in other towns. Eventually he started playing varsity soccer in school. Pete also encouraged him to teach the younger boys to play.

Today, Rafe Ramirez serves his community as a volunteer soccer coach. Four evenings a week he coaches intermural teams in the township where he lives. He's there when the children arrive at 6:30 and stays until 9 when they leave. During the varsity season he barely has time to grab a bite to eat after practice before he has to be on the field again. One of the teams, which he has been coaching for the past three years, is for boys under age twelve. The other team, which he just started coaching this year, is for girls under age sixteen. The soccer season runs from September through March, starting outdoors in the fall and then moving indoors in the winter. Rafe also coaches a traveling team of advanced players on Saturdays and several other children's teams in the summer.

Rafe realizes he could be doing other things with his time, and he also acknowledges that the world could get by if children did not learn how to play soccer. Nevertheless, there is much more to soccer, he feels, than simply kicking a ball around. Over the past three years he has maintained a close relationship with the sixteen boys on his team. In addition to the several dozen other boys and girls he has coached for shorter periods of time, he has been able to make a notable difference in these boys' lives. They have learned new skills and become better players, and they have also found in him an older brother: They listen to what he says, and some of them even dress in the same way he does. Rafe thinks it's "pretty neat."

The Trouble with Kindness

Tanika Lane, Amy Stone, and Rafe Ramirez are a few of the young people in America today who are trying to put their caring impulses into practice. They are in the process of gaining a more mature understanding of what it means to be kind, and we can only hope that their volunteer work will encourage them to be kind and caring as they shoulder greater responsibilities in their adult life.

Most people regard kindness as a virtue. They think that it is good when people take into account the needs of others and try to help them. Kindness, however, is always precarious. If it is rooted in a primordial human instinct, as the writers of the Enlightenment believed, it is nevertheless an instinct that is easy to suppress. The atrocities of the twentieth century—global war, mass destruction, genocide—bear sufficient witness to that.

Kindness is seldom easy to instill in children, as parents know, as it is usually overshadowed by petty jealousies, egoism, and self-interest. More often, it is suffocated by mere indifference as people become hardened to the realities of life. Well-intentioned men and women, regarding themselves as kindhearted and neighborly, can all too easily become preoccupied with their work, their hobbies, and their families. Although the bills are paid, the needy family next door remains neglected. Malnourished children become someone else's problem.

According to Tanika, indifference is the norm among most of the students she knows. Their attitude is "I got mine, so you can get yours." She is convinced that few people really care, "because any time you can see so many homeless people, how can somebody truly, truly care?" She points to the beating of Rodney King in Los Angeles as another example: "How can you beat somebody just because of the color of their skin?" she asks. "I think everybody is looking out for themselves these days; at least around me, they are."

Another student we talked to stated that people's indifference really bothers him: "At school, I find this most. I find that people really care very little one way or the other about people." He thinks this indifference pervades all corners of American life, including how people think about their jobs and how they treat one another at work.

Nationally, the view that indifference—rather than caring—is the norm is also widespread. Two Americans in three believe that people basically look out for their own interests, and only one-quarter believe that people are genuinely concerned about the needy.[1] Among teenagers, cynicism is more pervasive still: Seven in ten regard Americans as self-interested, and fewer than one in eight believe that people truly care about those in need.[2]

This lack of kindness is felt on a wide scale in our society, not only in countless violations of common courtesy on the highways and not only in the conflicts that tear families apart and lead to the abuse of children, but also in the glaring needs of the homeless, the hungry, the sick, the victimized, and the lonely. A cursory look at some of the statistics is enough to show how great these social needs are:

> In 1990, 31.7 million Americans lived below the poverty line. Of these, 3.6 million were children under five years of age. Another 7.5 million were children between the ages of five and seventeen.[3] This meant that for the nation as a whole, about one child in five lived in a family that was unable to provide adequate food and clothing.
>
> Official estimates (generally deemed by experts to be low) place the number of homeless persons in the United States at approximately 240,000, of whom 190,000 are housed in emergency shelters for at least part of the year, leaving approximately 50,000 whose existence is known only by their visibility on the streets.[4]
>
> Although the spread of AIDS has been difficult to estimate, one thing that is known with some certainty is that AIDS is now one of the leading causes of death among young people in the United States, ranking sixth among persons aged fifteen to twenty-four and third among persons aged twenty-five to forty-four.[5] Moreover, the rate of increase of AIDS-related deaths has been dramatic: In 1984, for example, 679 people aged thirteen to twenty-nine died of AIDS, but in 1990, that figure had risen to 4,745—a 600 percent increase in just six years.[6] The total number of AIDS cases reported to the Centers for Disease Control that year was nearly 42,000.
>
> The need for counseling about sexuality, sex-related diseases, and abortions among teenagers can also be inferred from the figures on abortion

collected by the Alan Guttmacher Institute in New York. In 1973, the
year of *Roe* v. *Wade*, 232,000 women between the ages of fifteen and
nineteen had abortions; by 1988, this figure had risen to 393,000.[7] In addition, nearly a million cases of syphillis and gonorrhea are reported
each year.

The need for support, counseling, and greater civic awareness is also evident from the fact that approximately 30,000 people take their own
lives each year and another 23,000 are murdered.[8] Each year, 30 percent of all households are touched by either violent crime or theft. In
addition, more than 2 million cases of child abuse and neglect are reported each year.[9] More than 15,000 of these cases involve sexual abuse,
and another 14,000 involve physical injury. The number of such cases
not reported is thought to be much higher.

Approximately two million young people between the ages of twelve and
twenty-one are victims of some physical or mental handicap or suffer a
learning disability that requires them to receive special help, and another two million children aged six to eleven fall into this category.[10]

These problems cannot be solved by volunteers, but volunteers can help
mitigate their suffering. For example, Megan Wyse's awareness that she cannot
do much to find housing for the homeless or to create jobs for them is quite realistic. Yet the example she cites of visiting a homeless man in the hospital
reveals the need for even small acts of kindness. She tells of another homeless
man she met at Pearl's Kitchen who had recently contracted HIV and was frightened and lonely. Megan was at least able to be supportive, and in the process, she
also benefited, as this man was a vivid reminder to her and her friends of the
dangers of drugs and unsafe sex.

In this sense, kindness is a social problem because there is not enough of
it. We need more people like Jason McKendrick and Megan Wyse who are willing
to devote a few hours of their time to the needy in their communities. Teachers and pastors, community leaders, and parents need more effective ways in
which to encourage young people to care for others less fortunate than themselves.

We realize how rare people like Jason and Megan—or Tanika, Amy, and
Rafe—are when we consider the results of recent studies of volunteering in the
United States. Although news reports of these studies are often upbeat—suggesting that America is a nation of helpers and that volunteering is the "in" thing to
do—a closer examination points to a more sober interpretation of the facts.
Judging from national surveys, nearly all Americans want to help make the world
a better place, are aware of serious social problems such as poverty and pollution

of the environment, and say that they would like to help the needy. But when they were asked whether it is important to them to spend time volunteering for community organizations, charities, churches, or other causes, the proportion responding in the affirmative drops to about half. Besides that, most people have other goals in life to which they attach a higher priority—such as being successful in their jobs, making money, and providing for their families—and those who say they value doing volunteer work place no less emphasis on these other goals than do people who do not value doing volunteer work.[11]

Thus the number that actually devote significant amounts of their time to volunteer work is quite small. On the surface, a majority of Americans—adults and teenagers alike—can point to something they have done, either in the past year or before, that counts as volunteer work: soliciting money door to door, visiting someone in the hospital, ushering at their church. In all, half of adults and nearly two-thirds of teenagers say they have done volunteer work within the past year.[12] Many volunteer activities, however, are not related to caring for the needy (for example, serving on the local arts council), and many others are concerned primarily with personal needs and the needs of one's own family (such as serving as a homeroom parent for one's children or as treasurer of one's homeowners' association). Moreover, some of the positive responses may be encouraged by the detailed ways in which questions are asked in surveys. In other studies—in which it is perhaps less obvious that having done volunteer work is a desirable response—the proportions drop to only 20 percent among adults and 13 percent among teenagers who are currently involved as volunteers.[13]

Even when all kinds of volunteer work are included, the picture of caring is often exaggerated by the fact that many people devote very little time to these activities. Although a majority of American teenagers claim to have done some volunteer work in the past year, fewer than one-quarter (23 percent) cite as many as ten hours a month, and only one in eight (12 percent) lists twenty hours a month. Students like Jason, Megan, Tanika, Amy, and Rafe—all of whom spend at least twenty hours a month volunteering—are, therefore, the exceptions rather than the rule.

Clearly, Americans need to learn better how to care for others and to be motivated to put their good intentions into practice. Community leaders, educators, and clergy need to discover how to better promote kindness. The fact that most young people already regard caring for the needy as a positive value is a place to start, and so is the fact that most people learn what it means to care by being cared for in their families and have some exposure to people who reach out to others beyond their own families. Community agencies, national service programs, churches and synagogues, and community service courses in high schools—all providing opportunities for volunteer work—also are valuable resources. There is, however, another dimension to the problem: Kindness itself is often subject to misunderstanding, corruption, and abuse.

What seems to worry the public most is the possibility that kindness is being abused by its recipients. Everyone knows the arguments: The smelly person who asks for spare change in front of Grand Central is a wino who is just wasting his life—and your money if you give him any—buying Mad Dog. He would rather take your charity than work. Or she lives in a shelter because her welfare check encourages her to do so.

People like Jason McKendrick who spend a lot of their time trying to help the needy are painfully aware of these problems. "There are some people," Jason admits, "who take advantage of us and just stay on the street." But he has seen enough of them turn their lives around that he feels the effort is still worth it. Sometimes the results are dramatic. For instance, Jason remembers one evening when the van stopped at Burger King to get some fries, and the guy behind the counter said, "Hey, you're the kids from Pearl's, aren't you?" And they answered, yes. And he said, "Yeah, you guys fed me for a month down in the park, you remember? Yeah, now I got me this job here every day. Got me an apartment, too. I'm back together with my wife and kids!"

"It was incredible, like whoa!" Jason says. "That's why I'm at Pearl's Kitchen today. Because people do need the food. And we're helping them." He is, however, confronted periodically by skeptics. He recalls: "One kid actually sat me down and said, 'I don't think what you do is right. Why do you do this? Why do you go up and feed the homeless? You shouldn't be doing this because you're encouraging them to stay on the streets.' I came back with 'These people starve. You can't just forget about them and they'll go away.' He's like, 'That's their fault.'"

Megan Wyse also worries about the possible misuse of kindness by the needy. "The shelter," she explains, "really is a dead-end place for these guys. They kind of take advantage of the fact that they're always going to get somewhere to live, and they'll always have someone to feed them. So they have no incentive to get up and get a job. They stay inside, some of them. Some of them do have jobs. Not enough to support themselves, but some have jobs. But some of them stay in all day and watch TV, smoke, then go outside and they get some stuff to drink, and then we feed them at night." She says it bothers her that the shelter encourages dependence: "They're not taking the initiative to go out and try to help themselves. So in that way, it's a crutch. What we're doing is worse for them, because they don't have the incentive to go out and get it themselves, because we're offering it to them, we're giving it to them. Even though it's not the ideal situation, it will do, if it means they don't have to do any work. So it bothers me when I realize that what I'm doing really isn't the best option for them." Nevertheless, Megan is also convinced that what she does is necessary for some of these people to survive at all.

Of greater concern than the recipients' abusing it, however, are the ways in which caregivers misuse kindness. Some of these ways are familiar: Kindhearted people donate hard-earned money to a charitable organization only to discover that its officers are fattening their own pocketbooks. Elderly believers who have always trusted their churches to be wise stewards of donations send money to television preachers who, unbeknownst to these donors, hire Madison Avenue firms to develop heart-wrenching appeals and set up bogus orphanages in the Cayman Islands to launder the receipts. Scandals of this kind have been reported in recent years with alarming frequency. So many of them have occurred, in fact, that the public's attitude has been deeply affected. In a national survey I conducted several years ago, for example, 75 percent agreed with the statement "Many charities fatten the pockets of their administrators instead of really helping the needy."[14] In addition, the donors themselves may inflate the records of their donations in order to avoid income or inheritance taxes.

These are the worst abuses of kindness, as they raise questions about whether the people involved—though seeming on the surface to value generosity—are really kind at all. In less dramatic ways, kindness is vulnerable to being subverted on a much wider scale. Good deeds are being performed, but for reasons that threaten to displace kindness, alter its meaning, or render it insignificant. A mother volunteers to help with the parent–teacher association bake sale because she knows it will look bad to the other moms in the neighborhood if she does not. A dad volunteers to coach the Little League team because his boss wants to see community service on his employees' annual reports. A little kindness will boost the company's image. High school students volunteer to help with the Special Olympics because it will look good on their college applications. Although they may have a good time, the intrinsic value of caring itself is diminished.

Everyone knows people like this: the businessman who volunteers for a committee at his church because he knows it will make him more visible in the community, the mayor who stops at the local soup kitchen for thirty seconds to get her picture in the newspaper, the college student who donates time to a health clinic in order to increase his or her chances of getting into medical school. Indeed, we know enough of these cases that we often regard them as typical. We also hold ideas about ourselves that reinforce cynical views of kindness. In the survey cited earlier, for example, 78 percent agreed with the statement "If I help others, it is likely that someone will help me when I am in need." Sixty-eight percent said that the statement "If I am kind, others will be kind to me" was a reason to be a kind and caring person. And 58 percent accepted the cynical view that "Being kind and considerate helps me get what I want in life" as a good reason to be a kind and caring person.[15]

Some would probably argue that the abuse of kindness is not worth worrying about. Serious breaches of the law, they would point out, are probably rare and, in any case, are subject to penalties already established in the civil and criminal codes. A preacher who steals from donors or a citizen who falsifies tax records can be tried for fraud. Others who stay within the law but who nevertheless exploit the kindness of others for personal gain may at least be subject to professional opprobrium and may fall under the scrutiny of muckraking journalists. Kindhearted physicians who overcharge for their services, for example, may find it hard to get referrals from other physicians or may be exposed on local television. The sort of abuse that consists only of self-interested motives getting in the way of genuine caring may be dismissed even more readily as a matter for concern. What is the problem, some might ask, if the motive is wrong but the outcome is right? At least the bake sale is held; the Little League team has a coach; and the Special Olympics has volunteers.

What makes these examples worrisome is that they diminish the meaning of kindness itself. Kindness ceases to be a virtue and instead becomes a mode of behavior that we learn to manipulate for selfish ends. Learning how to care no longer requires the cultivation of personal character but becomes a set of skills that will help us get what we want out of life. At the very least, such abuses of kindness lead to cynical attitudes that undercut the value of charitable behavior itself. Services may still be performed, but their symbolic value is lost because we no longer find ourselves admiring the kindhearted. At the worst, we become indifferent, telling ourselves that serving others does not matter so long as we are able to pursue our own goals in life. Even if community service and volunteer programs flourished, we would lose something valuable in our cultural heritage: We would have forgotten the reason for those programs, and having forgotten it, we would find it impossible to pass it on to subsequent generations.

Some might argue, nevertheless, that the problem is essentially one of individual failings. That is, a particular person happens to be greedy enough to bilk unsuspecting donors, or someone happens to have gotten so carried away with what the neighbors think or with the boss's expectations that he or she does good deeds for questionable reasons. If one assumes that, then of course it is easy to dismiss the problem on grounds that a few bad apples will not spoil the whole barrel. It is also logical to contend that the answer is to improve human nature (always a difficult proposition) but that in the meantime nothing much can be done other than continue to encourage people to be kind. The problem, however, is not fully encompassed under the heading of selfishness, as either a general failing of human nature or a fault of an individual person.

Kindness and Social Benefit

The full extent of this problem can be grasped only by realizing how often beneficial social ends are accomplished in contemporary society without kindness being involved at all. Consider the ways in which medical care is supplied to the poor and the elderly. Some care is provided by the thousands of volunteers who visit the sick or who work at hospices, by kindly people who help their neighbors, and by those who look after aging parents. Millions of needy Americans are given medical care, however, through government insurance and entitlement programs. The money required to maintain these programs comes from taxpayers, but most taxpayers are not motivated by kindness and, indeed, may not even think about what is done with their taxes.

The question that this example raises is whether kindness is no longer necessary. If so, it makes little difference whether or not we learn how to care. The uses and abuses of kindness are merely a sideshow to where the real action takes place: in legislative halls, in the personnel departments of businesses where decisions about employee benefits are made, or even in corporate boardrooms where ideas are generated that produce new jobs and the profits on which social programs depend.

Even if one acknowledges the other ways in which needs may be met in our society, a reasonable argument can be made that much kindness is still necessary, indeed, that the cultivation of kindness remains essential to the well-being of our society. Social programs always leave needs that can be met only through voluntary acts of kindness. Medical assistance programs—barely solvent as they are—leave much of the long-term, nonacute, and emotional care of those in need to be supplied by family members and volunteers. Economic growth may be the most effective stimulus for new jobs, but full employment is never achieved by economic growth alone (or by government job training and relocation programs), so tutoring, soup kitchens, and shelters for the homeless, all staffed by volunteers, are needed as well.

An even stronger reason for thinking that kindness is still essential to the health of contemporary society is that social programs depend on it. These programs do not simply happen or run on inertia or even come into being because of purely self-interested concerns. Rather, they presuppose some commitment on the part of leaders and the public alike to behave kindly toward one another. Things would be quite different if there were simply a callous attitude toward the poor, the weak, and the needy.

If these arguments make sense, then we are in a curious situation in which a value that is essential to the health of society is not always reinforced by social conditions and, in fact, may be eroded by these conditions. Kindness is necessary to mitigate social ills, to guide and humanize social policy, and to ensure common human decency. Kindness is a virtue that most people would not want to abandon openly. Yet the social programs we have established to care for the ills of our society make sure that certain needs are met whether or not anyone is motivated by kindness. Public policy presumes self-interest and tries to encourage it on the grounds that this pursuit will benefit everyone. Because much that passes for human decency is either legislated (as in the case of traffic laws) or encoded in the norms of everyday life (etiquette, for example), the need for kindness is minimized there as well.

We therefore have a serious problem in teaching people how to care for one another and, indeed, in even trying to understand what kindness is. One of these problems is that kindness is associated with private life much more than it is with public life. People are encouraged to express kindness in their families, through volunteer work performed in their leisure time, and in the casual relationships that are formed at work but that are not actually essential to their jobs. Schools, churches, community associations, and even businesses go out of their way to encourage kindness of this kind. Little of it, however, may be relevant to the ways in which the nation's business is conducted. Kindness exists, as it were, in the crevices between organized social life. People are likely to experience pressures and frustrations in trying to be kind. They may abuse the trust placed in them as caregivers or display kindness for what they regard as impure motives yet not grasp fully what the sources of these problems are.

My argument is that the use and abuse of kindness in American life are not so much matters of individual failings but of the way in which our institutions operate. Our institutions are organized both to encourage kindness and to abuse it. On the one hand, most institutions presuppose elementary kindness, foster the expression of kindness, and function more effectively when kindness is present than when it is absent. Schools function better when teachers and children are kind to each other. The world of business, competitive as it is, recognizes that kindness boosts employees' morale and improves customer relations. Most employees feel cared for at work and regard their work as a way of caring for others. Churches and synagogues depend on kindness to attract members. Charities specifically promote benevolence and giving. Even politics—often maligned for its lack of caring—tries to encourage volunteer efforts and presents foreign and domestic policy as an example of American compassion. On the other hand, many of these same practices systematically alter the meaning of kindness, seek to turn it to self-interested ends, and limit the extent to which it is likely to be effective. Schools urge competition among students and set standards of achievement that have little to do with kindness and may even demand so much effort that little energy is left for good deeds. Their efforts to promote community service may be so heavily laden with achievement norms or rules and regulations that little kindness is actually involved. Religious organizations and charities define kindness in a way that is likely to serve their own ends. For example, kindness may mean volunteering to clean the church basement or organize the monthly potluck, or in the case of charities, it may mean donating money or time. Businesses may encourage employees to be kind by participating in highly visible community organizations but be reluctant to give them time off to care for a sick child. Politicians may talk about compassion but do less after they are elected to promote it than their campaign promises would suggest.

In these examples, people still make a difference. A particular employee can choose to go the extra mile toward helping a customer or do volunteer work during his or her lunch break, and another employee can choose to grumble at everyone and make no effort to help anyone else. It is the institutional setting, however, that places certain opportunities in people's path, rules out certain possibilities, and nudges someone to choose certain options rather than others. For this reason, understanding how kindness functions in our society must take into account these institutional settings. Learning to care requires knowing more than just the psychology of the individual. It requires an understanding of more than simply the needs to which good deeds might be directed. It requires even more than reinforcing the value that people attach to caring and compassion. Learning to care must be grounded in the institutional realities of our society. It must recognize the opportunities that are present in our dominant institutions for expressing kindness. It must also be aware of the ways in which these institutions encourage kindness to be misused, abused, or redefined. Recognizing the opportunities and the potential pitfalls, people can then function better in institutional settings. They can also, when necessary, stand apart from these institutions, think critically about them, and perhaps ask whether kindness also needs to be expressed in other ways.

The reason to be concerned about the abuse of kindness, therefore, is that a better, kindlier society depends on it, as, indeed, do our notions of character, virtue, and what constitutes the good life. It is not enough simply to encourage more good deeds, more hours of volunteer effort, or more giving to charities as a way to promote kindness. Laudable as those efforts are, they may have very little to do with kindness and even less to do with the cultivation of moral character. They may, for instance, be motivated entirely by selfish interests and be directed toward leisure activities that actually benefit the donor more than the recipient. And indeed, there may be less visible ways in which kindness is also present in our society. For example, the extra effort that employees may make to help clients who are in a jam may be motivated by genuine kindness and yet never register in the statistics by which caring is normally measured.

Such behavior aside, it is nevertheless the case that simply getting more people involved in some kind of community service, and by any means possible, is certainly not the answer to achieving a better world. Rather, improving the quality of such behavior must also be an important part of the answer. And quality must be considered not simply in terms of how many clients are served but also by whether the behavior actually constitutes an act of kindness. In short, to have a kindlier society, we must have community service that is based on kindness; we must have social programs to help the needy and also to engender an ethic of kindness; we must have church dinners and visits to the sick and tutoring programs and also activities in which a deeper understanding of kindness itself is present.

Who Cares?

Much of what I have been saying can be encapsulated in the ambiguous meanings of the question "Who cares?" In conversation, the question is most often used rhetorically to mean that it makes no difference. In this context, indifference is an important feature of our society, as it indicates a lack of caring, an unwillingness to engage in kindness, an absence of virtue. The complaint of indifference is that the majority of Americans are unwilling to make any significant sacrifices to help those less fortunate than themselves.

This argument also suggests that indifference is built into the highly institutionalized character of our society. Indifference is now a possibility because much is done by institutions that depend on compliance and conformity rather than powerful or virtuous persons. It may offend our sensibilities as people to acknowledge this, but we know that the American political system continues to work reasonably well despite the fact that half the population seldom votes and 80 percent seldom become active in politics in other ways. Indeed, institutions thrive on a certain degree of indifference because they are organized ways of getting things done on a large scale whether or not particular people happen to be feeling virtuous on a given day. This is why many people who believe strongly in the need for a better society can nevertheless take a disinterested stance toward the question of kindness. In their view, kindness may not be as crucial as well-oiled institutions are. Social programs and economic growth, for example, may do more to help the needy than acts of charity can. Even volunteer efforts can be organized without relying much on the kindness of individual volunteers. Schoolchildren, for example, can be mobilized to clean up a park without having to learn about kindness at all. In this sense, then, kindness becomes problematic, not so much because indifference prevents it from being expressed, but because institutions (even caring ones) may be able to function without it. We may not like to think so, but at least we need to recognize that kindness is more complicated under these conditions than would be the case if we could be sure that genuine caring were available only from kindhearted individuals. If we believe that kindness itself is or should be an intrinsic virtue, then we need to consider whether it is really a part of the institutionalized ways in which people are now being encouraged to care for others or whether it is being neglected or abused as part of these efforts.

The indifference registered in "Who cares?" also raises another concern about kindness, arising from the ways in which institutions generate indifference and from the possibility that kindness is then regarded as a way of escaping this indifference. Institutions, I have suggested, function at least moderately well when there is a high level of indifference to them and toward particular roles within them. The reason is that specialization is the key to modern institutions and it is impossible without indifference to much of what else goes on in one's world. Most people, for example, are probably indifferent to the ways in which physicists spend their mornings. We have more important things to think about. We are willing to assume that physicists know what they are doing. By making this assumption, we can devote our attention to the specialized roles we are trained to play in our own institutional settings, for example, treating the sick or pumping gas. Most of us, in fact, find our specialized roles quite meaningful. In that sense, we are engaged rather than being merely indifferent. Yet specialization also corrodes the meaning we find in our specialized roles. It is easier to tell ourselves that what we do is interesting than it is to convince ourselves that what we do is truly significant; at least we have doubts. We know that we are expendable. Again, this is what institutions are designed to do: to ensure that tasks are performed whether or not a particular person happens to be there. In the process of performing our roles, we may be able to suppress these doubts, but when we momentarily step out of our roles, these doubts may well slip out. To protect ourselves, indifference may again come in handy. We tell ourselves that what we do doesn't matter that much to us, that it is not worth our full attention, and that it is not who we really are. We draw lines around the core of our being, the essential virtue we associate with ourselves, preventing it from being contaminated by the institutionalized roles we play.

Kindness takes on new meaning in this context. It stands in the crevices between institutionalized roles. It provides a way of escaping the inevitable boredom associated with indifferent role performances. Showing kindness to strangers becomes a way of fulfilling ourselves, of broadening our horizons beyond the specialized roles we play, of convincing ourselves that we are still alive, of meeting new and more interesting people. Is that virtue? If kindness is generated by these conditions, by the extreme indifference of modern life, then its meaning is surely different from the ways in which it has been understood in the past. We need to examine this meaning carefully to make sure that nothing important has been lost.

The other meaning of "Who cares?" is captured in questions such as "Does anybody care?" or "Which kinds of people can be motivated to behave in caring ways?" Considered in this way, the question usually assumes that caring is a good thing, perhaps because it is implicitly associated with kindness, virtue, or at least positive social consequences. The issue, then, is to find out who cares so that more caring can be encouraged. Indifference again provides a backdrop to the discussion. Those who do not care are assumed to be indifferent and in need of greater motivation.

If the question is rephrased, however, to mean "Who really cares?" then the matter becomes more complicated. We confront the possibilities that caring and kindness may not be the same thing or that caring is necessarily associated with such activities as volunteering and community service. If elementary kindness means ensuring that people have enough to eat and that one group does not brutalize another, then the path to kindness may wind through stuffy courtrooms and legislative halls rather than charitable agencies. Or if kindness is an individual virtue that enables someone to behave powerfully for the good of another, the more highly structured institutions that aim to provide human services in our society may indeed undermine, rather than encourage, kindness. We must ask ourselves, then, whether we want to—or even need to—use kindness as a way of promoting caring and, to turn the question around, whether some forms of caring may result in an abuse of kindness.

The tension to which I am referring is evident in the quotation opening this chapter. The character in Barbara Kingsolver's novel who makes this statement about elementary kindness is the main character's sister, an alter ego whom we never actually meet because she has gone off to Central America to fight oppression and injustice. The elementary kindness of which she writes (in a letter home to her sister in Arizona) is lacking where she is, insofar as there is not enough to go around and some people are being viciously destroyed, raped, and slaughtered, by their oppressors. It is the sort of kindness that her sister in Arizona takes for granted. The implication, then, is that such kindness, though by no means universal, is certainly widespread in the United States, brought about by democratic laws and economic stability more than by acts of virtue by individual caregivers. And the kindness that inspires hope, that allows the more virtuous sister to run along hallways of hope, happens—must happen—outside our own borders. Yet the puzzle that the story leaves for us is whether elementary kindness of the sort we so much take for granted in our own society can indeed survive without virtue or whether we too must search for ways of retaining virtue in the hallways available to us and, if so, what the shape of that virtue can be.

3

First Steps: From Family Ties to Specialized Caring

Home is where one starts from. As we grow older
The world becomes stranger, the pattern more complicated.

T. S. Eliot, *Four Quartets*

When Jason McKendrick was twelve years old, he saw a terrible accident in his neighborhood, empathized deeply with the suffering he witnessed, and vowed that he would always do what he could to help people in such circumstances. Ever since, he has been putting his energy into helping the homeless at Pearl's Kitchen. Or that is the way many experts would tell the story. They would link Jason's volunteering to a time of crisis and make sense of it by focusing on his empathy and pain. What actually happened, however, was much more ordinary.

Jason tells how he became a volunteer: "At first, I just went with Darcy, because she was my friend. It was actually like a social activity. I was going to talk with my friend. I didn't even *think* about what I was doing." Volunteering was just another activity that friends did with friends.

It was not until he got to Pearl's Kitchen that Jason began to realize what he was doing: "I was actually feeding the homeless and talking to them. That's when I really started to like it." Something clicked. "After that run, I went two other times, not for the social aspect of it, but just to go down and feed the homeless. That's when I really understood what I was doing."

Jason believes that his experience is not unusual. "There are a lot of kids in our school that will do that," he says. "They'll go to talk with their friends or be with their friends. Once they get down there, it's *totally* different." They discover that they are unable just to hang out with their friends because everyone has separate jobs. "They do their jobs, and then they don't necessarily meet back with their friends. They go talk with the homeless people."

Those who stay do so because they find the experience enjoyable. Jason, however, backtracks from the idea that he stayed just because he was having a good time. He admits he was scared the first time he went. "At first you get scared because you see a mob of, say, fifty or sixty people standing there wanting food, and you've got the food and you're to give it out and you get scared." Only when he started talking with the homeless people individually did his fear subside. He found they were people just like himself—polite, hungry, grateful for the food, interested in sharing their experiences. "They sit down and they talk with us. They tell us what they've been doing during the day." Jason pulls out a picture of one of the guys. "He has boxes all over the city. And each box has something different in it. Like a razor kit in one and there's clothes in another. They're just stashed throughout the city. I thought that was incredible."

Jason says the other reason he stays is that he really does want to help. Just seeing the number of people lined up waiting for food impressed him deeply. He remembers nights when the line in the park extended all the way down the block and around the corner—there must have been at least two hundred people who were depending on the volunteers from Pearl's Kitchen to keep them alive. Almost from the beginning, Jason knew this was a place where he could make a difference.

But there is more to the story than simply going with a friend and then deciding to stay and feed the hungry. Jason's first steps toward becoming a volunteer had taken place many years earlier. Like most people, he already knew what it meant to be cared for and to care because he had learned the meaning of caring from his family.

Jason's parents divorced when he was five, so he knows about relationships that go sour. But he also has been given a great deal of love. He lives with his mother and stepfather and sees his father (who lives only a few blocks away and is still friendly with his mother) every Wednesday and Sunday. Although he is not especially close to his stepfather, he describes both his natural parents as extraordinarily caring people and says he receives abundant kindness from them. Of his mother he says: "When my friends come in, we all sit down and we talk; she loves to talk with my friends and see what's wrong with them. Whenever I have a problem, she always wants to talk to me about it; she's very supportive." And about his dad: "All my friends, they know my dad. He's always cracking jokes. There's just a certain warmness about him. I don't know how to describe it. A lot of my friends walk away from my dad saying that he's a really nice guy."

When asked specifically how he knows his parents care about him, Jason explains: "My parents always take time for us" (that is, his older brother, younger sister, and himself). "In a busy workday, they'll always take time for us no matter what happened. My parents are very caring. I love my parents, my mom and my dad. Even if something was wrong, I always felt like they cared for me." At seventeen, Jason still feels especially close to his parents, noting that he can tell them everything and doesn't have to keep secrets, even from his stepfather and stepmother. He also credits his parents with having taught him the importance of caring about others: "My parents have always said you always treat people with respect, everyone, no matter who it is."

If Jason is typical, he has already learned about caring, and he raises both a significant possibility and a significant question. The possibility is that young people who do volunteer work already know a great deal about caring from their families and from other people who have shown them love and kindness; they do not have to discover it by doing volunteer work. But if this is the case, then what does volunteer work contribute? Does it deepen young people's understanding of caring? Is their understanding changed? Is it damaged in any way?

I believe the answer to this question is that volunteering is the route by which young people move from a primordial understanding of caring—rooted in family ties—to a more specialized understanding that will serve them better as they assume responsibilities in complex social institutions. Volunteering is thus an important link between having good intentions and being able to put them into practice. And becoming involved in volunteer activities as a teenager is the first step toward making the social institutions of adult society more compassionate. I would even go so far as to say that this is the main reason that young people should become involved in community service. By doing community service, young people make the critical transition from familial caring to a more mature understanding of kindness.

Of course, volunteering is not the only route by which this journey can be taken, but it is an attractive one because it is widely available to virtually all teenagers and because it presents young people with new challenges while preserving an emphasis on caring. Without volunteering, it is easy for young people to succumb to the pressures associated with self-interested roles and to adopt the attitudes of indifference that many of our social institutions encourage. Yet it also is possible that volunteering itself can lead people away from—rather than toward—a better understanding of caring. Thus we need to examine what it means to care and to be cared for, first within the family and then as young people begin to do volunteer work. We shall begin by considering how significant this journey is to the lives of young people and to the health of society.

Beyond Good Intentions

"In their actions," wrote Aristotle, "all men do in fact aim at what they think [is] good."[1] This assumption has long been the basis for thinking that society can be organized to good purpose; the question is how to transform good people into a good society. The difficulty is that well-intentioned people always seem to mess things up.

Restraint—delicately applied so that good aims do in fact achieve their goal—has generally been exercised at the two ends of the relationship between individual people and society. At the individual end, moral restraint has been the favored option, as it requires commitment, inner resolve, and a sense of duty toward oneself and one's neighbors. At the societal end, good laws and the political muscle to enforce them have been the preferred means of restraint. Aristotle himself helped frame social thought in these ways by dividing his major works into writing on ethics and on politics. Even today, in social debates, moral philosophy, on the one hand, and political philosophy, on the other, still are the prevailing categories of thought. After a prolonged period of social engineering, political maneuvering, and litigation, many analysts have turned again to the moral dimension and are asking about the obligation and responsibility of the individual person.

For the sake of argument, suppose that the world really is this simple, that the essential components of social order (or, if one prefers, of a healthy society, a good society, or, even—to risk the use of progressive imagery—a better world) are good people, on the one hand, and good institutions, on the other hand. Then it would make sense to be concerned about the moral instruction, moral literacy, and moral development of individual persons, to be concerned about the self and how to nurture or strengthen it in order to better understand its needs and realize its potential, and to make sure that people have responsible roles in society, such as exercising their civic duties, caring for the needy, feeding their families, and respecting the rights of others. It would also make sense to be concerned about the institutional life of society, especially to ensure that these institutions do not interfere with the freedom of people to develop themselves and to pursue their personal happiness as they see fit, to encourage the members of society to adhere to their moral principles and apply them to their public behavior, and to make certain that laws are just and that organizations are fairly and efficiently structured to provide peace, prosperity, and an equitable distribution of goods and services. When we state our arguments in this way, we see that they are in fact our concerns. Not only for sake of argument but also for much of what actually transpires in the public arena, we are concerned with the good of individual people and the goodness of our social institutions.

Let us, however, shift our attention from the two ends—individual morality and good institutions—to the middle. Suppose we focus less on the contribution that good persons make to social institutions and less on the space that social institutions create in which people can be good and more on the interaction between the two. Suppose that we ask what happens when good people start to perform tasks in social institutions. Do the good intentions or the moral principles that they may bring guarantee that these institutions will also be good? Is this individual sense of goodness simply lost, replaced perhaps by an entirely different set of norms, rules, and laws? Or is there some way of carrying an individual person's moral commitment into the institutional realm, even if this process requires some fundamental reshaping of what it means to be moral or good or right?

Posed in this way, the question merits careful consideration, as it points to the fact that individual goodness may have to be much modified as it moves into social institutions. It suggests that people may need to do more than learn to be good or to exercise moral responsibility or to behave ethically and that some of what they have learned as children may need to be relearned as they become responsible for social institutions. For example, we often think that the way to maintain fair practices in business and government is to make sure that people learn what it means to be fair while they are growing up; yet we also know that fair practices in business and government depend on more than this. They certainly depend on well-intentioned persons' learning how to pass laws and enforce them, but if my argument is correct, they also require well-intentioned people to learn that fairness means more than sharing toys with their playmates. That is, fairness must be reconceptualized to take into account the specialized roles that adults play in social institutions. For instance, it may mean that a physician offers a sliding fee schedule based on his or her patients' ability to pay and also contributes generously to charities that try to redress injustices in the community and pays more in taxes to ensure that social services are provided. These ways of behaving require that the fairness that people may have learned as children be retained but also transformed.

Reframing the question as I have done also suggests the need to consider the conflicts inherent in the formation of institutional life, that is, between the moral sensibilities that may be created in relatively uninstitutionalized, informal, or primary settings, such as the family, and the behavior required in highly formalized or complex contexts, such as the legal system or the contemporary workplace. Whereas one may allow people to develop deep bonds of trust based on extensive personal interaction, the other may depend more on strict adherence to rules that do not necessitate extensive knowledge of personal traits or situations. It may seem therefore that one can be more personable, genuine, and generous in one setting while at the same time having to remain aloof and self-absorbed in the other. We must examine these conflicts as a problem of greedy or dispassionate institutions bearing down on vulnerable persons and also from the standpoint of how a sense of moral commitment can be—indeed, must be—

retained in institutional settings. Practically speaking, the question of how good people can make the transition into institutional settings is essential to a wide range of pressing social issues, from ethics in business to the restoration of communities to the resolution of controversial policy debates.

Focusing too quickly on such practical matters, however, may prevent us from grasping the importance of the process to which I briefly referred. One way of appreciating its importance is to consider how the tensions between good persons and good institutions—and the transition from one to the other—are manifested in the mythic renditions of the human experience. Consider the biblical narrative of the fall of Adam and Eve. Their initial state can be described as one of innocent virtue, including harmony between themselves and with God and nature. After the fall, in which Adam and Eve gain the ability to discern between good and evil, there is tension in all their relationships as well as a greater division of labor, including one based on gender, and a requirement for greater effort to be expended. In the larger biblical narrative, moreover, the story of the fall becomes the basis of a continuing search for redemption and a new means of securing both individual salvation and the collective good. In short, the story moves from a sheltered microcosm in which goodness simply prevails to a wider, and more complex world fraught with a sense of loss and in which goodness can be attained only by undergoing an arduous pilgrimage away from the garden.

Many of the legends in our own heritage speak of similar transitions. The myth of modernization, depicting a nostalgic communal setting that has given way to more complex social institutions, is one story of such a transition. At a more popular level, this narrative can be found in personal accounts of leaving home, in tales of pioneer and frontier virtue and its displacement by corrupt politicians and bureaucrats, and stories about moving from farms and villages to cities and suburbs. Pulitzer Prize–winning writer Toni Morrison illustrates this transition when she talks about growing up in a small town. "You knew everything in that little microcosm," she says. "But we don't live where we were born. I had to leave my town to do my work here; it was a sacrifice. There is a certain sense of family I don't have. So the myths get forgotten."[2] Forgotten, to be sure but, we might add, also remembered. It is evident in Morrison's novels, for instance, that she has remembered a great deal about the small town in which she was raised. Yet the purpose of remembering is also to work out the tension we feel between that microcosm in which we knew everything and the world of loss in which we now live. What we have lost is indeed the sense of omniscience that comes with living in a microcosm. What we have gained is the freedom to grow and to experience the wider world and thereby to be more things for ourselves.

The transition from a world in which moral virtue is known—and indeed is so familiar that it can be taken for granted—to a world in which we have to seek ways to behave morally amidst complex and demanding expectations is thus a journey that people do not undertake without cost. The stories we create to make sense of these journeys begin with a sense of primordial goodness, of individual virtue that involves nurturing and good moral relationships, and of knowing how to behave. We also are aware that this state is temporary and not quite adequate in the wider world, that more effort will be required, that life will be more complex and more difficult, that there must be new structures and activities, and that these should be animated by primordial virtue and by an original moral vision but that they may not be so animated and, indeed, may corrupt individual persons and cause virtue to decay.

The transition from primordial virtue to responsible moral behavior—as we grapple with it in our legends and stories—represents a journey away from innocence and naive strength to a world in which innocence is no longer possible, self-reflection is needed, and greater effort is required. Role models become guides, and the sojourner becomes an apprentice. Stories become ways of resolving or maintaining the tension between one's origin and one's destination and of telling how one state is connected to the other. There is a sense of loss but an awareness of the necessity for growth. The self in the new world is weak, vulnerable, and lacking in self-confidence because nothing has yet been accomplished, so one must regain confidence by performing small tasks, learning new skills, trying out multiple roles, and thereby discovering one's uniqueness.

Caring for others is merely one dimension—but an extremely important dimension—of the transition that all of us must make in our journeys from home to the wider world. There is virtual agreement that a good society must include a strong commitment to caring, a sense of obligation toward others, and concern about the needs and interests of others. Caring is a basic virtue that most people learn to appreciate at home and then have to relearn at some cost to themselves in order to function as caring persons in a wider society. How this transition is made and how volunteering contributes to the process is best seen by considering what young people say about their families and their first efforts to make a difference in the lives of others beyond their families.[3]

The Family as a Place of Caring

They say the way to learn anything is one step at a time. They must have dancing in mind. Left foot, right foot, left foot, slide. Dancing has to be learned one step at a time because it does not come naturally. There may be something in the human spirit, some primitive urge, that compels us to dance, but to fulfill this urge we have to overcome enormous obstacles.

In this view, learning to care is like learning to dance. Children more or less endure the caring they receive from their families, the argument goes, because they are not yet mature enough to do things on their own. The primary human drive, however, is the capacity for self-preservation—what Rousseau termed the *first law* of human nature. "As soon as [the child] comes to years of discretion, being sole judge of the means adapted for his own preservation," wrote Rousseau, "he becomes his own master."[4] According to this argument, self-interest is the principle on which society must be based. Laws, for example, must be enacted to restrain the worst of human passions, and economic arrangements may be able to harness the desire for self-preservation to achieve common goals. The extent to which people can care for others is inevitably limited by this drive toward self-preservation. Caring is rooted in the *natural sentiment* of pity, as Rousseau called it, which is what makes animals emit "mournful lowings" for their dead, restrains violence among humans, and is the basis of benevolence and friendship.[5] Sympathy—the awareness of pain that Jason McKendrick might have experienced had he in fact witnessed a terrible accident in his neighborhood—is thus the basis for caring behavior.

But learning to care is not easy, according to this same argument, because the more we know, the more our reason works against the sentiment of pity. As Rousseau explains, "It is reason that makes man shrink into himself; it is reason that makes him keep aloof from everything that can trouble or afflict him; it is philosophy that destroys his connections with other men." So it is the more primitive or less educated that are the most compassionate: "It is the dregs of the people, the market women, that . . . hinder gentlefolks from cutting one another's throats."[6] Caring is like learning to dance, therefore, both because it is hard and because it runs against the more rational grain of modern civilization.

Recent scholarship recognizes that sympathy can be an important stimulus to caring behavior but also emphasizes how precarious it may be.[7] Sympathy by itself is a weak foundation on which to build a caring society. The voice of pity is easy to silence—as we recognize when we say that we become hardened to suffering by seeing it daily on the evening news or inured to the plight of the homeless by walking past them every day. Sympathy is also weak, as political scientist James Q. Wilson observes, because it springs from the same root that causes us to seek approval.[8] Knowing how painful it is to be excluded, we may go along with hate campaigns toward outsiders or tacitly assent to their mis treatment, all in the hopes of being accepted. If caring depends primarily on sympathy, therefore, it may well be a dance that is hard to master.

Listening closely to what young people say about caring, however, leads to the impression that caring is more like learning to walk than it is like learning to dance. It is not a sentiment that is quickly suppressed because it conflicts with one's primary drive for self-preservation but is, rather, a natural part of life that emerges early and develops to the point that most people take it for granted. Many of the volunteers we interviewed were thus convinced that their own caring was unexceptional; they believed everyone knew something about caring. Megan Wyse put it this way: "Some people might be afraid to volunteer and to take action or might not realize what they can do. But I think people are definitely just as caring as I am, especially with their friends and family."

We consistently found that the young people we interviewed felt cared for by their families and were generally close to their mothers and fathers.[9] We also know from information collected from random samples that the feeling of being close to one's parents and family is virtually universal in our society. According to a national survey conducted in 1982, only 7 percent of all Americans aged eighteen and older reported that they did not feel close to their mother while they were growing up, and 15 percent stated that they did not feel close to their father; only 3 percent did not feel close to either parent.[10] Consistent with this finding, our survey of teenagers nationwide showed that 94 percent regarded their family as a source of a great deal or a fair amount of personal satisfaction within the past year. Nearly everyone has some understanding of what caring means as a result of this closeness with their families.[11] Those who have experienced this caring and closeness most clearly, our data show, are the most likely to spend great amounts of time volunteering when they are teenagers.[12] We can, therefore, discover the qualities associated with caring by listening to what people say about their families.

For Rafe Ramirez, it was always the little things that stood out more than anything else. His parents never had much money. His mother did not work outside the home, and his father had a semiskilled job wiring mainframe computers for a manufacturing company. When the mainframe business began to decline, he had to shift over to maintenance, refurbishing offices, painting, and replacing light fixtures. His parents were unable to protect and coddle Rafe in the way that some of his upper-middle-class schoolmates were, but what they did give him was their love and attention. Rafe remembers when he was in grade school going to play Little League baseball. All the other parents dropped their children off and picked them up after the game, but Rafe's parents stayed and watched. A decade later, he can now point to those times as evidence that they really cared for him.

The two things that young people most often associate with parental caring are spending time together and talking. The amount of time spent together need not be long, but it must be time that both the child and the parents enjoy. Communication—talking—seems to be even more important. Parents and child need not discuss anything specific, but an element of trust and openness must be present so that the child feels comfortable talking to the parent. Megan Wyse explains: "If I had a problem, I'd feel very comfortable going to [my parents], and I probably would go to them. I think their advice is usually good. I feel that they would support me a lot in whatever I choose to do. They understand a lot of the things that I think and a lot of things that I do. I feel very close to them and I feel that we really share. We have a very good relationship in the way that they can trust me with things they have to tell me or things they want me to understand, and vice versa."

Sometimes such descriptions sound too good to be true—or healthy—at a time when young people need to become independent of their parents. Some of the more candid responses, however, reveal that there actually are limits to what can be discussed, that young people want to protect some of their personal secrets in order to develop their identities and avoid criticism. This need is especially evident among young people who feel that their parents intervene too actively in others' lives. For example, Tanika Lane says that she can talk openly with her parents and that she knows they care for her because they sometimes bring their problems to her. But she also explains: "As I get older, I don't tell my parents everything." She is especially cautious with her mother: "When I was younger, she would always say, 'You can talk to me. If you have a problem, you could talk to me. Come on. Talk to me.' And if I told her how I felt, she would holler at me or use it against me later on. So now I just say, 'Mom, can I express my opinion?' And then if she starts saying 'Well, I don't agree, and I'm the mother' or whatever, that's when I back off and say, well, I don't want to talk to you anyway."

Feeling cared for is thus not so much a matter of having to disclose everything as it is feeling accepted, trusted, and respected as a whole person. Feeling close to your parents means that they respect you and your opinions, including your needs and individual quirks, and that they respect you enough to take time for you and to treat you as a person. One student captured the element of trust especially well: "They listen to me. They allow me to be how I want to be. They trust me. They trust that I will be responsible."

Occasionally young people tell dramatic stories in order to demonstrate how caring their parents are. For example, one student told how his mother had taken in a friend who was being abused by his father; another student's parents had let a teenager in the neighborhood live with them while she was pregnant; others talked about their parents caring for them when they were seriously ill or in the hospital. Generally, however, young people focused on the little things their parents did for them. Some hint of sacrifice is often present; the child knows, for example, that the parent gave up buying something or was emotionally involved. The specific acts of kindness are, however, ones that show the parent having some fun or getting something out of the relationship as well. A typical statement would be that by Tanika Lane who says she was always impressed that her parents cared for her because whenever she was in a play at school or whenever there was an awards ceremony or something, they were always there. They cared how she felt and were there to share the experience.

When acts of kindness are small, ordinary, and mutually enjoyable, they show that caring is not difficult or exceptional but is a natural part of life. Most of the young people we talked to associated caring with their parents' basic personhood: Caring was just a part of who they were. As one young woman said about her mother: "She's just a very understanding person." And about her father: "It's just his being, his whole way of being." And because the whole person was involved, caring was inevitably personal or personalized. It was somebody tending a scraped knee, listening and saying, "It's OK," or reading a story and tucking one into bed.

I want to emphasize that caring such as this was not always the norm. Jason observed that there were times when he felt closer to his grandfather than to either his father or his mother. Tanika remembers when her parents nearly decided to divorce and how she was caught in the middle. Another student, raised in a single-parent family, remembers how her mother drank and became physically and verbally abusive. She remembers being hit repeatedly with the metal handle of the fly swatter. One year, things got so bad after being abused by her mother's boyfriend that she had to live with a neighbor. The rest of the time she went to school early and stayed late or just hung out on the street in order to keep away from her mother. Even now, she describes their relationship as very distant. She says she would talk to a teacher or a counselor about things before she would talk to her mother. Still another student was raised by a drug dealer who was a cocaine addict and described his occupation as gigolo and by a stepmother who went to jail for shoplifting. She recalls one day in grade school when she met two older children who turned out to be her brother and sister that her father had abandoned.

In these cases, young people were deprived of caring by their parents but generally found it in some other caregiver, such as a grandparent, an aunt or uncle, or a neighbor, and this care eventually encouraged them to reach out to help others as volunteers.[13] When Tanika's parents were fighting, for example, she grew close to a next-door neighbor who more or less adopted her (Tanika calls her "Aunt Yolanda"). She says the world was cold and harsh, but she felt blessed because Aunt Yolanda really cared for her. The young woman who was raised by an abusive mother also received care from a neighbor, a woman named Annie. She remembers the first time they met: "Annie came over here one night looking like something out of a horror movie. The guy she was living with had just beaten the crap out of her. He'd taken a skillet and hit her and hit her over the head. Her face was all bloody. So she took her son and came running over here. We took care of him while she was in the hospital, so I guess my mom thought she owed us. When they came and shut our electricity off, she told me to go live with Annie. I guess Annie was just real nice to me that year. She'd take me down to St. Vincent's and buy me things, just like for her own kids."

Even young people who were close to their parents often benefited from other adults who showed them what it meant to care (I discuss these role models in a later chapter). The important point is that young people gained firsthand knowledge of the value of caring. They learned about it naturally as part of their experience growing up, but it was not without texture or content. Caring was a virtue that reflected something about the whole person of the caregiver. Caring was nevertheless ordinary, and even though it required a genuine commitment of time and energy, it was nevertheless possible because it consisted of small deeds and kind words. Caring was also oriented toward the specific needs of the person receiving it, included respect and trust, and was mutually beneficial and enjoyable to the giver and the recipient.[14]

Parents as Volunteers

Parents sometimes wonder whether their offspring are even aware of the caring they receive, but the foregoing indicates that young people are indeed very aware of closeness and caring in their families. It is believed in some circles, however, that young people do not learn what it really means to care unless they see their parents helping others outside their families. When such help is offered, perhaps through volunteer work, young people realize an obligation toward others that extends beyond kinship. They may also see that caring consists of commitments that are more demanding, varied, or perhaps less enjoyable than simply tucking a child into bed at night.

Our interviews cast doubt on the assumption that children must see their parents volunteering in order to learn about caring—or, for that matter, to begin volunteering themselves. It makes sense that children whose parents volunteer would also become volunteers, and there is some evidence that young people are more likely to spend time volunteering if their parents also do volunteer work.[15] But there are so many other ways to become involved—schools, youth programs, religious organizations—that there need not be any connection. Moreover, young people are encouraged to care and to volunteer by seeing their parents helping others outside the family, whether or not this helping is formal volunteer work.[16] Among the young volunteers we talked to, their parents' volunteering ran the full gamut from those who had never done any such work (to their offspring's knowledge) to one couple who both were full-time volunteers, receiving only a subsistence allowance for food and housing in return for their efforts on behalf of a school for the mentally handicapped. In between, some parents had only become active as volunteers as a result of their children's becoming involved, whereas others had taken their children with them, and still others had done volunteer work only before their children were born.

The parents' volunteering did, however, influence the ways in which young people perceived their own volunteering. Those whose parents were volunteers saw their own volunteering as a natural extension of their family experience. The caring they put into their volunteering was like the caring they had received from their parents. For those young people whose parents were not volunteers, there was a sharper break. To them, volunteering was a way of distinguishing themselves from their parents and of pursuing their quest for a distinct identity. They felt they should be caring people because of the way they had been raised, but they were finding their own ways of putting this feeling into practice.

Whether or not their parents volunteered, young people also said it did matter a lot to know that their parents supported them, accepted what they were doing, talked to them about it, and sometimes provided transportation, advice, or some other form of assistance. Only a few of the respondents had become involved in volunteering against their parents' objections, and in these cases, they usually found support from a teacher or friend. Jason McKendrick was one of the lucky ones. He says his mother never did any volunteering, nor did his natural father or his stepfather. But once Jason started doing volunteer work, they became involved as a way of showing their support. His father, for example, has driven the van on runs to Pearl's, and his mother, an advertising specialist, has helped with fund-raising drives.

Most of the students we talked to thought their parents cared about people outside their family, whether or not their parents did volunteer work. Indeed, the students were often uncertain that what their parents did truly was volunteer work, and they sometimes forgot that their parents were volunteers, only to remember something later. The reason they were unclear about their parents' volunteering is that they thought of it simply as something a caring person did. Their parents were naturally caring—and so they helped others. Megan Wyse stated that neither of her parents had done any volunteer work, although both of her parents are in helping professions: Her father is a teacher, and her mother works for a philanthropic organization. Megan feels that both of them care deeply about people and points to their work as evidence.

Tanika Lane noted that neither of her parents did volunteer work, other than an occasional visit to her school, but she described both as people who care about the needs of people in their neighborhood. For example, not long ago an elderly woman across the street became ill with Alzheimer's disease, and Tanika's parents took care of her and her aging husband for several months. The way in which her mother is involved in informal networks of caring also is illustrated by the following episode: Tanika's mother was taking care of a baby during the day while the baby's mother went to school. The baby's mother was still living with her mother, who one day became angry with her and told her she could not live there any longer. On learning of the situation, Tanika's mother called her own mother-in-law and arranged for the girl to live there. Tanika concluded the story by saying, "I told Mom, hey, you're always getting involved in everyone else's problems. And she told me, 'So, I can help people if I want to!'"

Another young woman, Patti Evans, strikingly demonstrates that caring, rather than volunteering, is what children want from their parents. She said her mother was a woman who cared deeply about the needs of others but had never done any volunteer work. A few moments later she caught herself: "Oh, my mom did do volunteer work. What am I saying? She was in the Peace Corps. She was a volunteer down in Honduras. She speaks Spanish. In fact, she brought someone home with her. This was a long time ago, Orfi. And Orfi's been like another sister. And Orfi's like another member of our family. She's like an aunt, kind of, to me. She thinks I'm her baby. She's about four feet tall. She was there throughout my growing up. She used to live with us, until she got married."

Even when the parents are quite active volunteers, their children focus less on their specific roles when they talk about them and more on the diffuse commitment to caring that they associate with their parents' characters. A young woman whose parents served on a number of church committees and were involved in several other civic organizations, for example, admired both her parents enormously for the ways in which they helped people. But she said she could not recall any specific things they had done. She explained, "It's just so natural for them to be doing something for somebody else that I don't think of a specific person or a specific name."

Parents' volunteer work, therefore, plays an ambiguous role in encouraging young people to be more caring. When their parents are doing volunteer work, young people find it somewhat easier themselves to participate in volunteer activities. They do not regard volunteering as a role but instead as a manifestation of their personality. When their parents do not do volunteer work, young people still have a sense of what caring is from having received it and—in most cases—from seeing their parents help other people informally. This caring within the family, however, prepares them only partially for understanding what it may mean to care about needs in the wider world.

Exposure to People in Need

The outsider, observed Italian philosopher Giorgio Agamben, is one who stands at the door, not someone who resides totally in the beyond, but a figure who represents a passageway between our own dwelling and the world and who therefore gives us access to that which is different from ourselves.[17] One of the greatest shocks to young people's understanding of caring comes when they are first exposed to people in need. Such people are the outsiders, in Agamben's terms, who link us to a different world. In many societies, children do not regard the needy as outsiders because hunger and extreme poverty are all around them. But in our society, most children are insulated from such needs. Only later do they realize that the caring they have taken for granted is not part of everyone's experience.[18] If these young people were guided chiefly by sympathy—if caring were rooted in the natural sentiment of pity that Rousseau described—then their response would almost automatically be wanting to help. Evidence, however, suggests otherwise.

Fiction writer Gillian Roberts, basing the following exchange on her real-life experiences as a high school teacher in Philadelphia, offers an example of the reaction that homeless people may elicit:

> "Ever find one of them picking through your trash? Gross!" Suze flashed Clemmy a smile full of braces and smugness. They bonded, two rebels joined against the untanned, unpicturesque poor.
> "Don't you feel anything for them?" I asked.
> Indeed they did. They felt annoyance. Impatience. Disgust. Why don't those people *do* something for themselves? they asked.[19]

This example suggests that something besides mere exposure must be present to make certain that young people will have sympathy for those who are in need.

Part of what must be present—even in Rousseau's account—is *identification* between the observer and the person suffering. The more personal or intimate the connection is between the two, the more likely this sense of identification will be. Thus one of the ways in which volunteering can expand young people's ideas of caring is by bringing them into direct personal contact with the needy. Unlike Gillian Roberts's students, many of those we spoke with had come to know the homeless in a more intimate way.

The young woman I introduced who had been beaten with a fly swatter— I'll call her Sherry Hicks—is an example of someone whose attitude toward the homeless was dramatically changed when she actually started helping them. She recalls, "We went to the soup kitchen, and we helped fix food, and we helped serve. We waited on the people like they were in a restaurant to make it seem all the nicer. Then we went out there and we were actually talking to them. I had, I guess, the typical opinion, maybe, that oh, well, if you're homeless, then you're just a bum and you deserve it, because you didn't work hard." As she talked to these people, however, she discovered that many were hardworking, well-educated people who were on the street because the economy was in a downturn. Sherry's attitude was influenced by this new information, and she was also moved by the emotions to which she was exposed: "There was this one old lady, and she was just so happy to have someone talk to her, and to actually say, 'Well, how are you today?' that she started crying. She said usually people just shove her around because they don't care how she's doing. They just think that since she's on the street that she isn't worth anything. She just cried. I felt kind of weird at the time, because she was crying in front of me, but at the same time I just felt really good because I felt like even if I only asked how you were doing, or if I was just spending five minutes with her, at least those five minutes were worthwhile and maybe made her life a little bit better or a little bit easier."

Tanika Lane grew up in a low-income neighborhood, so she was exposed to the homeless at an earlier age when walking down the street, rather than as a volunteer. She also remembers, however, that firsthand contact with the homeless made her more sympathetic. When she was about nine, she recalls, she saw a whole family living on the street. "That's a little girl digging in a trash can," she remembers saying to her mother. Upon reflection, she says: "I was surprised, and I thought everybody got Christmas presents, and everybody had a mommy and a daddy live with them. Everybody had birthday parties, and everybody was just as fortunate as I am." But seeing the girl on the street made Tanika realize that the caring she took for granted was not universal. She remembers: "It made me more sensitive toward homeless people. My mom said it made me friendlier. I was already friendly. She said I began to give stuff away. Drastically different. You could have my sandwich, or my mom said I wanted to give the girl something— I forget. I was young. My mom said I gave her something that I had, and Mom said, 'See, you're spoiled. You go to McDonald's. You never know. That little girl she doesn't go to McDonald's.' So I said, 'Can I give her my cheeseburger?' She said, 'If you want to,' and I did. And she was, 'Oh, thanks.' Like I gave her a million dollars. 'Mom, she's happy over a cheeseburger.'"

Tanika's story shows that although a response may be sympathetic, it must be interpreted to the child, and generally, an adult is the one who supplies this interpretation. Exposure to the needy is thus a significant step toward developing a broader understanding of caring, but only if the situation can be appropriately interpreted. Parents who already are caring toward their children can supply this interpretation and thereby help young people understand better what it may mean to care for someone outside their own family. The young people we talked to had indeed been challenged to think in more complex ways about caring—well before they began to do any volunteer work—by confronting questions about poverty and homelessness.

A common reaction among young people, as they reflected on their first contacts with the needy, was to admit that they had been uncomfortable or afraid. They felt this way because they realized that the poor or the homeless were different from themselves—a fact that reflects the degree to which middle-class children are shielded from even seeing the poor. One young woman, for example, recalls meeting a poor family when she was in seventh grade: "I think I was mostly uncomfortable with it. As a little kid I was always uncomfortable about situations that I didn't understand and places I've never been before, so seeing things like that, it made me really unhappy." Young people also talked about disorientation and confusion as a result of the differences they observed. For instance, a young man being with people for the first time who had no address or phone number and who were begging for money, said he just "couldn't conceive of it."

Parents (or other adults) need to explain in such situations that there are reasons to treat the needy as fellow human beings, even though they seem different and perhaps scary. Patti Evans (introduced earlier) offered a useful illustration of this point: "Well, my parents always say that you have to look at the situation that people are in. You have to step into their shoes and see what kind of situation they're in. They've taught me to be compassionate. They've also taught me not to discriminate because of how a person looks, how a person acts. A lot of times when you're young, you say things like a 'nigger' or something. They'd always be right on me telling me not to say that. You just say it because you hear it. But they've always been real careful to teach me that. I'd say that's the most important thing they taught me: to look at the person's situation and step into their shoes and see where they're coming from."

Megan Wyse had learned about being kind to people from her parents, but this lesson was reinforced by the counselors she had at summer camp. She recalls: "There were some kids there who had severe learning disabilities, almost to the point of retardation. At first, when you're younger, you go and you make fun of these kids because you think they're just crazy kids. I remember the counselors making a conscious effort of pointing out to me that they're different, and that you have to really treat them nicely and be fair to them, and understand that they're not coming from the same background as you are."

If the needy or disadvantaged can be regarded as human beings just like oneself, the reality of their situation is also an important message that needs to be communicated. Many of the young people we talked to realized that the needy were people who lacked the basic necessities of life through no fault of their own.

On seeing poverty and homelessness for the first time, however, these young people often did not have much of a sense of what should be done—or even of what it was like to be in need. Their feelings were, in fact, less often ones of pain, prompted by the suffering of someone else, than of happiness or gratitude from recognizing their own privileges.[20] Their feelings naturally focused more on their own situation than that of the needy. Thus another valuable lesson that many parents tried to reinforce was that an awareness of good fortune—and gratitude for it—is important. Once one's own privileges have been fully acknowledged, then one may also feel able to help others.

The other lesson that many of these young people learned when they confronted the needy was that good intentions must be channeled into effective methods of providing care.[21] Many young people's first response was to fantasize about some heroic gesture that would fix the problem. But the counsel they received that led them to a more mature understanding of caring was to do little things that were possible, even if they did not fix the problem, and to think about additional ways of coping with the larger situation.

Megan Wyse learned this lesson from her father on a trip to Israel where she was confronted with people begging for money on the streets. She remembers: "My reaction was, 'Come on, Dad. Let's give them money! Let's give them money!' In the beginning, you would give money to everyone that passed by, but then you realize that you pass so many people, if you gave money every time, then you would have no money left. So my father explained to me that you can't give money every time you see someone, because there's a lot of people out there, and sometimes giving money isn't the best thing to do anyway. So my first reaction was give them money, help them out, and things will be fine. But I understood that it's not always the best idea."

In cases like this it was especially important that warnings against giving money not be interpreted as being coldhearted. Accordingly, Megan's father discussed poverty with her at some length so that she would understand some of the things that volunteers could do. Tanika Lane, as well, remembers that her mother "got on her case" to make sure she developed a caring attitude toward the poor. "I remember when I was younger," she says, "and we would go downtown and there's a lot of homeless people. People would ask for a dollar or a quarter. My grandmom, she would always say she didn't have it. I used to stay with my grandmom a lot, and being around my grandmom I would always say, 'Get a job.' Stuff like that, but my mom would say these people need help, Tanika. Some of these people were old doctors and lawyers, Tanika. They just need help. They didn't have the right direction, and you should be able to talk to people. You don't have to be so mean. I used to be a little cold-blooded, and I'd say, 'That's your problem. Don't tell me your problem. I got my own problem.' She gave me a whole, long lecture and told me how I shouldn't be and how I don't know where life is going to take me. I don't know all the problems. I felt bad because of the person I was becoming, and I was looking down on people. I realized I didn't used to be like this. When did this start happening? From listening to a lot of other people in school say, 'Tell 'em to get a job and stuff,' I started saying the same thing. When my mom chastised me, I realized that that's not a right attitude to have toward somebody who needs help."

First Efforts at Volunteering

By the time they started volunteering, most of the young people we talked to already had learned some lessons about the nature of caring beyond their own families. They had learned these lessons as a result of parents and other adults supplying interpretations that helped reinforce and clarify whatever feelings of sympathy they may have had toward people in need. Their volunteering then built on these interpretations. That is, as they began to volunteer, their movements shifted from walking to dancing. Volunteering required more effort and exposed them to the more specific ways in which caring can be put into practice. Young people learned that caring was not a matter of simply being open and relating without barriers—as it was with their parents—and they began to understand how to take pride in small accomplishments. But they did not start volunteering all at once. Most of them were drawn into it gradually by doing small acts of service in their schools and in their communities, often while they were still in elementary school.[22] Their views of caring were inevitably shaped by these activities because some activities provided positive experiences whereas others were largely negative.

Jason McKendrick's path to becoming a volunteer was fairly typical. He started doing volunteer work on a very small scale and for no reason other than someone's asking him. He remembers when he was a freshman that a teacher he had known from middle school asked him to join other students who were planning to help with the Special Olympics. Jason agreed simply because he knew the teacher. Once he was at the Special Olympics, however, he realized that he was having fun. He also met the other students at his high school (he knew few of them, being a freshman at a school of eight hundred) who did volunteer work, and one thing led to another. Jason learned about the Service Board and became involved in some of its activities. He also met the girl who enlisted him for Pearl's Kitchen.

Megan Wyse began volunteering at about the same time that Jason McKendrick did. She explained, "It was about four summers ago. I worked with the kids at the camp I was telling you about who had behavior disorders and severe mental disorders. We got paired up, and we worked with them doing whatever they wanted to do, depending on the child." She didn't think much at the time about why she was doing it, but she did find it enjoyable. "It was something that was very new to me, something that I was really interested in, just because it was something that was so new to me. So I think it was something I became involved in really to see what it was, to see what I could learn from it." She especially enjoyed working with people who viewed life differently from the way she did: "I learned a lot from people's mentality. Some of them, their mentality is like working with a child, that they're so fresh, and their ideas are so fresh about things. They see things so objectively, because they aren't warped by society the way some people are. And it was just sort of interesting to me the way they looked at things and the way they thought about things, the way they're so open about saying things because they didn't really know the difference between right and wrong or what's polite and what's rude. Although I might have been offended, I thought it was really interesting. It was fascinating just to see how their mind works."

Tanika Lane also became hooked on volunteer work as a result of working with the handicapped. "When I was in the sixth grade," she remembers, "I went to this camp for a week and we had to work on science and also had to work with handicapped children. I had never been really involved with the handicapped. I didn't alienate myself from handicapped people, but I just thought they were, like, prejudiced really. Then I got involved in pushing them around and playing with them." Tanika recalls how important it was to break the barrier between her own group and the handicapped children. "We didn't know the handicapped children were going to be there. At first, the handicapped sat on one side, and we sat on another side. It was like we were invading their privacy. We began to push them down to the pond and take them out. If they could get out, if they could walk, like play in the water, and they were like fun to be with. It was fun because they made us laugh. We didn't laugh at them, but they made us laugh. If you pick up a bug and you say, 'Look, this is a grasshopper,' for instance. They would repeat it—grasshopper, and they would like put it in their hand like they wanted to eat it. No, no you can't eat it. It was fun. It was innocent fun. We weren't putting them down. We were helping them, and they appreciated it. They loved us. They liked us back, and they showed us affection back."

Virtually all the young people who had worked with the handicapped said their experience had been positive. These young people enjoyed the time they spent volunteering because the handicapped children were having a good time and showed their appreciation. It was easy for first-time volunteers to see that they were making a small difference in someone's life. Other young people who had positive experiences volunteering generally emphasized something they enjoyed as well, such as learning to work with people or gaining a new skill. They did not volunteer because they were especially concerned about the needs of others. They already knew about caring and found it natural to say yes when someone asked them to help out. Their efforts put them in situations in which someone genuinely benefited from their help and they could learn from adults or other role models.[23] Because their experiences were positive, they were eventually drawn to become more active as volunteers, but sometimes only several years later.

When the first efforts at volunteering are positive, they generally provide connections between the caring that young people have experienced in their families and new understandings of caring that involve specialized roles—the kind of roles that people play throughout their lives. Even the simplest volunteer activities can serve this purpose. For example, a scout remembers that the first volunteer work he did was in the Cub Scouts when he was about nine or ten years old. His troop went along the highway picking up trash. The three things he remembers liking about it are revealing: being with his friends, realizing that he was a "nature lover," and feeling good about doing something helpful for the community. The last reflects the emphasis on being helpful and caring that he had learned in early childhood from his family. The other two were the beginnings of more specialized roles or ways of relating to others and of talking about himself.

Like the lessons from seeing people in need, one of the most important lessons that young people learn from their early volunteer activities is that small things count. The beginning of volunteering is, in this sense, the end of idealism, the end of childhood hopes that all problems can be solved and that the world can be made perfect. To volunteer is thus to begin experiencing realism. But volunteering is also the first step toward learning a new motive for caring—not to solve the world's problems and not to prevent someone else from suffering (and thus to reduce one's own pain), but caring as a way to make a small contribution. Doing one's part means playing a role, being part of something else, of working together, of feeling that one's part makes a difference because others are also doing their part.

A young woman who began doing things in the sixth grade with her church youth group captured the essence of this new understanding of caring: "You couldn't say, well, I'm going downtown to feed the homeless people and, therefore, there aren't going to be any more homeless people. You didn't see big results like that, but you saw little ones, and that was nice."

In some cases, first efforts at volunteering generated negative feelings, although much can be learned from these experiences as well. Young people talk about feeling coerced or pressured into doing something that was awkward or that they didn't understand. They also talk about doing things that had no immediate rewards, about feeling that they were serving an organization rather than helping people, and about experiences where they were subjected to danger or were not appreciated by those they were trying to help. The young people we interviewed did, of course, go on to become actively involved as volunteers later, but they were not encouraged to do so by their first efforts at volunteering. What they did learn was that volunteering can be purely a matter of performing tasks, of acting out roles, and of functioning impersonally in relationships so that little of the familial sense of caring is preserved.

One of the volunteer activities that many young people do as children is going door to door to raise money for some charity or organization.[24] It is unfortunate that this experience is so widespread because it is also one of the least positive. Few of the young people we talked to regarded raising money as a step toward becoming a volunteer or a more caring person. Instead, young people discussed these experiences without enthusiasm, as activities they were forced to do because they were in school or because they belonged to the scouts, a church, or some other organization. "Oh yes," recalled one young man, "we had to do all sorts of those, like for March of Dimes or whatever. Then in middle school, yes, I remember we had to do this jump-rope-athon. We had to jump rope to get donations. I've quit doing things like that."

In other cases, young people said they just went through the motions without any clear sense of why they were doing what they were. For example, one—whose first involvement was an Earth Day celebration during her freshman year—says she had no good reason to participate, other than she thought it would be "cool" or "neat." Three years later, she thinks that she really did not understand much of what she was doing that year. Another said, "Hey, we just went because it was a free party."

Young people generally had negative experiences, too, when their first volunteer efforts consisted of free labor needed by an organization but they did not directly benefit from helping. A young woman who started volunteering by helping at a child welfare agency provides an example: "It was one of my worst volunteer jobs. I wanted something that I could really make a difference with. I told [the man in charge] that I really liked to plan things. He said he understood and that he really wanted to put youth to work like that. I was really excited. He ended up making me enter things into his computer system, like hundreds of names into computers. They could have hired a secretary for that. It was really annoying."[25]

The fact that first efforts at volunteering can so easily be negative or meaningless experiences shows that special attention must be paid by those who wish to encourage young people to do volunteer work to make these experiences positive. One of the main problems we observed was that first efforts were often events isolated from the rest of life. Children were asked to do something but were given little explanation of why they should and were not encouraged to reflect on their experiences. They did not see a connection with the caring they knew about from their families and only sensed (perhaps implicitly) that volunteer work was different. They were not sure that this kind of caring was something they would enjoy or that volunteer work necessarily involved caring at all.

Those who had positive experiences were more likely to see that volunteering involved firsthand relationships like those they enjoyed in their families.[26] Such experiences could draw them into a caring relationship and yet lead to the realization that caring was important even if it were partial and specialized.[27] Volunteering was a way of preserving a personal understanding of caring and of making it suitable for the more complicated world of institutions outside the family. These young people were also encouraged to reflect on their experiences and thus to better understand what caring meant and why they should try to help others. We turn to these reasons in the next chapter.

4

Reasons to Care: The Multiple Voices of Modern Society

> In real life people talk most of all about what others talk about—they transmit, recall, weigh and pass judgment on other people's words, opinions, assertions, information.
>
> Mikhail Bakhtin, *The Dialogic Imagination*

On February 13, 1429, a seventeen-year-old girl set out on a dangerous journey. Disguised as a man, she traveled for eleven days, crossing enemy territory to reach her destination. Upon arriving, she was immediately seized and subjected to three weeks of questioning by the authorities to ascertain her intentions and the purity of her motives. Eventually she was given leave to return home, her request having been granted. She had asked no less than the right to raise an army and to lead it in battle against the enemy. A month later, her army raised and sword in hand (the sword having appeared miraculously in a nearby church), she arrived at a besieged city just in time to join forces with its defenders and turn away the attacking forces. Wounded, she nevertheless seemed always to be at the right place at the right time, anticipating her opponents' moves, and she inspired courage in her followers by her bravery and determination.

She was, of course, Joan of Arc, the maid of Orléans, and her struggles were only beginning.[1] For the next thirteen months she led her army in one battle after another. From Orléans they fought their way to Reims, where the English were forced to retreat and the French dauphin, on whose behalf Joan was fighting, was crowned as Charles VII. Other towns were captured and her army marched on to Paris, only to be repulsed by the duke of Burgundy, whose rival claim to the throne was supported by the English. Wounded again, she was forced to retreat but in the following spring took up arms again. This time she was captured and, after two attempts to escape, was turned over to the presiding religious authorities to be tried on questions of heresy and immorality. For three months Joan was interrogated. Although the trial itself lasted only a few days, she was convicted on seventy counts, ranging from wearing men's clothing to foretelling the future to claiming that her saints spoke in French rather than English. A month later, having refused to recant on threat of torture, she was sentenced, and on May 30, 1431, Joan was burned at the stake.

Events have been kinder to Joan of Arc in death than they were in life. Twenty years after her execution, her sentence was annulled. A campaign soon began, which eventually was successful in the twentieth century, to have her declared a saint. Mark Twain once described her as "the most extraordinary person the human race has ever produced."[2] Certainly her leadership in the battle at Orléans is credited with providing the turning point in the Hundred Years War. Historians marvel at her courage, her valor in battle, her conviction, the singlemindedness with which she pursued her aims, and even the tenderness she displayed toward friends and enemies alike.

What motivated her will never be known for sure. The desperate times in which she lived—her family, her village, and the surrounding region had been at war for generations—undoubtedly steeled her resolve. Once propelled by her initial successes on the battlefield, she became a public figure with few options but to continue fighting for her cause. She herself claimed to have been driven since the age of twelve by voices, audible ones that she associated with the three saints whose statues adorned the church of her childhood. Yet much of what we know of these voices comes from the uncertain record of her trial. What remains undisputed is that Joan bore the mark of the genuine prophets and saints, unswerving in the mission that it was her destiny to pursue.

The Problem of Motivation

The sense of mission that drove Joan of Arc is seldom evident in our own society. Indeed, we are tempted to call people like her zealots or fanatics and to worry about the passion that drives them, especially when they claim to be motivated by audible voices inside their heads. Yet it is also true that we remain convinced of the importance of motivation. We want young people to do things not just because they have been told to but because they have good reasons for their behavior. A significant part of learning to care is understanding why one is— or should be—interested in the needs of other people.

In this chapter I examine the reasons that young people give for becoming involved as volunteers and what they say about their motivations. I argue that the process we saw in the last chapter—of gaining a primordial sense of caring in the family and then discovering how to play specialized roles as one begins to volunteer—is also evident in the ways in which young people talk about their reasons for caring. Teenagers who have begun to do volunteer work are well equipped to understand their motives for wanting to help others. Several prominent languages or frameworks are readily available in our culture for explaining why we should care about others. These frameworks are nearly universal and therefore legitimate to draw on in accounting for one's own behavior. They are, however, learned specifically from interactions with one's parents and other adult role models. They are thus a primary language that young people learn in conjunction with the caring they receive as children and in early encounters with people in need.

Ironically, contemporary young people are very much like Joan of Arc. Although few young people nowadays speak with the sense of divine mission that inspired Joan of Arc, modern teenagers are still inspired by the voices that ring inside their heads, and these voices are indeed multiple and yet uniform in their message. The reasons that young people give for wanting to help others are expressed in *scripts*—formulaic strings of words—that they have heard others use and that they have remembered, repeated, and internalized. Sometimes they can identify the exact source of these words. In other cases, teenagers shift their inflection when they repeat certain phrases, to indicate that they are quoting something they have heard. How they differ from Joan of Arc is that few young people nowadays believe that the voices they hear are speaking to them with divine authority. Nevertheless, the students we interviewed did regard their reasons for caring to be authoritative.

As young people mature, they retain these primary frameworks of understanding, especially when they are put into caregiving situations. Volunteering is an effective way of preserving these reasons to care, because volunteers are frequently asked—and ask themselves—to explain why they are trying to help others. As they mature, however, they are also subjected to social processes that cause the moral authority of these reasons to erode. The fact that many different voices speak is sometimes a problem because it raises doubts about which reasons are actually the best. Modern culture is a cacaphony of voices, about caring and also about self-interest, personal preferences, success, and fun. Young people are faced with sorting out the balance between these voices and the ones encouraging them to be concerned about the needy. Becoming involved in volunteer work also poses a challenge of its own: Because specialized ways of caring may seem arbitrary and insignificant, young people must develop a secondary language of motivation that explains why they happen to be involved in a particular activity.

Megan Wyse's description of why it is important to her to be a caring person provides a concrete example. She describes her family background as a "sheltered microcosm" and attributes her volunteer work to a desire to break out of that microcosm. "I was in high school," she says, "and I didn't even realize that there's so much poverty here in the city; I was never really exposed to it before." She admits that one of her reasons for becoming interested in helping the homeless was simply "curiosity and understanding things I'd just never been exposed to, to really understand how people live that way, and why they live that way." She adds: "It was really curiosity, I think, that drove me initially." She says she started developing personal relationships with some of the homeless people, however, and that process, she emphasizes, involved breaking through the "barrier of them being homeless and you not being homeless." Once she had this "one-to-one personal" orientation, the importance of caring blossomed. She recalls: "I almost felt like it was required, like it was something I had to do, like it was an obligation." Then, needing to supply a reason for feeling this way, she observes: "I was really blessed with going to a good, private day school, and having a family, and having the option of going to a university, so it was my obligation, my way of appreciating all this and saying thank you by working with these people."

We see in this example that motives can change, as they are a matter of reflection and interpretation. As Megan became involved in volunteering, she was forced to reflect more deeply about her reasons for caring, and she found that these reasons were mixed. She drew on language about curiosity, as if helping others were no different from traveling to another country or learning something new in biology. She also talked about obligation, thereby grounding her interest in caring in something deeper and more authoritative than curiosity alone, and she stressed the differences between her life and the lives of the homeless but saw in these differences a need to pay something back and to show her appreciation for what she had. As she articulated these reasons, she was drawing on the multiple scripts—the voices—available to her by virtue of the settings in which she had been reared.

The connection between Megan's reasons and the voices to which she had been exposed is evident in the way she talks about her parents. She believes her parents exemplify caring because she has seen her father helping people as a teacher and her mother working hard to raise money for the needy and other causes in Israel. Although neither parent has done volunteer work, Megan regards them as helpers. There is also an interesting thread of "sameness" and "difference" that runs through her description of her parents' helping behavior. When she was in the second grade, one of her classmates became ill with cancer and died. She remembers her parents visiting the child in the hospital several times and later comforting the family. The story hinges on the fact that the two families had much in common and yet were fundamentally different in respect to the one's bereavement. She also tells about her grandfather—whom she describes as the most compassionate person she knows—giving lectures about racial tensions. Her choice of words is instructive; she says he talks about "harmony in a world of difference."

Megan's sense of harmony and of differences among people underlies her perception of why she feels it important to care for others. An absence of differences is how she understands caring within her family: She talks about closeness as a lack of barriers and of being able to share and to reciprocate. Sameness also extends beyond her family, for example, as she describes how her parents moved in order to become more a part of the Jewish community and as she remembers her camp counselor's emphasis on sharing. Her realization of sameness, however, also includes overcoming differences, such as learning about the handicapped children at her camp and developing a personal relationship with the homeless. Megan associates her sense of curiosity with these differences as well, observing that she was intrigued with the differences among people as she lived in various communities while growing up. Even her sense of privilege—especially making plans to attend an expensive university—grows out of this recognition of differences.

When Megan offers a general statement about why people should be caring, it is thus not surprising that she talks about reaching out to others, connecting with them, and drawing them into a common circle: "I think it's very important for people to be there for other people. I think it's very important that everyone understands that they're not alone and there's always someone they can look to for help. It's a very crucial part of human mentality to not be alone and to be part of a group. I think if someone doesn't have that, and he's really on his own, and he's on the street, it can be a very lonely life. I think that it's almost an obligation to fulfill that part in someone's life that they might not have fulfilled."

At one time, reasoning and motives were considered to be wholly mental processes. Now these processes are understood to be heavily influenced by their cultural, historical, and institutional settings. The reasons that people give for wanting to help others and their motives for caring cannot be divorced from the contexts in which they live and the languages they have learned. Although a person like Megan Wyse regards caring as natural—and certainly desirable—it is meaningful to her because she has developed a language that helps her explain its significance to herself and to others.

In this sense, language is not so much like English or German but, as Robert N. Bellah and his colleagues suggest in their book *Habits of the Heart*, "modes of moral discourse that include distinct vocabularies and characteristic patterns of moral reasoning."[3] It is clear that Megan Wyse understands her reasons for helping others in a *moral* framework, that is, as an obligation that is right and good. I would venture that this understanding is embedded in her personal experience—so much so that it is a primary obligation—but also that it depends on the various vocabularies she has learned from her parents, at school, and in her religious community. These vocabularies give her several overlapping moral frameworks.

Frameworks

A framework of understanding is perhaps unnecessary in order for a person to perform a particular activity. As we have seen, young people often become involved in volunteer work without a clear sense of what they are doing. Having a framework of understanding does, however, make one's behavior more meaningful. And behavior that is meaningful is more likely to be sustained over a longer period of time; it is more likely to be considered personally fulfilling because one can see its implications more clearly; and it is more likely to be regarded as an expression of one's values, commitments, and personhood. When we say that an action has meaning, therefore, we are referring to the ways in which a person subjectively perceives it.

The process of learning to care must include an effort to make caring activities meaningful. Rather than commandeering young people simply to raise money or to perform other unpleasant tasks, community leaders, teachers, and parents must pay close attention to the frameworks that young people develop in order to make sense of their behavior. Some of these frameworks are, as Megan Wyse exemplifies, associated with the symbolic acts of kindness of parents, grandparents, camp counselors, and other role models. These acts become symbolic, however, only when they are interpreted.

When we listen to what young people say about their caring activities, we gain the impression that their behavior is indeed subjectively meaningful. But we determine this only because they put their feelings into words. That is, they use scripts to talk about it, and these are not scripts they invent from scratch, but strings of words they have heard, repeated, and internalized. Although their specific choice of words varies, broad themes can be identified. In Megan's case, for example, her words about showing appreciation and saying thank you for the privileges she has been given point to a broader framework of understanding.

A framework need not be spelled out in detail, but it must provide a context, a category in which to place caring and to explain why it is good to be a caring person. Frameworks are often used without thinking about them. They are habitual, remaining in the background of our thinking while we focus on more specific issues, and they are rooted in common, everyday ways of interacting and behaving. For this reason, we may have trouble articulating them, especially when an activity such as caring, as I have suggested, is rooted in early family experiences. One young man, for example, stated that he could not explain his reasons for being caring: "I have trouble saying why. I believe that almost everything in life that you do and the way your decisions are made are pretty much how you are raised. It's like if you were raised to think that that was important, you just feel it, and there's not like a definite reason for it. It's just one of those answers that's 'just because.' I don't know of a better answer than that." Frameworks are nevertheless powerful because they invoke certain ways of classifying the world even before we begin to speak about it. They are thus broader than motives. A motive gives us an account of why we engage in a specific form of behavior, whereas a framework points us toward the plausibility of an entire category of behavior.

Frameworks generally carry a sense of obligation, as they do for Megan Wyse, or of moral authority: Caring is conceived as being right because the framework is universally accepted or indicates some universal feature of the human condition. Megan's arguments, for example, emphasize both her view that human need is something that should always be addressed insofar as resources allow and her belief that humans have a natural need for community and a natural desire to escape loneliness. As we shall see, young people reflect the uncertainties inherent in our culture by toning down their arguments about the universality of their claims. Frameworks are often arbitrary and are defended primarily on the basis of personal experience rather than being rooted in abstract or metaphysical assertations about the human condition. Their legitimacy is, however, strengthened by the fact that most people are exposed to more than one such framework. If one seems to falter, therefore, another can be cited.

Judging from the people we talked to—young people and adults alike—caring is most often defended in terms of one or more of the following frameworks: humanitarianism, the pursuit of happiness, reciprocity, and self-realization. Each of these frameworks is so readily available in American culture that teenagers are likely to have been exposed to one or more of them in a number of different settings. The better they can articulate their reasons, however, the more likely they are to understand the significance of caring. We shall consider each of these frameworks, therefore, to see how it makes sense of caring and how it may need to be modified as young people mature.

Humanitarianism

In popular usage—news stories, speeches, charitable appeals—humanitarianism means supplying aid, such as food, clothing, and shelter to victims of war or natural disasters. The goal is to eliminate pain and suffering. More generally, humanitarianism combines a feeling of compassion or sympathy with a value that attaches importance to helping those toward whom one feels compassion. In the survey, the responses expressing these notions suggest consistency within the humanitarian perspective.[4] Humanitarianism also connotes a common bond that ties all people together and obligates them to help one another. Humanitarianism is thus the awareness that no person can live happily and effectively as an island; it is the awareness of fundamental human affinity that sometimes motivates great acts of heroism on behalf of people in grave danger.[5]

Megan Wyse was drawing on a humanitarian framework when she underscored the troubling commonality between the homeless and herself. Another student, a young man who had won an award for his community service activities, explicitly used humanitarian arguments to explain his involvement: "I believe in humanitarian thought," he observed, "and that explains why I am involved in community service." For the past four years he has visited the elderly in a nursing home. Like himself, the people he visited were Jewish. But he denied that this was the reason for his interest: "I'm involved because they are people who need help. They have no family. So I help them. I write them letters. I visit them." Extending his argument beyond himself, he explained that in his view, everyone should do what he or she can to relieve suffering.

Although humanitarianism focuses on specific groups or persons who are in need, it also stresses the basic equality of people and thus legitimates efforts to redress inequities. A young woman who said she had learned most of her ideas about caring from her mother is an example of how often equality may be emphasized. "My mom's always been one for equality," she remarked, "that, more than the needy. I was always told that people are equal. It goes past race to people who aren't economically as well off as we are. Because they came from disadvantaged backgrounds, economically anyway. And my parents have always instilled in us the sense that 'You are lucky, but don't expect it.' Just because people don't have any money doesn't mean they're any less of a person than you are."[6]

Humanitarianism, more so than the other frameworks we shall consider, also tends to evoke the language of moral duty or moral obligation.[7] Young people who felt a need to help suffering or disadvantaged persons often described it as an obligation built into the very nature of things. Sina Mesnar, a young man of Turkish origin who devotes much of his spare time to visiting and feeding the homeless in the suburb in which he lives put it this way: "You understand that everyone has a moral obligation. We're connected in a way that we have to help one another. If not with material goods, if not with food, just by stopping and saying hello, talking to them, showing that you care. To see them as human beings, because a lot of the time it's simply ignored by many of the people. Aside from giving the food, I've been talking with the homeless and that especially helps them because they usually don't have people to talk to. They're obviously by themselves continuously. It's a way in which they can open up to you."[8]

Although humanitarianism is often framed in terms of moral obligation, it should not be understood strictly as a moral absolute or even as an expression of altruistic or selfless commitment.[9] Because young people do not learn about humanitarianism in the abstract but in their families, they realize that their duty to help others may be limited by circumstances and that there is likely to be something in it for the caregiver as well as for the person receiving help. Listen to the way in which one young woman explains why it is important to care for others: "Because we have the duty as human beings to be decent, compassionate people with the people around us, with people all over." But then she says: "We owe it to ourselves, to the world, to everyone, to work to make the world more just and to enable people, everyone, to live a decent life." And when she is asked what she would do to enlist others in caring activities, she stresses duty less and focuses more on what people might receive: "Tell people that it'll be fun and rewarding for them, too. That while it'll be fun for them and rewarding, they also have a duty to contribute to others and to contribute to society and to make things better."[10]

The Pursuit of Happiness

If humanitarianism is a self-evident principle on which to base caring, so is the pursuit of happiness, especially when humanitarianism itself is defended on the basis that it is mutually enjoyable and beneficial. From Jeremy Bentham to John Rawls, political philosophers have argued that individual happiness and the good of others are not incompatible but are in fact linked. Many of the teenagers we interviewed explained that they helped others because it was a way of spreading happiness. They felt good when someone cared for them, so they assumed others would feel good if they too received care.[11]

As we saw in the last chapter, when Jason McKendrick went to Special Olympics, he was surprised that he had a lot of fun. Not long after this, the same teacher who had invited him urged him to do something with a group that was helping handicapped children. He and some other students went to the place where these children were housed and entertained them (Jason is a talented pianist). He says, "I had a lot of fun doing that, too." Asked if there were other reasons, such as doing volunteer work in order to build up his résumé, he answered no, that he was just doing it for fun, for himself.

Another young man, Jim Grayson, spent the last three summers as a volunteer counselor at Boy Scout camp. He had been a camper himself for several years and had had a lot of fun. He recalls that when he was eleven, "I liked the counselors and stuff, and I looked around as a scout then, and I said these guys are out here, they're having fun, it's a really nice place, and once I'm fourteen and I'm old enough, I want to work here." This is a case in which having benefited first from some volunteer activity, one then goes on to participate, at least partly as a way of extending the fun. Although this can be a fairly selfish form of motivation, there may be an element of caring present as well. Jim Grayson adds that he also "wanted to make an impact on these kids" because a lot of them were from poor, inner-city neighborhoods and were outdoors in the summer for the first time. What made the experience "fun" for him was the fact that these kids were getting so much from the experience. Jim also was moved by being able to pass something along to them that then repeated itself. He remembers one boy in particular who was from a very disadvantaged background but was quite eager to learn in order to help other kids.

Jim Grayson's story is significant because his account, like many of the others that emphasize happiness, does not focus exclusively on happiness. He recognizes at least implicitly that helping others is good for its own sake—whether or not one has fun doing it. He is also aware, however, that one of the ways in which people can sometimes be helped is by helping them have fun and that this kind of activity is likely to be fun for the caregiver as well as for the recipients. Happiness is thus something that depends on the well-being of others. One's own happiness is likely to be greater if others also are happy. Sina Mesnar adds this argument to his account. Besides his feeling that helping others is a moral obligation, he also believes that listening to the homeless talk about their hopes and expectations is a way of maximizing their—and his—happiness. "That way," he says, "you feel good, and at the same time the homeless person feels good too."[12]

Volunteer work, I should note, is especially effective in perpetuating the happiness framework as a reason for caring. The young people we talked to generally associated the caring they had received in their families with happiness. It made them feel good to be cared for, and as we saw, they often talked about types of caring that had made their parents feel good as well. Their happiness was sometimes temporarily interrupted when they came into contact with people in need. Thus, doing volunteer work became a way of restoring and extending the happiness they had experienced in their families. They liked volunteer activities that put them in direct contact with appreciative recipients because they could then see that they could make other people happy. Moreover, they were often given options that allowed them to choose volunteer activities they thought they would especially enjoy.[13]

Sina Mesnar thought a great deal about his reasons to be a caring person. When he was in the seventh grade, he started volunteering occasionally to feed the homeless at a downtown soup kitchen. The next year a friend of his father's became homeless, so Sina acquired a more personal view of what it was like to be in need. In the ninth grade he joined an activist club in his high school and started to do more with homelessness and illiteracy. A year later the woman who was president of the club graduated, and Sina inherited her job. For the past three years he has worked to keep the club going and to expand its activities into new areas, such as cleaning and painting low-income apartment buildings, renovating a shelter for abused women, and running the van to feed the homeless twice a week. As he talks about his reasons for caring, he emphasizes the connection between volunteering and what he has experienced in his own family. He also demonstrates that it has taken thought on his part to develop this connection and that he is now able to see that volunteering reproduces some of the happiness he has known in his family but that the satisfaction comes not only from knowing people personally but also from simply doing one's part to help improve the world. Asked what the best reason to be a caring person is, Sina responds: "It's a good thing because you're helping another person. It's in a way like helping a family member or something like that. It's a good thing because at the same time you're giving help to this one person, you're also receiving a huge reward, huge satisfaction. Simply you're just not letting this problem continue. Maybe even if you're dealing with one person, at least you're attacking the problem, the cancer. At least you're doing something. It's beneficial on both sides."

Asked whether he thinks everyone should be caring, Sina elaborates: "I think they need to be compassionate, because they have to understand that the individual by himself cannot do anything. They have to understand that it's a close-knit family. Even though how different we all may be—our thinking, our looks, our everything—underlying it all, we're connected. Each person is responsible for the next because you don't know what will happen later on in life. Everyone is responsible for the next. I presume that's our moral obligation that we have towards one another."

Reciprocity

"Reciprocation among distantly related or unrelated individuals," writes Harvard sociobiologist Edward O. Wilson, "is the key to human society."[14] It is not surprising that another way of understanding why we care for others is to emphasize this key. Megan Wyse's observation that she feels a need to show her appreciation for the good things she has received in life by helping the homeless is an example of reciprocal reasoning.

Although this framework has much in common with humanitarianism, it comes up often enough in discussions of caring that it is worth considering separately. Indeed, it differs from humanitarianism in one fundamental respect: Whereas humanitarianism emphasizes people's basic equality, reciprocity stresses the special privileges or unique resources of a few. The teenagers we talked to, for example, mentioned the material comforts their parents had been able to provide. The adults sometimes discussed the opportunities their parents had given them or other marks of good fortune, such as a college education, health, or being raised in America.

In an affluent society like ours, an emphasis on good fortune is often a way of acknowledging privileges that do in fact make it possible to help others.[15] A young man who has grown up in a comfortable—but not wealthy—family, for example, describes his reasons for caring: "I was very lucky in the way I was born. I could have been born to any parents. I could have been born into any situation and I feel gifted that I was born in the situation I am. And I don't feel that that's a right. I feel like that's a privilege and that it is my right and my duty to share that with others." Asked to cite the best reason to be caring, he answered: "To give others the chance to experience the same sense of somebody caring for them that you have."

People who have not enjoyed material advantages, however, are not exempt from emphasizing the opportunities they have enjoyed and the fact that people need to help one another if they can.[16] Tanika Lane has never been economically privileged, but listen to how she explains why she values helping others: "It shows that you can give a little piece of yourself to somebody else. That you can give something back. I don't know where my life may take me. I might need some help and somebody that I helped, they might be there to help me. So I feel as though it's like a chain. Almost like a food chain. It's like we pass it on. Somebody passes it on to me. It just continues. It's never ending."[17]

Reciprocity sometimes means that one cares for someone else in hopes of receiving help in return—caring is thus like insurance. Part of what Tanika says sounds like this. Other young people from relatively low income backgrounds sometimes realized that they someday might be in need, so helping their neighbors or classmates was a way of buying insurance. In most cases, though, the reward expected was psychological rather than material. And even this reward seemed sufficiently self-serving to some young people that they denied its importance, even though they acknowledged it was part of their thinking. A young man who was quite poor—his family had been homeless for a year—offered this as a revealing example of the limitations of reciprocity when it focuses too much on oneself: "Like they all say, you do something for someone, you always get something back. You're repaid." Having stated this as a reason to care, however, he retreated to an argument that stresses paying back more than receiving: "But I really don't think much about that now. It was just something in me that always wanted to help someone else, because people have always helped me during my lifetime. So I thought that it was time to give something back."

I should emphasize, as Tanika's statement suggests, that reciprocity generally does not focus on paying back the specific people who were the source of one's own good fortune. In most of the cases we examined, one's parents were this source. But young people learned from their parents that kindness could be repaid by helping others. The term *serial reciprocity* is thus used to describe this understanding of caring.[18] Serial reciprocity is perhaps best expressed in the phrase *pass it on*. Caring is like a chain, linking people together as they receive help from one direction and give help in another direction.

Rafe Ramirez is another student who expressed his reasons for caring in this way. He says he mainly wants "to give a little bit back to the people who have helped me." Referring to his parents and to his coaches, he explains: "I've had a lot of people be kind and generous and help me, and I feel I should be like them and show other people that they can do it, too. And maybe the next person, somebody I help down the line will—it's just kind of a chain effect."

I should also stress that reciprocity can easily be combined with arguments about humanitarianism and the pursuit of happiness. Although one may feel it is a duty to pay back the good fortune one has experienced, it is thus possible to recognize the genuine needs that are being served and the happiness one receives in return. Nikki Unger, one of the young women who rides on the van with Jason McKendrick to help at Pearl's Kitchen, shows how these various frameworks can be combined to explain her interest in helping others: "The reason I wanted to [help the homeless] and be a social worker is because I was given so much. I have a very loving family, and I have everything I need in terms of physical needs and a great education and everything. I have more than enough to give to somebody else. I always felt best giving my time. I have money and I can give money to things, but that's not always what is needed most. What makes me feel happy is knowing that I'm helping someone else. I guess my one main need is to feel like I'm needed. That's what makes me happy is when I'm doing something where I know they really need me there, and where I'm really helping someone. When somebody says 'You really made a difference,' that's what makes me happier than anything in the world. I guess it's a feeling *I* like to get, and often knowing that I'm making somebody else feel better is what makes it really important for me to do volunteer work, whatever it is."

Although some reseachers argue that personal caring and an interest in social justice on a wider scale are quite different, Nikki Unger also reveals that the reciprocity framework can be a powerful way of combining the two. When one's own comforts are acknowledged as privileges, the idea of paying for those privileges can reinforce one's awareness of the rights and needs of those with fewer advantages. Nikki explains the connection in this way: "It's not right that people should have to live in bad conditions when so many people live in good conditions. I mean extra good conditions. Why can't we kind of meet somewhere in the middle where everybody has a satisfactory, comfortable standard of living? It could happen. It's possible, I think. And I think when I have so much that I have extra to give. I have extra, because I have so many caring people around me, I have extra caring to give to somebody who doesn't have very much, and I can give it to them. That's why it's important to help needy people. I mean, why should somebody be unhappy when I'm so happy and I have something to give?"

Nikki Unger also illustrates the point I made earlier about voices. In the foregoing, she is speaking in her own words. If we ask, however, where these words come from, we will find that her mother has been a decisive influence. Nikki says that her mother has always told her how privileged she is and has emphasized "be willing to give and to always be willing to lend a helping hand." "I guess the main thing my mom taught me," Nikki adds, "is not to be selfish. That's always been her biggest lesson to me. Like, if I think, oh, this person doesn't like me. She goes, 'Well, you're thinking about yourself. Think about how you're making this person feel. You've got to think about this person. Just never think of yourself. Think of somebody else.'" Refecting on these words, Nikki remarks, "Of course, sometimes I get upset because I want her sympathy, and I want her to say uh-oh. Instead she's saying, 'Well, what is this person thinking? Are you sure that they don't have a point? Are you sure you're thinking of how they're feeling?'" As Nikki repeats her mother's words, she uses a high voice to indicate that the words are someone else's. Then she continues in her normal voice: "When I back away and I think of how unselfish she is, I really admire that. I wish I could be more like her. And I wish I could follow the idea of not being selfish more closely. I work as hard as I can at it. I work very hard at it, and of course, there are some times when I could work harder at it."

Examples like this are not uncommon. They indicate how deeply our understanding of caring is embedded in the primordial caring we have experienced and seen modeled in our families. Nikki, in fact, stresses that her desire to reciprocate by helping others is directly related to the good feelings she has received from being cared for herself: "I know how good it makes me feel when somebody's kind and compassionate to me. And when people who need so much *more* and have so much more need, I know how good it's going to make them feel when they don't get much and they need so much."

Self-Realization

Self-realization appeared somewhat less often in our interviews but is nevertheless a distinct addition to the others. It emphasizes the personal benefits gained from helping others but focuses less on happiness than on growth. It derives, implicitly at least, less from utilitarian philosophy or popular conceptions of having a good time and more from psychological conceptions of the self and its capacities to be nurtured and to grow. The main idea is that people can achieve their full potential only by facing the challenges of caring for others.[19]

The best example of self-realization as a rationale for caring comes from a young woman named Frieda Katz. She is a classmate of Megan Wyse's and is a member of the same Social Action Club. Frieda has been spending between four and six hours a week during the past year at an AIDS hospice for the terminally ill. She cares for the children of people with AIDS, helps cook meals, does laundry, and talks to the patients.

Frieda became involved mainly because of her mother. Several years ago, her mother was diagnosed as having a tumor that might be malignant and would need surgery. The tumor turned out to be benign, but the episode forced Frieda's mother to rethink her values and her lifestyle. Having in a small way faced the possibility of her own death, she decided to help people who were dying with AIDS. A year later, Frieda followed her mother's example. The way that Frieda describes her reasons for caring underscores her own personhood and that of the people she is helping. Asked to give a general argument about why people should care for others, she responded: "Everyone is a person. I guess it should make you look at what you have, not take it for granted as much and realize that food is just something everyone should have. No questions asked. That they're entitled to it as people. That we should just do our part to help." She added that the goal of caring should be "to be the best person you can be personally, individually. Ideally, if everyone did that, there'd be a lot of great people around. If you realize that you as one person can help so many, and everyone did that, people would be much more accepting. I'm sure people would be that much happier, not only because they have actual food or help or whatever, money, but feel better about themselves as people."

As a framework of understanding why one should care, self-realization is sometimes part of the specific relationships that caregivers have developed with those they are helping. In Frieda's case, she sees that AIDS patients are often subject to criticism that dehumanizes them and demeans their personhood. Although she has experienced many deeply moving encounters, the one that stands out most vividly for her is one of the AIDS patient's caring for someone else. One day a man came to the hospice seeking food and clothing. And, as Frieda recounts the story, "He was saying all these awful things—fag and dike and all you disease-ridden people. I mean, I didn't understand why he came in. I was just ready to say, Go to hell, get out of here." Then Marty, a gay man who was one of the AIDS patients, intervened. "Marty just sat the man down and talked to him for like forty-five minutes. I was so surprised that someone could insult you so blatantly, and it was so personally offensive. I was offended, and it had nothing to do with me. Again, I didn't have the HIV, and I wanted to kill him. But Marty sat there and he explained everything. By the time the man left, Marty had given him food. He'd given him clothes. The guy wasn't exactly persuaded, but he wasn't saying anything, and he said he was sorry as he went out, and I was really surprised. I couldn't believe it. It gave me—this sounds corny—but it restored my faith in humanity."

Self-realization is clearly an emphasis that depends as well on the way one has been raised. Like the other frameworks, it is not an abstract philosophical argument that people have learned from books but is a more vibrant, fluid, and personalized outlook that has been internalized from the interaction and conversations that young people have had with their parents and other role models. Frieda's mother had never done volunteer work before she began helping at the hospice, nor had Frieda's father. Her parents had also been separated for several years while Frieda was little, so she bears some resentment toward them for that, and she admits she occasionally has conflicts with her mother. Nevertheless, they showed a great deal of love and kindness to her and her brother and taught them to respect others, to be tolerant, and to be concerned about human suffering. It was the idea of respecting herself and of respecting others in the same way that seems to have come through most clearly.

Thus when Frieda describes what her mother taught her about caring, she says, "Be nice to people, but draw the line against being used." And she describes her mother now as "a force for a lot of other people." Words like *power*, *personality*, and *strength* frequent her remarks. Her definition of being close to her parents is that she is learning more about them, including their problems and struggles. Frieda also emphasizes self-respect and respecting others when she talks about AIDS patients. For example, she says that seeing AIDS patients as persons—including their vitality as well as their pain and their zest for life—

has been especially moving. And she says that it troubles her even more when her friends at school say negative things about AIDS patients. She also feels she is realizing more of her own potential as a person. She understands better, she feels, that she has the power to help others. And her sense of tolerance has deepened. Frieda noted that she was always tolerant "in a bookish way, like being politically correct," but that now she knows more about how to be accepting in specific situations.

The self-realization framework often focuses on the giver by emphasizing the personal growth that results from giving (including new skills and a sense of accomplishment), but this framework sometimes extends to the recipient as well, as it does in some of Frieda's remarks. The argument is that other people have the right to realize their own potential; thus, helping them to do this is a good thing. For example, a young man who does volunteer work at a hospital put it this way: "I think that needy people have just as much chance, or should have just as much of a chance, as the ones like us who aren't as needy, to go out and succeed in the world and that there could have been any number of reasons why they're so poor now. It could be like a medical problem, and I think that those people should be given another chance. Knowing that my kindness could help somebody open up and tell them or tell somebody their problem and that once they have their problem out in the open, they can deal with it and it could heal them." When asked why she volunteered, another teenager answered: "To help other people realize their potential and what they can do and help them feel better about themselves."

A sense of how widespread these frameworks are among teenagers nationally can be obtained from the survey. When asked whether various statements represented "a major reason" to be kind and caring, for instance, more than two-thirds (69 percent) of those who had ever done volunteer work responded positively to a humanitarian statement: "I want to give of myself for the benefit of others." Almost this many (64 percent) responded positively to a statement reflecting the pursuit of happiness: "It makes me feel good about myself when I care for others." Nearly two-thirds (65 percent) gave a similar answer to a statement that sought to capture the reciprocity framework: "Helping others is a way of paying debts for the good things I have received." About the same proportion (63 percent) expressed the idea of self-realization: "Helping others makes me a stronger person."

These figures also suggest that most teenagers have more than one reason to value caring.[20] When teen volunteers in the survey were offered a list of twenty reasons for volunteering, 95 percent selected at least one as a "very important reason" for their own involvement, but nearly as many (89 percent) said at least two of the reasons were this important to them. Indeed, four volunteers out of five said at least three of the reasons had been very important to them; two-thirds of the volunteers said at least five reasons had been this important, and more than one-quarter cited ten or more of the reasons as being this important.[21]

As we have seen, the teenagers we talked to often shifted from one framework to another as they described their reasons for caring. Nevertheless, the frameworks are sufficiently independent that they could emphasize one more than the other. Some people were clearly more oriented toward a humanitarian framework, whereas others volunteered more for the fun of it or as a way of realizing their own potential.[22]

The Wrong Reasons

Some experts continue to argue that caring is such a natural feature of human life that reasons to care are not important. According to them, people should simply do what they can to help others and not worry about the meaning of their behavior. The problem with this view is that it fails to understand that people need reasons for what they do. Although frameworks may be taken for granted most of the time, the foregoing examples show that young people who become involved in volunteer work find themselves thinking about their reasons and having to defend themselves to their classmates.

The importance of reasons is also evident in the fact that young people are critical of those who do good deeds but for the wrong reasons. Rafe Ramirez, for example, contends that some of his classmates become volunteers for purely selfish reasons and then fail to carry through on their commitments: "They want to make themselves look good. It's kind of a self-image thing. They say they'll do it, and then they don't, because when they said they'd do it, it made them look better. Then when it comes time to do whatever they said they would do, they feel, oh, no, I just was saying that, I don't have to do that."[23]

The fact that people are concerned about wrong reasons suggests that certain reasons are still considered right or proper. However, the ways in which wrong reasons are discussed also point to one of the difficulties inherent in contemporary society. The reasons with which we grow up tell us that caring in general is right and good, but these reasons do not guide us in expressing those values. As we mature and learn to play more specialized roles, our primordial frameworks must be modified so that they tell us not only that we are caring people in general but also that the specific activities in which we are engaged are connected to the value we place on caring.

Rafe Ramirez's statement about his classmates demonstrates two of the ways in which young people often modify their understanding of caring as they mature. One is our tendency to do (or say) things that strategically enhance our image. As we function in more complex settings, we discover the importance of managing how others perceive us. Playing specialized roles also allows us to present different aspects of ourselves in different situations. I shall say more about this in a later chapter, but I want to underscore here that image management can also lead away entirely from caring, toward either cynical forms of helping behavior or such norms as success, advancement, and monetary attainment. The other tendency implied in Rafe's statement is that reasons on the whole are downplayed in comparison with results. Of course, Rafe believes that good reasons lead to good results. He does, however, imply that the results are more important: That is, if the results were good, the reasons would not matter. But when what people do is judged in terms of results, they may lose sight of the reasons to be caring in the first place.

Motivation as Process

Given the tendencies to which I have just alluded, it is important to people who may be engaged in caring activities to use scripts that help them link this behavior with their more fundamental sense of why caring is important. Motivation, I argue, can usefully be understood as this kind of script. Young people's accounts of their motives for becoming involved in volunteer work connect their understanding of themselves as caring persons (and as persons who have received care and who value it) and the specific activities in which they are now engaged. Motivation is thus an ongoing process. It is not, as it has commonly been assumed, a preexisting psychological state that propels people to take certain actions but a process of interpretation by which people make sense of what they are doing.

This view of motivation is consistent with a number of emerging perspectives in the social sciences (phenomenology, cultural anthropology, poststructuralism, linguistic theory) that argue that we create ourselves through the webs of language in which we live. We are not the heroic warriors we once thought ourselves to be, conquering new vistas with strength welling up from within. Nor are we the weak, oversocialized products of social forces beyond our control that so many social scientists of an earlier era liked to describe. We are more like spiders, spinning out threads—"webs of significance," Clifford Geertz calls them—that connect us to our surroundings.[24] Each thread, moreover, is temporary, attaching us momentarily to what we are doing and providing us with a reason for doing it. As we move on, we find that these reasons are provisional, so we improvise, coming up with new interpretations as we make our next moves.

Jason McKendrick, we recall, stated that he was propelled into helping at Pearl's Kitchen by going with a friend and that only sometime later did he begin thinking about his motives. For a while he told himself that it was fun, and then he realized he was helping because he cared about the needy. Periodically he still reflects on his motives as he rides the van home on Thursday evenings. Doing so helps him connect himself—the self that he is at that moment—with his activities.

Besides musing about our activities just to make sense of them to ourselves, we are often asked to account for ourselves to others. One of the results we repeatedly observed of young people's becoming involved in formal volunteer work was that they had to devise such accounts—in classes, on résumés, and in interviews. Volunteering not only involved young people in new experiences; it also required them to articulate their motives more clearly. Volunteers were forced to make explicit their primordial frameworks and to link them with the changing activities in which they were engaged.

Chandra Lyons is a second-generation flower child—her parents were devotees of the 1960s' counterculture—and she spends two evenings a week at an inner-city community center helping children learn art. She grew up in a commune and has attended an alternative school for the past eleven years. She explains her motivation for volunteering in this way: "I've always been interested in the city. There's something like calling me there. 'Chandra, come to the city.' [Voices again.] It was like my dream when I was thinking about a project to do, to go into the inner city and do what I'm doing. I didn't think it would happen, but it did. I told my dad. I'm like, 'This is what I want to do,' and he's like, 'Oh, you should talk to Sam Jones.' So I talked to him, and he gave me the phone number of a woman called Angelique Dexter who works with the Amateur Boxing Association, which is another movement with the inner-city kids. I got in touch with her, and she's a member of this community center. She brought me over there, and I had an interview with the director. He totally grilled me with questions. It was the most intense interview I've ever had. It's like college interviews are nothing compared to what he asked me. It was really good what he was asking me. Like he said, 'What if I said you were too young and too white for this job?' Or 'If I gave you a class in an hour, what would you do?' Or just like ones which really had to make you think so that he would know that I wasn't just doing it in passing or whatever. So then he said, 'When can you come in? Can you come in twice a week?' I said, 'Well, I'll have to check with my teachers. See what they say.' So then I checked it out and figured that I could come twice a week. Get another study hall. So then I started going, and every time I don't come in, I hear a lot of grief about it." She adds: "I also know that I've been very lucky in my life to know how to do the things I do. When I was young, I learned a lot of little craft things which I find are very useful in my life now. I wanted to be able to share that, and I wanted these kids to know of outlets to express themselves, such as painting. It's my outlet, one of them, painting and writing."

The first point to observe about motivation, then, is that the ways in which people talk about their motives for caring are generally quite ordinary. People focus on their everyday experience, on commonplace activities and relationships. Their accounts make their behavior seem routine or unexceptional, only occasionally painting it as heroic, but always individualizing it by stressing the particular circumstances that guided the speaker into a particular course of action. In Chandra's case, there are hints of motivation as an initial predisposition (her dream to be in the city and her desire to pay back society for her privileges). But her motivation is more clearly associated with the process of moving from those predispositions to working at the community center. Chandra explains herself by reporting some of the conversations that shaped this process.

In other cases, the same pattern is evident. Motivation is not so much a predisposition as a sequence of events. Descriptions of motives are thus stories that show how one thing leads to another. Rachel Farb, a student who works with the blind, offers a detailed description of this kind, beginning with a seemingly routine event initiated by her guidance counselor: "IIe handed out pamphlets and I sort of threw it in my school bag, and I said, 'I'll look at this later, who knows.' And then the more I thought about it, the more I realized that I was so bored that I came home every day and I wouldn't do anything. And I said, I need something to do and this just sounded like a great idea. I figured that I could do something that would help me get over my fear of the handicapped and still work with people who were able to handle themselves. They gave me a list of things to pick from, all these different hospitals and everything and I just saw Overbrook School for the Blind and I said, 'You know, I would really like to do that.' My aunt does volunteer work for the blind, and I knew she really enjoyed it. She translates text books. I said, 'Well, I'd really like to work with mentally handicapped people instead,' but I knew how much she enjoyed it and how much she got out of it, and it just sort of stuck out of the page and looked at me. And I said, 'Well, might as well sign up and try.' And I did. It was all very informal and just sort of on a whim and I always joked with my friends. I'll tell them, 'Just from signing up from this one little thing, I now have no time.' I mean, I have none. I am running around all the time and just doing all kinds of things."

The second point is that descriptions of motivation usually do not emphasize the frameworks of understanding that I have described but presuppose those

frameworks, keeping them in the background and yet referring to them implicitly and obliquely in ways that reveal their existence. Jason McKendrick's
friend Nikki Unger illustrates this point especially well when she talks about her
motivation for working with inner-city children. As a high school senior, she
looks forward to her career goals and also backward to the values she learned as
a child. The burden of her statement is to demonstrate not so much what propelled her actions from within but how her behavior makes sense in relation to
her past, present, and future. She says: "I guess since I was a freshman, or maybe
even before that, I always wanted to be a social worker when I got older. There
are so many avenues of social work that you can do. There are so many different
things that are needed. I've taught Sunday school, and I babysit all the time, and
I always thought that that was my best—that's what I had to offer. I loved working with kids. That was one of my favorite things to do. And so I thought maybe
that's how I would do it. I wanted to get experience." She adds that a conversation with her father was pivotal: "So one day I was talking and I said, 'I really
want to be a social worker, and I do things at school and around here, but things
that aren't really getting me the kind of experience of the things I want to do,
like working in the city and getting experience with kids in the city.' And so he
said, 'Well, let me talk to [the director] and see if she needs any volunteers because that would be perfect for you to get experience.'"

Nikki's account is thus quite ordinary. It shows that her involvement in
volunteering was the result of a natural progression that started in her childhood and that will, one hopes, carry forward into her career. The voices she
hears as she repeats her conversation with her father, like the voices that drove
Joan of Arc, help guide her.

It is significant that young people have opportunities to spin stories about
the connections between themselves and the fundamental virtues of caring.
Volunteer work is one occasion in which such stories can be encouraged. Most
young people, as I have argued, already know what caring is, but they need to
be able to articulate their reasons for thinking that it is important. As they talk
about these reasons, young people discover that caring is something that they
do value and that efforts to help others are not simply an imposition on their
time or a distraction from what they would rather be doing. They also relate
stories that help them update their experience. These stories help them see that
caring is not simply a vague experience in one's childhood but an ongoing
process of selection and effort. It is never driven by only one motive or by purely
altruistic ideals but is contextualized and made meaningful by conversations and
interaction with significant others.

The stories we tell about our motives for caring are modern and help us
adapt to the pressures of living in a complex and highly institutionalized world.

Unlike Joan of Arc, our voices do not spring from a single tradition, and our saints do not reside in the single village of our youth. The voices that guide us still carry authority, encouraging us to be concerned about others as a moral obligation, but these voices are multiple and replaceable. We recognize that we choose particular scripts from a wider repertoire of reasons and accounts and that these scripts are thus arbitrary. Our specific ways of caring also are arbitrary because we have selected them, as Nikki Unger says, from "many avenues." We cannot defend them on grounds of principle. About all we can do is show that one thing led to another. But if we can do even that, we have accomplished a great deal. We know that despite the indifference built into the specialized roles we play, our primordial values are still connected with those roles.

5

Serving God?
Kindness and Transcendence

> The spiritual condition of modern civilization . . . is characterized by loss: the loss of metaphysical certainties, of an experience of the transcendental, of any superpersonal moral authority, and of any kind of higher horizon. . . . Only through directing ourselves toward the moral and the spiritual, based on respect for some "extramundane" authority—for the order of nature or the universe, for a moral order and its superpersonal origin, for the absolute—can we arrive at a state in which life on this earth is no longer threatened by some form of "megasuicide" and becomes bearable.
>
> Vaclav Havel, *Disturbing the Peace*
>
> I would describe myself as a person who was so afraid of remorse and afraid of God, that he had to act in a way that other people called heroic.
>
> Vaclav Havel, *Faith Under Fire*

These two statements—written by Vaclav Havel before he became president of the Czech Republic—capture the dilemma we face in trying to figure out how religious faith relates to kindness in our society. In the first statement, Havel describes the uncertainties that many of us feel about the sacred. Some people doubt the existence of God at all. Others regard the existence of God as an item of faith but are unsure what authority that belief holds over their lives. They question whether the existence of God can provide them with absolute standards of right and wrong, but they nevertheless think that religious faith is necessary in order for life to be bearable. Havel's second statement suggests a connection between the loss of transcendence and kindness. Paradoxically, uncertainties about the existence of God do not result in good deeds' being abandoned. Instead, we strive all the harder to perform "heroic" acts in the hope that they will compensate for our lingering doubts about God. Kindness may thus be a way of finding transcendence, but this form of caring may also serve ourselves more than it serves others.

The changes that have overtaken our religious sensibilities can also be seen in the example of Joan of Arc. Although we hear voices, we no longer believe that they speak with divine authority, and yet we have not given up the possibility that such voices exist. Indeed, most of us believe in God, most of us pray, and most of us claim a religious preference. Young adulthood has typically been a time of questioning. But if American teenagers question their faith, most have nevertheless been reared with some exposure to a faith tradition, and most claim to believe in some of the teachings of their church, synagogue, or mosque. These teachings, moreover, include statements about the value of kindness. The faithful are counseled to be of service to their religious communities and are called to love their neighbors—if not their enemies as well.

If it is important to be kind and also to understand what kindness is, religious tradition is a part of our heritage that can scarcely be ignored. Religious conceptions of kindness may not be communicated in public schools or in secular community agencies, but they remain a significant part of what young people understand caring to be. Especially if caring is rooted in the family and religious practice is part of early childhood experience, then religious conceptions of caring may be important. They are, like the messages communicated to us by our families, part of the primordial meaning of caring that we learn early in life.

We also must reckon with the implications of Havel's argument about the loss of transcendence. If religion has been a framework for understanding caring in the past, perhaps its strength is now eroding. We are, as Havel suggests, less sure of metaphysical statements about the universe or human nature. We have trouble not so much with finding ways to care for our neighbors but with finding the moral authority with which to legitimate our behavior. Perhaps we are replacing the absolute religious injunctions of the past with self-interested ways of thinking about kindness. Perhaps we are also turning kindness into a device for silencing our doubts about the existence of the sacred.

Tanika Lane illustrates how difficult it has become for young people to think about the relationship between faith and caring. As we saw, she was raised going to church, and she is still active, teaching Sunday school and doing community service work that is partially sponsored by her church. She believes that God had something to do with her becoming involved in LEAD. In fact, the day she heard the announcement about LEAD over the school intercom, she felt an impulse to respond that she couldn't quite understand. In retrospect, she says, "I really think it was God leading me." But she also admits, "I don't know how."

The best evidence regarding religious belief among teenagers nationally is that it is widespread but badly defined, impersonal, and seldom put into practice. Nearly all teenagers believe in the existence of God, yet fewer than one-third feel they have ever experienced the presence of God, and not many more than this

pray, read the Bible, are able to name correctly the four gospels, regard their religious beliefs as important, or believe that religion can answer today's problems.[1]
Teenagers, it appears, buy into the adult mythology of American culture that says
religion is something respectable that people should practice (three-quarters say
regular church attendance is a mark of citizenship, for example). In their own
hierarchy of values, however, religious faith generally falls much lower than
such virtues as hard work, self-respect, and independence.[2] Another telling indication is the amount of trust that young people place in religious organizations.
Although this trust is still high relative to that in many other organizations (especially government), it has slipped well behind that in secular organizations
concerned with humanitarian causes. For example, nearly twice as many young
people express a great deal of confidence in environmental organizations as
they do in religious organizations.[3] Young people are, on the whole, unwilling
to dismiss religion out of hand (only two in ten, for instance, declare that religious beliefs are simply unimportant), but they are quite willing to concede that
religion is less important to them personally than it is to their parents and grandparents.[4]

In view of these patterns, a devoutly religious teenager like Tanika is more
the exception than the rule. When she was twelve, her interest in church started
to diminish, but two years later she was more actively involved in church than
ever. The reason was that an aunt started taking her to a new church. In the
process, Tanika experienced a religious conversion. She recalls: "I accepted Jesus
Christ as my savior. I began to find that Jesus was the answer. A lot of times I was
involved in religious groups, but they never did anything for me. But when I accepted Jesus Christ as my savior, it seemed like a lot of empty spaces were filled.
My life changed. It was a life-changing experience, and now I can't get enough.
God is so good. I can't get enough."

In contrast, the majority of teenagers become less actively involved in
religious groups. At age twelve, nearly two-thirds are members of a church or
synagogue, but at age seventeen, fewer than half are still members. Regular attendance at religious services also drops off markedly, whereas nonattendance
doubles. Significantly, the proportion identifying themselves as religious conservatives (about one-fifth) remains constant, but there is a massive shift in the
dominant orientations, from religious centrism to religious liberalism.[5]

The diminishing impact of religious commitment is also evident in the
motivations that teenagers cite to account for their volunteer activities. Nationally, only one-third of American teenagers say that religious or spiritual concerns were an important reason for their volunteering. This figure is higher, of
course, among teens who are actively involved in churches and synagogues.
Even among those who attend services every week, however, fewer than half
list spiritual concerns as one of their important motivations. More, in fact, list

other motives, such as expecting enjoyment, wanting to feel needed, or hoping to acquire new skills. And this group is no less likely than the unchurched to mention instrumental reasons, such as enhancing one's résumé or making useful career contacts.[6]

Still, for a minority of young people, religious commitment is a relevant consideration for their volunteering. Indeed, there is evidence that those with a strong religious faith are more likely than other teenagers are to value helping the needy and to be involved in caring activities. Thus, for two reasons, we need to consider the specific ways in which religious understandings bear on the meaning of kindness. One is to clarify the connection between faith and caring for the minority who are strongly guided by their faith. The other is to see why, for the majority of young people, faith is not a more compelling reason for caring.

Considering these issues also gives us an opportunity to address the larger and, in my view, more important question that Vaclav Havel implies: What can compel us authoritatively to be caring? That is, can we still believe that caring for others is an absolute, morally binding truth? Or do the complex, relativizing processes by which we become absorbed in social institutions necessitate a different understanding of caring? We may, as we saw in Chapter 3, learn the value of caring as part of the natural process of being cared for in our families. As we move into adulthood, however, we need reasons to be kind in the more diverse settings in which we find ourselves. We have the frameworks that we considered in the last chapter to guide us, and we can construct accounts of our own motives—after the fact. Yet none of these may seem particularly compelling. If Havel is right, we must learn to understand caring in a way that remains morally compelling but allows us to be caring in the complex, specialized roles we must play in our society.

The ways in which young people make sense of their religious inclinations permits us to consider this larger process. Exposure to religious diversity erodes the moral authority of our beliefs, yet this exposure also results—for many young people—in a more individual way of linking our values to our caring activities. These individual conceptions must be reinforced by interacting with others (more on this in the next chapter), but they permit personal values to be connected with the specialized roles we must play as adults. In the process, we may regain a sense of transcendence and of moral authority that we can carry into these specialized roles.

Faith and Caring

The ways in which religious faith undergirds caring for those who are devout believers can best be demonstrated by listening to more of what Tanika Lane says about her faith. Asked why her faith is important, she explains simply that it is her "foundation" in life: "It's what makes me me. It's important to me because I live by what I believe. I try to stand on the word of God. I don't just say, I believe or whatever. I try to live the life that God has for me." Her guiding assumption is that her beliefs should be put into practice.

This assumption rests on a clearly articulated set of beliefs about God, Jesus, and personal salvation. Tanika summarizes these beliefs: "I believe that Jesus Christ is the savior. He is the son of God, and that he came and died for our sins and rose again on the third day. I also believe that he is living in me. That he is my guide. He leads me, and he cares for me and we have a personal relationship." Her language about Jesus and about God is nearly the same as the creed she recites weekly at her church. "I think God is omnipotent, omniscient. I think God knows everything. He is not a stupid God. God is in control of everything. God is great, and God loves everybody. He loves us. He loves me. He loves you. He loves everybody."

Tanika's belief that God loves everybody is the key to her own emphasis on caring for others. She thinks God expects her to follow him and depend on him, and she believes that the things she does should have a purpose. The love she sees embodied in Jesus helps her identify this purpose: "Jesus is the light of the world for me. Jesus is my salvation. I feel that Jesus died for my sins, for the wrong things that I did in my life, that I do in my life. Through him there is forgiveness. Jesus died on the cross for something. He was innocent, and he didn't do anything, and I feel that he died. I really love Jesus. I really put my trust in him. There's no words for the way I feel about it—I love him. I really do. I think this really helps people to become more caring, because the Bible says, 'Love thy neighbor as you would love thyself.' I think you should just hold that to heart every day."

As an example, Tanika poses the question, and then answers it, of how to behave if she is confronted with someone she dislikes: "I'm supposed to love her like I love myself, and I look at her for what she just said to me. I know nobody is perfect but God. I could sit here and say, oh yes, I love. A lot of times I can't stand people like that. But I try to love them. I try to be caring. Even when people smack me in my face, I try to not withdraw and become angry."

The main ingredients of Tanika's faith are a set of firm beliefs about the reality of God, the divinity of Jesus, and the authority of Jesus's teaching about loving one's neighbor. These beliefs convince her that everything she does should have a purpose and that some activities, for her at least, are morally right and others are morally wrong. As she says, "I always want to have a purpose, and if I don't have a purpose, I don't want to be there. If I don't have a purpose, I don't want to be involved in it at all. That's why I don't include myself in a lot of things because I see no purpose."

Loving other people is a general principle that Tanika tries to apply to her life. To learn how to do this, she relies heavily on prayer: "I pray daily. I pray several times daily. I pray about different things I'm going to get involved in that they won't lead me in the wrong direction. I prayed about this interview."

Tanika also seeks guidance by involving herself in religious activities and with other religious people: "I read the Bible. On Sundays I go to church. Mondays I go to Bible study. Wednesdays I go to Bible study." Praying and studying the Bible give her strength to be kind. She also gains reinforcement, of course, for the specific volunteer activities in which she is engaged.

Among teenagers nationally, there is evidence that active religious commitment and volunteering consistently go together. Teenagers who are members of a church are more likely to value volunteering than are those who are not church members. Those whose mothers and fathers are church members are more likely to value volunteering than are those whose parents are not members. Those who identify themselves as religious conservatives are more likely to value volunteering than are those who say they are moderates or liberals. Those who attend religious services more often are also more likely to value volunteering. On all these measures, the religiously involved are ten to fifteen percentage points more likely to value volunteering than are the religiously uninvolved. So, it appears, something about religious involvement is important. Yet the strongest effect of all is not so much involvement itself but whether the person is both involved and deriving personal satisfaction from that involvement. In fact, those who say they derive a great deal of personal satisfaction from their religion or spirituality are nearly three times as likely to value volunteering as are those who derive only a little satisfaction from this source.[7] In other words, religious involvement must be meaningful, as it is for Tanika. Teenagers who are dragged to religious services by their parents or who attend simply out of habit are unlikely to be motivated to care for others as a result of these experiences.[8]

Religious commitment influences actual caring behavior as well, not just the likelihood of saying that volunteering is important. Among weekly churchgoers, for example, the average number of hours devoted to volunteering per month is 8.7, compared with 6.3 for those who attend several times a month and only 4.7 for those who seldom or never attend. Part of the reason for the relationship between religious involvement and volunteering may, of course, be that the volunteering takes place in religious organizations or is for religious causes. There is, however, a broader connection as well. The more that young people value their religious commitment, the more likely they are to volunteer even in nonreligious settings, such as schools and community agencies.[9]

On the whole, these patterns resemble those found in studies of adults. Those adults who attend religious services regularly are more likely to do volunteer work, even in organizations that have no connection with religious causes, and these differences cannot be explained by differences in the gender, age, or social class of those who attend religious services and those who do not.[10] Other research suggests that being in Bible study groups, such as the one that Tanika attends, or participating in other fellowship groups encourages people to do volunteer work in their communities. This research also suggests that being a recipient of caring in these settings and feeling that one is experiencing the love of God are particularly conducive to becoming a volunteer.[11]

From our interviews with teenagers, it is also clear that feeling cared for and experiencing God's love are often important reasons for becoming involved in volunteering. We need, however, to make the connection more clearly between religious commitment and what gives authority to the idea of caring. Our interviews suggest two connections.

One is that religious involvement takes place in a kind of enclave—much like the family and often an extension of one's family—and that this enclave shields the person from wider, more diverse, and potentially more confusing ideas. In Tanika's case, a group called Teen Haven provides her with an enclave of this kind. She meets with this group every Monday, Tuesday, and Wednesday evening. "They pick you up," she explains, "and take you to Bible study those evenings. They also take you on different trips on Friday nights. We might go bowling or skating. We have Bible studies. We learn about the Bible. We have lessons. We have a movie night where we watch a Christian movie. We have a night where we have worship and we all get together and one person comes and speaks to us all." She says all of this helps keep her faith strong.

Groups like this supply the voices that ring inside people's heads, reminding them of the words that express their beliefs. In Tanika's case, it is thus not so much a matter of having a vague sense of believing in God but of living inside a swirl of phrases that tell her about Jesus, salvation, and her purpose in life. As she prays, she repeats these words, and they become real again and again. Her participation in Teen Haven becomes an occasion for seeing, moreover, that the words are not just her own but are externally real. In addition, the group affirms her, giving her an identity that is closely associated with her faith. She says, "It's so fulfilling. It's like I don't want to do anything else. They respect me. They want to know how I feel about something. They want to ask me questions. They really love me. For as long as I've been involved in Teen Haven, it's been fulfilling. That's the only word I would use."

This example helps explain one of the broader patterns I referred to earlier: that self-identified religious conservatives are more likely to value helping the needy than are teenagers who call themselves religious moderates or liberals. Religious conservatives are more likely to belong to fellowship groups and to receive social support for their religious beliefs in other ways. For example, three-quarters of religious conservatives are church members, compared with only one-third of religious liberals. The conservatives are also more likely to have mothers, fathers, siblings, and friends who are church members than are moderates or liberals.[12] Religious conservatives are thus not only more likely than religious liberals to value volunteering, but they are also more likely to regard helping the needy as a moral obligation. Apparently the social support they receive for their beliefs give these beliefs added authority.[13] Religious conservatives who are involved in volunteering also are more likely than liberals to cite their faith as a reason for becoming involved.[14]

The other way that religious involvement gives authority to caring is by emphasizing the believer's duty to God. This sense of duty—to demonstrate the love of God—is evident in Tanika's remarks. A ninth grader who tutored homeless children at a shelter run by his church provides another example of how Jesus crystallized his resolve to be caring more than his more general beliefs about God did. This ninth grader described God as "a spirit that is nice, who wants people to love each other, care for each other, do right and not do wrong, be the best person that they can, and do as well as they can to their ability." Of Jesus, he said: "He's the son of God to me, and he's like a close friend to me, really. I feel closer to him than God, because he was like a youth, the son of God."

Another young man showed how being in a supportive religious setting helps reinforce beliefs in Jesus, which then give moral authority to the need to serve others. He had attended the Methodist church all his life with his parents; his friends belonged to its youth group; and he admired the pastor. He asserted that his faith is "everything I live for." Jesus is central to this belief: "Jesus Christ is my savior and through him I have a life after death. My only mission right now is to bring others to know him and I enjoy knowing that I have him as my savior."

Those who believe firmly that Jesus is their savior may, as this example suggests, define caring for others as bringing them to know Jesus, rather than feeding the hungry and clothing the naked. Yet the teachings of Jesus also focus sufficiently on taking care of physical needs that most of the teenagers we talked to who believed in Jesus did more than proselytize. One young man, for example, walked each winter throughout the city in which he lived giving sweatsuits to the homeless. He felt this was part of what it meant to serve Jesus. As he explained, "I don't believe we're just on this earth fighting to save our own butts. There's more to it than that."

Both the protective enclave and the authoritative figure of Jesus are increasingly problematic in our society, however. Few of us are able to surround ourselves with people who believe just as we do. And in more and more cases, our own parents and siblings have been reared in different faith traditions. When they have been exposed to different religions, even those who describe themselves as Christians find it harder to believe that Jesus is the only route to salvation, and they may also find it difficult to identify with Jesus. "Those of us who profess to be Christian," writes philosopher William Barrett, "might do well to remember that the central figure of the Christian religion is a man nailed to a cross."[15] And therefore, Barrett suggests, any sense of identification with the Christ must include an acknowledgment of both the suffering around us and the fact of our own suffering. Or, as Mother Teresa says, we must see Christ in the poorest of the poor and, in so doing, see ourselves. That is, many Americans may find Jesus a perplexing figure, even though they may assert their belief in his historical existence.

The Erosion of Moral Authority

Turning from the minority of young people who are devoutly religious to the majority who remain only somewhat interested in religion reveals more clearly how the moral authority of religious tradition has eroded. It is still possible to draw implications from religious teachings about being kind to our neighbors. But it is hard to defend these arguments as absolute truths. Instead, we must resort to situational arguments that emphasize expedience, and we rely on arguments that emphasize our own needs.

Amy Stone, the student who organized the AIDS rally at her high school, exemplifies what I mean by an erosion of moral authority. Because of her own illness, she is a strong person and has shown initiative in a number of ways—the AIDS rally, delivering Meals on Wheels, visiting nursing homes, and counseling teenagers about drug abuse and pregnancies. She exudes a certain degree of moral authority in her speech. Yet the way she talks also shows that she finds it hard to speak with absolute conviction, even about being kind. For instance, she talks about her volunteer work as if it were simply a hobby or a personal interest, and she is unwilling to insist that everyone should do volunteer work or even that everyone should care for other people who are in need.

The incipient erosion of moral authority is especially evident in Amy's views of religion. She attended church every week while she was growing up and still attends at least twice a month. She went to Sunday school and was an active participant in youth group. Because she lives in the South, she receives a great deal of social support for these activities. Even now, she says her prayers every night before going to bed, and she believes in Jesus as the son of God and as her personal savior. She regards Jesus as a model of caring and tries to be like him. In all these ways, she is deeply involved in Christianity. Indeed, Amy was one of the most involved of all the teenagers we interviewed. Yet she does not regard Christianity as a universal truth that implies binding moral obligations. She relativizes it by saying that people who happen to have been raised as Christians should try to defend it and follow its rules but that others need not believe it. She does not extract principles of virtue from Christianity that may be universal to all religions. Indeed, Christianity does not often enter Amy's discussion as a reason to be kind and caring. Instead, she allows other language from the wider culture to influence how she talks about Christianity. For example, in discussing the Good Samaritan, she suggests that the main point to be learned is that helping others will "always pay off."

The loss of metaphysical certainties, as Vaclav Havel calls them, is particularly evident in young people's remarks about God. It is common to say that God exists but to assert that God does not really expect anything. God is a libertarian who affirms personal freedom and the right to do one's own thing. For example, one student—acknowledging that her pastor probably wouldn't like her answer—says she believes that God decides when you are to be born and when you are to die but leaves you alone in between. She admits that her image of God depends mostly on what she has seen in movies, even though she reads her Bible three times a week and prays every day. "There was some movie I saw, and it was about this lady. The people in the movie were in heaven. And they called the God the He–She, and the God had like a little woman's voice and a little man's voice."

This student also imagines that God is a distant entity that mainly wants people to look out for themselves. She explains: "I kind of see a God that's just colorless. When I was little, I used to lay down and look up at the sky. For some reason, I would always imagine that I see eyes. I don't know if I really saw them or if I was just imagining I saw them. I would just imagine that those were God's eyes, and God was just colorless, but he was always looking down on everyone, and he was concerned with everyone and what was happening in everyone's lives. But he knew enough that he wanted you to try and make it on your own, and when you were down to the last straw and you didn't think you were going to make it, he would give you that little extra push to make it."

God is still a force for goodness, encouraging people to be kind to their neighbors, but this God is neither specific nor active in guiding behavior. People are supposed to make their own decisions, taking their cues largely from immediate circumstances. Insofar as God is relevant at all, it is as an invisible therapist. It may be impossible to care for others because of one's own anxieties.

Taking these worries to God frees one, so to speak, to be more interested in other people. The same student, for instance, argues that religious faith makes one more caring "because it gives a way of people being able to take their problems somewhere and leaving them there." She adds: "Like if you feel something really bad about yourself, or if something's going really wrong, you can just in a sense take your problems there and leave them there, and go continue with your life. I think God allows you to do that."

Another student—a young woman who had run away from home and who now volunteers at a shelter for runaways—also talked about God as a means of gaining personal strength. She had been raised as a Catholic, had gone to church regularly, and talked at length about her religious beliefs. She believes in God because "you need something to believe in, something to get you through." She thinks it "isn't possible to get anywhere without God." Asked what she thinks God is like, she answered: "He or she makes you get through, is looking out for you, and is there to help." But this is very much her own, personal view. She is unwilling to speak in universal terms about God. For instance, she says, "I don't try to push it on anyone else; that's their own choice, but I know for me that that's my way of making it through every day." Consequently, she is reluctant to argue that belief in God is necessary in order to be a caring person or that God necessarily makes it easier to help others. "I think it's just the individual," she explains. "If you're born to care about some-body, it's a quality that you have. It doesn't matter whether you're religious, or what religion you are, it's just there. If you're going to help somebody, you're going to do it."

Faith, then, may be helpful, but it does not provide a reason to be caring in the first place. As long as God expects nothing of people, they must find other grounds on which to make their choices. Another student shows how this line of reasoning may be articulated: "I don't know what God is like, to tell you the truth. It's hard for me to believe that he's a man because he could very well be a woman. I just think that there's someone up there running heaven. I don't believe that heaven is like these big gates and that you have to stay in purgatory until you enter it or you get sent to hell. I don't believe that. But I believe that there's someone up there running it, so to speak. I don't think God expects any-thing of anybody. I think he just wants you to be yourself. I do a lot of the stuff I do for myself. I work with the kids to help them, but it also makes me feel good."

Some of the young people we talked to made it clear that their churches were failing to give them clear messages about God. They learned to think of God only as a vague reality that holds things in place. One young man offered a poignant example: "I went and had a talk with the preacher to make sure I was Presbyterian," he recalls. He said the preacher told him about some "old scholar who kind of said the universe is the God." The main idea was to acknowledge that "there's never going to be a guy before you who says, 'Hello, my name is God.'" Thus, when asked about his own views of God, this young man ventured: "It's kind of hard to describe. It's kind of there, and I think if you live how Jesus wanted you to live, you're basically living the right way. I think Jesus was basically a perfect guy, but I'm not sure or I don't think he was divine, sent from God who was up in space somewhere. I don't think he sent Jesus. I think Jesus was a man."

Whether they had learned them at church or elsewhere, other students talked in similar terms about God. One, for instance, stated that he believes there must be a God, not a "master of puppets," but a being that keeps things generally under control. Therefore the authority of God is to provide a background to life that includes being kind and fair with other people. It does not supply scripts for specific situations or a language that one should use to explain particular activities. This student commented: "Like some people, they can't think of a better answer, so they'll say, 'Well, that's the way God wanted it, so he wills it.'" He disagrees with that view. He also asserts that his own religious beliefs are important "in some places." Asked to explain, he offered that he is "not one to believe that religion should shape your entire life."

The main reason that religious arguments fail to provide metaphysical certainty is that so many young people today are products of the religious diversity characterizing our society and are, in addition, the offspring of parents who were influenced by the radicalism of the 1960s. A young woman we talked to in Maryland offers an apt case study of these effects. Her father, an African American, was raised in the Catholic church, no longer attends, but says that his daughter should be a Catholic if she decides to be anything. Her mother, who is Jewish by birth, occasionally holds a seder for the family but was unable to take the children to Sunday school because of her husband. She had also been a member of est and practiced Buddhism for several years. Her daughter does not remember exactly what Buddhism was, only that it was "something really strange" and that she once had a birthday party at the temple when she was little. Then she remembers that for a while her mother had a lot of "born-again" Christian friends and turned "sort of fanatical" in that direction.

The daughter, now a high school senior, does not attend religious services anywhere. The reason, she says, is that she would be all alone. She doesn't know anything about a particular tradition and would feel uncomfortable going by herself. She summarizes her beliefs about religion by saying that there is probably "something out there," which she hopes will make it easier to face death, but she is not sure what it is or how to think about it. Interestingly enough, she does believe in God and admits she prays, so she would appear rather orthodox in a

Gallup poll. Yet she says it is hard for her to believe that God is doing anything more than sitting back and watching while humans destroy themselves, and she says her prayers are little utterances inside her head, like "Please God, let me get into Yale" (a prayer, incidentally, that was answered).

Being exposed to many different faiths—or at least to many different expressions of the same faith—is part of contemporary society. Some people are exposed to multiple faiths within their own families, but even those who are raised by same-faith parents cannot escape being exposed to multiple faiths at school. In the wider society, institutions are also composed of people from widely varied backgrounds. Part of playing a role in these institutions—as an employee, shopper, student, voter, or volunteer—is thus to rub shoulders with people having different faiths or no faith at all.

The value of this diversity, according to some scholars, is that people are then free to choose their own faith and, having chosen, that their faith becomes more meaningful to them. This view may be correct from one perspective: If one looks at the religious groups themselves, one will find many people who are deeply committed to these groups because they have chosen to be members of them. Tanika, for example, is more actively committed because she experienced a conversion and joined a new religious group, rather than simply staying in the church her parents sent her to as a child. Yet from a different perspective, not all the effects of religious diversity are positive. Listening to what a cross section of young people say about their faith, we see that exposure to religious diversity undermines their confidence in the truth of religion itself.

One student described her religious views in this way: "I believe in many different things, but I don't like to categorize myself and I don't even like to say that I'm agnostic because really all I am is just what I believe in and that's many different things. And if I categorize myself as many of my relatives do, as a Jewish person, I really would consider myself lying because I don't believe in everything that they say and I don't believe in everything in any religion. There's a lot of religions where I'll take things that I believe in. I believe in lots of things from different religions." She was sufficiently aware of different religions to pick and choose. What was ultimately true for her, however, was what she decided for herself.

Rafe Ramirez shows how religious diversity reinforces the view that a person must choose what is true and is ultimately alone in making these choices. Rather than living in an enclave as Tanika Lane does, Rafe feels as though he is confronting the universe by himself. He went to church regularly until he was fifteen, but his mother and father belonged to different faiths, and he attended church mostly to have fun with his youth group. He still says his religious beliefs are important to him, but the reason, he explains, "is that you basically go through life by yourself. You find yourself in situations in which you cannot count on your friends. All you can count on is yourself, and that may not be enough. So you need something besides yourself to depend on." For him, that something is God. Life is set up so that whatever happens is "basically up to you." But God is there to "support you" in whatever you decide to do. God neither controls nor judges. God simply knows that people are sometimes going to do what is wrong and accepts it. Rafe feels no particular need to go to church to find this God. In fact, he stays away from church because the preacher always seems to be asking him for money when he goes. Sometimes Rafe still reads the Bible because he likes the stories. He also has a little guardian angel pendant that he wears around his neck. After a friend of his died, somebody gave all the members of his soccer team these guardian angels, and he's worn his ever since.

Rafe feels he basically has his "head on straight," and so he has not felt religious beliefs pushing him one way or another. When he was in confirmation class, he learned about Jesus's saving people from their sins. He thinks this is a nice idea but not very relevant to how one actually lives one's life. Instead, he likes to think that Jesus is a spirit who is always around. His presence is evident just in the things that happen: "Like maybe you learn something. Or you make a decision and find you have done the right thing." Rafe calls these "little Jesuses." Otherwise, religion has a very small place in his life. He does not feel that it has made him more caring. "If you are going to be caring, you just are," he explains. "It doesn't make any difference whether you are a pastor or just someone walking down the street."

Other young people we talked to were left completely on their own to decide whether or not they wanted to adopt a religious faith. Jason McKendrick, for example, was raised by parents who did not believe in God and who did not attend religious services. They did not try to teach him that religion was false or that he should be an atheist. Rather, he was brought up simply to believe that whatever he wanted to think about religion is fine. Jason believes that there may be a connection between his volunteering and some transcendent reality in the universe—the possibility intrigues him—but he has no framework in which to make sense of this connection. For instance, he recalls: "My friend said something the other day about the community service that I do. She said, 'Oh, you were touched by God' or something like that. 'Since you do all this, that means that you are touched by God.' And I go, 'Wow, I don't understand the association there. If you do, please explain it.'"

Exposed to comments like this, Jason cannot help speculating that religious faith provides a reason to be kind. His views, however, register ambivalence. He thinks that faith may be important to some people, but he is unable to draw any universalistic conclusions about caring on the basis of religion. Like Vaclav

Havel, Jason is also convinced that religion may generate good deeds for the wrong reasons. He asserts: "Religion makes people want to do stuff to impress someone else, impress God or whatever. I don't know if I understand the religions exactly, but it makes a lot of people—how do I want to word this?—not want to do sin. It makes a lot of people be on their best behavior because they feel that someone's watching them at all times."

Signals of Transcendence

The loss of the transcendental, in Havel's terms, supplies an impetus to perform deeds of service, not acts of service to God, but ways of convincing ourselves that goodness, order, or a sense of right and wrong still exists. Although it is possible to engage in caring behavior for other reasons, many of us, it appears, may regard it implicitly as a way of saving ourselves—and our world—from chaos. We need to understand the implications of this quest. Because caring gives us glimpses of the sacred, we may be able to carry a morally binding sense of kindness into the complex roles we perform in social institutions. Yet there are dangers to be recognized as well.

Coined some years ago by sociologist Peter Berger, the phrase *signals of transcendence* refers to the ways in which brief experiences of the sacred occur in the midst of everyday life.[16] Although such signals can appear in any time or place, the idea takes on added importance in a society such as ours. Signals of transcendence, as Berger conceives of them, must be viewed against the backdrop of highly institutionalized social experience. Life that is routine, predictable, and divided into many compartmentalized roles typically becomes unidimensional. Rather than providing spaces in which chaos rules or mystery prevails, life of this kind takes place on a single plane dominated by standard definitions of time and space and governed by practical considerations. Signals of transcendence break through that reality at odd moments and compel us to recognize that there is more to life.

Play is one of the signals of transcendence that Berger discusses. He suggests that play temporarily suspends the rules that ordinarily govern reality. There is, for example, a different clock that runs during the game and that tells how long each period should be. Many games—basketball, football, baseball, tennis—also have a special space in which the game is played. Psychologically, play also breaks through the seriousness of everyday life. The game itself may be played with utmost seriousness because winning is important. Winning, however, is not a matter of life and death.

Perhaps more than anything else, play is a signal of transcendence because it allows the players to break through the limits that govern most of their roles.

In everyday life these roles are highly circumscribed. A young person is a student, and so during first period, for example, must play the role of algebra student, then during second period, the role of biology student, and so on. Each role may be quite boring, both because the tasks involved are narrowly defined and because their connection with the rest of a person's life may be tenuous. Play provides an escape. It, too, consists of carefully prescribed role behavior. But the game itself is more self-contained, supplying its own logic and its own intrinsic rewards. If nothing else, it offers an alternative reality to occupy for some of the time. It may also do more than that: teaching one how to have fun, not to take life so seriously, that there is more to life than work, and that one's horizons should be extended.

Rafe Ramirez finds that coaching soccer does all these things for him. The secret is that he is teaching children to play, and so he feels better able to behave like a child himself and to have fun the way children do. "It doesn't take much to amuse me," he explains. "I can entertain myself in any situation. I'm thinking like a little kid. So, when it's a real boring situation, I can find something to do that's dumb to most people. It's like childish, but it passes the time. It helps me to see the way I used to when I was their age, and remember how much fun it was back then. When you have to take on more responsibilities, that creates a lot of stress in everyday life. So what I figure is if I can act like a little kid, it relieves some of the stress of everyday life."

Other young people who had worked with children also talked about play—and the joys of childhood—as a kind of epiphany. For example, a young man who spent part of his summer doing construction work as a volunteer among Native Americans in Oklahoma admitted that what made it special for him was the kids. There were three of them. They liked to hang around and watch whenever the crew was building something. One little boy was living with his aunt because his mother had died recently. Nobody had seen him smile since the funeral. Then gradually, he began to lighten up again. The smile came back. It felt so good to see him smile that everyone else smiled too.

A simple smile need not be regarded as a signal of transcendence, but smiles, hugs, and warm expressions of gratitude were often said to be evidence of something deeper in life because they were so rare in everyday life. These small episodes of human contact became symbols of some greater goodness in the universe because they broke through the indifference and competitiveness of ordinary life. A young man who tutored homeless children offered one of the many examples of how a small episode took on special meaning because there was a different and more deeply human element to it: "I met a four-year-old girl named Sarah. She was the youngest student I ever had. She couldn't read or write, and within three days she could read small books, like *Cat in the Hat* and

Green Eggs and Ham. She read a couple of read-along books that I had on tape. I taped my voice, reading a book and taping it. She read along with it." He remembers how good that made him feel. "It was touching to me because I had done something for someone. It was just spectacular for me. I had a great feeling about it."

The sad or traumatic events that occur as a result of volunteering can also send signals of transcendence. These events break through the security that our institutions provide most of the time. Work, for example, is a place where goals are pursued, where the sick are absent, and where accidents seldom happen. Volunteering may remove us from the shelter of our institutions long enough to interact personally with someone who has no home or to care for someone who is dying. We then see that there is a reality from which even our institutions cannot protect us. A young woman who had worked as a volunteer in a hospital, for example, cried as she remembered a ninety-four-year-old woman she had gotten to know. "I would go in and visit her every day. She was so neat. And then she died. That was awful for me, because I got so close to her." Death suddenly became real. But in the process, the value of everyday life was also elevated. With the right instruction, we can learn to appreciate our hospitals, our schools, and our work.

The awareness that one's own life could end at any moment also led a number of the people we studied to be more caring because they did not want to have lived their life in vain. They wanted to leave a mark for good, even if it were only a small mark. And it dawned on them that they had better do it sooner rather than later. If they waited, for example, to finish school and then make a difference by treating sick people or by teaching, they might never have the chance. Rafe Ramirez was one such person. He told us that his volunteer efforts were significantly influenced two years ago when a classmate, and friend, died: "He was a real free-spirited guy. Never really cared what anybody else thought. Was very open with parents, other kids. We'd go to soccer games, we were on the same team. We would go to soccer games, and the cheerleaders would be doing cheers, and all us kids would be sitting there, because they wanted us to get into it, and we'd all just kind of be sitting back. And he'd always be right up there getting into all the cheers with the cheerleaders. Kind of a free-spirited guy. He was killed in a car accident when he was sixteen, and it just kind of made me realize that I don't have that much time. There's not a lot of time out there. So that kind of affected me a lot. Made me realize that life's pretty short. Can be, anyway. So I figure I'll do what I can when I can do it. It's really changed the way I look at life."

The danger—as far as religious communities are concerned—of volunteering becoming a signal of transcendence is that these signals may ultimately fail to point to anything beyond themselves. The joys of caring thus become good feelings and nothing more. Or an awareness of the frailty of life changes one's outlook, but not in a way that can be put into words. Many of the young people we talked to, for example, saw the joy—or sadness—they had gained from volunteering as an enriching experience, but few had found beliefs that gave them certainty about the nature of the universe as a result of these experiences.

This danger notwithstanding, there is a valuable lesson to be learned from the ways in which young people talk about their volunteer experiences in relation to their ideas about transcendence. This lesson is that people must, in fact, take responsibility for their actions. Moral authority may not be inscribed in the universe if this means a list of rules to be followed with blind allegiance. But few of the young people we talked to denied the reality of a more general sense of moral authority—one that required them to make informed choices, to do good to the best of their understanding, and to include service to others as part of doing good.

The authority that religious inclinations contributed to teenagers' thinking about caring was thus expressed primarily in a humanitarian framework. In the survey, those teenagers who were church members were more likely to emphasize humanitarian reasons for their volunteer involvement than were teens who were not church members. Similar effects were evident in those teens who actually volunteered through their churches. And smaller, but positive, effects were evident in those having parents, siblings, or friends who were church members. In short, the more closely a teenager was connected socially to a religious organization, the more likely he or she was to give humanitarian reasons for caring and volunteering.[17]

The idea of helping those who are in need seemed to be, as we saw in the last chapter, universally valid. When pushed to say why it was valid, some teenagers resorted to religious arguments. For example, one student remarked: "As a Christian I believe [caring] is a good thing because it's what God wants us to do. We're all equal in life and we need to show care to other people and not treat them unequally, not treat them as if they're just someone less fortunate and tough luck for them." Or as another student put it: "It's something that we were bound to do. God wanted us to do something like that, so I think that we should do what he wanted us to do." But these arguments were secondary. It helped to think that God wanted people to care for the needy, but if God did not exist, helping the needy was still an idea that seemed to make sense.

Some of the students we talked to, in fact, argued specifically that humanitarianism was really the underlying principle in religion, not the various teachings on which religions differ. A young woman who had grown up attending a Presbyterian church, for example, commented: "The stories and doctrines are small differences and really don't change that much how people act in terms of general behaviors. I mean some religions don't eat meat, but I'm talking about like just general. Most religions, though, preach to be kind and compassionate to others." She said she wasn't sure if there were any one religion that was right, even for a particular person, and she was sure that "very few people follow everything about their religion." As for herself, she noted simply, "I have my own personal religion which helps me."

A conception of moral authority that focuses so much responsibility on the individual person is, ironically, compatible with living in a complex world but also difficult to sustain in such a world. The reason that young people emphasized making up their own minds, regarding both religion and helping others, was that they were being trained to behave responsibly in a complex, diverse world. Their experiences with volunteering contributed significantly to this process. They learned not only to play responsible roles but also to talk about them in the language of contemporary society. They were reluctant to defend their activities in terms of absolute religious truths or even to make universalistic claims about the propriety of helping others. As Amy Stone did, it was more common to talk about personal preferences, special interests, and unique circumstances. Yet it is difficult to defend caring behavior entirely in these terms, because such arguments apply equally to studying, watching television, playing games, and hanging out with friends.

The difficulty of making moral choices entirely on one's own is thus a reason to reconsider the idea of protective enclaves that we discussed earlier. Although living in a homogeneous enclave is not easy for most of us, it is not impossible. We found young people who had been able to develop (or maintain) strong attachments to their faith communities, even though they remained actively involved in the wider and more diverse settings in which they lived.

One reason that it remains possible to identify strongly with a distinct enclave is that many of these enclaves are more internally diverse and more supportive of individual freedom than outsiders may realize. Megan Wyse is an example of someone who is deeply integrated into a distinct religious community and yet who finds a great deal of room for diversity within that community. As we saw, she derives much of her identity from the Jewish community. She attends a Hebrew day school and participates in activities at her synagogue. Her faith has an objective quality because it is part of her physical surroundings. Asked whether it was important, she answered: "It's what I eat, it's what I do, it's who I date, it's everything." Community and the legacy it stands for are especially important to her: "Our survival was based upon the fact that we are such a tight community and we have so many strong traditions that brought us together. I really believe much more strongly in tradition, and custom, and the family aspect of Judaism. So I think I'm much more community oriented in terms of religious belief instead of God oriented. So it's more of a community for me."

This community reinforces Megan's sense of the value of caring. It tells her that caring is more than simply a personal preference or something she does from self-interest. But the community also encourages her to be herself. She says: "I think each person is created for a certain purpose. What the purpose is, you don't really know, but your goal is to fulfill that purpose." Another indication of her individuality is that she brings in ideas that would be alien to Judaism traditionally. Elaborating on her idea of purpose, for example, she asserts: "If you don't fulfill it in your first lifetime, then you can fulfill it in your next lifetime, but you'll keep on being rejuvenated and reincarnated until you fulfill that certain purpose, whatever that mission is that you're created for."

It is also clear that Megan's community is a substitute for the more absolute sense of divine reality that may have guided people in the past. As she observes, her faith is more community centered than God centered. What this means is revealed in her comments about prayer. She says she prays every night: "I thank God for things that I have received, I ask God for things that I want or that I want for my friends or my family, and ask for forgiveness for things that I think I've done that I would like to ask forgiveness for." Asked whether she thinks her prayers are answered, she responds: "I don't think so. I think really I'm just praying because maybe it makes me feel like I can somehow change things, and it makes it feel like there's someone for me to answer to. But I don't think that they're necessarily listened to."

Without clear directives from God, Megan nevertheless constantly receives reinforcement from the religious community itself for thinking about kindness. She says the value of caring is built into the 614 mitzvot that she has studied at the Hebrew academy: "There's a lot of laws that they have that we learn about. Things like if you're a farmer and you're harvesting a field, you have to leave a tenth for the poor to eat from. You have to give 10 percent of whatever income you have to charity, no matter what it is, a minimum of 10 percent. A lot of the holidays involve inviting people into your home that don't have anything to eat. There's also laws dealing with helping people who are poor, comforting those who are sick, orphans, widows, things like that. So the big foundation, like the backbone of Judaism, I think, is helping other people."

The other reason that distinct enclaves made sense to some of our respondents, without seeming oppressive to them, was that pragmatic arguments outweighed ideas rooted in absolute metaphysical certainties. For many of the young people we talked to, religious beliefs are not a set of teachings about the mysteries of life but a set of practices that ensure a safe, happy, and worthwhile lifestyle. In this view, you believe what you do because it keeps you out of trouble and because it puts you in contact with good friends. It is consistent with this view that you should be a good person and do a little to help others. The notion of reciprocity that we considered in the last chapter is part of the logic: You yourself have benefited from the lifestyle practiced by the religious community, so you try to promote it and extend it by helping others. The religious community, then, may not be grounded in ultimate authority, but it has a pragmatic appeal. It is an enclave that protects one from the uncertainties of the wider society. It encourages an orderly, decent life, and to the extent that this life is attractive, it promotes helpful behavior both in the community and for others who may be in need.

One of the students we talked to is an example of someone who participates in a religious community of this kind. He went to an Assemblies of God church when he was younger and for the past five years has attended a Baptist church. He goes to church every Sunday morning, attends Sunday school regularly, and on Sunday evenings participates in a youth group. Asked why, he says: "I go because I found that what they talk about and the beliefs and way of life associated with it are basically the only things that actually work in life. You can get into drugs or popularity or whatever you want to get into in life. I've seen it with friends. I've seen it with Christians who have done it before they've turned to Christianity, and it does not work. If you live the way they're talking and live the way the Bible tells you to or whatever, or even to a portion of that, your life is just so much different than it would be if you don't, because if you turn away from it, then anyone that cares about you will see it. Sooner or later you're going to see it because it's happened to me before. As soon as you go back to it, then everything is basically OK. It's not peachy keen because you're a Christian and you're under God or whatever. It's not everything is cool. It's not like God is going to strike you down with lightning, but really it's the only way that works."

This young man can recite his beliefs as if he is quoting from a prayer book. For instance, he says: "I believe that Christ came and died for my sins on the cross, rose from the grave on the third day, went back up into heaven, and is preparing a place for me. I believe he sent his holy spirit to be with me and every other Christian on the face of this earth to comfort them and to help them in their mission until he gets back and takes us all back up to heaven with him. And that my purpose in life is to share the good news of Christianity with any other person who doesn't know it." Still, it is his community that is most important to him; the beliefs hover over it like angels. When asked what it is about faith that makes people care for others, he does not appeal to theological verities but to the pragmatic evidence from the community of faith: "I've seen it happen in people's lives, myself included."

Examples such as this suggest that assertions about the loss of metaphysical certainty, such as those of Vaclav Havel, may be accurate and yet overlook an important characteristic of American life. The pluralism of our society makes it difficult to hold religious beliefs as absolute, universal truths. We relativize and personalize our beliefs, juxtaposing ideas from different traditions, asserting our right to judge their validity, and refusing to judge the validity of others' beliefs. A stance such as this makes it hard to say that we should help others because there is an absolute or sacred mandate for doing so. Rather, we connect kindness and transcendence in less dramatic ways, finding "little Jesuses" in giving away a sweatsuit or in the smile of an elderly person who is near death. These small epiphanies remind us that caring is a good thing but allow us to live in a complex and highly institutionalized world. We are able to perform small acts of kindness in the diverse, specialized roles we play. Yet we are not compelled to function entirely as lonely individualists, either. We can still find shelter and encouragement in communities of faith. These communities may not inspire our commitment because we think they convey metaphysical truth. They do, however, inspire commitment because they help us remember our past, because they show us examples of how to be caring, and because they promote a lifestyle that works.

6

Contexts: Schools, Community Agencies, and Churches

It is tempting to think that the problems that we face today, from the homeless in our streets and poverty in the Third World to ozone depletion and the greenhouse effect, can be solved by technology or technical expertise alone. But even to begin to solve these daunting problems, let alone problems of emptiness and meaninglessness in our personal lives, requires that we greatly improve our capacity to think about our institutions. We need to understand how much of our lives is lived in and through institutions. We need to understand how better institutions are essential if we are to lead better lives.

Robert N. Bellah et al., *The Good Society*

Institutions are embodied in individual experience by means of roles. By playing roles, the individual participates in a social world. By internalizing these roles, the same world becomes subjectively real to him.

Peter L. Berger and Thomas Luckmann,
The Social Construction of Reality

Our primary sense of kindness, I have been arguing, is an intuitive understanding that comes in most cases from interacting with our families. We learn that kindness is a feature of intimate, firsthand relationships that involve our whole being and are based on trust and knowledge of our needs as persons. We are also exposed to arguments—humanitarianism, the pursuit of happiness, reciprocity, and self-realization—that reinforce our intuitive sense that kindness is a good thing. As we prepare for adult life, however, we are increasingly exposed to social institutions that require us to behave in ways different from those we learned in our families. We learn to play specialized roles, behaving as algebra students, for example, and to interact with others in these roles rather than relating as whole persons. We learn to bracket kindness or to give it new meanings, and we learn that self-interest and competition are the dominant rules rather than trust and cooperation.

In this process, we are exposed to diverse circumstances that make it harder for us to behave with certainty about the moral rectitude of our actions. Sacred authority becomes less absolute and more contingent on particular experiences. Volunteering and community service, I have suggested, are a valuable way in which to retain our primordial sense of the value of caring and also to modify this understanding as we learn to play specialized roles. Volunteering teaches us ways in which to be kind that are limited, that pertain to strangers, and that do not require an investment of our entire being. Ways to talk about our motives become more situational, providing accounts of how we became involved in particular avenues of service. Transcendence also becomes more situational, linking our specialized actions with fleeting glimpses of a reality even more fundamental than the one implied by the institutional roles we play.

Implicit in this argument is the fact that volunteering takes place in institutional contexts. Schools, community agencies, and religious organizations make up the bulk of these contexts. Young people help the homeless because there are school programs like the ones in which Jason McKendrick and Megan Wyse participate. Or they work through a community agency such as the LEAD initiative in which Tanika Lane participates or the soccer teams that Rafe Ramirez coaches. An AIDS rally like the one Amy Stone organized depends on the resources provided by her school and a number of civic organizations. In other cases, young people may work alone or start programs from scratch, yet these sooner or later become part of institutions as well. The reason is that little can be done in our society by working entirely by ourselves.

As young people engage in volunteer work, they are put in situations in which they learn to play roles in institutions. As Berger and Luckmann point out, these roles become part of who they are and how they see the world. The hope of educators and community leaders is that young people also learn, as Bellah and his colleagues suggest, ways to think about institutions that make these entities better and our society stronger.

We must turn next to the question of exactly what young people learn as they participate in volunteer organizations. Do they gain a new understanding of kindness? Is this understanding subverted by the humdrum requirements of institutional life—by the need for efficiency, order, impersonality, and specialization? Or is it possible to gain a new understanding of kindness that carries over to the other roles we must play in our society?

I want to consider these questions by discussing, first, the importance of institutions, second, the ways in which schools, community agencies, and religious organizations facilitate caring, and, third, the common and variable understandings of kindness that emerge in these settings. As before, I believe that language is crucial. Thus, it is important not only to consider the obvious fact that young people perform volunteer service mostly in organized contexts but also to emphasize the less obvious fact that young people learn new scripts for talking about caring. These scripts make sense of caring less as a personal virtue and more as a feature of programs and roles. Let us begin with a specific example.

From Inspiration to Institution

There was nothing unusual about watching the evening news, except that Tucker Aims never did. An aspiring seventh-grade party animal, he had better things to do, like hang out with his friends, listen to Minor Threat, Black Flag, or an old Jimi Hendrix tape. But that particular evening it was too rainy for anyone to be out, so Tucker was alone, watching television in his bedroom at his parents' mansion in Parkhurst, South Carolina. The local newscasters were spouting their usual drivel, he recalls, but something caught his attention. Runoff up in the park. Apparently some land had been stripped, and now with all the rain there was serious erosion in one of the creeks that ran through the park. Jesus! Why couldn't the highway people take care of it?

The more he thought about it, the more stupid it seemed. Anybody could fix something as simple as that. There were probably things like this going on everywhere. You just needed to motivate people to do something about it. Plant a few trees. Recycle. Clean up the beaches. It was an intriguing idea. How could you do it? Images flashed through his mind. Playing football in the park on Saturdays with his friends, Little League baseball. That was it! Make it competitive. The wheels were churning now. Notebook in hand, he curled up on his bed. An hour later he had it figured out.

"This isn't bad," his father told him when Tucker ran downstairs to show him. The idea was simple. Have a national contest, and give an award to whoever had thought up the most imaginative environmental project during the past year. Tucker worked out a point system to make the contest fair and focus it on kids his age, so in that way, they'd get involved. He even had an inspiration about what to call it. They would name the award after his grandfather. The old man always told him he'd never amount to anything if he didn't get serious. This would show him!

Thus came into being the Foster Aims Medal for the Environment or, as Tucker called it, FAME, the brainchild of a single thirteen-year-old sitting alone in his room one night. Five years later it was still going strong. Boys from all over the country were sweating away on weekends trying to win it. Trees were being planted. Cans and plastic were recycled. Beaches were being cleaned. It really happened. It was proof that one person, even a Jimi Hendrix fan, could still make a difference.

But there was more to the story. Even before Tucker ran down the stairs that night to tell his dad, he knew he could not handle the program all by himself. There had to be some way to let other kids know about it. It would work better, too, if kids could compete as teams, as they did in sports. Another image came to him: the scout uniform hanging in his closet, the badges. That was it. Indeed, the next day he and his dad drove down to the Boy Scout headquarters and tried to sell them on the idea. Make it a national contest that the scouts would administer. Troops would compete against one another. The scout leaders said, fine, but you do the work. So for the first year, Tucker did do the work. He called scout leaders all over the country, telling them about FAME. And in his bedroom, he kept records of all the troops' activities, tallied up their points, and sent the information to the scouts, who announced the award. By the second year, Tucker had proved that the program would work. But he also realized that it was too much for him to administer alone, so he turned it over to the scouts, who incorporated the medal into their system of badges and awards.

This story illustrates the importance of individual initiative and, even more, the significance of organizations. The few people who start their own programs generally rely on other organizations to help them, and most of the people who perform acts of service to their communities do so through formal organizations. They participate as volunteers, work with others they have met through the organizations in which they participate, and draw resources, such as facilities, transportation, expert guidance, or even photocopy machines, from these organizations. Even the small acts of kindness that people do for their friends and neighbors are likely to be shaped by the organizational contexts in which these friends and neighbors are known. Reflecting on his own experience, Tucker Aims summarized: "It's hard for someone just to do it by himself. You basically need an organization to get it done."

Schools as Contexts for Service

For young people, the one organization in which everyone is sure to participate, is the school.[1] Recognizing this fact, the promoters of community service have turned increasingly to the schools as a mechanism for mobilizing volunteers. Service clubs, community service requirements, internships, and in-service learning are among the initiatives currently being advanced, and these initiatives are beginning to bear fruit. Nationally, about one-quarter of all teenagers who are involved in any kind of volunteer activity say that some of this work has been performed as extracurricular activities at their school, including tutoring, helping with youth programs, volunteering for artistic and cultural programs, and organizing environmental projects.[2] Many of the young people we considered in previous chapters worked on community projects through their schools: Jason McKendrick and Megan Wyse, helping the homeless through school-organized programs; Amy Stone, organizing an AIDS-awareness assembly at her school; and so on.

Our conversations with young people revealed that service clubs are one of the most popular ways of drawing students into voluntary activities through their schools. Service clubs enlist students voluntarily, just as athletic, scholastic, or musical groups do that meet after school or during free periods. The students we learned about were engaged in a wide variety of activities—from organizing cleanup days for the school to staffing tables in the lunchroom offering information about social needs in the community to participating in programs for the homeless or for tutoring the handicapped. How service clubs function is described in the following example.

When Zia Hillier was a freshman, she was chosen to represent her high school at the President's Youth Leadership Forum in Washington, D.C. Approximately one hundred students from across the country attended the conference, whose purpose was to promote community service in high schools and voluntary organizations. Zia realized that her school offered students no opportunities for becoming directly involved in community service. Some clubs encouraged service within the school itself, but none put students in personal contact with the homeless, the handicapped, and the needy. So she started a club called the Youth Outreach Unit (or YOU) to promote such opportunities.

By getting students directly involved, Zia's hope was to change attitudes rather than merely provide services. "The people you help," she explained, "become human beings; they're not just statistics or charity cases." Her first step was to meet with the school's administrators to win their approval. Then she organized an activities fair to let students know about the club, when its meetings would be held, and what its purposes were. Their first major activity was a coat-and-blanket drive for the homeless. Serving as coordinator not only for the school itself but also for all the schools in the county, YOU collected one thousand coats and blankets. Then, to advance its aim of offering direct involvement, YOU organized a Christmas party in one of the city's low-income sections. Students baked cookies, went around to stores soliciting donations of toys and other gifts, and then worked with a community agency to put on the party itself.

Three years later, YOU is starting to have a wider impact on the high school. It has not been very successful in attracting members (only twenty in a school of twelve hundred). It has, however, exposed a larger number of students to various forms of community service. They have gained experience working with the elderly, the homeless, the handicapped, and inner-city children. In addition to hosting parties and clothing drives, they have taken homeless children on field trips, done cleaning in shelters for the homeless, and are currently sponsoring a foster child in Bangladesh and are hoping to start lobbying in the nation's capital in behalf of children's causes. The children especially have made a difference in the volunteers' lives, Zia says, because they "latch onto you so quickly" and they have "so much hope and courage."

The great advantage that service clubs enjoy over other ways of enlisting caring activities is that they make community service a *social function*, a peer activity around which informal pressures can be organized. Although participation remains voluntary, the members' behavior can be molded by example and by the expectation that students must do certain things in order to win the approval of other members. Indeed, the desire for approval is one of the strongest forms of motivation at this age (perhaps at any age), and service clubs merely focus it on community spirited activities. Consequently, service clubs can elicit a certain number of hours of participation each week simply by making these hours a condition of active membership, and they can confer special honors on those who do more.

Tucker Aims speaks in precisely these words as he describes the service club he belongs to at his high school: "It's a lot like a fraternity, and you really do get to be friends with the people in your club. There's a minimum. You've got to work at least fifteen hours per quarter, volunteer work, so you've got to do sixty hours a year. That's in our club. In each club it's different. So there's really a lot of work that goes into it."

The activities are sufficiently diverse that members do not feel compelled to do something they dislike. Tucker observes: "We babysit for kids. We also work at Special Olympics. Anything anybody approaches us with. Lots of times we work at haunted houses around town at Halloween. That's always a fun thing to do, to be the monster." But the club makes it clear that people must serve in order to belong: "You have to write a little article. We have a sheet, and it kind of asks about service and volunteer questions. Would you be willing to come to meetings? Would you be able to do volunteer work? What are some of your ideas for volunteer work? Stuff like that." The club also has a tryout day— a kind of audition that prospective members must pass. Tucker admits the process is a bit intimidating because the older members ask a lot of questions to test personalities and see how people will respond to odd situations.

The club also exercises discipline by threatening to expel members who do not live up to its expectations—and carrying out these threats. Tucker feels this is important to do, "because it's also something social. You get kicked out of the club if you don't do enough work. That happens lots of times. What you basically want is to have people who'll have fun so you have fun when you have parties and people who will do the work, or someone who's just responsible and can, like, keep track of those hours."

Among other students we talked to, such practices were considered common. Many of the larger high schools had more than one service club: some that admitted only young women, some that were for African American students, some that were for "artsy" students, and some that focused more on politics. As a result, members could choose fellow students with whom they liked to associate and then encourage at least some participation in useful activities. As one student explained: "If we let someone in who's cool, we'll do that too, but if they don't do the work then they're kicked out."

Another way in which schools promote voluntary service is through internships. These are generally part of the formal curriculum and are designed to give students hands-on experience in working with the handicapped, teaching, tutoring, or developing vocational skills. Patti Evans (whom we met briefly in a previous chapter) is an example of a student whose life has been deeply influenced by her participation in an internship program. A senior in a medium-size town in Pennsylvania, Patti has been involved for the past two years in an educational internship program that her high school started six years ago. Last year she worked as an assistant for a sixth-grade teacher. The experience consisted mainly of photocopying materials for the teacher, and Patti found it very unrewarding. She did, however, learn about some opportunities through the program that she hoped would be more challenging. One of those was the handicapped program she is helping with this year.

Patti currently works with a class of six handicapped students who are mainstreamed only to the extent of being in the same building as the other high school students. They have their own teacher and mix only occasionally with the other students, for example, in the lunchroom or in activities such as art, gym, or music. Patti spends one forty-minute class period each day working one-on-one with the students. She receives credit for this participation, just as she would for a regular class. In addition, she voluntarily helps the six students by bringing them individually to her own classroom during study periods and by tutoring them from time to time during lunch period or after school. The students are quite severely handicapped. Only two of the six can walk. Only one can go to the bathroom; the rest are in diapers. None of the six can talk. One has seizures every day. Patti is nevertheless able to make a significant difference in their lives. She helps them do physical exercises that help them relax and enable them to do art work. She has earned their trust so that she can take them to gym class. She is beginning to learn sign language. The internship has also had an impact on her. When she began, she thought she would like to be a teacher in a regular classroom, but now she wants to major in special education.

Besides service clubs and internships, a growing number of schools are also establishing obligatory service requirements. We will examine the extent, strengths, and weaknesses of these programs in a later chapter, although we will briefly consider here the one at Megan Wyse's high school. Her school requires all students to do community service during the last six weeks of their senior year. After regular classes end in April, students work on various service projects from 8 o'clock to 3:30 every day.

The idea, Megan explains, "is that everyone has to somehow give back to the community what they've been building up for so many years." The activities range from working at a hospital to tutoring kids that come from disadvantaged backgrounds. Megan is considering an inner-city hospital for her project. "They bring in women who are at high risk for whatever reason—poverty, drugs, HIV positive—and help them with prenatal care up to the point of delivery," she explains. "So I'd be working probably the social and medical aspect of it for six weeks, which would be very interesting. I can pick any agency that I'm interested in and call them up, and if they're interested, I can do volunteer work. We have an interview, and they tell us what we can do. We're not doing things like filing or anything. We're going to do something that's beneficial to us as well; otherwise we can't do it. I can't just work at an agency and just staple all day and answer phones. I'll be doing something that really is part of the agency, something that's really going to benefit people and that I can learn from."

In discussing the service activities of schools, we should also mention the role of support groups. These may be part of the curriculum, run in conjunction with community service or internship programs, or operated separately as training units. Their function is not to engage members directly in service activities but to prepare them for service by cultivating personal skills or to deal with the emotional impact of other voluntary efforts.

Tanika Lane regards her involvement in LEAD as a kind of support structure that has enabled her to do other things. She remembers: "We had to get up and talk about ourselves, so we won't be shy. At first, it was to get over the fear of talking in front of people, and then we just began to talk about what makes us angry. That really helped us get along. Somebody came in and observed, and they said, 'Is this therapy?' We said, no. This is LEAD. And they said, 'Oh, this looks like therapy,' because we sit in a circle, so it won't be like a classroom atmosphere. One of our main things is unity. With so many people, you have to be unified. You can't be, 'I'm going to do this and if you don't like it, I don't want to be in it.' We learn to get along and say, 'Well, Tanika is better at this. No, Anginette is better at this, so let her.' We learn to be loving and caring to one another."

Patti Evans is also part of a support group. Hers is composed of the special education teacher, herself, one other intern her age, the art teacher, the home economics teacher, and one of the school administrators. The group does not meet regularly, and its purpose is not to provide emotional support on either a regular or a special basis. It does, however, offer resources that interns like Patti can draw on. For example, it meets periodically to discuss objectives and evaluate accomplishments. These meetings give Patti a chance to hear the professionals reflect on what is happening and to gain a broader perspective on the overall program.

Schools are thus a way in which students can gain exposure to a variety of helping and service activities. Lest it appear that schools have become bastions of kindness, however, we should also acknowledge the problems that remain. Many of the students we talked to said it had been difficult to enlist large numbers of their classmates in community activities. Academic pressures account for some of this indifference. Alcoholism and drug abuse are still problems of considerable importance among teenagers. Sexual harassment is quite widespread, and racial tension continues to prevail in many high schools as well.

One of the African American students we interviewed provided valuable insight into what it is like to experience racial tension firsthand. As a result of busing, she is one of one hundred African American students, nearly all from low-income neighborhoods, who attend a high school of sixteen hundred in a wealthy suburb on the north side of town. She says it has been hard to fit in because of these income differences. The white middle-class students can spend hundreds of dollars going to the prom; she is lucky if she can scrape together $3.00 to buy a ticket for a football game and then may not have transportation to get there. The income differences are aggravated by racial tensions. She tried to start a racial awareness club, for example, but was disappointed to find that it only made the problem worse. She explains: "Any time you have more than one black person together, there's going to be a problem. That's just the way things are. I think a lot of it has to do with, like, in my calculus class, Reese and I are the only black students, and that's outstanding for a calculus class in this area. Usually you're the only black person in your advanced class. Like in my English class, I've been the only black student since freshman year. Usually they're only used to seeing one of us around. So any time they see more than one of us around, they usually think there's going to be a problem."

Apart from sexual and racial conflicts, high schools also continue to be places in which selfishness prevails. One student supplied an example when talking about her classmates' reactions when a friend threatened to commit suicide after having broken up with her boyfriend: "We should just tell her to f— off;

she's so psychotic." Another said, "I told her to go ahead. I just wanted to see if she'd do it."

These problems notwithstanding, schools nevertheless play an important part in transforming students' views of caring. The impulse to care that students bring from their childhood experiences is often naive and idealistic. Participating in service clubs or internships is one way of expressing this impulse but confronts students with the realities of playing specialized roles.

One of the realities that Zia Hillier discovered is that service clubs compete with one another for members. Caring is thus connected to the need to make membership attractive and to the competitive spirit prevailing in most institutions. Another reality is that organizations—especially ones involving public trust—are averse to taking risks and thus emphasize what can be done, but not necessarily what needs to be done. Jason McKendrick, we recall, spoke of the difficulties that his service club had encountered in securing permission to work in the inner city.

Many of the students we talked to found themselves torn between idealism and the realities of program requirements that focused volunteer efforts on the school rather than the wider community or on the local community rather than a community in some other part of town that needed the help more. For instance, Zia Hillier remarked: "I think if you're going to volunteer—you know it's nice if it's really close to you, but if what's really close to you happens to be just cleaning up your sidewalk, then I don't think you're that effective, and you shouldn't really say that you're trying to do community service. Community service should be about giving to other people. If it's just convenient for you, then you're not really giving anything."

Another reality that students often run into is the school's subculture. All organizations have such subcultures; that is, certain attitudes are implicitly condoned. Zia's high school again provides an example. She says that it is customary for students to sign up for service clubs because it will look good on their résumés but then not to do any work because nobody checks. Another commonplace is to express concern about minorities in the abstract but not to be tolerant in practice. She says it would be hard to volunteer for a gay rights organization, for example. "I strongly believe that everyone should have whatever rights they have. But a lot of people in my school make jokes about it. And if you say something like, 'Well, that's not true. That's a really nasty thing to say,' then people are automatically like, 'Well, you're gay.' And then they equate it with something bad. If somebody just called me a homosexual, then I'd just suggest to them that they're incorrect. But it doesn't matter to me if that's what they believe. It's a pretty negative attitude."

Customs such as these, together with teasing about being a "do-gooder," curb some of the enthusiasm of volunteers in schools. Many of those we talked to found these norms disturbing, yet other norms that the students learned helped them to be of service. These were often expressed in the scripts that young people learned to use when talking about their volunteer efforts. As we saw in Chapter 4, these scripts offer ways of describing one's motives for being interested in a specific kind of volunteer work.[3] They also reflect the particular organizational contexts in which they are used.

In the schools, the most distinctive script we observed emphasized the connection between caring and education. This script equated caring with teaching and with being helped through learning. Thus, transmitting knowledge to someone is one way to know that you have made a difference. This assumption, in turn, is rooted in the idea that recipients will then be able to help themselves, to achieve more, and to be more self-sufficient. A young man who tutors clearly expressed these assumptions when he described why he likes this activity: "When you're talking to the students and they finally understand something, they just get this look on those faces. I don't know how to describe it. It's just the most awesome thing you can ever see on someone's face. They're just like, 'Wow! I understand! I can do this!' It was just like the most awesome feeling that I helped someone else go beyond what they felt they can go beyond. It was just awesome!"

Another part of the educational script is that the volunteer learns as much as the recipient does. A student who tutors the blind offered the following example of this script: "I was tutoring in Braille, which I know very little, so I was only able to help him to a certain point. Basically we learned Braille together. He's much better at it than I am at this point. I'm learning at this point in my high school career, half of these things I'm still learning."

Thus it makes sense to be caring, even if your abilities are limited, because you learn things that will help you be more effective in the future. Yet it is also clear that considerations of effectiveness and efficiency come to prevail over more personal orientations. In the same case, the tutor said it had bothered her when the supervisor transferred a pupil to whom she was close to another tutor who had more experience.

Because schools are in business to educate, a script such as this also serves their organizational purposes, as it encourages young people to channel their caring impulses into something that the organization can support. Indeed, we found that schools also protected these impulses by focusing them on activities that could be performed at the school itself. As will be evident when we turn to community agencies and churches, the idea of "community" is an important way of channeling such activities. Schools use this idea by calling themselves communities. Students told us, for example, that their school was a microcosm of the wider community and that it was important to serve in it. They felt they understood the school's special needs and thus should focus their efforts where they could be most effective.

Community Organizations

Besides schools, community organizations are an increasingly common context in which young people learn new meanings of caring. Leaving aside volunteer work done in conjunction with schools, as many as one teenager in five is a volunteer for some kind of community organization, not counting churches or synagogues.[4] Many of the programs run by schools depend on community agencies as places where young people can actually engage in service activities. But community agencies also draw young people directly into service programs and activities. These agencies can sponsor a wider variety of activities than most schools can, and they can put volunteers into direct contact with a more diverse range of social needs. Two examples illustrate some of this variety.

Like Zia Hillier, Nikki Unger is active in several service clubs at her high school. She heads an organization called Students for Environmental Awareness and is active in a club that seeks to promote greater concern among students about the needs of people in less developed countries. Most of Nikki's volunteer work, however, is conducted through organizations outside her high school. Several are political activist groups that try to monitor human rights violations. One, for example, has worked through diplomatic channels to pressure the government of Haiti to pay more attention to human rights. Another one raises funds in conjunction with ceremonies commemorating such events as Martin Luther King Jr.'s march on Washington or the death of Archbishop Oscar Romero in El Salvador.

Most of Nikki's current volunteer activities are centered on an organization called Help the Children. It is a community agency sponsored entirely by private donations and volunteer time and based on the special needs of children being raised by grandparents, other relatives, or neighbors because their own parents are dead, in jail, addicted, or absent for some other reason. Its activities include counseling the natural parents so that they might again be able to care for their children and counseling the current guardians about needs and issues that have arisen in becoming temporary parents. Help the Children is, in many respects, like thousands of other self-help groups. By bringing people together who have unusual needs, these groups share homespun advice, provide emotional support, and serve as conduits for information about medical assistance or other public programs. Help the Children relies more on outside volunteers than do most self-help groups because some of its clients are indeed suffering from extreme dysfunctions and most are seriously disadvantaged in terms of income, jobs, education, and other personal resources.

Nikki plays a small but crucial role in the activities of Help the Children. She babysits. Every Saturday morning, when parents and guardians come for counseling and talk-therapy sessions, Nikki is there to look after the children. It sounds simple, but it is a big job. Usually, she is responsible for forty children, nearly all of whom are younger than twelve, and many of whom are preschoolers. She entertains them, provides snacks, changes diapers, and maintains order for the three hours they are there. She also organizes special events, such as a recent Christmas party. Counting the actual time she is there, the time it takes to commute, and the several hours each week buying supplies and planning games, she spends at least twenty hours a month doing this.

Nikki remembers how nervous she was the first time she went to Help the Children but says she became hooked almost immediately. "When I first came, I was afraid, since they're basically all African American children. I thought maybe there would be some animosity, and I was a little worried the first time I went down. Even with the first two kids who I rode up with in the elevator, they were really outgoing, and by the time I got upstairs and there were more and more kids coming, they were all trying to jump on my lap and everything, and they were very, very loving children. It made me feel like it was really worth it, since probably some of them don't get as much love at home, since the parents aren't there, and they've experienced a lot of hurt. How needy these children are for love more than anything else! It made me see how it was very valuable time that I spent down there, when I could give what love I have and they were so eager to receive it."

As this example shows, one advantage of many community agencies is that they are located where the needs are. Help the Children is located in one of the poorer sections of a large city, which makes it possible for people who are unable to care for their own children—of whom there are many in this part of the city— and for those who are serving as guardians to attend meetings regularly or simply to drop in when problems arise. This means, of course, that community agencies must operate through networks that draw volunteers from other neighborhoods. Most of the volunteers at Help the Children, including Nikki, drive or take public transportation from middle-class suburbs located ten to twenty miles away. Nikki usually drives but sometimes rides with her dad, who now serves on the board of the agency and is in charge of its finances.

Nikki herself is a key link in the network that connects Help the Children with potential sources of volunteers. The teacher in charge of the Service Board at Nikki's high school is helping her organize a field trip for the children. This will require some additional volunteers from the high school. The teacher is also trying to recruit more African American students to work with the children. She thinks it is important for them to have African American, rather than white, role models.

Nikki's church provides another link: Not long ago Nikki arranged to have the director of Help the Children speak at her church, and as a result, some of the parishioners donated money. Community agencies are often part of networks that pool their resources to meet a wider array of needs as well. The building that houses Help the Children, for instance, also includes a job placement center, an office that provides information about low-interest loans, and an agency that recruits volunteers with skills in construction to help homeowners renovate and make improvements on their houses.

Sherry Hicks also does volunteer work for a community agency that focuses much of its attention on children. Living in the same community that she serves, she provides a contrast with Nikki Unger's commuter-style volunteering. At 5'8" and weighing nearly 200 pounds, Sherry is a commanding presence wherever she goes. Her mother is white and her father, whom she never knew, is black. She lives in a small single-family house with her mother and younger brother in one of the poorest sections of a medium-size midwestern city. The house is surrounded by projects—the "red" ones behind and the "brown" ones down the street—and by vacant lots, and there is broken glass everywhere. "You can drive down Lincoln Street at night," Sherry observes, "and you can just see tons of young males and females that should be studying and making the grade, and you can just see them hanging out, not doing a thing. A lot of them are selling drugs up there, getting into violence, getting into gangs." The neighborhood has declined significantly since an electronics assembly plant that had provided work for many of the residents relocated to Mexico. Sherry's mother considers herself fortunate still to have a job at a factory that makes home appliances, even though she was laid off for two full years and is now lucky to work six months of the year. As a high school senior, Sherry has had the most education of anyone in her family: Her father quit school after eighth grade, and her mother ran away from home when she was a freshman.

Every Sunday evening for the past four years Sherry has sought refuge from what she describes as a very unhealthy home environment. She walks five blocks to the old Hacker building near the center of town. It used to house a whites-only club. Now it is the home of IMPACT, a place where inner-city kids can come and swim, play games, talk, get help with their homework, and just hang out. It is operated by Youth Resources, a pilot program established six years ago by the National Crime Prevention Council. With funding from the Department of Justice and a large private foundation headquartered in the state, as well as donations from United Way and a number of local businesses, Youth Resources sponsors numerous service projects, promotes efforts to combat drug abuse, and trains young people to take leadership roles in the community. Sherry has been involved with many of the Youth Resources programs. A two-year winner of the top-GPA award at her high school, a member of the state mathematics team and the National Forensics League, and a state prize-winning member of the woodwind ensemble, she has served on the Youth Resources board of directors for two years and as its president for one year, represented her region at the governor's commission on drug abuse, and played an active role in the Youth Resources Teen Advisory Council. With committee meetings some mornings at six o'clock, and all-day sessions on Saturdays, she often devotes a dozen hours a week to these activities.

Sherry's volunteer work at IMPACT on Sunday evenings consists of spending three hours each week working with elementary school children. Each week she develops and teaches a project, such as coloring pictures or writing essays dealing with alcoholism, learning physical exercises, or making Thanksgiving decorations for people in nursing homes. She also organizes special activities, such as visits to hospitals, litter patrols, day-long tutoring programs every other Saturday, or—one of her favorites—an all-night "lock-in" that gives the children an opportunity to play and to "sleep over" with their friends in the safe environment of the IMPACT building. She organizes these activities with seven other volunteers her age, three from her own neighborhood and two each from other parts of the city. They also have an adult supervisor, currently a pastor from one of the neighborhood churches.

Sherry recalls clearly the first time she came to IMPACT. It was right after they had moved into the old Hacker building. She remembers that the building was cold, stank from having been boarded up for several years, and had mushrooms growing out of the cracks in the floors. All that has changed, thanks to the hundreds of hours of cleaning, sanding, painting, and carpet laying put in by volunteers. The building is now a place that commands respect and instills pride—at least most of the time. Sherry also recalls the night that things nearly got out of hand. Not realizing what they were getting into, the volunteers had planned a race for the children that required carrying an egg on a spoon as one of the games, but some of the kids had other ideas. Sherry recounts, "So they started throwing them, and we had eggs all in our hair, and all over ourselves." She yelled at the perpetrators, "If you don't stop, then you will have to leave, because we won't tolerate that behavior." But they replied, "You're not going to make us leave, because our parents aren't coming. So there's nothing you can do to us." Eventually things got so bad that some of the kids had to be driven home. That, however, was not the end of things. When one boy's mother heard what had happened, she started hitting him, prompting the IMPACT sponsor, who was from a different part of the city, to intervene, thus alienating the mother. Sherry remembers the mother shouting, "Well, I don't see why you white people should come in here and do anything anyway. You don't know anything about black people." Eventually the mother was drawn into IMPACT's activities; the boy started doing better in school; and the racial tension subsided, but only because there were volunteers like Sherry who were part of the neighborhood itself.

Just as it is in the schools, one way in which caring is promoted in the more formal contexts of community agencies is by providing familylike experiences. That is, young people perform specialized tasks but preserve their primordial sense of caring because the agency itself becomes a surrogate family. In many cases, small groups of fellow volunteers who care for one another are an important part of community agencies. Because the volunteers work together, share common interests, and establish bonds of trust, volunteering becomes a place to receive as well as to give.

Sherry Hicks reveals the value of such support when she talks about working long hours with an IMPACT group for several weeks planning and organizing an antidrug camp for teenagers in the neighborhood: "Mike came to us and he was talking to us. He said, 'Well, I have something that I've told Nancy.' Nancy is our youth director. 'She's helped me with it, but I just feel that I trust you guys enough that I can tell you and know that you won't laugh, or think I'm funny, or think I'm weird.' So he told us about how when he was little how he got molested. He was telling us all these things, and everyone just started crying because we were just so close and we loved each other so much. So that, it just made the gateway just open, because then I was telling stuff from my past, about getting beaten up and abused and all, and everyone else was telling stuff, stuff that really hurt us but that we didn't feel that we could tell anyone else, not even our parents, not even our best friends, no one. Here we were, most of us were seventeen, finally after seventeen years just being able to let it all out and know that no one's sitting there judging you because of what happened before, and knowing that all the rest of the people in the room supported you, and appreciated you, and loved you."

Out of such experiences, volunteers are motivated to keep serving. They serve a wider variety of people and do so in more specialized ways than in their families, but for the same reasons—a sense of commitment to others in the organization who care deeply for them. Such caring can be, as Sherry Hicks's story shows, quite profound. In a different way, community agencies also encourage service by providing recognition. This kind of support may be more ephemeral, but it can be highly motivating, especially in a competitive world that teaches us to value such recognition.

Community agencies have become special places in which to gain recognition for acts of service. In schools, recognition is more likely to be given to those who excel academically and in sports. Community agencies, specializing in service, can link recognition more directly to service. Rafe Ramirez, the soccer player who does volunteer coaching, is one example. He explains: "I got a scholarship through the soccer club. They gave me $250. What they did is they made an award. I don't remember what they called it, but it was a scholarship where they would give $250 to a player who has come through the system and given back a lot to the club. They started it two years ago, and a guy named Fred, who I used to play with, he's a year older than me, he goes to college, he received it that year. It was really neat. He was up there in front of everybody, and he received the award at our banquet. It was pretty neat. I was like, wow! That would be neat to get an award like that. That was a $500 one. Now, the next year they decided that they've split the $500 into $250 each, a male and a female, someone who's come through the league and then given back a lot. So they gave me and this other girl in my class the award that year at the banquet. It was really neat. I had no idea I was getting it."

This example shows how awards given to leaders one year can motivate other volunteers to work hard in hopes of being recipients in future years. Such awards, of course, link caring with a competitive spirit. But recognition can be used to promote a cooperative spirit as well. Rafe Ramirez offers this example as well: "My team had given me a big plaque with their picture on it and all their names on it. They gave me that plaque last year. And one of the parents takes pictures, is a really great photographer, and he took many pictures through the whole season. He made little plaques and little stands, and he gave me one of them, and he gave me a set of the film of all this stuff, and it has pictures of all the kids, and me coaching the kids. It was really neat. I liked it."

Sherry Hicks provides another example of how community agencies can use awards to encourage caring. In this case, recognition is given to the recipients of volunteer efforts, which in turn reinforces the enthusiasm of the volunteers: "I think the reason I've stayed is because I can see how much good it is doing. Like last night, we had the Pride Awards banquets, and a lot of the kids that come to the tutoring program that are in middle school, they were up there getting awards for having a 3.0 [GPA] or better. That just made me really proud to see that, because a few years ago, you would have seen black students up there getting awards for their 3.0s, but it would have been the black students on the East Side, or the North Side, and the West Side that have money. It wouldn't have been those from the inner city."

Like schools, community organizations also supply specialized scripts that volunteers learn to use when talking about their activities. If schools promote an educational script, community organizations will use language about the community itself as a way of defining and motivating caring activities. This script builds on the primordial moral sensibilities learned in the family during childhood. It nevertheless is a new language that must be learned if participants are to function effectively in the context of community agencies. And like any new language, it requires giving up some of the earlier idioms that were part of their primary speech and to translate old meanings into new ones. It focuses the participants' understanding of what it means to care, turning them into volunteers, into servants of the community. It selectively emphasizes certain activities, thereby neglecting others, and, most important, gives participants meaningful ways in which to talk about these activities. To serve effectively in community agencies, one must not only engage in certain activities but also learn the community script.

The most important elements of the community script are phrases that stress the community as the object of care. Helping still means caring for particular people, and it also means service that somehow contributes to the betterment of a more collective entity, such as the neighborhood, the city, or a section of the city. Listen to how Sherry Hicks describes IMPACT: "What we do is we work in the community and we put on programs each month for the other children that live in the inner city, and it gives me a chance to meet my neighbors and to help out with the people in the inner city."

A second feature of the community script is language that emphasizes programs. These are organized activities, formal means of helping others, as opposed to purely individual, spontaneous, informal acts of caring. From its emphasis on programs, it follows that the community script also underscores effectiveness. Outcomes are important. It is not so much the process that counts but seeing that something actually happened, that events really took place, that programs were carried out, and that people participated in activities. This does not mean that persons were necessarily helped or that evidence must be gathered to show that lives were changed or the community actually improved in some measurable way. It does mean, however, that volunteers must not be idle. They must identify specific activities as their goals and then carry out these activities.

For example, a project involving younger children in Sherry Hicks's community is described in its literature in the following language: "Fourth-grade students will collect gallon milk jugs, clean them, and cut holes in the sides. Clean, recycled bags will be put into each milk jug. The jugs and a potted flower will be given to apartment dwellers in the neighborhood." The description further notes that 114 children will be involved and that there will be 310 recipients. It says, too, that the entire project will cost $777.50. Caring, in short, is redefined in the very specific terms of these activities.

A project description of this kind is not generated simply because someone happens to write it down in this way. If this were the process, there would be much more variation in how projects are described. Instead, these are scripted accounts. They follow a pattern, are highly stylized or formulaic, often come from the professionals who head up such projects, and are thus transmitted formally to the volunteers who participate in them. Twenty-nine other projects in Sherry Hicks's community are thus described in almost the same language as the one for milk-jug flower pots. Indeed, the same computer template could have been used to supply the appropriate headings. That volunteers learn these scripts is also evident in this example. The children themselves are required to come up with proposals for new projects, although they can ask adult sponsors for assistance. The adult sponsors show them the scripts that have been successful in securing resources for previous projects. If such scripts seem to neglect the more primordial understandings of caring that come from families, they nevertheless prepare young people to think about caring in the more orderly ways required by large, complex social institutions.

Another feature of the community script is that activities must be organized rationally. They must not be based simply on emotion, on feeling sorry for those in need and trying to help them, but must involve planning. In addition to specifying goals and activities ahead of time, this kind of script must also include something that does not always have to be a part of planning, namely, the use of incentives, a reward system of some kind, and a formal mechanism for inculcating skills or extending the work of volunteers to others. That is, a logic is built into the community script that rewards desirable behavior and tries to perpetuate the agency's work.

Sherry Hicks demonstrates this logic: "We do things like have tutoring programs where we help them with their schoolwork, or we'll take them to Holiday World if they've gotten good grades all school year, or we'll just do different activities each month, like we'll throw an Easter party. Then also we put lessons with everything we do. Like the Easter party this year, besides making baskets for them, we made them in turn make baskets for elderly people, and the home across the street from our building." Note that the children that her program tries to help are thereby encouraged both to be worthy by making good grades and to be of service by making baskets for others.

Churches and Synagogues

Religious organizations such as churches and synagogues are like other community agencies in that they provide services to the wider community and generally do so free of charge. These organizations, however, deserve separate consideration because they draw on the special languages of faith, as we saw in the last chapter, and because they include activities that only partly resemble the services performed by secular agencies. Religious organizations are also a primary setting for volunteering, enlisting the services of nearly 30 percent of all teenagers.[5]

An example: "We were visiting the Committee of the Displaced. They operate a clinic which two years ago was raided and everyone was captured. We passed by this little boy who was like nine years old, and he had been hit by a mortar that was dropped on his community. That was one of the times when I just like—I don't know if I cried or not, but came close to it. It was probably a U.S. mortar. And seeing this kid lying there almost, I guess, dead. I assumed he lived, but really damaged by this mortar from our government. That was my country that supplied the mortar that did that. That's, I guess, one of the few first eyewitness experiences I'd had with the war."

The person speaking is Jackie White, a seventeen-year-old who attends a largely middle-class high school. When Jackie White was eight years old, her parents started attending the Methodist church. They were baby boomers from the 1960s who had been deeply influenced by those unsettled times. Her father had lived in Latin America for a while, worked at various odd jobs, and then pursued a career as a guidance counselor in the public schools. Her mother had been in VISTA, worked for the American Friends Service Committee, and raised three children before deciding to make a midlife switch into nursing. They live in a three-bedroom row house in an older, racially mixed section of the city. As a small child, Jackie's father had been sent to a conservative Baptist church every Sunday but, after receiving a spanking one Sunday, refused ever to go back. Her mother was Lithuanian Catholic but had never been taken to church except on holidays. They joined the Methodist church because it was involved in causes they believed were right. Jackie's parents became active members of its Social Action Committee, which tried to put into practice religious teachings about equality, reconciliation, and social justice.

When Jackie was nine, the church took in a Guatemalan refugee family, giving them sanctuary, legal assistance, and financial aid. Through her parents, Jackie became acquainted with the family. She felt comfortable with them, started attending the meetings at church that were being held on their behalf, and listened to their stories of injustice and oppression. It was that experience, Jackie says, that made her feel comfortable being part of "the movement" and being involved in an activist church. Soon afterward, she and her mother became active in an organization called Going Home. Its aim was to help Salvadoran refugees in both Central America and North America relocate in El Salvador. At thirteen, Jackie raised most of the money needed for the refugee family from their church to return to El Salvador.

After that, her parents' interests shifted, but Jackie continued to be concerned about the situation in Central America. She started working for the Committee in Solidarity with the People of El Salvador (CISPES) and another organization called Sister Cities. CISPES supports human rights, land reform, and social justice, especially by promoting the activities of the Farabundo Marti National Liberation Front/Democratic Revolutionary Front (FMLN), the coalition of political and military groups that fought the El Salvadoran government for twelve years and, following the peace accord that ended the war in 1992, is currently a legal political party. Sister Cities is a humanitarian organization that connects former political resistance groups in local communities in El Salvador with groups in the United States willing to support the local schools, churches, health clinics, and diplomatic efforts in these communities.

Jackie says she does "whatever comes up" to help these organizations. Right now, she is organizing the national tour of a Salvadoran FMLN leader who is coming to the United States to speak to Congress and to visit CISPES groups and other organizations around the country. Jackie's job is to arrange meals and lodging for the woman and to help coordinate her speaking engagements. She arranged a similar tour for another Salvadoran leader a year ago. Jackie also has visited El Salvador three times, spending time with FMLN groups, unions, women's organizations, and refugees, taking them money and material goods, and trying to strengthen the ties between those groups and organizations in the United States. Hardly a day goes by when she is not involved in these projects in some way, perhaps just by making a phone call or two. But the work varies a lot, depending on specific projects. She figures she may spend about twenty hours per month on average.

Jackie's experience is one of the ways in which religious organizations contribute to the wider efforts that take place on behalf of needy people both in the United States and around the world. It would be misleading, however, to suggest that international efforts such as this are the norm. More typical are efforts that focus on the needs of the religious community itself or that can be carried out locally with a relatively small investment of time.

For instance, at Beth El congregation, a Conservative temple in New Jersey, the teacher of the seventh-grade Hebrew school class had an idea several years ago: Besides teaching the children Hebrew and Jewish history, she wanted them to gain a more intimate sense of their tradition. To that end, she obtained the names of residents of a Jewish nursing home not far away and organized a pen pal program. Each of her students chose one of the elderly residents and wrote him or her a letter. They told their pen pals a little about themselves and asked them some questions about their lives and what it had been like being Jewish in an earlier generation.

One of the boys in the class, Sid Gerson, wrote to an eighty-eight-year-old man who had spent most of his life building bridges. Sid's interest was aroused, and so he decided to go visit the man in person. Their relationship continued for five years. Finally, at age ninety-three, the man died. Sid had become like family to him. Having no children of his own, the man referred to Sid as his grandson. And having just lost his grandmother, to whom he had been very close, Sid had found a new grandparent. Sid's experience also influenced others. Before he graduated from Hebrew school, he organized the Well Wishers Club, which encouraged other students to stay in contact with their pen pals. What the teacher had envisioned as a one-shot project therefore turned into a lasting service.

This example points to another important feature of caring. Of all institutions, other than the family itself, religious congregations probably do the most to encourage involvement by the entire family. As a result, they provide settings in which young people can work with their parents on service activities. Such experiences give young people a chance to continue the traditions of kindness they have learned in their families and also to learn from their parents how to be caring in more specialized roles. The consequences are enormous. When the children are the first ones in their families to become involved, their parents may be drawn into caring activities when they might not otherwise be. When the parents are initially involved, they may bring in their children. Moreover, the children have occasion to see their parents helping others and thus to regard them as caring people. Parents also have an opportunity to explain to and reinforce their experience for their children.

Sid Gerson's involvement with Well Wishers was greatly facilitated by his parents. Both his mother, a counselor, and his father, an attorney, went along when Sid visited his pen pal. They provided transportation and also stayed and visited. Several times they all went out to eat together. Sid's mother also helped him plan and organize the Well Wishers program for other students. When asked to think of one time when he was impressed that his parents really cared for other people, Sid chose their involvement with his pen pal as the best example. "Whenever I went," he recalls, "they went with me, and they were very pleased to be with him. They loved talking with him. They thought he was a terrific person, a very funny person, a very sharp person, a very good thinker. They didn't just say that to his face, they said that to me when I was away from him, too."

Whether or not the parents are directly involved, religious congregations often function much like families. Caring is thus motivated less by abstract theological principles than by people becoming immersed in a community from which they derive part of their core identity. Jackie White says that she probably first became involved just because she wanted to attend some of the meetings her mother was going to, and then later, she developed a theoretical language about social justice, change in El Salvador, spiritual hope, and the cause for which she was working. When she is most reflective, however, she talks less in these abstractions and more about the experiences she has had and the lifestyle she has created.

Jackie explains, "I think it's just through the whole involvement, meeting people and hearing the stories and making friends and coming in very close contact with the culture through the food that the refugees made and their passions, like one of the dances they did for us at religious services that we had, and music. So, for me, it was developing at an early age a close bond with Central American culture as well as Central American people and politics. And the justice of their work, of their cause. And also, particularly in later years as I've gotten more involved with CISPES and with El Salvador, just how hopeful and how exciting, particularly El Salvador is, and how much of a chance it is to really make a change."

Then, as if realizing that she is again moving to too high a level of abstraction, she again shifts to the level of experience: "Just all the friendships I have with Salvadorans, with North Americans; I feel an incredible bond with a lot of people from both countries that I've worked with. I mean, certainly visiting there and meeting people and a lot of the anecdotes, and the spirituality, and a lot of things. It's so much more than political work. I've internalized a lot of it: the poetry and the literature and the dances and the music and the culture. It's just become a big part of me, and I eat tortillas and beans. So, that's been really important, the spirituality and the culture and also kind of an activist culture that we have, which is kind of a fusion of North American and Salvadoran culture, as well as political culture that has kind of all come together to be a very distinct culture of our own that is really comfortable for me and it's really like home."[6]

What it means to say that a community is "like home" is that caring is received as well as given.[7] People relate to one another in informal and spontaneous ways, and as a result, they feel stronger.[8] Each person's activities are amplified, becoming more significant because others are contributing as well. And one's beliefs are amplified, too, becoming louder as one hears them played back in the conversations of others.

Jackie White is a good example of how such a community reinforces her sense that what she is doing makes a difference and is right: "Just knowing that my church supports this work—and advocates this kind of work—justifies the work. When I question the validity of putting energy into it, I think of my church and my family and my upbringing and my religion and also the Salvadoran spirituality. These are various things that have been important to me." She adds: "I guess I've almost become religious as a result of the work rather than the other way around, although the religion is also backing for my work."[9]

The religion is important to her, Jackie comments, because it helps justify what she is doing. But her beliefs cannot be divorced from the context in which she has learned them. Indeed, the church gives Jackie more a context for believing than a set of beliefs. It exposes her to a certain range of ideas about God, nature, Christ, and human relationships. From these, she has selected ideas that make sense to her: "I've been raised in a very liberal Methodist church which is more God and nature centered than Christ centered. The church has been very active in various civil rights issues, political issues and rights issues, and antiwar issues. I guess that's kind of given me a foundation for a very liberal view of religion or very liberal religious feeling, as well as being political, a lot of my political beliefs. I've also adopted a lot of liberation theology, which I guess is a brand of Catholicism and liberal Christianity that has come out of churches in Latin America, and I guess other parts of the Third World that take the Bible into people's daily lives. My interpretation of liberation theology and therefore my own religious belief is to see God in a more Quakerly way of him/her, whatever, being everywhere, and that the Christ is more a symbol of the struggle for human rights and justice and that he's a symbol of the martyrs of anyone who's died for those ideals."

Like the young people we discussed in the last chapter, Jackie White finds reinforcement for her beliefs by participating in a religious community, but this community is permeable, allowing her to express her individuality and to be a caring person in her own way. As a result of this permeability, she is able to piece together her own beliefs about God from a variety of religious traditions. Having done so, she is unsure whether she really understands what God is—for example, she admits that she could "come up with some high falutin' answer" but would not be able to articulate fully what she senses intuitively about God.

Jackie's community is also sufficiently permeable that she is attracted to non-Christian ideas, especially ones that send out signals of transcendence in the natural world. She explains: "I don't know if I'd call myself pagan, but I am very centered around nature, and nature is very important to me. I don't know if I worship nature, but I appreciate nature. I guess I do believe that God is the spirit in all of us—I don't know if that's Quaker, pagan, whatever—and that he, it, she is, it's just the spirit that is everywhere and maybe it's the paganist god that is the spirit in the trees and the grass and every natural thing and in humans, and in human qualities and love, and struggle—everything is God."

If religious congregations function like families, like informal communities, they also function like formal organizations. Indeed, they are often as highly bureaucratized as schools and community agencies are. Thus, they too offer ways in which the more familial sense of caring with which young people grow up can be molded into the kinds of service activity that are more characteristic of the institutional world. In the United States, both tradition and size contribute to the formal complexity of religious organizations. Churches traditionally have tried to follow the principle of doing all things in an "orderly and decent" manner. They have relied on formal governing bodies, both in the congregation and at the regional and national levels, to do this. As religious organizations have grown larger, they have also initiated more formal programs.

Valley Presbyterian Church illustrates both these tendencies. Following the traditions of its denomination, it is governed by an elected committee, or "session" of lay leaders who serve three-year terms as "elders" of the congregation. This groups makes all major policy decisions. A number of "councils" or subcommittees handle specific tasks, such as finances, home visitation, and the Sunday school program. Over the past ten years, Valley Presbyterian has grown steadily, adding about 100 new members each year and thus bringing its total membership to approximately 3,700—a number that makes it the tenth largest Presbyterian church in the country and puts it among the top ten percent of all U.S. churches in size. For this many members, the church has created more than twenty councils to run its programs and has drawn up a long list of specialized ministries, ranging from ministries to the elderly to inner-city projects to a youth program to an environmental concerns committee.

Jill Daugherty, a junior, is currently a member of the session at Valley Presbyterian Church. She is one of two young people in the congregation who serve in this capacity. Unlike the older members, she will serve for only a one-year term. She volunteers ten to fifteen hours each month to the session's work and to some of the church's specialized ministries. The one she is most active in is the Older Adults Council, with which she has been involved ever since she was in the sixth grade. Through the church's youth program, she was asked to participate in an Adopt-a-Grandparent program, and from that she went on to help with various activities associated with the elderly. She has visited nursing homes, taken Easter flowers to shut-in members, and organized field trips for the elderly.

Because Jill's volunteer work has been centered on these highly organized programs of the church, the scripts she uses to talk about her motivation follow the "one-thing-led-to-another" logic we saw in Chapter 4. She explains that she was already involved in the church youth group and had been asked to do some service projects through it; then she became friends with the daughter of the pastor in charge of older adults and decided to see whether she would enjoy working with the elderly; also, she did babysitting for the woman who was this pastor's assistant.

Jill's language does not exude caring and compassion; indeed, these terms are almost absent. Instead, she talks about work ("I work with the Older Adults Council"), service ("I serve on the 50-Year Reception Committee"), joining ("You can join different committees"), attendance ("I attend monthly meetings"), leadership ("I led the discussion"), and even requirements ("Everyone on session is required to be on one of the councils"). Although she is engaged in a caring activity, she is learning a new language to talk about this activity—a language that she will continue to use when she embarks on a career or participates in community activities as a volunteer.

Those people who serve in formal programs can also do so "in role," that is, as representatives of a particular program rather than simply as whole persons. They can present themselves in an official capacity, using their role as a way of both gaining access to new situations and legitimating their presence.

A particularly striking example of such role behavior is evident in Jill Daugherty's account of a recent expedition to take flowers to elderly members of her church in a nearby nursing facility. Having observed an older woman who seemed to be in a great deal of pain, Jill went to the nurses' station to find out more. "I introduced myself and said, 'I'm an elder at the Valley Presbyterian Church,' and I asked her [the nurse] what the name of the woman was over there and what was the matter with her." Upon learning that the woman was dying, Jill continued to behave in her announced role. "I said, 'Well, does she have a church?'" The reply was no, so Jill responded by having some flowers (left over from those given to the church members) delivered to her room. A week later the woman died. And the story ended, Jill recalled, with the woman's son sending a thank-you note to the church.

Jill could have responded in any number of ways, of course, or done nothing at all. By playing the role of session member, she did something, but her role also defined caring in a way consistent with the church's programs. Asked why this event had been meaningful to her, Jill gave further evidence of this orientation: "because we were able to fulfill our responsibility to her in that way." Only as a second thought did she add, "She was hurt and we took care of her."

In churches, as in schools and community agencies, people who value caring learn that serving on committees and programs is a way of behaving in a caring manner. In the process, caregivers must play restricted roles and yet make some connection between these roles and their impulse to care. They develop a new language and map it onto the old one. It is important that they be able to preserve some of the primary language of caring that they learned in childhood. They must also ignore any doubts they may have about the actual benefits of the programs to which they contribute.

Being part of a formal organization is a way of feeling efficacious. You feel that your small part does in fact matter because others in your organization are working to address other concerns. (For instance, Jill says that it meant a lot to her—after becoming aware of the immensity of the problem of AIDS—to discover that a committee at her church was concerned with helping AIDS patients.) In the process, the organization in which you participate becomes the seat of primary power—the way of truly making a difference. You become less powerful (an issue we will consider in a later chapter) but also more efficacious by identifying with the organization.

The Process of Redefinition

Much of what happens to caring when young people volunteer in their schools, communities, and churches occurs incidentally. The pressures of trying to care in organized ways simply reshapes the meaning of caring. Young people find out that a desire to help others is not enough, that this desire must be expressed in a way that draws people together, that attracts at least halfhearted participation, that can be done safely and within limited time frames, and that contributes to the purposes of the sponsoring organization. In the process, young people learn new scripts that encourage them to be caring, not merely because it is good to care, but because caring is a way to have friends and fun, to develop their skills, to educate people, to contribute to the community, and to express their interests. Many young people, as we have seen, experience this process as one of growth. But their comments also reveal that the process is fraught with violence. They bump into realities that violate their primordial understandings of what it means to care. Because these experiences can be troubling, it is important for organizations to provide occasions for guided reflection on them.

The most effective programs we studied did offer such occasions for reflection. Young people were given opportunities to talk about what they were experiencing and to express their misgivings as well as to affirm what they were learning. Feedback and evaluation sessions were particularly effective in doing this. These sessions focused on those who were providing volunteer services. As the young people talked, they were able to define their experiences as valuable, even though the consequences for the recipients might have been minimal. The experience no longer was a casual event but one that linked caring with the students' new understandings of who they were.

One student was particularly candid about the benefit of such occasions for reflection. She said her school not only encouraged community service but also required the participants to meet periodically for reflection. Sometimes a guest speaker provided information, training, or a pep talk. More effective, however, were the times when the students simply shared their own reactions. "We had a reflection period after school and mostly everybody attended. Everybody shared their experiences, their disappointments, their feelings about the reactions of teachers, and their happy thoughts. It was really nice. Everybody opened up and said what they learned." In this way, everyone learned new scripts.

7

The Drama of Helping: Stories and Role Models

> We have no pleasure in thinking of a benevolence that is only measured by its works.
>
> Ralph Waldo Emerson, *Essays*

The scripts about caring that young people learn when they volunteer are indicative of the roles in complex organizations that most of us play during adulthood. These scripts give us a way of making sense of our behavior in terms of organizational goals (such as education or service to the community), the appropriate means of obtaining these goals (for example, developing specialized skills), and the criteria by which the behavior is to be evaluated (especially its efficiency and effectiveness). All this sounds very rational, as it fits one conception of organizations that indeed emphasizes their rationality. Volunteering is thus a training ground for life in the world of organizations. If it teaches us to be kind, it does so by molding our kindness to fit the demands of organizational life.

Recent studies of organizations, however, challenge the view that these entities are essentially rational. The newer view is that organizations are places in which myths are constructed.[1] Rationality is simply one of these myths. In this view, scripts are even more important than I have suggested thus far. Scripts make us think that organizations are rational when in fact they may not be. An organization chart, for example, is important to trot out when prospective employees are being recruited, but old-timers know the organization seldom operates according to this chart. In the newer view, ceremony is everything. Organizations, like people, put on a good face, appearing to know what they are doing when the realities may be quite different.

When using this newer view to make sense of what happens when young people start to volunteer, we would say that they do, indeed, learn new scripts about goal-oriented, efficient behavior, but they may not be guided very much by these scripts. That is, if they feel like being kind, they will be, and they will do so without much regard for new ideas about organizational goals or rational procedures. In short, there isn't anything important going on. The tension that I have emphasized between primordial caring as a person and the more specialized caring of a role player in an institution is largely a nonissue. People simply finesse the question by learning to use multiple languages for what they are doing.

There is an irony here. The newer understanding of organizations is an attempt to show that culture—symbols, rituals, ceremonies—is more important than we thought. But in effect, this understanding makes culture less important. In volunteering, the important thing is to help out, doing good works in any way possible, rather than being concerned with particular scripts to make sense of kindness. In the newer view, people do whatever they want to, using organizational resources when they can, defying the rules when they have to, and only after the fact making up stories to explain what they did.

I take the trouble to mention these alternative views of organizations in order to set the stage for arguing that there is a third way of understanding what is going on when young people become volunteers. In any organization, I believe, there is real tension between the sensibilities that people bring with them as persons and the demands and expectations to which the organization subjects them. People do not simply become happy warriors, so to speak, as the old view suggests. Nor do they construct stories willy-nilly, doing whatever they feel like, as the newer view suggests. Rather, they not only talk about skills; they learn them. They not only express their impulses to be kind, but they express them in new ways. Learning to care is, as I have maintained, a real transition that requires unlearning some of what caring meant in one's childhood and yet seeking new ways of expressing caring that are appropriate to institutional settings.

The view I am proposing suggests that there are mechanisms for handling the real contradictions that people experience between their personal inclinations and their behavior in social roles. Among these mechanisms, I believe, are the stories we tell and the role models about whom we tell our stories (or who "enact" our stories). Our stories permit us to play specialized roles while retaining our sense of personhood. Our role models show us that it is possible to perform well and still be human. In short, because we feel conflicted, we tell stories. What we tell, therefore, is neither beside the point nor totally arbitrary. Instead, our stories are an important way of making sense of what we are doing.

In addition to learning new scripts about caring, I shall show in this chapter that young people find role models to emulate and stories to tell as they participate in service activities. The role models and stories complement the new scripts, and together, these ways of thinking and talking begin to reshape the meaning of caring. Role models, like organizational scripts, move caring from their primary setting in the family to their new location in the schools, community agencies, and churches. Role models demonstrate that it is possible to be a person and still play a role. They show that caring focuses on specific needs but goes beyond meeting them. Stories punctuate the ordinariness of institutional behavior, giving it added meaning.

Even if stories and role models work in concert with organizational scripts, they nevertheless help resolve some of the problems that arise in learning new scripts. The concern with efficiency, competition, and pursuing one's interests may, as we have seen, be troublesome to those who engage in volunteer activities because they want to reproduce the personalized caring they have experienced in their families. They worry that something important is being compromised. They feel ambivalent, just as people do when they give up one way of life to pursue a better one. And just as anthropologists find when they study groups in transition, this ambivalence is expressed in the rituals and beliefs that people construct to make sense of themselves.[2] This is why drama becomes important. The dramatic actions of role models demonstrate that the personal touch is still present. And the telling and retelling of stories is a way of resolving one's tensions.[3]

Stories of Service

When I was growing up, one of the events that had a dramatic influence on my and several of my classmates' thinking actually happened thousands of miles away. It had nothing to do with events that the wider culture has chosen to remember from that period—the Korean War, the civil rights movement, the death of James Dean, or the popularity of hula hoops and Elvis Presley. Yet it was widely publicized at the time. It was the death of five young men who had gone to Ecuador as missionaries. Barely out of college, they flew into a remote section of the Ecuadorian jungle and set up camp. They soon made friends with the people who lived there and started telling them about Christianity. They also learned about a neighboring group who did not welcome contact with outsiders and were considered dangerous. Deciding to refocus their efforts, the young men gradually initiated contact with this other group. They flew over and dropped gifts, then went on foot and left gifts, and finally established personal contact. At first their relations were amicable. Then, inexplicably, the missionaries were killed. Of course, I did not know these men personally; I was influenced by them because of the stories that were told about them.

Many of the young people with whom we spoke had been influenced by stories as well. Megan Wyse, for instance, said she had always been fascinated by the story of Gandhi. This story had convinced her that one person could really make a difference in the world. She had come to appreciate this fact more recently by reading the story of another person who had made a difference. "This sounds very backwards," she apologized, "but I wrote a paper this year about Dr. [Joseph] Mengele, the doctor in Auschwitz." She said this experience had made her realize how much power a person can have, even if it's not used for good. She added, "I think he inspired me to be really aware of things, conscious of things, and shows really the strength one person can have." Sina Mesnar, the young man who started working with the homeless after one of his father's friends became homeless, also talks about Gandhi but mentions the story of Che Guevara as having been even more influential. Sina admires people like this for standing up for what they believe, going against the grain, being idealistic, and being concerned about human suffering.

Other young people talked about public figures such as Dr. Martin Luther King Jr. and Mother Teresa.[4] Although a few admitted that they could not relate to Mother Teresa (because she was celibate or too dedicated), many regarded her as the most compassionate person in the world. A young woman who did volunteer work for an emergency medical team and served as a volunteer firefighter provided an example: "I took my confirmation name as Teresa, after Mother Teresa," she remarked. "I really admire her. I was asked to describe my role model one day in class and I honestly said 'Mother Teresa' and described why. The whole class laughed at me. It bothered me, and yet we started talking about it and got into a very interesting discussion. Other people admitted that from learning about her, from me telling them and I came in the next day with a report on her and her actions, that they admired her, too. They might not necessarily want to be like her, but they admired her. I think she's a very giving, caring person. She's assertive in her beliefs. She'll stoop to the bottom of the earth to make a difference for someone. When I said that I get down on the floor and play with people, she gets down on the floor and washed their feet. She does not consider helping other people demeaning. She has everybody on the same level."

Some of the volunteers we interviewed had also been moved by learning from their families or churches the story of the Good Samaritan. Nikki Unger, one of the young women who volunteers at Pearl's Kitchen, for example, teaches Sunday school and has attended a Presbyterian church all her life, so she knew the Good Samaritan story by heart. It's a story, she explained, about "a man who was beaten up by robbers in the road, and was laid at the side of the road, and was suffering. One man went by him, and he pleaded for help and the man wasn't concerned and said he had more important things to do, and he kept walking. Then the next man walked by. The beaten man along the side of the road pleaded for help, and he had more important things to do and he continued walking. And the third man came by, and he heard the victim's pleas for help and picked him up and put him on his donkey and carried him to the inn and gave the person at the inn money to take care of him and to bathe him and to get his wounds fixed. And the Good Samaritan came and checked on him and helped him to get better." She said she often thought of this story as she observed her fellow students feeding the homeless at Pearl's Kitchen.[5]

But it was more common for young people to recount stories from their own experience. They were less likely to have read a story that inspired them to become caring than they were to have started doing volunteer work and then experienced some event that they could put into story form, remember, and reuse when they needed inspiration. Sherry Hicks offered an example. She was talking about a "lock-in" at the neighborhood center where she volunteers. Part of the activity was having a speaker who explained to the children that people should share and be kind to one another. She remembers that there were fifty or sixty children present and that she was fixing snacks when a fellow volunteer came running to say that there was something she should see. "So I went upstairs and there were some children arguing. Then there was this one little girl, and she said, 'Now what did you guys just learn? You know you're not supposed to be doing this!' She was just sitting there going through everything they were supposed to have learned, and I was just like, well, if we didn't get through to anybody else, at least we got through to this one person, and she'll help us change things."

A story like this is, we might say, a "reconstruction" of an event. When word first spread about the deaths in Ecuador, there were many questions about what had actually happened and why. Some reports emphasized the brutality of the deaths themselves. Other accounts speculated on what might have gone wrong, and still others provided background on the men and their families. The stories that survived stripped away many of the extraneous details. Gradually, the dominant story that emerged was told by one of the widows. Within a few months, she herself established contact with the people who had killed her husband and lived among them. The story provided a capsule summary of what happened and also an interpretation of what the event meant. In this case, it became a story of forgiveness and love.

In Sherry Hicks's case, the story she retold was a story of hope. As she explained, "So often you don't see the good you do, and you lose sight of what it is that you're doing. Also, sometimes no matter how much you do, you don't feel like you've done anything. Just seeing that one little girl sitting there telling the other kids why they shouldn't be arguing and fussing—it let me know that some people are listening, and they're getting the message." Being able to remember an event like this makes her feel better about what she does. "It just might make our society a little bit better in the future."

The Functions of Storytelling

But what difference does any of this make? Everyone tells stories. We can spin tales of rock stars and of athletic contests just as easily as we can of people helping their neighbors. Some scholars—who contend that stories are the key to our culture—say that we tell stories simply because they help us organize our experience chronologically. For these scholars, the essential feature of a story is that it places events in a temporal sequence. Yet the stories that volunteers tell are often quite disorganized, but not because they lack skills as storytellers. As the examples I have reported indicate, many of these young people are extremely articulate. But they feel it is important to emphasize certain moments in their stories, rather than reconstructing an exact sequence of events. Moreover, they tell stories that are homey, not the kind we might expect to see in the movies or to read about in novels. Their stories may, in some instances, be considered inspiring, but often they are about rather ordinary experiences. Thus, we must look closely at these stories to understand what they do.[6]

One of the most important functions of storytelling is to bring something abstract down to earth so that it can be understood at several levels, viscerally as well as intellectually. The need to do this is especially evident when the problem being addressed is of such immense scope that its contours become difficult to comprehend. Inequality, social justice, human rights, or even death and suffering on a large scale may be difficult for the average person to grasp unless a story is told that shows, in capsule form, what is happening on a broader plane.

For example, Jackie White told about an event she witnessed in El Salvador that helped her understand the scope of the suffering there better than did all the statistics and political analyses she had read. The story is about a vigil for the dead, one of thousands held periodically throughout the country. The atmosphere of such vigils is traditionally one of sadness and mourning, but in El Salvador they are usually celebratory. In one village, for instance, it is customary for the living to dance on the graves of the dead, and people take pictures of the dancers. This, incidentally, was not something Jackie had experienced personally but was a story she had heard from a friend. Yet it moved her, and she remembered it and retold it. For her, it was especially poignant when her friend said that the villagers had told him it was their way of showing that "life overcomes death." Jackie's own conclusion was that "you probably need that kind of spirit in a country where 75,000 people have been killed."

Storytelling can also bring abstract ideas down to earth by making the events more relevant to the context in which people live. This means that different stories have to be told in different situations—and that the same story may need to be modified. Sherry Hicks provides an example of this when explaining how she would tell the Good Samaritan story to the children in her neighborhood. "I would say there was this little boy who was walking home from school. He had stayed after school for an after-school club. He was on the basketball team. He was walking home to get to his parents' house. While he was walking home, this guy shot him and took all of his money so he could go buy drugs. He was laying there on the street, bleeding. The guy had left him there. So this first person came by, and he was a Vice Lord. He just kind of looked at the boy and picked him up to see if there was any money left, and then he went off on his own separate way and left the boy there. The boy was really in pain and was really hurting. So then another person came past. This guy was a basketball player. He walked up to the boy, and he was like, 'Oh, man, you want to go play some ball? You want to do this? Let's just hang out. Aw, you hurt. Well, let me go find somebody else.' So then a third person would come past, and this person wasn't the brightest person in school, wasn't the most athletic, he didn't belong in a gang. He was just a normal person, just like you or I or anyone else. He stopped and he helped the person, and he went and dialed the operator in the phone booth that was near there and told the ambulance that someone was hurting. He saved the little boy's life, because he went and called the ambulance."

Often another function of stories about caring is, ironically, to diminish the nature of caring. Perhaps it is because of the elevated expectations that surround caring that such stories are needed. They show that caring need not involve great sacrifice or heroism but can be demonstrated in small acts of kindness. One of the stories that Jackie White loves to tell provides an example. She tells about being in San Salvador attending a mass vigil for the dead one evening, accompanied by a friend who was a Salvadoran refugee she had known in the United States, when they were approached by an old Salvadoran man whose dress revealed that he was a peasant. She recalls, "He reached in his bag and took out a lime. He asked us, 'Do you want a lime?' I was ready to say, 'No, I don't have any money. No, I don't want it. No, thanks,' and just kind of brush him aside. And then we realized that the guy was just offering us the limes that he had. He told us that he had come in from the countryside that day from his home, and he had picked the limes off the tree near where he lives to bring to the people and to give them out to the people at the vigil as a little gift. He was just really sweet. It was just really touching, really humbling." This story shows that even little things can be tokens of great caring.

This story is remarkably similar to the one Sherry Hicks told about the little girl encouraging the other children not to argue. In both cases, small acts of kindness become tokens of caring. Such stories are especially important in complex, institutionalized contexts. As we come to play specialized roles—even if these roles are to help others—we may not be sure of their consequences, and so it becomes easy to feel that what we do makes no difference. In this way, we become indifferent, telling ourselves that the energy we expend is not worth it or excusing ourselves from becoming involved because the problems are too large or others are more capable than we are. Stories about small acts of kindness demonstrate that one person can still make a difference. They do not "prove" it in the way that a scientist might prove the effects of a chemical reaction. Instead, they demonstrate it by providing a dramatic instance that serves in the absence of proof.

Once we recognize this important function of stories, we can understand why most of the stories that people tell about caring seem mundane. Caring is, of course, considered in both the popular press and scholarly circles as something heroic. If we really want to understand caring, for instance, we must read about rescuers who risked their lives in Nazi Europe to save Jews. Or we must examine the lives of Gandhi and Mother Teresa. Some of the young people, as we saw, were in fact inspired by such stories. But more of them admitted that these stories were too distant from their own experiences to be meaningful. Tucker Aims, for instance, expressed it well when he noted that the great deeds of such people "usually don't inspire me because what they're doing is on such a different scale that I feel like it's something completely different." In contrast, mundane stories make caring possible—even within the busy world in which we live, the world in which people often seem to make little difference in comparison with the large-scale institutions that rule our lives.

I can perhaps demonstrate this point by contrasting the stories of two of the young women we met in the last chapter. Sherry Hicks, as we saw, is exposed daily to the raw edges of life in the inner city. Institutions are certainly present in her environment, but they often do not function effectively. She—like Jackie White in El Salvador—has seen people bleeding in the streets. Her stories sometimes focus on small victories, but many also have a kind of heroic quality. For example, her story about converting the Hacker building into a neighborhood center is truly dramatic, as is her story about the racial conflicts at the center (or her own triumph over economic adversity in becoming a top-flight student).

In comparison, Jill Daugherty—the young woman who serves on the session at her suburban Presbyterian church—lives in a more fully institutionalized world. She can rely not only on her church but also her family, school, the hospitals in her neighborhood, and her neighbors themselves to lead orderly and predictable lives. Even though she is a caring person, she is so much a role player in her church that her activities are quite ordinary, and she has nothing very gripping to relate about her experiences. In fact, one of her most memorable experiences as a volunteer is about visiting a woman with Alzheimer's who was confused and thought Jill was her granddaughter. Jill recalls, "It was nice to know that I could go and see people who needed some comfort in times when she was in a lot of pain and she was refusing her medication. She just wanted to die. She didn't want to continue on the way she was." Yet, for Jill, this story was about a moving experience, and we should not think less of it because it contains nothing particularly heroic. Indeed, it functions in the same way that Sherry Hicks's story about the little girl does—demonstrating that caring can still happen in the sanitized worlds in which we live.

Yet another function of storytelling is to encapsulate a sense of belonging. Most of us leave home—literally and figuratively. There is, as I have argued, a sense of deep movement in this transition. Not only do we move out, establishing our own residence, marrying, raising our own children, and making new friends; we also move away from the primary bonds of caring and attachment that we have known as children and take up residence in complex and impersonal social institutions. High school students generally have not yet left home physically, but they are squarely in the midst of doing so psychologically. They already know that others will never be as close to them as their families and that they may never again feel "at home" in the same way that they did only a few years earlier. So one of the attractions of volunteering is that it provides a halfway house, a home away from home, where close bonds can develop similar to those of one's family. The support groups that we considered in the last chapter are an example of such portable homes.

Some of the stories that arise in the context of doing volunteer work are thus narratives about these homes away from home. Here is one example, a story told by a young woman about sitting in a hotel room with a group of international students that she had taken on a field trip: "We looked awful because it had rained that day and here were these students who had really just met this year; they didn't know each other all that well and they wouldn't probably see each other after this year and here they were in this little cramped room, singing songs. They didn't know the words to the songs; everybody was just humming along and clapping, and it was sort of a representation of the whole world. Here were all these people that expand across every continent you could possibly think of, and they were all in this one room singing together. Forgetting everything that's gone wrong in their countries and all the problems and the wars, and they were all just sitting there singing. I just remember feeling that this is where I belong. It just sort of came over me and the songs were extremely—they were corny songs to anybody else who was listening, but

I think to everyone in the room it was just sort of a symbol of how when people from every other country get together and really just communicate on a different level, a peaceful level, they really can accomplish something. And it was in an unfamiliar place, they had no idea where they were, they couldn't see where they were, they couldn't adapt to it and this was their way of adapting. It was wonderful."

This story is unusual because the speaker recognizes that the episode has an important symbolic dimension. Indeed, she adds that the experience was, for her, "a representation of how people can come together." Other speakers were generally less reflective about their experiences. But they, too, told stories about feeling at home—perhaps especially when they were working with children who reminded them of themselves, among handicapped people who were especially friendly, or, most commonly, among fellow volunteers who had bonded together (like Jason McKendrick and his buddies on the van) by spending time working on projects, attending retreats, and demonstrating kindness in one another's presence.

I want to emphasize that these stories take on a special significance because of the transition from a person's real home into the more specialized world of institutions and roles. As I have argued, the latter requires new kinds of behavior. Indeed, it does not overstate the case very much to say that there is a contradiction between the rationally orchestrated, goal-oriented, impersonal behavior required in most institutions and the nurturing behavior we associate with our families of origin.

Stories of belonging are a way of resolving this contradiction. They allow us to carry some sense of elementary kindness into the indifferent roles expected of us in social institutions. We can tell these stories because it is possible to find enclaves in our institutions in which we can still behave as if we are at home or among friends. But these are enclaves. They consist of the odd time when a rainstorm forces us to sit in a hotel room and sing, or they are the occasional camaraderie that may emerge at a party or even at the funeral of a coworker. They contrast with the bureaucratic structure of the classroom or the office, so we package these experiences by telling stories about them. Our stories remind us that the world of institutions is not entirely cold and calculating after all. It can also be a world in which kindness is preserved.

Storytelling also resolves the contradictions we experience as we move into institutional roles, by convincing us that we are still whole persons rather than becoming nothing more than the roles we play. This dilemma is the counterpart, for the individual person, of what I have just been describing in regard to groups, homes, and our sense of belonging. As we become bit players in social institutions, we may lose not only our sense of belonging but also our sense of having a self. I do not want to exaggerate this point. From a different perspective, we of course gain a stronger sense of who we are as we develop skills and begin to occupy a distinct niche in an institutional space (I can say, for example, that I am a doctor). But it is also the case that we become more and more identified with the roles we play, to the point that we may ask, Who am I? I may wonder, for example, if I can still be someone who is loving, artistic, and playful, or if I can be only an A student, a chemistry major, or an aspiring engineer.

Being a volunteer, I have suggested, is a way to be a caring person, but it is also a limited role. In addition to being an A student, for example, I am a tutor or a helper at Pearl's Kitchen. Even in this context, then, we may experience the tension between being a person who wants to care about people and having to express that impulse through a specific role. Again, storytelling is a kind of drama—theater on a small scale—that helps us resolve this tension. As we tell stories about our volunteer experiences, we can demonstrate to ourselves that it is possible to still be a person, even though we may be playing a role.

The following account, told by a young woman who was tutoring a blind student, illustrates the point I am making. Describing her pupil, the young woman remarked: "She's very timid and she's just a very quiet individual and initially she smiles a lot, but you have to really initiate a conversation with her in order to get anything done. And I'm used to talking, but it's sort of nice to have someone actually start a conversation with you, and I worked so long just to try and get her to initiate a conversation."

From some other parts of the young woman's account, we know that the problem of getting her pupil to talk was actually a symptom of the conflict this young woman was experiencing between functioning simply as a tutor and trying to relate to the pupil on a more personal level. Her story continues: "One day, I don't remember what exactly happened, but we were getting ready to prepare for one of our lessons and I had left the book at home and we really had nothing to do. She wasn't used to doing homework with me yet, so she couldn't really do that. And I said, 'Well, would you like to play cards, or would you like to just talk?' And she said that she would rather talk. And this seemed to be the most amazing thing.

"I thought about it afterwards, the reason that she talked and everything that she told, and I guess it didn't occur to me how amazing it was while I was talking to her. But I thought about it, and she had told me about her private life and the places that she had been. She asked for my advice on things that were happening to her and a boy that she knew back home, and it was simply the most amazing thing. I couldn't really imagine why she opened up to me, and I came up with two reasons afterwards: one, the other student that I was tutoring her with—I was tutoring the two of them together—he wasn't there that day. And I figured well, maybe she's not real comfortable talking in front of him. And then it really occurred to me that the real reason was that she had gotten used to me and had learned to trust me. It was the greatest feeling! I rushed home, I called my supervisor. I was thrilled! She talked! And she initiated the conversation, and she trusted me enough to ask my advice on something that was really personal to her and something that really meant a lot to her."

When listening to a story like this, we can grasp only a little of why the experience was so thrilling. Viewed from the outside, the account may even seem trivial. On closer consideration, however, this is a memorable experience for the young woman telling the story because it was the first time she was able to break through the role of tutor and relate to her pupil on a more personal basis. Talking about private matters was evidence that a degree of intimacy had been established. The experience itself was important because it opened doors for more intimate interaction in the future.

We must also recognize how important the story is. It provides a convenient summary of the experience, one that can be remembered and retold. When volunteering on other occasions becomes bleak, regimented, or routine, this story can be taken out and used as a reminder that one can still function as a person and, in that capacity, can still be the caring person one wishes to be.

Bringing Stories to Life

I observed earlier that young people sometimes told stories about heroes of caring, but more often they told stories about themselves or about ordinary experiences. The fact that heroes are too distant from most of our lives to inspire us very much points to another important feature of caring: We need some way to bring these heroes down to earth. The same is true of the abstract frameworks—such as humanitarianism—that may give us reasons to be caring. We have to relate to these ideas at more than an intellectual level. We do this as we grow up because our models of caring are family members, more so than the heroes or ideas we have read about. As we grow older, however, our experience may become increasingly removed from our intellect. We live at one level and study abstract ideas or public figures that have very little to do with our experience. Stories, I suggest, are a way of bridging this gap. Nonetheless, stories must be brought to life.

The men who died in Ecuador would have had no meaning for me had it not been for my great aunt Amanda. I did not know these men—I only read about them in *Life* magazine and saw the pictures of their bodies—but I did know my aunt. She was the link between the men in Ecuador and me because she, too, had been a missionary. All her life she worked in Africa, living in a wooden hut she constructed herself, three days' ride by motorcycle to a town of any size. That summer, when she came home on furlough, I heard her stories, saw her eating African food, and sensed what it might be like to live in another culture. She was neither a public figure nor one who saw herself doing anything heroic, but she was able to spark my imagination as I watched her, helped with her yard work, and listened to her stories.

The young people we talked to generally constructed their own bridges between stories and reality. They told their own stories, which were more real, even though they were distillations from reality. And because they were distillations, they depended on having models—other people who also told stories and enacted them.[7] After Nikki Unger retold the story of the Good Samaritan, for instance, she mentioned that Jason McKendrick was, to her, a living example of the Good Samaritan. She remembers specifically seeing Jason walk five blocks to carry a dinner to a homeless man who was too sick to come to the park. For her, Jason made stories of caring come alive. Like the apprentices in traditional societies who learn skills as adolescents—and like the participants in all rituals of gaining adulthood—the volunteers we studied had guides.[8]

Tanika Lane's guide was Miss Gillis, the director of LEAD, a beautiful woman in her late twenties whose picture could grace the cover of *Ebony* or *Vogue*. Tanika says she admires Miss Gillis because she is "so down to earth, so to speak. She really relates to us, and she doesn't say, 'Well, when I was sixteen, sneakers were two cents,' stuff like that. She really understands us, and she has children of her own, and I really like the way we have discussions and the family atmosphere."

Tanika finds it difficult to explain exactly what it is about Miss Gillis that makes her special ("Words can't describe her"), so she tells a story: "There was one girl who talked about the incident of her father dying in front of the class, and Miss Gillis cried. She's always there. She wants to know what's wrong. She cares. If you have a problem, she listens. She knows that we're hungry sometimes after school, and brings food. Also—just the fact that she gave up her job and she's spending all her time with us, even though sometimes we don't give her any feedback. It might be a tired day. We're the reason why she continues the program, and some days we know we send her home with a headache, but she comes right back."

Rafe Ramirez's guide was Angel Marquez. "He definitely showed me that caring can make a difference," Rafe told us. Angel was in his mid-thirties when his son was killed. After that, Rafe recalls, Angel started doing a lot more in the community, including coaching soccer. "He felt like he had to give something back," Rafe explains. "He started up a memorial fund for his son, and he uses some of it to sponsor a soccer tournament for the club. He foots the whole bill. He is also into helping the handicapped. He's been doing that for a couple of years."

Rafe is especially impressed that Angel has been able to help without much in the way of training or background. Angel had never coached before and had never worked with the handicapped. Yet by reaching out, he has demonstrated that anyone can make a difference.

In both of these cases, the guide was someone who was known personally and could be emulated. Tanika also admired Oprah Winfrey, for example, and says it would be wonderful to have a career in the media like Oprah's. Tanika can identify with Oprah to some extent, especially because she feels Oprah overcame disadvantages to become famous.[9] But because Tanika knows so little about Oprah, Miss Gillis is a much easier role model to follow. The same is true of Rafe. He has read about Mother Teresa, for example, but Angel Marquez is a real presence in his life.

Role models are like parents in that they care for you, rather than simply showing you how to care for others. It is important, however, that these role models are not parents. As we saw in Chapter 3, some young people (Tanika was one) do not learn very much about caring from their parents, so to them, other role models are especially important. But even for young people who have loving parents, other role models often stand out as exemplars of caring. They do so because parents are supposed to care for you—it is part of their job description. But others are simply busy adults. Thus, if they stop to care for you, it has special meaning.

Rafe Ramirez was one of a number of young people who talked about a memorable time when he had been cared for by someone other than a parent and, as a result, had come to a broader understanding of caring. He recounted the following story: "I got into a car accident one time. It felt like I was all by myself for a while. It was right in front of the school, and there were a lot of people I knew around, but it just felt like I was all by myself. A friend's mom really helped me through that. She happened to be the first person there because she was in the area. I was real nervous, and I was shaking all over. I couldn't stand up. I was like sitting down, and I didn't know what to do. My friend had called my parents for me. I told him, 'Call my parents. They'll come out here,' but it's a fifteen-minute drive to the school. So she was the first one there, since she was picking him up. She says, 'Don't worry. It's just a car. You're more important than the car.' Like a lot of people can say that and it's like, yeah, yeah, right, whatever. But she really gets you to believe it."

This example is revealing because it shows that a role model need not care for a person over a long period of time. An episode such as being comforted after an accident can stand out and become evidence that the world is not all bad. Generally, however, it does help if the role model is someone with whom you interact over an extended period of time. Indeed, such models are helpful not only because you know more about them and they know more about you but also because their very persistence is compelling. Sina Mesnar, for instance, says this is what impresses him most about the woman who runs the community agency for which he volunteers. "She basically goes out every night, and she's always working with them [the homeless]," he explains. "You get depressed to see these people's situations. A lot of the time it gets extremely frustrating that you can't help them. You see that she keeps on going on, keeps on doing. She's persistent, and she doesn't want to give up."

Much of what inspires us about role models seems to be random—the unexpected comfort after we have an accident, the person who just happens to coach our soccer team, or the woman we admire when we do community service. We are attracted to specific role models because they reach out to us or because we feel some affinity between our personal history and theirs. But after examining the numerous stories we heard about role models, we can also draw some generalizations.

First, role models frequently have some specialized skill that we hope to learn by watching them and by doing similar things. Jason McKendrick provides an example. He says that the teacher who is in charge of the service board overseeing his work at Pearl's Kitchen has been his role model. What he admires most is her skills at organizing people and projects. "When she wants to get something done," he says, "she will go and get it done. Her organizational skills are incredible." A young woman who volunteered at a community center admired one of the leaders there, a teacher, because she could help children with math: "She's like, 'Oh, I'm a math teacher, come on over." Other students talked about skills their role models had taught them, such as knowledge about how to work with learning disabilities, information about applying for grants, and skills in dealing with political issues.

Second, role models are likely to be admired, not simply because they have special skills, but also because they demonstrate virtue. I discuss the nature of virtue more fully in Chapter 9, but we can examine here something of what it means, by noting that role models seem to have special qualities as persons. Their skills, however, consist less of special knowledge or techniques than interpersonal skills that can be carried with them and transferred to new situations.

Young people talk, for example, about the leadership abilities, the authority, the persuasiveness, or the persistence of the people they admire. It used to be that we would have termed these *character traits*, but I am not sure that we completely understand anymore what these traits are. On the one hand, they are quite common—the traits we try to cultivate in our children or among students. On the other hand, they are rarely understood to be the critical links between our personhood and the specialized roles we are asked to play in social institutions. Yet they do seem to serve in this capacity. A trait such as authority becomes attached to us because it is a diffuse part of the way we behave; it is distinctly "ours." But it is also a trait that becomes evident only in the roles we play. We exercise authority over other people. What we see in a role model, then, is a way to carry our basic personhood into the complexities of institutional life: The traits we emulate in these role models thereby become attached to our personhood and yet allow us to function better in whatever specialized roles we may be called to play.

An example will help clarify what I have in mind. Sherry Hicks says that one of her role models is a young woman who also volunteers at the neighborhood center. Although the young woman is only a year older than Sherry, Sherry looks up to her because she has a "special quality." Choosing her words carefully, Sherry explains that this quality is best described as authority. When distinguishing it from knowledge or power, Sherry points out, "It isn't the kind where she's like, 'Well, I know. I'm in charge of all you, and so I have power over you.' Her authority is, 'Yes, I'm in charge of you, but you lead me and you tell me where to go.'" Sherry associates this kind of authority with caring because it is responsive to the needs and interests of those over whom one exercises authority. To illustrate, Sherry tells about a time when she and her mother had gotten into an argument. Sherry came to the neighborhood center visibly upset. Her role model knew that something was wrong and sat with Sherry long after curfew in order to let her talk it out.

This was a memorable experience for Sherry because it taught her something new about caring. Her role model had a special quality that was not simply a personality trait; it had been developed in the course of doing volunteer work, and Sherry thought she could learn it as well. If she could, then she could be more caring in whatever roles she might play as an adult. This was a type of kindness that she could carry with her.

Third, role models do in fact play roles but, ironically, impress us most when they step out of these roles. In a small way, Sherry Hicks's story also demonstrates this point. The other young woman was playing a role, helping out because getting acquainted was part of what it took to be a volunteer at the neighborhood center. Indeed, both Sherry and the other young woman had been elected as officers at the center, so there was a special need for them to get acquainted. By staying after the curfew, however, the young woman violated one of the rules. She thus demonstrated that caring may be part of playing a role but may also necessitate breaking out of the role. For Sherry, it was a memorable experience because the other young woman had, in fact, gone beyond the call of duty.

Patti Evans offers one of the clearest examples of how role models step out of their roles when she describes the teacher in charge of the internship program in which she participates. Patti admires the teacher not only because of her skills in working with handicapped students but also because the teacher relates to them as a person and not simply as a teacher. Patti observes: "She's a very, very caring person. She gives whatever she can to these kids. She tries to give them the best that they can get. Like with Bill. She goes to visit him at his group home during vacations. She takes him out even when they're not in school. She'll go to his house and pick him up. Only two live at home. Bill lives in a group home. So she'll take him out and spend the day with him. She brings her kids to school to meet the kids."[10]

We should note, too, that Patti's teacher provides a way for Patti to comprehend what Mother Teresa may be like. Patti has never met Mother Teresa, but what she admires about her is the same thing that she admires about her teacher. Indeed, she makes the connection explicitly: "Mother Teresa has devoted her entire life to other people. She goes everywhere to help people. I think she changes people's lives for the better. I really admire her for doing that. Just like I admire my teacher. She makes these kids' lives better. Mother Theresa makes other peoples' lives better."

Tanika Lane also showed how stepping out of normal role behavior can solidify the relationship between role models and their admirers. Her model was her English teacher in the seventh grade. Tanika admired him because he made the students in his class work hard and because he coached the drama club. Mostly, though, she admired him for relating to her as a person. She recalls that when she was sulking after not having gotten the part she wanted in a play, the teacher came over and talked to her at a more personal level than ever before. "He pulled me aside. He really talked to me. He told me about not having flaws in my character and being a well-rounded person. That really made a difference in me." Another student, also talking about a teacher who he admired, summarized: "He tries to relate with you, and rather than trying to keep that strict teacher–student relationship, he lets that stray a bit."[11]

Fourth, role models effect their magic on us by caring for us and also by telling stories, which begin to reshape our thinking about life and about ourselves. In other words, we learn by both seeing and hearing. We hear stories that we can incoporate into our own accounts of ourselves. The stories supply us with scripts to account for becoming involved in a specific activity. And in the most influential cases, these stories also begin to shape our identity. I can illustrate this process by reintroducing Jim Grayson, the high school senior we met in Chapter 4 who has spent the past couple of summers as a volunteer at a Boy Scout camp and who is currently serving as an assistant scout master.

Jim Grayson's path to becoming a scout leader started when he was in the seventh grade and attended summer camp himself. There he came under the influence of a man who has become his role model. He remembers: "There was a guy who worked at the pool. His name was Jack. I talked to him sometimes, and he seemed like a really rough guy. A lot of kids got the impression that he's mean. But then you watched him work with the scouts. He goes in there during his free time and at nights and stuff, and he's teaching these kids how to swim. You can really see that he cares about them in his own sometimes rough way. He talks to them really tough in the beginning, but then you see him work with these different kids who are having trouble and he's a really nice person. The kids who work with him that way really like him, while some of the others just sit there and they see the rough parts."

At first, Jim saw only the rough parts, too. But Jack became a "significant other" for Jim by literally redefining his identity. "I was taking the canoeing merit badge," Jim explains. "Jack's sitting there talking to us. I'm leaning on my paddle. He goes, 'First rule, never put the tip of your paddle into the dirt.' So I sat there, I listened to him. This is a good idea. I didn't really realize that I'm sitting there doing it. First thing I know, he calls me brain dead. I have a nickname forever now. I'm Brain Dead. And he uses it for stories. For example, I was working up there as a counselor in training one summer, and he's sitting there talking to these scouts, because he wants to make them laugh. He was telling them a story. 'A scout I had up at the lake, boy, talk about brain-dead people.' Then he winked at me. I was impressed that he still remembered me as Brain Dead."

Finally, role models come in multiples and tug at us from different directions, so the special value of volunteering is that it places us in contexts in which we rub shoulders with a particular kind of role model. Many of the young people we talked to mentioned fellow students, perhaps a year or two older than they were, as role models. They admired them because they were knowledgeable about popular music or good at sports. Teachers were frequently mentioned as well, some of whom were admired because they cared deeply about their students.

Volunteering, especially when it involved work at community agencies, exposed young people to role models that they would not have met in other contexts. Although these models seldom did anything that their admirers found truly remarkable, their very presence in voluntary organizations defined them as caring persons. As they related in ordinary ways with younger volunteers, these volunteers felt affirmed enough to want to continue volunteering.

An example that demontrates this last point comes from a young man who raised Seeing Eye dogs as part of a service project organized by his 4-H club. When asked to name the most caring person he could think of, he named the woman who was in charge of the project. She had never saved lives or performed other heroic deeds, but she was there—donating her time to help young people and giving him guidance and reinforcement. "She'll just come over to me. She won't tell me I'm doing anything wrong, but just give me some pointers on how I can improve. I can see where she's coming from."

The Symbolism of Caring

We learn, then, as we listen to volunteers talk about their experiences and their role models, that caring is not what it has often been described as being. The standard view is to assume that caring for others is such unnatural behavior that it must be inspired by role models who soar high above our heads. We see, however, that the most effective role models are generally close at hand. Because they do ordinary things and relate to us as ordinary people, we can truly follow their example. They nevertheless provide continuity with what we have learned about caring in our families. As we saw earlier, our parents did not inspire us to be caring by performing heroic deeds, either. Rather, we learned that caring might mean going the extra mile but that it did not necessitate going into outer space. Our parents showed us the meaning of caring by relating to us as whole persons, sometimes stepping out of their roles as parents just to be our friends. Role models do the same thing. We admire them because they stopped being teachers or coaches or pastors—or volunteers—long enough to listen to our problems and talk about their own. If we stop to think about these role models, we realize that we can demonstrate elementary kindness in any context. For example, I can be an accountant, computing tax figures all day, and still make the extra effort to console a coworker or explain something to a client for the third time.

We also need to recognize that kindness is fundamentally symbolic. It may deliver the goods, too, for example, by helping someone learn to read or keeping the homeless from going hungry. But, as Emerson says, we do not judge benevolence only by its works. We judge it, as we have seen, by the minor triumphs that stand out in our memories. It is the gift of limes on a street in El Salvador that moves us. Such events are symbolic because they carry deeper meanings and make us think of something other than the act itself. A gift of limes is a symbol of goodness in a world of carnage. It tells us that we are not alone in trying to help, that others—perhaps the recipients of our care—are also concerned enough to care for us.

Volunteering is thus a special kind of bridge between the family and friends who show us what it means to care and the wider world in which caring so often appears to be absent. By volunteering, we do our part to make the world better. We perform deeds that are intrinsically beneficial to other people. We may learn skills that will make us more effective in other roles. We even gain experience at working in complex organizations—and come to terms with new scripts about efficiency, effectiveness, and specialization. But probably without fully realizing it, we also learn that the real world—the institutional world in which we spend so much of our time—is built primarily on stories. It functions not so much by getting the job done but by giving us a chance to tell stories about what we have done. Volunteering teaches us that kindness can be part of those stories. We need not live in a world organized entirely by indifference, by competition, or even by rationally deliberated decisions. Rather, we live in a world of ups and downs, of routine punctuated by occasional triumphs, and by the tenuous bonds that link us meaningfully to our co-occupants.

8

Engendering Compassion: Men, Women, and Social Change

> Women must shape their own activities outside of institutional supports, negotiating and rethinking strategies that will allow them to be effective in ambiguous and sometimes marginal positions.
>
> Arlene Kaplan Daniels, *Invisible Careers*

When considering the ways in which young people move from primordial to role-specific understandings of caring, we must confront the issue of gender. Young men and young women are about equally likely to experience caring in their families and about equally likely to become volunteers during their teenage years. At the end of this time, they are also about equally likely to say they value helping other people and want to work at something that will make the world a better place in which to live. But the process by which young men and young women gain a new understanding of what it means to care is quite different. Because mothers play a different role in teaching their offspring about caring than fathers do, young people learn early that caring is gendered. Moreover, young women associate caring much more with their changing understanding of themselves as persons, whereas young men are more likely to associate caring with the accomplishment of specific tasks. Thus, some of what I have been arguing about the need to relearn the meaning of caring during young adulthood can be better understood by considering the differences between young men and young women. That, at least, is what I want to demonstrate in this chapter.

Mothers and Chicken Soup

It is hard to talk about caring without mentioning chicken soup. The old standby, grandma's recipe for curing the flu, gout, postpartum blues, and whatever else may be wrong, still conjures up images of warmth and well-being.[1] Experts on folk medicine proclaim it to be the surefire remedy for clogged sinuses (if not lumbago and indigestion), and some encourage saving spare hunks of fat for burns and nosebleeds (but warn against using it for herpes). In the twelfth century, Maimonides was already advocating chicken soup as a cure-all for the "black humors" (including, he thought, leprosy). And good etiquette still dictates carrying steaming crocks of the brew to sick neighbors and, in some communities, serving it at wakes or as a first course at charity luncheons.

There is endless variation in how the soup should be prepared and served, all indicative of particular customs, beliefs, and ethnic traditions. The Jewish penicillin, as some call it, requires whole chickens (bones included) and is better with matzo balls; Mennonites insist on whole-egg noodles; German immigrants served it on mashed potatoes; Hungarian gypsies use it to cure a hangover; Russian peasants believe it works better if ample amounts of garlic are mixed in; Burmese hostesses serve it at the end of an evening's entertainment to help restore emotional balance; Chinese and Koreans have their own dumplings and spices; south Indians invented a version of it (mulligatawny) to keep their British rulers happy; and Irish families include it in traditional Christmas meals.

The apparently universal quality of chicken soup is that it is always gendered: Women (mothers, grandmothers, aunts, neighbor ladies, church women, rabbis' wives) fix it; men are biologically incapable of doing so unless they forgo the medicinal virtues and serve it canned. Chicken soup is thus a metaphor for the gendered quality of caring itself. Women have always been the nurturers, the caregivers, the considerate neighbors, the preparers of chicken soup. As one young man lamented, "I don't know what I'll do when I leave home. Mama won't be there with her chicken soup!"

Apart from the obvious connections in the family between caring and motherhood, formalized volunteering has long been a gendered activity as well. Historical studies, for example, show that women in nineteenth-century towns and cities were involved in a wide range of voluntary activities, including ladies' auxiliaries, women's clubs, civic associations, benevolent societies, temperance movements, and a variety of informal service and neighborhood activities.[2] Some evidence, which we shall consider momentarily, suggests that women are still more actively involved in volunteering than men are.

Some people might contend that the gender differences observed in historical studies were a temporary aberration, rooted in middle-class women's withdrawal from the labor force between the 1870s and 1950s. If so, the inclusion of women in the labor force in the past several decades might signal the end of such involvement. Yet this conclusion seems less likely when we look at evidence from the past showing that just as white middle-class women were, working-class women, immigrant women, and women from racial and ethnic minorities were actively involved in volunteer associations. Indeed, writes one historian, "the notion that voluntarism emerged as a consequence of the rise of domesticity and the attendant increase in women's leisure time is not borne out."[3] Thus we must continue to ask how gender roles are learned and how this learning affects the nature of caring.

As we saw in Chapter 3, young people learn about caring from both their mothers and their fathers. But the lessons learned tend to be different. Mothers are perhaps more likely to be the primary sources of emotional support—the person who bandages cut knees or who makes chicken soup when the family is sick. If there is a primordial image of caring that involves intimacy, trust, and whole-person relationships, it is likely to be an image with a female face.

On the whole, young people of both sexes felt somewhat closer to their mothers than to their fathers, and national survey data support this generalization. In one survey conducted among adults, for example, two-thirds of the respondents said they felt very close to their mothers while they were growing up, but only half said they had felt this close to their fathers.[4] According to other data, most teenagers, especially females, get along with their mother better than their father.[5] When asked in an open-ended question to name anyone in the world whom they regarded as an example of compassion, moreover, seven times more teenagers mentioned their mother than they did their father. The closeness and caring of mothers in comparison with that of fathers are also evident in the degree of animation with which young people talk about their parents.

Jamal Harris is one of the many young people illustrating this difference in the way that they perceive their mothers and fathers. Jamal is a remarkable young man, now a freshman, who has been tutoring children after school and on Saturdays in the low-income housing development in which he and his family live in a medium-size midwestern city. Jamal's father is a mechanic, and his mother has a telemarketing job. Both parents love him dearly, and both do what they can to help the neighbors. In commenting on his parents' caring, however, Jamal speaks much more enthusiastically about his mother than about his father. For example, Jamal describes his mother as a caring person "because she always goes out of her way to help people. Even when she doesn't always have something, she usually goes out of her way to help others."

Jamal gives the following example: "Like when one of her friends needed some help with their funeral, they needed money and stuff, she gave it to them.

Or if somebody needs help with food or something, she would give it to them." His father, he says, is caring in some ways and in some ways not. "Like sometimes somebody asks him for something, 'No, because when I needed something y'all wouldn't give it to me,' and that kind of way." His most memorable time of seeing either of his parents helping someone outside the immediate family also involves his mother instead of his father: "My mom, because when our next door neighbor's mother died, and when my friend died—she was in kindergarten, and the house caught on fire; they tried to get her out, but she burned up—she helped the mother and everything, helped her to get through it, and then she helped our next door neighbor with the funeral arrangements."

Mothers are also perceived to be helpful in a more interventionist way than fathers are. That is, mothers go out of their way to care for people around them, whereas fathers are more often described as people who simply enjoy being around other people. Whereas mothers actually help their children or their children's friends, fathers are admired for being gregarious, liking to do things with people, liking to spend time together, or being someone with whom one can have a good time—indeed, dad is just a regular guy.

As an example, consider what a young man named Scott Hastings says about his parents. Scott's main volunteer activity is raising Seeing Eye dogs as part of a project that his 4-H club sponsors. He feels very close to his mother and recognizes that her helping with the 4-H club is what makes it possible for him to have a puppy at all. She goes out of her way to be at home when he cannot be there, and she devotes extra time to the club. In contrast, Scott's father does no volunteer work and is basically ambivalent about having a puppy. Yet Scott insists that his father is a very caring person. When asked to explain what he means, Scott says, "My best friend, this is Joe, my dad loves him. Joe loves my dad. For example, our family likes beef jerky, and we were eating some of it in the car one day and Joe was with us. And my dad's like, 'Yo, Joe, don't you want a piece?' He's like, 'No way! I don't want shoe leather.' And I was like, 'Come on, try some.' My dad was giving him a hard time about it, so he finally took a bite and he really liked it."

On the surface, seeing one's father joshing a friend may seem like pretty weak evidence that he is a deeply caring person. But the point is not to question the sincerity of such a statement; rather, it is to show that one's father can be caring simply by being a buddy.

Jason McKendrick talks about his parents in a similar way. He describes his mother as a warm person who goes out of her way to do things to help him and his friends. She likes to talk with his friends and to find out if anything is wrong and how she can help them. Jason says she is very supportive of both him and his friends. He also maintains that his friends love his father. But the reason they do is different: "My dad's funny. He's always cracking jokes. There's just a certain warmness about him. I don't know how to describe it. A lot of my friends walk away from my dad saying that he's a really nice guy."

Part of the difference among these examples may be that males view their fathers differently than they do their mothers. We see some of this when we listen to young women talking about their parents. Consider Tanika Lane. She says it bothers her sometimes because her mother tries too hard to help. For example, someone may not even be aware of having a problem, and her mother says, no, we've got to help her. In contrast, to show how her father cares for people, Tanika says that he likes to go over to his cousin's house to watch basketball, and when he does, he sometimes takes along some of the kids from the block.

Zia Hillier provides another example. She says that she feels especially close to her mother and knows that her mother will be supportive and try to help her no matter what the situation may be. "She's really a friend when I need somebody. I always know that my mom is my best friend." Zia describes her father as a caring person, too, but does not consider him particularly warm. "I guess my dad I feel kind of distant to because I can't tell him really, really personal things. And sometimes I feel kind of like he takes the attitude that he knows everything."

Another reason that caring has different meanings for boys and girls is that the small acts of helping through which children become directly involved in caring are gender specific. One way in which children learn about caring for others is by helping with small chores around the house. Among the young people we interviewed, we found that both boys and girls had performed such chores when they were children. But we also found that girls were somewhat more likely to have done so than boys. Indeed, none of the girls we interviewed said they did not help around the house, whereas some of the boys made it quite clear that they refused to do such things. We also discovered that the person for whom household chores were done was the mother. For example, young people would carry out the trash for their mom or they would tell their mom that they would clean their room on Saturday morning. Thus, it is clear that the link between caring in the family and one's parents carries gender connotations.

Still another important difference is that young people tend to associate maternal caring with informal, spontaneous, and voluntary acts of kindness, whereas paternal caring is more likely to be associated with formal duties, especially work. This is true even when both the mother and the father are employed and do virtually the same work. Jim Grayson is an example. Both of his parents are teachers. But when he explains why he thinks his mother is a caring person, he talks about her "whole attitude," says that she "goes out of her way" to help people, and mentions how she has invited people into their home. In contrast, he says his dad is a caring person because "he couldn't do that kind of work if he didn't care about people." The reason that this difference is important is that by identifying with their mothers, young women are more likely to think of caring as something that emanates from their personhood, whereas young men are more likely to choose their fathers as examples and talk about caring as part of a role they must play. It will become more evident later in the chapter that young women and young men actually do differ in these ways.

Apart from nurturing within the family itself, young people are also somewhat more likely to see mothers than fathers caring for people outside the family. When only one parent does volunteer work, for example, that person is much more likely to be the mother than the father. These differences also are accentuated by the offspring's gender. That is, boys are more likely to say that their father is involved as to say that only their mother is involved, whereas girls are much more likely to say that only their mother is involved.[6]

What also is significant is the effect of the mother's, as opposed to the father's, volunteering. Among students whose mother (only) had done volunteer work, the proportion that themselves valued volunteering was as high as that among students whose mother and father both had done volunteer work. Among students whose father had done volunteer work (but whose mother had not), the proportion that valued volunteering was slightly lower than for students with no parent who had done volunteer work.[7]

These sources of gender differences in understandings of caring are doubtless changing as the result of broader changes in American society. The single change to which all young people have been subjected is the growing inclusion of women in the paid labor force. Young people who reached adolescence before 1975 had about a fifty–fifty chance of having been raised by a mother who was not employed outside the home. Conversely, young people (including our respondents) who reached adolescence during the 1980s or early 1990s had only a one-in-four chance of having been raised by a mother who was not gainfully employed.[8] In addition, public opinion concerning the appropriate roles of men and women has also shifted dramatically toward the greater inclusion of women and a greater awareness of the need for gender equality. Insofar as gendered understandings of caring originate in traditional relationships in the family, they also may show the diminishing impact of gender differences.

When women take full-time jobs, they spend less time on volunteer activities, at least in comparison with the time spent on volunteering by women who work only part time. Marital dissolution and instability may also take its toll on volunteering, judging from the fact that married women are more likely to do volunteer work than single or divorced women are.[9]

The larger effects of these changes on children's attitudes toward caring is, however, likely to be mixed. On the one hand, children with working mothers may at, some level, feel less cared for by their mothers or may be less likely to see their mothers engaged in informal or formal voluntary caring activities, such as taking chicken soup to the neighbors. On the other hand, the vast majority of working women are employed in the rapidly growing service sector, and a majority of the most visible helping professions are still overwhelmingly populated by women. For example, as of 1991, 94.8 percent of registered nurses, 85.9 percent of elementary teachers, and 68.0 percent of social workers were women.[10] Thus the possibility of young people's associating caring with being female is still quite likely.

Teasing

In her study of women volunteers in California, sociologist Arlene Kaplan Daniels found an undercurrent, or "covert" imagery, of volunteering that was often negative and that created misgivings on the part of even the most actively involved. This undercurrent reflects many of the changing assumptions about gender that have emerged in the past half-century with the inclusion of women in the paid labor force. It includes concern that volunteer work is not as important as "real" work, that participation in community activities takes valuable time away from pursuing one's own career, that caring for others is an old-fashioned role that should be replaced by paying greater attention to one's own needs, and that volunteering is a kind of "do-gooder" or "socialite" activity encouraged by middle-class husbands as a way of elevating their status in the community rather than an activity that made any real difference in alleviating social problems.[11] The implication of Daniels's research is that young women may also have a harder time learning how to care when they become involved in community service projects, because of either self-doubts or the criticisms of their peers.

Although schools have tried to become more neutral in the messages they deliver to boys and girls about what desirable behavior is, differences remain— as evident in the much-discussed discrepancies between girls' and boys' performance in basic math and science skills. Opportunities (and in some cases requirements) for community service have been made available to young people regardless of gender, and as we have seen, young men and young women are often involved in similar kinds of activities (such as feeding the homeless or tutoring the handicapped). But there still are informal pressures for young men and young women to become involved in different volunteer activities and to experience these activities in different ways.

One of the clearest indications of these informal pressures emerged in response to questions we asked about teasing. We asked our interviewees whether they had ever been teased about their volunteer activities. We also asked if they could think of cases in which other students had been teased. We found that about 70 percent of the young people we talked to had been teased, that virtually all of them could cite specific examples of having been teased or of having heard others teased for their caring and volunteer activities, and that young men and young women were about equally likely to have been teased or criticized. If schools are doing more to encourage community service, there is still a subculture in most schools that sends different messages about the value of caring. What is most important to our purposes, however, is that young men and young women—though experiencing criticism about equally—were teased for quite different reasons.

Young men were teased for doing volunteer work that was deemed to be childish, too closely linked with one's family (especially one's mother), naive, immature, and not sufficiently manly. Even activities that were exclusively male were sometimes subjected to these criticisms. A young man who worked with the Boy Scouts, for example, admitted that classmates tease him: "It's kind of like the wimps or something. That's the way a lot of people see it."[12] Another young man says the environmentalists at his school are criticized because it seems like a "sissy thing to be." He says his friends tease him about being a vegetarian, too, because eating meat is a more masculine thing to do. Attending an inner-city high school where gangs are prevalent, another young man—who works with the homeless—admits that people tease him because he isn't doing things that are sufficiently risky or isn't hanging out with a gang.

Young women, in contrast, were criticized for trying to perform caring activities that were undeniably adult, specialized, and helpful. Their classmates questioned whether these were appropriate ways of caring and whether there was something deviant about the self-identity of people who would be involved in such activities. Young women were thus exempt from teasing as long as they demonstrated caring in traditional, familial ways, such as helping their friends or listening to someone with a personal problem. But the signals they received about specialized, adult caring activities were more ambiguous.

For example, a young woman who received a Woman of Achievement award from the Girl Scouts for a variety of volunteer activities, including working on the local rescue squad, said she had been made fun of and criticized afterward. She said classmates questioned her motives, expressed doubts about the appropriateness of her having received this recognition, and asked if she didn't have better things to do with her time. Another young woman who did volunteer work as a counselor for Planned Parenthood said she had been criticized, not for trying to help people, but for not doing so in a way that paid like a real job: "You're wasting your time. Get a job where you can actually get paid. Earn some money."[13] And a young woman who does volunteer work with the homeless admits she has been criticized "for being too nice." In all these cases, the teasing reflected uncertain norms about how to combine an ethic of caring with the expectations associated with adult roles.

The effect of teasing on young women and young men alike was not to discourage them from doing volunteer work in the future (most said they simply "blew off" the criticisms) but to alter the ways in which they talked about their activities. Young men tried to redefine whatever activity they were involved in as a specialized role requiring skill and that would lead into a career or that would have transfer value in the future. Raising Seeing Eye dogs, for example, was privately a way of having a puppy but to one's friends was an act requiring adultlike responsibility, knowledge of special diets and training, and possible preparation for work in animal husbandry. Young women, in contrast, redefined their volunteer activities as special interests or hobbies. The rescue squad volunteer, for example, said she responded to criticisms by comparing her volunteer work with other afterschool activities: "I just kind of blew it off and said, 'You do what you do and I do what I do.' Some people said, 'Why don't you do sports?' I said, 'Well, I care about this as much as you care about your football game. You make yourself feel good by staying in shape and I make myself feel good by doing this.'" Her way of derailing criticism was thus to say, in effect, this is my personal preference, who are you to criticize? But in so doing, young women also left open more ambiguity about what was appropriate role behavior and retained a stronger link between their self-identity and their activities.

We also observed that these ways of talking were reinforced by differences in how the volunteer activities in which young men and young women participated were organized. Fewer than one-third of the young men said that their close friends did volunteer work, whereas more than half of the young women reported that their close friends did volunteer work. This difference alone suggests that young men are more likely to go off by themselves to do volunteer work, whereas young women are more likely to do things together with their friends and thus to receive some support from them.

In both our interviews and the national survey, we noticed some differences that in fact corresponded to this pattern. Young men went off on their own to be with the elderly (like Sid Gerson), initiated their own programs (like Tucker Aims), or were sometimes the only one from their high school (like Rafe Ramirez) who participated in an activity sponsored by a community organization.

In contrast, young women were more likely to do their volunteer work at their high school or a church or synagogue (like Jackie White and Jill Daugherty), and when they organized their own activities (like Amy Stone and Zia Hillier), they were likely to enlist their closest friends. There are, of course, many exceptions to this pattern. As a statistical generalization, however, it does appear that young women who volunteer are more likely to surround themselves with friends than are young men.[14]

This difference again matched some of the differences (as we shall see momentarily) in the ways in which young men and women talked about their volunteering. The reason that young men were able to go off on their own to do volunteering was often because there were structured organizations in which they could play specialized roles—scout leader, soccer coach, volunteer carpenter, and so on. These roles permitted them to do something for a short time each week that was largely removed from what they did when they were at school or at home. Conversely, young women usually did volunteer work— whether in structured roles or in more ambiguous circumstances—in the presence of their friends from school, who knew them in other contexts. The volunteer role was thus less segmented from the rest of life, and so they had to invest more of their personal identity in the volunteer experience.

Levels of Involvement

Do any of these differences influence the volunteering itself? Research studies give mixed answers to the question of whether more women than men are involved in caring activities. A 1989 survey of teens drawn from a representative national sample showed that 64 percent of females had done some kind of volunteering within the past year, compared with only 51 percent of males. In 1991, using nearly comparable questions, a national survey of teens found virtually no differences between females and males.[15] Nevertheless, female respondents were more likely than males to say that volunteering was important to them.[16] Another national study found that teenage women were about 10 percent more likely than teenage men to be involved in caring activities such as helping the poor, the sick, or the elderly. Although this last study could be construed—as could the others—as showing more similarities than differences between young women and young men, it nevertheless revealed that young women were three times more likely than young men were to say that they would volunteer for community service if their school helped them find a way to do so.[17]

Studies also show mixed results for adults. A 1989 survey asking, "Do you, yourself, happen to be involved in any charity or social service activities?" found that 32 percent of the women were involved, compared with 29 percent of the men—barely a significant difference statistically. According to another national study of adults, however, women were more likely than men to have given time within the past year to helping the poor or the needy and to say that they highly valued helping others.[18] Still another national study estimated that women devoted approximately one hour more each week to volunteer activities than did men—a small but significant difference, especially when totaled for the year and when figured that this hour amounted to about 60 percent more time being given by the average woman than by the average man.[19]

This last finding suggests that some of the inconsistencies in patterns among teenagers may also be resolved by focusing only on data that measures involvement with some level of refinement. According to the Independent Sector survey of teenagers, for example, white teenaged women devoted approximately 1.5 hours more per month on average to doing volunteer work than white teenaged men did and, among volunteers only, about 2.5 more hours per month. This means that a slightly higher proportion of women than men are very extensively involved in volunteer work. The same is true for blacks, although only at the most active level of involvement.[20] The same survey also showed that 57 percent of females, compared with 40 percent of males, receive a great deal of satisfaction from doing things for others.

If some evidence suggests that young women are more actively involved in volunteer work than young men are, then even more evidence shows that volunteering and other kinds of caring activities differ between the sexes in their variety and meaning. According to one of the adult surveys mentioned earlier, for example, men were more likely than women to have lent money to their friends within the past year, saved someone's life, given money to a beggar, and helped someone having automobile trouble, whereas women were more likely than men to have donated time to a volunteer organization, cared for someone who was sick, gone door to door to raise money, tried to get someone to stop using drugs or alcohol, helped a friend through a crisis, and taken care of an elderly relative in their home. These differences conform to many of the conventional images of gendered behavior, of course, but they also indicate that women may be involved in activities that are more nurturing, personal, and long lasting. Other data reveal that women are also more likely to value nurturing and caring activities than men are. Although a majority of both claim to value helping the needy, for example, fully one-third of the men admitted this was not very important to them, whereas only one-fifth of women did.[21]

Among teenagers, our qualitative interviews also show that young men and young women differ to some extent in the kinds of volunteer activities in which they participate. Many of the service clubs and community agencies that young people joined in their high schools were either predominately male or predominately female, and so as a result, the activities sometimes differed. For instance, Tucker Aims's environmental project enlisted boys because it was organized in conjunction with the Boy Scouts. Scott Hastings, the young man who raised Seeing Eye dogs, did so because several of his close male friends did the same thing and because they found support through their 4-H club. Although the 4-H leader was a woman, none of the young people were girls.

As we did in the other studies, we found in the survey that young women were somewhat more likely than young men to be actively involved in their churches and synagogues. As a result, young women were also more likely than young men to volunteer for activities such as teaching Sunday school classes or helping with children's programs at their churches. We also found some evidence of gendered activity related to the nature of the task or of the clientele. For instance, Sid Gerson's volunteer work with the elderly consisted of visiting an elderly man; another young man mowed lawns for the elderly; another put up drywall and dug ditches for low-income housing projects.

In the teen survey, young women were more likely to be engaged in a wide variety of direct personal caregiving activities than young men were. When adding up those who had cared for the sick, helped someone stop abusing drugs, visited someone in the hospital, helped someone with a crisis, cared for an elderly relative, and tutored someone—and counting those who had done four or more of these—we came up with 18 percent of white males and 27 percent of white females, and 18 percent of black males and 39 percent of black females.

In regard to the meaning of volunteering, we must consider what young men and young women had to say about their volunteering in greater detail and also consider several clues in the survey. For example, by a margin of 46 to 32 percent, females reported that enjoying volunteer work was a very important reason, suggesting that volunteering and caring are defined more often as a legitimate way of having a good time for young women than for young men. This pattern of responses also makes it somewhat more socially acceptable for young women to volunteer and creates expectations of getting more out of it for oneself emotionally. The survey also showed that young women are somewhat more likely than young men are to say that what was important to others they respect was an major reason for their volunteering—indicating that peer support may also be particularly important to young women.

Rights and Responsibilities

One of the best analyses of the differences in emphasis between women's and men's understandings of caring is Carol Gilligan's research on moral reasoning.[22] Gilligan argues that women tend to be more relational and thus stress responsibility and mutuality more when talking about moral dilemmas, whereas men tend to be more competitive and thus emphasize individual rights more. Gilligan's work is suggestive but was not developed specifically in regard to questions about caring. Its main implication, nevertheless, is that talk about caring is likely to be gendered in a way that allows women to be somewhat more concerned with caring for the needs themselves, whereas men are more likely to be concerned about such rights-related issues as equality and social justice.

In my earlier research on adult volunteers, I asked open-ended questions specifically designed to test Gilligan's ideas about rights and responsibilities. In one hundred qualitative interviews, my colleagues and I probed understandings of caring and of justice to find out whether people perceived conflicts between rights and responsibilities and emphasized one more than the other. Most people regarded the distinction as a false dichotomy, arguing that any clear sense of caring involved both a sense of one's responsibility for another person and a sense of that person's rights. There were no noticeable differences in the responses of men and women.[23]

Our qualitative interviews with teenagers took a somewhat different approach, encouraging volunteers to talk openly about their motives for becoming involved and how their involvement had influenced their ideas about caring and social justice. The main difference between this approach and Gilligan's is that my concern was with the ways in which people actually experienced and talked about their activities, and not with responses to hypothetical ethical dilemmas. Again, we found no gender patterns in the data. Young women were likely to mix ideas about responsibility with ideas about rights (a pattern that Gilligan's more recent research also has begun to reveal), and perhaps more significantly, young men also combined both ideas, and their language did not depend heavily on the kind of volunteering in which they were engaged.[24]

Indeed, the most revealing aspect of the ways in which young people talked about rights and responsibilities is that both ideas are part of the typical response to human needs, although either sex can be guided to focus on either rights or responsibilities, or both, depending on what kinds of role models are present to guide the person's behavior. For example, Sherry Hicks remembers going on a field trip with her high school to Washington, D.C., and, for the first time in her life, being shocked by seeing a homeless person begging on the street of the nation's capital. "He must have been in the Vietnam War," she recalls, "because he would always say things about the war and stuff. We were told not to give anyone money because it would create problems, especially by being a tourist it would create problems. We would go past him every day, and I just wanted to give him all the money I had, because he just looked so sad." This, in Gilligan's terms, was a *connective* response underscoring her desire to be of assistance. But a sense of anger was also part of Sherry's response: "I was mad because here we were, in Washington, D.C., and there were all these people with no place to go just laying around with bags." In Sherry's case, the high school counseler warned her against following her desire to provide nurture.

Jill Daugherty had a similar reaction, although she was only in the seventh grade when she first became aware of the homeless. Coming home angry at the injustice of the situation, she talked to her mother, who tried to channel Jill's reaction in a more nurturing direction. Jill responded dutifully and took Christmas cookies to an elderly man in the neighborhood whose wife had died recently.[25] Later she became involved in a more structured community service program that reinforced the concept of equal rights that her mother had also taught her as a child. Today, Jill hopes to go to law school after college and work in the area of social justice. She also lobbies whenever she can on behalf of gender equality in her high school.

One could object that volunteers are not the best group in which to test these ideas about rights and responsibilities because they are, after all, oriented toward caring in the first place. For this reason, it might be better to draw data from a more representative cross section of the population.

Further doubt on Gilligan's thesis is cast by the responses of teenage men and women nationwide to a question that asks directly about the trade-off between rights and responsibilities: "We all have the right to concern ourselves with our own goals first and foremost, rather than with the problems of other people." If men are more oriented toward rights, and women to responsibilities, we would expect the men to agree with this statement more often and more strongly than the women would. In fact, gender was related to the responses in the direction suggested. However, despite the large number of cases in the survey, the differences were too small to be statistically significant.[26] Furthermore, the study showed no relationship between the responses to this statement and those to the statement considered in an earlier chapter about having a moral duty to help those who are suffering, revealing again that young men are as capable of combining ideas about rights with ideas about responsibilities as young women are.[27]

Selves and Roles

The clearest differences between young men and young women emerge not in talking about rights and responsibilities but in talking about roles and selves. Deborah Tannen's research on conversational styles shows both that women and men use language quite differently and that these differences are themselves indicative of deeper contrasts in the ways in which women and men perceive themselves. Her work is especially relevant to questions about the gendered nature of caring because the differences she observes actually focus on supportive relationships. Women, Tannen argues, approach conversations as "negotiations for closeness in which people try to seek and give confirmation and support, and to reach consensus." At the heart of these negotiations are efforts to prevent being pushed away, to preserve intimacy and avoid isolation, and to signal friendships and approval rather than power and accomplishment. Men, in contrast, use language in a way that discloses their orientation toward accomplishment, their concern with achieving goals, their desire for status, and their proclivity to compete and oppose.[28]

These observations are consistent with the idea that women are inherently more nurturing than men. I want to suggest another interpretation, however: Women are more likely to regard caring as an expression of their selfhood, whereas men are more likely to associate caring with the specific roles they may play. This interpretation is consistent with some of the things we have already observed in talking about mothers and fathers. Young people, for example, see their mothers as more inherently and genuinely caring and credit them with relating personally and with going beyond what may be required in specific roles; conversely, fathers are less likely to be credited with warmth, with relating as whole persons, or with going beyond the call of duty, but they are likely to be seen as caring because of the work they do and the skills they use in their work (including volunteer work).

Tannen's emphasis on language suggests that young men and women also pick up some of these gender differences in the ways that they talk about their own caring. In particular, her argument that women speak in ways that negotiate closeness, I believe, is an indication that women think of themselves as being invested in their caring relationships and use words that signal this involvement. Men, in contrast, are more likely to use words that distance themselves from their caring, showing instead that it is defined by the roles they play and is thus governed by norms of goal attainment, competition, and status.

Support for this interpretation comes from the responses to our question asking young people to talk about good reasons for becoming involved in volunteer work. First, young women used more words to talk about these reasons—about forty on average, compared with thirty for men—and since both used between two and three sentences on average, this difference meant that women used longer and more qualified sentences and that men's were shorter, more succinct, and more declarative or unqualified. The more important difference, however, was that women were about five times more likely than men were to use the word *I*. The reason for this difference is that women qualify and personalize their statements much more than men do.

What these differences imply is that for women, caring focuses more on the self and includes statements about the relationship between oneself and one's situation, whereas young men speak about caring in less personalized terms that include abstractions and generalizations.

Another indication of the different ways in which young men and young women talk about caring comes from another question in our qualitative interviews, which asked the respondents whether they thought that everyone should be kind and compassionate or whether it was all right if some people were not. The question gave the respondents an opportunity to give an unqualified generalization, to favor a more qualified response, or to use their own words to suggest qualifications. Only 10 percent of the young men said that they didn't believe everyone should be kind and compassionate, whereas one-quarter of the young women immediately opted for a more qualified response. Moreover, of those who thought everyone should be kind and compassionate, only one-tenth of the young men offered any qualifying remarks, whereas one-third of the females did. The overwhelming tendency among male respondents was thus to make generalizations, whereas female respondents were more evenly divided, but a majority offered qualified responses.

An example of an unqualified response came from a young man who, when asked whether everyone should try to be kind and compassionate, answered, "Definitely, because if we were all kind and compassionate we wouldn't have all this hatred and violence now. If everyone worked together, it would be just a peaceful place." Or as another young man responded, "Everyone should try and be kind and compassionate towards others, because then it would probably be a better place to live in."

An example of a more qualified response came from a young woman who answered the same question by asserting: "I think everybody has a kind and compassionate side to them. People don't let it out as much as they should. Everyone should try to be that way. However, there are some people who have a greater sense of it than others. Not everyone can be the same." Another young woman gave a similar response: "I think it's OK if some people aren't, because I don't think everyone was made for the same purpose in the world, and that may not be their purpose. I think it's best to do what they feel is right for them." In both of these cases, the qualification depended on recognizing human differences.

In other cases, young women also put themselves more directly into their response. For example, one commented: "It's not OK [to be unkind], but I understand. Some people feel like they have no reason to be. Some people are abused physically and mentally, and they don't feel like they have any reason to be kind or compassionate. I can understand." Another remarked: "I think everyone should try, but it's inevitable that not everyone will succeed. I don't succeed all the time, that's for sure."

Judging from these and other examples, the logic of caring evident in the young women's responses is to connect the person in a web of meaning to her individual circumstances by talking about motives and reasons in personal and situational terms. In contrast, young men are more likely to talk about their own circumstances separately from the generalizations they offer and to use abstract language that does not take into account their individual circumstances. Young women, it appears, invest a sense of themselves directly in the ways they talk about caring, whereas young men associate caring with specialized and diverse roles that can be detached from themselves and that require generalized language.

Although some of the difference may simply be attributable to gendered patterns in the use of language more generally, we should point out that the languages used to talk about caring also suggest differences in understandings of roles and selves. The language that is more commonly used by young men makes the occupants of roles more readily interchangeable. That is, a role is like a fixed position in society that can be filled by one person, then another and another. Thus, different people can presumably show kindness in different ways depending on the various roles they may play. The language used by young women focuses more on the differences attributable to persons and circumstances. Thus, it may be ideal for everyone to show kindness, but some people may be prevented from doing so and may be excused from having to be kind because of their backgrounds, personalities, or the situations in which they find themselves.

There is also some evidence in the national survey that women regard volunteering more as an expression of their selves than men do. When asked about their reasons for volunteering, women were just as likely as men to mention the more instrumental or role-specific reasons, such as making contacts helpful to one's career or enhancing one's résumé, but women were significantly more likely than men were to emphasize expressive motives, such as feeling needed, feeling compassion toward people in need, and gaining enjoyment.[29] We will consider the personal consequences of caring in the next chapter, but we should mention here that women also seem to find caring for others more personally rewarding than men do, as least judging from how many say they receive a great deal of personal fulfillment from doing things for other people.[30]

In other surveys, women and men give many of the same reasons for being kind and considerate or for becoming involved in volunteering. There is, however, some indication that women are more likely to stress giving of themselves as a value in its own right, whereas men are somewhat more likely to stress giving as a way of getting something that they want in return.[31] One could, of course, interpret these differences to mean that men are more selfish than women. I suspect, however, that the pattern is probably another indication of the ways in which men and women put together their caring with the roles they play. If women associate caring with their sense of selfhood, then it makes sense that they should regard caring as an intrinsic value. If in contrast, men associate caring with the specific roles they play, it makes sense that their view of caring would depend more on the instrumental logic that generally governs such roles.

A more nuanced picture of the different motivational languages that may govern the caring behavior of men and women comes from a set of questions I included in another nationally representative study. The question read, "Imagine the following:_____ is a person you met on a recent business trip. S/he calls and asks if s/he can spend a couple of hours with you discussing a personal problem s/he is having. How likely or unlikely would you be to meet with her/him under each of these conditions?"

For male respondents, the person in the story was named Harry Jones; and for female respondents, Mary Jones. Five different conditions were described: (1) S/he says s/he'll pay for your advice; (2) S/he works for one of your competitors; (3) You've struggled with the same problem and really know what s/he's feeling; (4) S/he could be useful to you at some point in your career; and (5) You discover that s/he grew up in the same neighborhood you did.

Men and women were alike in two respects: They both were more (and equally) likely to say they would meet with the person if they had grown up in the same neighborhood, and they both were less (and equally) likely to say they would help out if the person worked for one of their competitors. In other words, gender made little difference when positive norms of community, on the one hand, or the negative norms of competition, on the other hand, were invoked. Men and women did, however, differ in two other ways: Men were more willing than women to be swayed by instrumental motives (expecting to be paid or to reap career benefits); women, in contrast, were more likely than men to be swayed by empathy (having experienced the same problem).[32] The differences should not be exaggerated, however. Both men and women were more likely to say they would help because of empathy rather than because of receiving some tangible reward. Nevertheless, women tended to be somewhat more oriented toward the former and men toward the latter. Again, then, women seem to make a greater investment of self in caring, and men, a stronger element of calculation.

How can we make sense of these differences? There are a number of reasons that young women may invest more of their selfhood in caring and young men focus more on roles. One reason is that young women may be socialized early to think of themselves as nurturing, whereas young men may be taught to achieve and to aspire to positions of status. Another reason may be that different relations develop between children and their parents—young women feel greater continuity with their mothers, enabling them to carry more of a caring identity into their adult roles, whereas young men break their ties with their mothers as they mature, making it necessary to develop more abstract notions of caring. Still another reason may be that young women emulate their mothers and young men model themselves after their fathers. If this it an important factor, it nevertheless begs the question of why mothers and fathers are viewed differently in the first place.

An interpretation that also helps us clarify the larger argument we have been considering about selves and roles is that suggested by Arlene Kaplan Daniels's statement about women's shaping their activities outside institutional supports and in ambiguous contexts. Daniels has in mind the middle-class women she studied who had taken up volunteer work instead of paid employment. For these women, caring was often in transient contexts that were sometimes viewed with skepticism by men and by women who were employed and, of course, that did not result in steady remuneration. It is quite possible that many of the young people we studied had witnessed such ambiguities when observing their mothers. For example, although most of these young people's mothers were employed, some of them were not; some were full-time volunteers; others split their time between part-time work and volunteer activities; and still others had taken years out from working to raise their families or to do volunteer work.

We see even more direct evidence of the differences between mothers and fathers in the ways in which their offspring talk about their parents' styles of caring. As I mentioned earlier, fathers were seen either as caring by going off to work and helping people by doing their jobs well or just by doing what came naturally when they were not at work, such as being a fun-loving guy who got along well with the neighbors. Mothers, in contrast, seemed to devote more energy to their caring activities. As perceived by their offspring, mothers showed kindness by taking time off from work to take someone to the doctor, staying at home in order to care for an elderly relative, going beyond the call of duty in intervening in the life of a friend, and breaking through the facade of everyday life more often by showing grief and crying. Again, then, mothers seemed less likely than fathers to care simply by relying on institutional supports and by staying within the confines of institutionalized roles.

Whether young women themselves experienced caring in the same way as they perceived it in their mothers is less clear. It is evident, first, that they tended to identify with their mothers (or other female role models) and for this reason alone may have developed a gendered conception of caring. Moreover, there is some evidence from our interviews that young women also experienced the ambiguities of roles and institutionalized support systems that Daniels observed in her study.

Many of the young women we talked to, for example, had counseled friends about pregnancies, sexually transmitted diseases, sexual harassment, date rape, and sour relationships, whereas few of the young men mentioned having such discussions. For young women, these sessions were often described as being uncomfortable because it was unclear what they should say and there may not have been professionals to whom referrals could be made. In addition, many of the young women had become involved in volunteer work that required them to create their own programs, rather than being able to rely on readymade programs. As Amy Stone did, they had to improvise in order to initiate AIDS awareness, or as Zia Hillier did, they had to start their own service club. Although they were, as we saw, teased in different ways than boys were, they were, nevertheless, subject to criticism on issues that were particularly important to them—especially on matters of women's rights and sexuality.

Megan Wyse, for example, says she has never been teased for doing volunteer work with the homeless or the handicapped, even though only one or two of her immediate friends also do volunteer work. She says she has, however, been teased for taking part in a club devoted to women's issues. "Women's rights is a big issue at our school, and there's a women's issues club that I'm involved in that sometimes guys make fun of. They try to start men's clubs that just mock women's issues clubs. They make fun of the whole concept of militant women." Another young woman observed how difficult it has been to do service work concerning AIDS and sexuality. "With the condom issue I got my share of comments. People assumed I was more promiscuous than I was. Also, they're constantly saying fag and drag. That's just how they use the terms of a lesbian and a homosexual. They're just terrible. High school people are so insecure about their sexuality anyway."

The connection between all this and investing one's selfhood in caring is that an investment of selfhood is a way of coping with ambiguous institutional settings. That is, if one is uncertain that a formalized role will make it possible to be caring, then caring must be supported by a clearer sense of doing it because this is who one is. Or put differently, one must retain more of the primordial sense of caring that one learns in childhood—the understanding that caring is personal, intimate, and an expression of one's whole self—because the roles that one plays do not show clearly how to be caring. Indeed, it becomes less possible to assume that one is caring simply by fulfilling one's duties, working hard, or preparing for life in a complex institution. As we have seen, young women find it necessary to use more words to describe their caring activities, to refer more often to themselves, and to take more time to explain the linkages between themselves and their settings.

If this interpretation is correct, it has important implications for understanding the different ways in which young women and young men learn to care. Although the activities in which the two are engaged may be quite similar on the surface, the ways in which these activities are experienced may be quite different. Young women may be more likely to carry a significant piece of their self-identity with them and to invest it in their service activities. Young men may be more likely to concentrate on learning structured roles in which they can demonstrate caring and yet distance themselves to a greater extent from these roles. One strategy is not necessarily better than the other, but the differences need to be understood if either strategy is to be effective.

Because young men and young women must relearn the views of caring that they developed as children, it is important that both have opportunities to reflect on the ways in which they, as persons, are caring and also on ways to demonstrate kindness in specific roles. Insofar as young women are more likely to focus on the former and young men on the latter, it may be valuable to have them discuss together their different perceptions. It may also be useful to encourage frankness about what they have learned from their mothers and fathers, explicitly paying attention to the gendered messages they have learned about caring. Young men and young women will probably continue to choose different kinds of volunteer activities, but schools may be able to break down some of the traditional stereotypes of these activities. Candid discussions of the ways in which volunteering is gendered may also be helpful in overcoming the teasing to which volunteers are subjected.

Those who are in charge of community service programs must be particularly sensitive to these gender differences. Playing ambiguous roles is associated with what Mary Field Belenky and her colleagues termed in another context the development of a "subjective voice."[33] This voice, though perhaps regarded as weak or unauthoritative by the standards of law or science, is nevertheless an important way of retaining personal power and of staying "centered" amidst ambiguous role demands. The subjective voice is, incidentally, used most commonly when telling stories—which again brings us to the importance of stories as ways of resolving the dilemmas associated with learning how to care in new situations. And storytelling, other research indicates, is especially common in small support groups that encourage intimacy and trust—groups that are more commonly made up of women than men—and that permit one's self-identity to be refashioned as situations change.[34]

The other implication of this interpretation is that we can now refine what we have been saying about the transition in young adulthood from primordial caring to a more institutionalized sense of caring. The model we have suggested to this point assumes that institutionalized roles are uniformly well defined and therefore unambiguous. One thinks, for example, of an organization chart and a set of job descriptions that establish the expectations for a particular role (such as "bank teller" or "Red Cross volunteer").

Many roles are defined in this way and are supported by the resources of corporations, government bureaus, schools, large nonprofit agencies, and other formal organizations. There are many exceptions as well. Other roles are ambiguous and unsupported. People find themselves, for example, without child care or ways of caring for elderly relatives. Or they take a new job only to find that they have to work out the job description from scratch. Although there may be a transition toward assuming specialized roles as one enters adulthood, it is never possible to rely entirely on the expectations of these roles. One still has to have a strong enough sense of self to know how to be caring. The tension between self and roles is thus ongoing and, for this reason, deserves closer consideration in the next chapter.

9

Building Character: Vulnerability and Virtue

I have arrived at the age of grief. . . . It is not only that we know that love ends, children are stolen, parents die feeling that their lives have been meaningless. . . . It is more that the barriers between the circumstances of oneself and of the rest of the world have broken down, after all—after all that schooling, all that care. Lord, if it be thy will, let this cup pass from me. But . . . the cup must come around, cannot pass from you, and it is the same cup of pain that every mortal drinks from.

Jane Smiley, *The Age of Grief*

In the United States hardly anybody talks of the beauty of virtue, but they maintain that virtue is useful. . . . They show with complacency how an enlightened regard for themselves constantly prompts them to assist one another. . . . The principle of self-interest . . . cannot suffice to make a man virtuous; but it disciplines a number of persons in habits of regularity, temperance, moderation, foresight, self-command; and if it does not lead men straight to virtue by the will, it gradually draws them in that direction by their habits.

Alexis de Tocqueville, *Democracy in America*

Asked how she feels about herself after she has been doing volunteer work, Tanika Lane responds, "I feel full inside. I feel joy." She says she feels this way when people tell her they've read one of her essays about drugs in the free newspaper and been touched by it or when people seek her out for advice because they respect her opinion. "It just makes me feel good inside to reach out and help somebody," she says. "Sometimes it just feels too good to be true."

In talking with teenagers, we discovered that this was a common response, that it made them feel good to help others. Jason McKendrick, we recall, sat in the van that evening after helping at Pearl's Kitchen and experienced what he and his friends called a *helper high*. Jason explains what this feeling is like: "After you feed everyone, you get in the van, you sit down and you just feel really good for what you just did. I mean, you feel bad for these people, but you feel really good with yourself, because you just went out and you helped them and you fed them." He pauses and then asks: "Do you know what I mean? It's hard to explain. No one can explain the feeling that you get, so we call it the thirty-second helper high." Others spoke of similar feelings—feeling important, warm inside, fulfilled.

This language sharply contrasts with the way Alexis de Tocqueville talked about kindness when he visited the United States in the 1830s. His word was *virtue*. He recognized that people did not associate virtue with beauty, as they did in his native France, but he insisted that good habits, including caring for one's neighbors, cultivate virtue and that virtue, in turn, was tantamount to being a person of character, not a momentary rush of good feelings.

Many of us still think of kindness, as I have suggested, as a virtue. Indeed, one of the things educators hope to instill by involving young people in community service programs is a stronger sense that kindness is, in fact, an item of virtue. Nonetheless, the young people we talked to seldom used this word. If they are learning virtue by doing volunteer work, they seemed not to realize it.

We must, therefore, clarify what we mean when we say that kindness is a virtue or that doing volunteer work helps build character. We must look closely at the ways in which young people do understand the consequences of caring activities for themselves, and in doing so we must ask whether there is some meaning of virtue that can be rediscovered or rehabilitated. But before we can make sense of the language that young people now use to describe the consequences of caring, we must take a brief excursion into the broader meanings that virtue has held in the past and ponder some of the ways in which these meanings must now be rethought.

Kindness as Virtue

The basis for considering kindness as a virtue is historical. Kindness—taken to mean some of the same things as love, charity, and benevolence—has long been regarded (along with faith and hope) as one of the three great "theological" virtues—and, indeed, in much of Western thought as the highest of these, as depicted, for example, in the New Testament. The four "cardinal" virtues identified in Greek philosophy—justice, prudence, fortitude, and temperance—have often been associated with kindness as well. The cardinal virtues were regarded either as traits of caring behavior itself or as means by which kindness could be achieved in social relationships.

Throughout history, although much debate has focused on the ways in which kindness should be expressed, the basic assumption that kindness should be regarded as a virtue has itself seldom been questioned. For example, it was argued in some societies that enslaving certain races or ethnic groups was actually a kindness and in other societies, that slavery was considered a great evil, but in no case was it believed that kindness itself was a vice instead of a virtue. In our time, we still think this way. The extreme kindness of Mother Teresa, for example, is taken to be a mark of virtue, even by critics who may want the needy of Calcutta helped by other means.

If kindness is still regarded as a virtue rather than a vice, our understanding of virtue has nevertheless changed. We still think of virtue as something good, but we are less sure of how to identify it than we were in the past, and we are reluctant to try to determine its presence or absence in others. Consequently, virtue has, as it were, retreated into the dark, interior recesses of the self. Virtue is harder to see, harder to understand (even in ourselves), more closely associated with our private feelings about ourselves, and, for this reason, more affected by the shifting moods that come and go depending on the circumstances in which we happen to be at any given moment.

When Tanika Lane says she feels good inside, she is expressing much of our contemporary understanding of virtue, even though she does not use the term itself. It is significant that she focuses on her feelings, that she locates these feelings inside her, and that these feelings seem to reflect something about who she is. Her feelings are good in the sense of being pleasurable and good in a moral sense: They tell her that she has done something right. These feelings are very much her own, and if we were to reflect on them, we would conclude that virtue is also understandable only in relation to her as a person. Yet as Jason's comments reveal, we know that these feelings are quite ephemeral. If they reflect who we are, therefore, they are an indication that we are quite ephemeral, too. We know, as Jane Smiley suggests, that we inevitably will come to an "age of grief," despite all our caring, and that we will be overwhelmed by feelings of quite a different sort. If we feel virtuous at one moment, we also know that we are vulnerable.

It is the interplay among these feelings of virtue and vulnerability—and the ways in which acts of kindness may alter the balance among these feelings—that I want to examine. I want to suggest a way of thinking about virtue that contradicts our common assumptions about it and then use this perspective as a way of understanding what it means to say that caring activities help us build character.

Rethinking Virtue

As a starting point, let us go back to another historic meaning of virtue—as power—in which it is a quality or force that helps a person produce some desired result. Broadly speaking, this meaning of virtue is evident in the phrase by virtue of—for example, when we say that something happens by virtue of something else or when virtue is used to describe something that is efficacious, such as the virtue of a medicine. In these usages, virtue implies the power to make something happen. If virtue is a personal trait, then we might also speak of it as a kind of personal power. Virtue, for instance, might be revealed in the personal power it takes to stand up for somebody who is being victimized or in the fortitude it takes to say no to drugs or unsafe sex.

In a more traditional setting, an example that establishes the connection between virtue and power is the biblical account of Jesus healing a woman who had suffered for twelve years from an untreatable flow of blood. In the account given in the Gospel of Luke, the woman touches the hem of Jesus's garment and is healed, then Jesus turns and says, "Somebody touched me, for I perceived power going out from me" (Luke 8:46). This is the contemporary translation in the New King James Bible. But power and virtue are used interchangeably in translating this verse. In the original King James Bible, for example, the verse reads, "Virtue is gone out of me."

So we can talk about power, but what do we mean by it? We tend to associate power with people and to say that a person has been born with power or has developed power. This makes sense if we are thinking about power as a way of discussing virtue. Virtue is thus a moral trait—an attribute of the person displayed in his or her personal attitudes and behavior. A virtuous person is someone who has inner strength, perhaps one who has strong convictions or who has exercised enough willpower to have mastered a difficult skill or performed a difficult task.

But power can never be understood solely as a characteristic of an isolated person. Instead, power always derives its meaning from social relationships. For instance, one nation has power in relation to another, or one person exercises power over another. Power is also conferred; that is, power is something we recognize because social institutions tell us that certain people or organizations have it. A singer such as Madonna has power, for example, because the recording industry and the media tell us she does. Or to take a different example, a Nobel Prize winner has power not just from being smart or hardworking but because the scientific or literary community confers power on that person.

This last example also shows that a social understanding of power can help us rethink the meaning of virtue. We might say, for example, that a prize-winning scientist is not only powerful but also virtuous (a virtuoso of science).

Virtuosity in art or music easily falls into the same category. The same is true of the so-called cardinal virtues. A virtue such as courage (fortitude), for example, must be socially recognized and legitimated. For instance, war veterans are generally recognized for their courage. But the same individual act can be considered courageous in one setting (say, in a popular war) and foolhardy in another (such as in an unpopular war). Another way in which society determines what we recognize as courage can be seen in the language we use to talk about alcoholism. At one time, recovery from alcoholism was largely a private matter; now, however, with the advent of Alcoholics Anonymous and other support groups, we talk openly of the courage required in recovering from alcoholism.

We can use the idea that virtue is power and that power is socially conferred, then, to ask the following question: What kinds of social arrangements are most likely to confer this sense of personal power on an individual person? That is, what type of society needs its members to function as powerful persons? In short, what conditions create strong people?[1]

The answer is that strong people are most likely to be needed in societies that have relatively few institutionalized resources with which to sustain people or accomplish collective tasks. The rugged individualism of American lore fits this description quite well—as long as it is restricted to its origin, namely, the pioneers, explorers, trappers, hunters, and frontiersmen and -women of the nineteenth century. In that period, the American frontier provided little in the way of organized social life on which people could rely. Families raised and processed their own food, built their own dwellings, schooled their children, and buried their dead. They did not have enforceable laws, standardized systems of weights and measures, and regulatory agencies to make sure that the food they consumed was pure or to protect them from being cheated at the market. Noon whistles did not blow to tell them when to stop for lunch, and retirement plans did not take a portion of their monthly check for savings and insurance. The relative weakness of their social institutions was compensated by the relative strength of the individual people. Temperance and prudence took the place of factory schedules and insurance schemes. By common agreement (that is, the culture-defining capacity of families and churches), people were credited with the power to demonstrate these traits, and those who did were deemed virtuous. Regularity, temperance, moderation, foresight, and self-command, as Tocqueville put it, were the marks of the strong, virtuous person.

In comparison, our own society has less need for strong, ruggedly self-sufficient people. Prudence in saving one's money, for instance, is less important because of massive old-age and disability insurance schemes. Some people may do marginally better than their neighbors if they exercise caution in their financial dealings, but those who do not will nevertheless survive, and so will the society. Other institutions govern, protect, and guide much of the rest of the activities on which people and societies depend. Educational systems coerce the young to learn what the culture has to offer. Legal systems, lawyers, and police stand ready to curb violence and injustice; we are not encouraged to form our own vigilante committees. Medical care, therapists, and undertakers stand ready to carry out other necessary functions. We depend on supermarkets to have food available when we want it and on government inspectors to ensure its quality; we do not have to raise our own livestock. In short, people can now be relatively weak because of the strength of their social institutions. This is not to say that institutions run by themselves or that they function effectively all the time. But there is a vast web of institutional resources that most of us rely on so much that we simply take them for granted.

The changes in our society during the past century and a half is, in fact, nothing less than a remarkable shift away from the self-sufficiency of the rugged individualist to what might now be termed the insufficient self. The inner strength that was once required in the absence of powerful social institutions has now atrophied in the face of rising institutional strength. As a result, we often feel insufficient, weak, and powerless, and we are—at least in terms of many of the traits, skills, and moral rigors on which our forebears depended. Yet many of these personal virtues are no longer necessary because institutions have been created to take care of us. Indeed, the need for strong persons has declined in the same way that the need for strong muscles has declined. Society can now get by without very much of either.

The past has not died easily. Although we no longer need strong muscles to dig ditches, muscle-building programs flourish. Although the society could get by without such programs, vanity encourages some of us to develop strong muscles just to prove we can. In a similar way, programs have also emerged to help us cope with our sense of insufficiency. We attend self-help groups and talk about our feelings of vulnerability, our uncertainties, our indecision, our desire for fulfillment (as if the self were a vacuum needing air), and our efforts to grow and to develop ourselves. Partly we do this because we compare ourselves with the past and sense—rightly—that something has been lost. Partly also we do this because our institutions, despite encouraging us to be weak, nevertheless fail us all too often. We may not need courage to cross the open plains by ourselves, but we may still need it to recover from alcoholism.

If virtue is like inner strength, then the implication of this argument is that it, too, has atrophied over the past century and a half. A society of rugged individualists conferred virtue onto the men and women who personified it. They were courageous because no institutions existed to protect them. They needed faith and hope to face the future because no institutions could reduce the inevitable uncertainties of life. Prudence, temperance, and justice depended on the people who were assumed to be committed to these principles in the absence of laws to enforce them. In contemporary society, virtue is discussed avidly, like personal growth and muscle building, but may well be less significant as a social factor because of the growth of strong institutions.[2]

Strange as it may seem, much of what has been happening to the individual person in our society is just the opposite of what many of our theories have taught us to believe. That is, society requires us to be self-sufficient, and if anything, people are too individualistic and too preoccupied with their own interests and desires. These theories tell us that society is breaking down and that strong—virtuous—people are what we need to put it back together. In contrast, the argument I have just outlined implies that institutions do nearly everything for us and that if we feel weak, it is because we can generally get along by letting institutions have their way. But what does all this say about virtue (including kindness)? Let me suggest three implications before turning again to our considerations of kindness among young people.

First, we may be better people than we think. We may not be particularly virtuous, but we do get along most of the time because our institutions protect us from our worst vices and because we can do good things without being very strong individually. This is why we can have a lot of kindness in our society without much virtue. Mother Teresa is an exemplar of virtue, but most of us know we cannot live the way she does. Still, we can be neighborly in small ways. We can get good feelings from helping at the homeless shelter without having to sacrifice our lives to it. And because voluntary organizations carve up the work, we can do little and still feel it matters. We can, in short, be indifferent to suffering much of the rest of the time because we have institutions that encourage elementary kindness.

Second, and perhaps curiously, we need to consider the possibility that virtue is now more an attribute of institutions than of individual people. That is, virtue has perhaps not so much diminished as been transferred. Consider the self-sufficient cowboy. The virtues he needs are no longer necessary because people can depend more on social institutions. But this does not mean that the cowboy's virtue has simply disappeared. Although the courage it took to fight villains singlehandedly is perhaps unnecessary now (perhaps even to the average soldier who sits thousands of miles from enemy lines operating a computer), courage is still a virtue that we hope characterizes our military system as a whole.

Similarly, the cowboy's prudence in taking adequate food and clothing on a cattle drive is not needed by today's bureaucrats, who know that they will simply be reprimanded if they do not arrive at work on time or that their bank will notify them if they overdraw their account. We do expect our economic system, however, to be organized in a way that builds in these incentives and punishments. Prudence is thus an expectation associated more with the institution than with the people who happen to work in it. This does not mean that imprudent persons will be rewarded in the same way as prudent ones will. But it does mean that someone who manages to get to work on time most mornings and who seldom receives an overdraft notice from the bank will not be regarded as a person of particular virtue. The reason is that most of the power needed to encourage this behavior is now located in the institution instead of the person. In regard to kindness, we thus need to find ways not to engage in heroic deeds of caring but to behave kindly in the roles we play and to make sure that our institutions preserve and embody the value of kindness.[3]

Third, the kind of virtue (or strength) that people need now is different from the heroic or rugged virtue that we associate with the past. We may not need to be strong, for example, but we may need to do things once in a while that make us feel strong. That is, it helps, as we suffer from feelings of inadequacy, to experience symbolic victories periodically. If kindness happens routinely, for example, we may still need special times when we can feel good about helping others. We also may grow stronger when we perform deeds of kindness. But the most valuable kinds of growth may be those that show us not that we are invincible but that we are vulnerable. And we may also benefit especially from experiences that help us perform well in institutions, rather than encouraging us to get along without institutions.

My argument does not imply, I should note, that we necessarily regard our institutions as being compassionate, but we do worry about whether they are, how they should display compassion, and which ones should take the lead in this area. Businesses are criticized for not doing enough to promote kindness, but they are widely regarded as an institution in which kindness may not be entirely necessary. Voluntary associations, charities, and churches, in contrast, have become the specialized institutions with which kindness is associated. Their very existence reassures us that kindness is alive and well. People may be kind in their daily lives, but there is less virtue attached to this behavior because so much of the power on which kindness depends has now been transferred to institutions. Etiquette, for example, is a way of institutionalizing common courtesy in everyday life so that kindness ceases to be a virtue and becomes a matter of simply following the rules. Similarly, community service programs in schools ensure that the charitable sector as an institution receives sufficient labor, but the students who participate in these programs may not be particularly kind or particularly virtuous in other ways.

This is why, as I suggested, we may have a great deal of elementary kindness in our society but relatively little virtue. The kindness existing in institutions and the good deeds that individual persons contribute to the maintenance of these institutions. Those people, however, need not be virtuous themselves and, except for the few who provide symbolic representations of virtue, are not likely to be perceived as people of virtue. Ironically, then, the very institutions that promote kindness in our society are in the business of stripping away virtue from individual persons. But this is no fault of their particular leaders; in fact, this is what institutions are supposed to do. They are ways of organizing social relationships so that they depend less on the discretion or strength of particular people and more on the orchestration of large numbers of people. We realize that caring can take place, sometimes quite effectively, without an individual's virtue being very strongly developed. Yet we also know that in this process we lose much of the meaning of kindness. We lose it as a way of teaching children the meaning of virtue, for example, and we lose its connection with building character. As with any aspect of our society, there are both costs and benefits to the ways in which we organize our lives. We feel ambivalent about our institutions and about virtue, and so we must examine carefully the relationships between the roles we play and the persons we aspire to be.

But we need to come back to the young people we talked to and listen to what they say about themselves in order to see how these broader observations work out in real life. As always, real life is more complicated than any of our theories. We can also see that young people are learning valuable lessons about the kinds of virtue that are sorely needed in a complex society such as ours.

Becoming Strong

I shall start by considering what it means when young people say that their volunteer work has made them feel stronger, and I shall do this by returning to the case of Amy Stone. We interviewed no cowboys—no rugged individualists who exemplified the kind of personal strength it takes to live without institutions—but Amy Stone comes close, ironically because she was institutionalized for part of her life. This experience, we could say, proves how easily people in our society can get along when they are weak: Institutions are in place to do everything for them. The more decisive impact of Amy Stone's being institutionalized, however, was that she was cut off from virtually all other forms of support. She was, in this more important sense, very much alone and was forced to be self-sufficient to a greater extent than any of the other teenagers with whom we talked. She thus provides one sense of what it means to be strong.

As we saw in Chapter 2, Amy Stone had serious allegeric reactions to food while she was growing up and was forced to be hospitalized on a number of occasions during her childhood. Strength is a recurrent theme in Amy's remarks about herself and in her understanding of what it means to be a caring person.

For instance, when asked what she likes best about herself, she says she likes the fact that she is "a strong person as a result of everything that has happened to me." She cherishes her individuality, and she defines individualism as being a strong person. In fact, the sort of individualist she admires and strives to be is "someone who can stand on her own two feet and not be dependent on anyone else." She likes being independent because being dependent on somebody is "scary" and makes her think she is "sinking" or "failing." It worries her when she depends on someone else to get the job done, rather than doing it herself. She also says that helping other people is a way to "grow." This, in her view, is because everyone is naturally selfish, so it takes effort to be kind, and the harder one tries, the more one will grow.

The best way of explaining why caring is a good thing, Amy believes, is that "it shows that you're a strong person. You have to be a strong person to give that much time and give that much of yourself, because you are giving of yourself. It also helps you grow as a person as well." Most of her role models, moreover, are people who struck out on their own, endured hardship, and had to prove themselves strong. She admires Mother Teresa, for example, because she is "totally devoted." She admires Harriet Tubman for risking her life to help liberate slaves. She admires Mikhail Gorbachev for, in her view, overturning the Communist system. And she regards Hillary Rodham Clinton as one of her role models—" a very strong lady."

Being a strong person, a person of character or of virtue, means that specific acts of kindness naturally follow. I do not mean that kindness occurs effortlessly. Indeed, the AIDS awareness rally that Amy organized at her high school took a great deal of effort. It was also a memorable occasion in Amy's life.

Kindness is a dimension of character and seeps into other activities rather than being limited to formally organized events, such as a rally or doing volunteer work. Several years ago, for example, there were some handicapped children in Amy's school, and she just quietly started having lunch with them and tried to become their friend. Another time she found someone willing to lend her an eighteen wheeler and (almost singlehandedly) loaded it with old clothes, food, and relief supplies for hurricane victims. On another occasion, one of her classmates, who was married, shot and killed his wife after she threatened to break up with him and take their baby away. Amy found herself deeply involved in doing a lot of informal grief counseling among her fellow students and also working to prevent the episode from being depicted by the media as a racial incident.

How does one come to be a strong person? In Amy's case, by experiencing a lingering illness. But what was it about her social relationships that was affected? If virtue is, as I have suggested, somehow more obvious when people are self-sufficient than when they are dependent on social institutions, then Amy would seem to contradict that generalization. Because of her illness, she was very much dependent on other people. Indeed, the environmental health unit to which she was confined might be viewed as a symbol of just how dependent she was. I believe, however, that it should be regarded as a symbol of something else. In the manner in which Amy actually experienced it, the environmental health unit serves much better as a symbol of protection than of dependency. That is, it was an enclave that shielded her from the institutions on which ordinary people depend. Its sterilized interior can be regarded as an image of the contrast it provided with the institutionalized world. To be sure, this enclave could not have existed without nurses, physicians, technicians, hospital administrators, accountants, and a host of other institutionalized roles. The six-year-old Amy did not experience them in this way, though. Rather, she experienced herself as being alone, needing to be strong, self-sufficient, and brave.

The effect of Amy's illness was, I believe, to set her apart from other institutionalized relationships as well. She could not do what other children did. She regarded herself as different. Even now, she sets herself apart from many of the activities in which teenagers normally engage. For example, she hates to shop and seldom watches television. It is revealing that she also mentions role models who stand out less as representatives of institutions and more as deviants with respect to those institutions. For example, she singles out her piano teacher who supposedly was a good piano teacher and, we discover, also played the organ at Amy's church. But what Amy remembers most about her was that she was an alcoholic, that she didn't quite fit in, and that she was nevertheless someone who cared about her. It wasn't the piano lessons that impressed Amy but the fact that the teacher spent time with her afterward—out of role, so to speak—just talking. Amy also singles out her pastor for the same reason. In fact, she says specifically that he "goes beyond his duties." She does not admire him because he preaches well or runs good church programs but because he went to her softball games and has taken her to the doctor.

The specific nature of Amy's caring activities, it seems to me, clearly reflects these life experiences. She does things that depend little on organizations and that fall in the margins of established social institutions. Indeed, many of her activities seem to be motivated by a kind of defiance of these institutions. Her AIDS rally, for example, seemed to run on the energy she derived from being rejected by the school board, health commissioner, and local newspapers. Although it drew on resources from the school and from a volunteer agency such as the AIDS Task Force, it was not a regular part of any of these organizations. Amy's role as student body president gave her the authority to organize it. Rather than trying to work through the ninety-member student council, however, she relied on a handful of volunteers. Although it was also a one-shot deal, she hopes that the next student body president will carry on her work. Nonetheless, although Amy used the rally to mobilize interest for several months both before and after, her energies did not extend to building some structure that would ensure continuing interest.

The hurricane relief effort that Amy organized had some of the same characteristics. Although it started as a student council project, it wound up being mostly her work and that of about five other volunteers. All of her caring activities at school, in fact, have been carried out with little institutional support. Amy mentioned one or two teachers who have helped, but no organized programs of community service and no clubs to promote social action. Indeed, she estimates that out of a thousand students, only about ten do any kind of volunteer work or community service. Amy herself has done some formal volunteer work, for example, delivering Meals on Wheels with her mother, singing in nursing homes with her church choir, and helping with a community cleanup day organized by the school.

It is the less organized activities that seem to mean the most to Amy, such as the time she found a boy crying who had been caught shoplifting and went with him when he had to appear in court. Or the countless times when she has counseled fellow students about pregnancies.

Even though her activities fall outside normal institutional routines, Amy is nevertheless the recipient of much social reinforcement. Being student body president, of course, is an honor as well as a responsibility. It defines her as someone who can—indeed, is expected to—make a difference. Last year the sheriff's department selected her to visit elementary schools in the county and give talks about the dangers of drug abuse. Recently, she received the Jefferson Young People's Award from the American Institute for Public Service in honor of the work she has done on behalf of her community. There are, in other words, people who define her as a strong person.

As a person who is socially defined and recognized as a person of strength, Amy exudes a certain degree of authority in her speech. She says, for example, that it is very important for her to do what she believes is right—a word that few of the teenagers we spoke to were willing to use. She regards it as a matter of principle never to hurt anyone else and always to respect others' opinions. She believes it is inevitable that people will disagree about things, but she also cherishes conflict and thinks it is important for people who disagree to enter into debates with others. In these ways, she holds strongly to the minimal moral convictions of a liberal society. Tolerance, respect, diversity, and even obedience to the law and to norms of social order under most circumstances are matters of unquestioning and uncompromising loyalty for her.

Amy's language also indicates that the moral authority we associate with people of virtue is tenuous in our society. Although she prides herself on being kind, she seems unwilling to say either that kindness itself is a mark of character or that it is something to which all people should aspire. Instead, she falls back on other arguments, more common in American culture, to explain her behavior. For example, being of service to others is something she likens to playing sports or being active in school clubs. It is just an interest of hers, what she does, like a hobby. She is equally reluctant to say that there is any morally binding reason that people should care for others. Those who do not, she thinks, may simply be too busy or have other interests. She does believe there may be something instinctual about caring. But she thinks this instinct may be suppressed most of the time because the economy forces people to look out for themselves.[4]

Amy Stone is, then, a person of exceptional strength, a virtuous person and yet—perhaps because of this strength—a person who fits uneasily into the structure of contemporary society. Her kindness may eventually be routinized as part of a career in one of the helping professions. She says she would like to become a doctor or a social worker, for example. Still, she is nervous about efforts to institutionalize kindness. She realizes, for instance, that detachment is part of what it takes to be a good doctor or a good social worker, and she is afraid that she cares too much about people to play that role. In the more immediate future, she is planning to attend a college that will require her to do community service. She doubts, however, that this will be the main way in which she tries to be a caring person. It is as if she recognizes at some deep level the tension between kindness as a virtue and the more limited manifestations of kindness that may be part of organized social life.

In Amy's case, personal strength primarily means self-sufficiency. She does not believe it is possible—or desirable—to be a loner who has no friends. But she does believe it is important to do things largely on her own and not to depend on institutions to get things done. Most of the teenagers with whom we talked, in contrast, described strength in ways that helped them get along better in institutional roles, rather than being able to do without institutions. A person of strength is thus not an individualist who constantly bucks the system but someone who has achieved an organic relationship with the communities in which he or she interacts. Weakness is to approach one's roles with only an instrumental focus ("getting the job done") or to let social institutions define one totally. One moves beyond weakness by developing a sustaining relationship that includes oneself in one's roles and that transforms cold institutions into life-sustaining communities. Thus, as one writer observes, "the community is an essential organ of the self, but not the sum of that self."[5]

Jackie White, the young woman who works with revolutionary organizations in Central America, expressed this organic notion of personal strength most clearly. When asked whether she considers herself an individualist, she replied, "Probably half and half. Part of it is that I believe in the good of the whole or community, and I try to incorporate that into my daily life. But I also look out for myself. I act on selfish impulses and also have ideals which are for the good of the whole and for the good of society." Elaborating, she explains that she holds only a qualified belief in individual rights. She believes that individual liberties in the extreme are dangerous and that a massive institutional bureaucracy that commands total allegiance, such as a Stalinist regime, is dangerous. She thinks that many of the social problems in the United States—drugs, crime, AIDS, broken families—arise from people stressing only their rights. This is why she tries to strike a balance between defending her own rights and emphasizing community-mindedness.

Jackie also tries to find a balance between functioning independently and recognizing her inevitable dependence on others. "I certainly depend on a lot of people for a lot of things," she admits, "particularly because I'm living at home and everything. So I do take a lot from a lot of people out of necessity, out of the norm of society, out of laziness, out of whatever. And I also like to be on my own and to be responsible for my own—and it's usually not my own money that I'm using when I'm on my own—but to have that sense of independence." She says that even her volunteer work is an example. It takes initiative to carry out these activities responsibly, but she also realizes that she is able to do this work because of her church, her family, her school, and other voluntary organizations.[6]

Another meaning of personal strength that seems particularly suited to our context emphasizes the individual person's responsibility to scan the environment and to make informed choices. Nikki Unger, for example, told us that she is learning more and more that she has choices to make. She does not see herself a nonconformist who chooses to do things just because nobody else is doing them or who makes choices without seeking advice. Instead, she considers herself an individualist who takes responsibility for her actions but also pays attention to what others are doing, learns from their example, and chooses to let others influence her.

Scanning the environment also means that a strong person is one who knows how to work with other people, rather than doing everything alone. The environment consists not so much of challenges to be faced but of interpersonal resources to be cultivated. For Jason McKendrick, the struggle has been to overcome the feeling that he should do everything by himself. He says this way of behaving is "not a strong point" for a successful person; instead, "you should be able to work with other people. It's something that you have to do in this world. You can't be individualistic. I always figured the best way to do something is to do it yourself. I always do things myself. Ever since I got into Pearl's, though, I've had to distribute jobs, delegate responsibility and stuff like that. So that helps me."

A related connotation of personal strength is to be able to adapt to a changing environment, which Tanika Lane demonstrates. She says her volunteer work has taught her that she can relate to anybody regardless of "color, rich, poor, no home, a home." It just makes her feel good about herself knowing that "I can get along with anybody, even people who really work on your nerves." Having an attitude like this makes her feel more powerful. Whenever she gets to feeling like a replaceable part, she knows that if she is replaced, she can always move on to something else. A young man made a similar point in talking about how his volunteer work had broadened the range of people with whom he feels comfortable. "I can get along with a great variety of people. You have, like, your 'artsy' people. I can get along with artsy people. I can get along with the 'techers' from the tech school, as they're called. My friends aren't in, like, one social group. I've got friends from, like, all these different social groups. I have friends from camp. I've got friends down in the city."

One must be flexible but at the same time be anxious about becoming too adaptable. A person of virtue must still have a center of gravity. Behavior must be genuine rather than only a response to the demands of the moment. For instance, Tanika remarks that she will do anything in any situation to help people, but most of all she wants people to know that she is not a fake. This is a quality she has learned through her volunteer work. It bothers her especially when caregivers are simply playing a role rather then caring from their heart. "I try to ignore those people who really don't care," she says. "People will sit there and say, girl, I love you to death. You know I love you, and they really don't. I mean they are fake. I don't like phony people. I try to be real."

To retain this sense of self-identity, a person of character must sometimes be unwilling to play expected roles. A young woman who works with handicapped students at her high school illustrates this point in the following story: "We were in lunch. There was a whole table of guys. We wheeled a couple [of handicapped] kids in. We were sitting around. And that whole table, all except for about three guys, got up and walked to the other side of the cafeteria, because they didn't want to sit near these 'retards' who drool. We had Jen in, and Jen can't eat on her own. Jen has to be fed. Her food has to be mushed. And sometimes food will fall out of her mouth, but she can't help that. So as soon as I saw a couple of them, I went up to them and I said, 'Why did you guys all get up and leave?' They're like, 'Oh, no reason.' And then I said, 'Why did you guys all get up and leave? Because you did not get up and leave until we came in.' They said, 'Oh, it just grosses us out that they sit there and drool and stuff.' And I said, 'Well, do you know why they drool?' And they're like, 'No, but it's disgusting.' I'm like, 'Maybe you should ask why. Maybe you should try and understand that these kids can't help it.' Then they're like, 'Uh.' And then they didn't say anything. So they probably felt like teeny, you know. Probably felt like a little piece of dust, because they realized that their actions were stupid. I told them, 'You guys are just being ignorant.' And I walked away." Being able to do this made her feel stronger. She was not conforming to the normal student role and acting like everyone else; instead, she was challenging the normal expectations.[7]

As this story suggests, part of what being a strong person now entails is a willingness to speak up. Indeed, it was interesting in our interviews to observe how frequently young people talked about learning to speak up. In the background of their comments was an image of a mass society dominated by the media and a babble of smaller, insignificant voices all saying the same thing. Part of playing one's role effectively was thus to find a way to be heard. Sherry Hicks was one of the students who made this point most forcefully in talking about her volunteer work: "It's made me more able to speak up and say what's on my mind and say how I feel, and I don't let people just push me over all the time anymore. A few years ago, I would have been the mousey one sitting in the back, not wanting to talk, having a question, but just sitting there holding my question in because I didn't want everyone to turn around and notice who I was or think who I was. I didn't think I was that important, but now I feel like I'm important enough that if I have a question I don't care whether I'm sitting in the back or in the front, I'm going to ask my question so it gets answered."

Personal strength, as defined by the young people we interviewed, also included a sense of one's potential contribution to the wider world. That is, although the roles that one plays may be small in themselves, one can still feel efficacious because small acts add up to greater accomplishments. Jim Grayson, the scout counselor, explains the personal strength he has felt when talking about these contributions. "I'm not just one of those people who seems to lead a nothing life—who never does anything for anybody else and who thinks only about themselves. I can help some of these kids and teach them what I know and hopefully make them a better person and somehow influence even the future of the country." He adds that being a counselor has given him more confidence in his ability to influence other people. "The more people you work with, the more confident you are working with them. Because you start off at the beginning of the summer, you're kind of like pulling back a bit. When you first start it, you're not necessarily ready to just take charge of these kids right away. But then you grow used to it, and you're sitting there, and you know what you're going to do, and you become more confident in yourself and what you're telling these kids."

Finally, and perhaps most important, a person of character is someone who performs his or her duties responsibly and yet realistically. This kind of person does not try to do everything alone—indeed, is not simply a caregiver—but works with other people to make things happen. Tanika, for example, knows that journalism is only one way to make a difference in the world, but she feels it is realistic to think that she can make a difference in this way. "If I write down my opinion about drugs," she remarks, "other people look at it and they might say, 'Well, I don't agree.' But if I wrote it down, I leave a mark on them." A highly institutionalized society such as ours needs people like this who are willing to do their part—shouldering a small piece of the world, recognizing that what happens depends on them but not taking on the whole world.

Another example of this kind of strength is Scott Hastings, the ninth grader who raises Seeing Eye dogs. He says he has not really changed as a person but feels he has become more responsible: "It was a lot of responsibility placed on my shoulders. I was also a counselor, and so I was responsible for all the kids that were in my group. That was just a lot of stuff on my shoulders that I'm not always used to, but the only way I can get better at it is with practice." He adds: "There's no one else to blame but yourself, so I've become much more responsible."

In all these ways, then, the young people we talked to felt that they could be strong, even in a society as complex as ours. Their volunteer work reinforced this sense of personal strength.[8] It did not make them self-sufficient or convince them that they could move mountains, but it did strengthen their conviction of the need to balance their own interests with the needs of others, to scan their environment and adapt, to recognize their ability to make contributions to the good of society, and to feel confident that they could work effectively with others. These were the ways in which volunteering built character.

I should note, too, that volunteering does not simply build character in these ways by giving young people opportunities to learn more about themselves. Like other forms of power, as I have suggested, these redefinitions of oneself come about partly by being conferred. Volunteer agencies confer recognition on caregivers, which helps them think of themselves as responsible people who can make an important difference in their communities by working with other people and by doing things that do not require a great sacrifice or huge investments of time.

Consider Tucker Aims, the young man who invented an environmentalism award. He admits that he spent a lot of time administering the award when he was in seventh grade, and he has stayed involved in environmental projects much of the time since then. For example, he participates in a local Adopt-a-Park program, which means that he picks up trash there periodically, and the town council has called on him a few times to organize volunteers for other cleanup projects. Sometimes, he acknowledges, he would rather be playing football with his friends but instead has committed his time to some volunteer project. He also says, however, that these activities do not dominate his life. He still enjoys listening to Jimi Hendrix, plays two sports, and makes good grades. Indeed, he admitted that he has not thought much about his scout project since he was in junior high, that he seldom participates in scouting anymore, and that he has pretty well "scaled back" on his volunteer efforts during the past year.

Despite Tucker's tendency to downplay his activities, there is nevertheless a sense of realism in his speech, compelling the listener to conclude that in fact his behavior was not all that extraordinary, heroic, or self-sacrificing. Yet consider the recognition that Tucker has received: the Hornaday Award from Boy Scouts for environmental work, the Young Citizens' Award given by the governor of his state, a full four-year tuition scholarship for college that comes with the governor's award, the Chevron Conservation Award (which includes $1,000), two Take Pride in America awards administered by the federal government, a congressional volunteer award from the U.S. Congress, a presidential award for environmentalism from the White House, and the honor of being named as one of former President George Bush's "thousand points of light." Tucker is proud of these awards, displaying some of them prominently on the wall of his bedroom. But even he thinks they may appear excessive: "Some of my friends think I just swindled my way into them." Yet it is also clear that recognition, even on a smaller scale, is important to legitimating the sense that young people can, indeed, make a difference.

Exotica

With these understandings of personal strength in mind, we can also make sense of one of the other things that teenagers liked best about their volunteer experiences. Many of them said they particularly enjoyed the chance to do "exotic" things—such as meeting new people, broadening their knowledge, or even doing things that were risky. We need to put these responses in perspective. Institutionalized society provides narrow, sheltered enclaves in which to live. Algebra class may be the prime example or, for older people, working at the office all day. The family itself may be a narrow, sheltering place consisting mostly of routines, such as eating, sleeping, doing homework, or watching television. Such enclaves are deadeningly real. But we also know that they are only part of reality and therefore feel inauthentic when we live in them all the time.

One way to escape from narrow, sheltering enclaves is to live in the fantasy worlds created by television and movie stars and athletes (or, for that matter, drugs and alcohol). Such worlds can make us feel alive by taking us out of the inauthenticity of everyday life and filling us with passion and new experiences. Statistics on the schedules and consumer habits of young people suggest that these sources of escape are widely used, even though surprisingly few of the people we talked to said they had occupied themselves in these ways.

Jason McKendrick, for example, plays the piano, listens to music, likes to tinker with old cars, and jogs for exercise, but he has never been particularly drawn to rock music or sports. He says he mostly just listens to whatever is on, plays sports when he feels like it, and seldom watches television. Megan Wyse likes to play soccer, sing, write, talk to her boyfriend, and be with her girl-friends, but she has never had an obsession with a musical group and seldom watches television (which she says is a waste of time). Tanika Lane is similar. She enjoys singing, being in school plays, and participating in the drill team at her church, and she has been trying to write a novel about a girl that sounds a lot like herself. She notes that her activities after school keep her busy enough that she does not have time to hang out with a gang as a lot of her friends do. She also says that she has never much liked popular music or sports and regularly watches only one television program. Rafe Ramirez, of course, is pre-occupied with soccer, but he manages to combine it with his volunteering, to do well in school, and to have time for a few friends.

Most of the young people we talked to would not have had time to do as much volunteer work as they did if they watched television four or five hours a day or been too preoccupied with rock music and video stars. They did, how-ever, gain a sense of the exotic from their volunteer work. For instance, Jason McKendrick says that what he enjoys most about helping at Pearl's Kitchen is the stories the homeless tell. It is like "adventure reading," he says. "Each time it's different, and you never know whether to believe them or not. That's the fun part of it. You've got to figure out, because sometimes they'll just tell you flat-out lies." He especially likes the stories about homeless people being chased by the police, getting thrown out of their makeshift homes in the sewers and under bridges, only to return a few days later. He revels in the fact that the cops are always being outsmarted. Running through his narrative is a kind of fasci-nation with the violation of law and order.

Zia Hillier, talking about the volunteer work she does on Saturdays with inner-city children, offers another example of the lure of the exotic. "It really interests me," she says, "because of what they have to go through, because these are kids that have had gunshot wounds, their parents have been killed, they walk to school and they're offered drugs every day. There's something in them that just drives them. It's really interesting for me to meet a bunch of kids with that much courage. Also, they're much different from the kids I'm used to around here."

One reason that these exotic experiences were especially valued among the teenagers we talked to is that such experiences help clarify one's identity. In developmental terms, late adolescence is a time of individuation. Young people detach psychologically from their parents and try to establish their own identities. They may be very much like their friends and yet do things and wear things that help set them apart. We observed this need for an individuated identity in the ways that young people talked about their volunteer experiences and also in their comments about themselves, in the ways they decorated their rooms, and in the ways they dressed.

Megan Wyse is a good example. She wears a small nose ring that has become a symbol of her struggle to be herself. She says she got it partly because her parents didn't want her to. She also prides herself on being a vegetarian. This, too, has meaning because her parents were opposed to the idea. Speaking more generally, she says she tries hard not to compromise her own convictions, dislikes conformity, and thinks it is good to go against the grain. The people she most admires, she explains, are "people who do things because they feel it's important, not necessarily because other people think it is important." Her volunteer work at Pearl's Kitchen reinforces this sense of being a person who is pursuing something that she, herself, feels is important. "Sometimes when I'm doing my daily things, going to school, and getting up in the morning, and doing all the things I do, I feel that it's basically worthless," she says. But her volunteer work is different because it "makes me feel like I'm doing something important. I'm not living a life that when I die nobody's going to remember it."

Another function of these exotic experiences is that they are ways of gaining confidence that one can actually play roles in less exotic circumstances. Megan Wyse also illustrates this point. In talking about her volunteer work, she ventures, "I think it gave me a better idea of what I really can accomplish, that I've never realized before that I really can make such a difference. I think I realize that one individual person really has a lot of power to heal a lot, and that power can be underestimated, depending on what you do with it. So I've realized that there's a lot of things I can do if I just do it. You really can make a difference by helping people, putting them into a shelter, helping them get a job, or even just to smile, to give them some kind of personal relationship. I realize that there is a lot of power in individual work, and depending on how you use it and use your potential, then it makes a big difference."

Exotic experiences also have a symbolic role. They tell young people that role behavior does not constitute all of life, that there can still be adventure, intrigue, escape. Caring activities thus become a way of convincing ourselves that we are still alive, a problem that—if not one of the existential maladies of modern life itself—is at least symptomatic of living in an institutionalized world governed by impersonal routines and responsibilities. Leaving the world of home, with its attendant emotional force, is like the experience of Camus's "stranger," whose alienation lies in his inability to register what might otherwise be regarded as normal human emotions in the face of his mother's death, his falling in love, his act of murder, and his imminent execution.[9] In caring for others, we realize that we can still feel—we assure ourselves that we have not become deadened to the trauma and to the misery of life.

Rachel Farb, a young woman who spends several hours each week doing volunteer work at a nearby school for the blind, shows how caring can provide relief from the routine of ordinary life. "I was really bored at school, everything at the school, all the clubs and all the activities, nothing interested me," she admits. "And this [volunteering] seemed to be something that I could really put all of my energy into and really get involved with, enjoy, and not sit back and say, this is boring, we're not doing anything, we're not accomplishing anything." Even though volunteering is not the way she spends most of her time, it convinces her that even ordinary people can make a difference. As she explains, "I figured that if I could find something that was not restricted by the school and wasn't run by people at the school, then I could actually do something and not be bored."

The danger of focusing too much on the exotica of volunteering is that it ironically makes caring into an escape from the routine responsibilities of everyday life. The caregiver then becomes like one of writer Christina Garcia's characters who "stayed on the fringe of life because it was . . . more dignified there."[10] The caregiver also may use the homeless or other needy people in order to escape the boredom of ordinary life. Tucker Aims offered evidence of this danger as he talked about his reasons for participating recently in a Habitat for Humanity project: "To be perfectly honest, the main reason I chose Habitat For Humanity was less to help people and more so I could get to go down and see what it was like down there."

Making a Difference

Nearly all the young people we talked to say they especially cherished the feeling that they were able to make some difference in the lives of the people they were helping. When asked whether his feelings about himself had changed in any way, for example, Rafe Ramirez responded, "Realizing that I can make a difference." Then, referring to the boys on his soccer team, he added: "They do listen to me, and I can actually get through to them. It gives you a little bit of self-confidence to realize that you can make a little bit of a difference."

But why does "making a difference" make any difference? Why is it important? In our society it is easy to feel that nobody makes a difference. Some days as I sit at my desk writing, for example, I ask myself whether it would make any difference to anyone if the book on which I am working was never published. Or for that matter, whether it would make any difference at all if there were one less sociologist in the world. It is easy to answer no, because there are thousands of people who could readily step in and take my place. Our institutions make this possible. Each of us performs rather limited, specialized tasks, and many other people besides ourselves have been trained to do these them. There is also a great deal of redundancy in our institutions. Furthermore, the world would get by without some of these tasks being performed at all. Others would readily be taken over by competing institutions. Nonetheless, we all are trained to believe that our worth is contingent on what we accomplish. Even though we may not make much of a difference, we believe that we should make a difference.

If it is easy for adults to have these frustrations, young people are even more likely to have them. An adult may at least have the training to make a difference in people's lives—say, by performing surgery to save a patient's life or by defending someone in court—but someone who has not yet received specialized training is less likely to feel that he or she can make a difference. Adults may also believe that they make a difference because of the responsibilities they have shouldered. For example, a sociologist may make no difference to the wider world, but if she quit his job, her family would certainly feel the difference when it came time to pay the bills. Young people without such responsibilities may be more inclined to feel that they truly make no difference to anyone. Their parents could get by without them. Their teachers may compliment them on getting good grades, and yet it may make no real difference whether they do or not.

The value of caring is that the effects of one's behavior can at least be seen directly in the activities of another person. A homeless person takes a plate of food and smiles. A nine-year-old goes into the soccer game, kicks the ball to a teammate who scores a goal, and later says to the coach, "Did you see me? I did just what you told me to do!" A friend sits down at the lunch table and says that she has more respect and understanding for the handicapped students you are working with. In each case, the "difference" may be small, but it does reinforce the caregiver's self-confidence. Making a difference is a way of affirming that the individual person matters.

Rachel Farb demonstrated the significance of feeling that one is actually making a difference when she described her volunteer work with the blind. "I think I've just gained a lot more courage for myself," she remarked. "I never really thought that I could accomplish anything. I always did well in school, but I never strived to do anything important and [the volunteer work] made me feel really important and it made me feel useful." She said it has helped her a lot just to know that the students with whom she is working respect her. "They respect me for giving my time and not caring what everyone else might think about blind people and just giving myself and spending time with them and just enjoying their company."

Jackie White also shows how doing a little can make a big difference, even in the wider world. "One of the most exciting things has been the peace accords which were signed in El Salvador after years and years and years of work," she observes. "I participated in this work personally and so many people who were in it for years and so many Salvadorans had died for it." She remembers how excited she was when she heard the news: "I was walking along with a group of friends from CISPES and Sister Cities. All of a sudden someone stopped us. Like, oh my God. I thought it was something lying on the ground they were talking about. It turned out I looked up at the newspaper box and the first article was 'Salvadorans Agree to Halt Civil War.' It was just like, wow! Oh, my God!"

Good Feelings and Bad Feelings

Finally, we must return to the good feelings of which Tanika Lane and others spoke. These are, as I have pointed out, quite common and are among the most cherished aspects of volunteering for most young people. Good feelings are pleasurable, and although they are ephemeral, they nevertheless are small confirmations of the fact that one is a good person.

I want to emphasize that good feelings must be kept in perspective. Volunteering is by no means the only way in which young people can get good feelings. Nor are these feelings necessarily conducive to becoming firmly committed to caring activities. In our survey, the vast majority of teenagers said they get at least a fair amount of satisfaction from their schoolwork, from their leisure activities, from their families, and just from doing nice things for themselves. The fact that most of them also derive satisfaction from doing things for other people, therefore, is just an extra. Indeed, half those who get a great deal of satisfaction from doing things for others are already deriving this much satisfaction from several other sources; only one in seven is not.[11]

Moreover, the good feelings that come from helping others may not be any more special than those coming from other kinds of gratifying experiences.

When students were asked how good they thought they would feel under a variety of conditions, they were most likely to say they would feel very good if they received an A on a hard test and if they had been given $500 for their birthday. Only slightly lower on the good-feelings barometer were those associated with getting concert tickets for their favorite group or receiving a thank-you call from a friend they had helped. In comparison, the good feelings associated with other kinds of imagined helping behavior all were somewhat lower; for instance, from giving a dollar to a beggar, from helping clean up the park as part of a school project, from having spent an hour helping a handicapped child play ball, and even from having spent a week in Mexico helping the poor. It is perhaps significant, however, that the feelings imagined from the more serious kinds of helping behavior were somewhat more positive for those students who had actually spent a lot of time volunteering than for those who had not.[12] In other words, active volunteers may find it more personally rewarding to help others, or having helped others, these volunteers may know better that it does feel good. In any case, volunteering is a source of gratification for many young people who become involved in it. Indeed, among all volunteers in the survey, 54 percent listed personal satisfaction as one of the very important benefits they had received—and this percentage was higher than for nearly any of the other benefits mentioned.[13]

One of the most obvious sources of good feelings is what might be called simply the joy of giving. Caregivers feel happy because they have been able to help someone specifically and to see the personal consequences of their help. For example, Jim Grayson sits for hours at a time with individual scouts teaching them how to tie knots or helping them earn a merit badge in cooking or use a compass. He reflects, "There's that feeling that somewhere you helped this kid on his way to either gaining his Eagle or that just in some way you've influenced this kid somehow, and hopefully for the better and that he'll be a better person later for it. Every kid that comes through there is touched somehow."

The joy of giving is a way of reminding oneself that role behavior is not all that matters. Quite often, the young people we talked to experienced this joy most forcefully when they stepped out of their roles—even as volunteers—and related to someone else on a purely personal level. Nikki Unger, for instance, says that working with underprivileged children gives her better feelings about herself than just doing her schoolwork, but she also emphasizes that it is being able to relate as a person—even when she is volunteering—that is most rewarding. "There was this little girl, and she just came and she sat on my lap and she wouldn't get off my lap. Everywhere she went, she took me by the hand with her. Either I made a big difference to her, or she just doesn't have a whole lot else going on in her life. But it really made me feel good." In fact, Nikki believes that just being accepted by someone else is the most rewarding part of her experience. "I didn't have to do hardly anything for them to love me, and they were receptive to me, and that made them so much more able to give love back to me. That's just a very good feeling to me."

But the joy of giving is also a way of remembering that one can still be human—and kind—even within the constraints of the institutions in which we live. Institutions teach us to play specialized roles, but they do not require us to play by the rules all the time. We can exhibit kindness in small ways to those around us. Indeed, having experienced the joy of giving, people are sometimes encouraged to seek out roles in which they can reproduce these feelings more regularly. Carl Bryant, the young man who gives away sweatsuits to the homeless, is one example. When he was in junior high, he remembers his family helping a poor family in the neighborhood. "Their shack burned down and she had kids; she had no husband. We ended up bringing things. There was just something involved in giving—that whole feeling. You know, when you get that initial reaction, like, 'You can't be doing this for me. How could you be doing this for me? Nobody's ever given me anything.' It was just a special feeling." Carl recalls his own reaction. "I needed this feeling. It was almost like a high, just the feeling of giving, the joy. So I said to my parents, what can we do? We ended up buying seventy hooded new sweatshirts from Hanes. And that Christmas, like two weeks before Christmas, we went around downtown in our station wagon, and we handed out sweatsuits to the homeless on the streets."

It is also important to recognize that even though good feelings are pleasurable, they are not the result simply of doing good deeds. Good feelings require us to have a framework in which to make sense of them. Indeed, the same experience can be part of the joy of giving for one person and simply a duty for another person. Carl Bryant, for instance, makes an interesting admission when he explains how he responds to some of the recipients who ask him why he is doing this. He tells them, "I am a Christian and I believe in the joy of giving." And when pushed to explain why he likes helping others, he says, "I don't know, it's just something that makes you tingle inside, it's something that makes you feel like you made a difference. You've impacted them, and as a Christian that's what we're on the earth to do. That's what I believe we're on the earth to do is to help other people who are less fortunate and be a part of their lives." In other words, he has a religious framework—and is involved in a church—that helps him define the experience of giving as one of pleasure.

Having a framework that emphasizes the joy of caring also makes it possible to overlook some of the less pleasurable aspects of caring. As another student observed in talking about his volunteer work with the handicapped: "It's hard to get along with people who are drooling and can't eat or can't sit up straight or can't talk or can't sing or are ugly and wearing glasses that you can't see through. There are all sorts of aversions, but you have to look through all that. And part of the joy is that you can look through all that."

Without a framework for translating the temporary joys of giving into deeper meanings, these joys may actually diminish with time. Especially when volunteering is motivated by a quest for exotic experiences, the routine is likely to catch up with one sooner or later and turn one's activities into less exciting adventures. The "helper high" that Jason McKendrick and his friends experience at Pearl's Kitchen is an example. Jason recalls a time when he no longer experienced this feeling: "It stopped. Things got to be too much of a job instead of enjoyment, and I started to take things too seriously. I had to work on clockwork. I had to get things done, and it wasn't as enjoyable for me." He says that the good feelings didn't come back until he was able to lighten up, view the activity less as a job, and remember the reasons he had gotten involved in the first place.

Thus we come again to the importance of stories, role models, and frameworks that can help us interpret our experiences as sources of good feelings. In the family, these experiences may seem natural—so natural in fact that we take them for granted. Laughter, happiness, and love may be expected. In the institutions where we work, shop, or vote, however, such experiences may seem less common, compared with norms that tell us to be rational, competitive, self-interested, and indifferent to the needs of others. Having stories to tell ourselves about the joy of giving and having ways of accounting for our caring behavior are important if such behavior is to be part of these institutions.

Patti Evans, for instance, finds that she sometimes gets bogged down in the routine of working with the handicapped, but when she does, she reminds herself of some small episode that made her feel good. "You know, when you go in, if you're having a bad day, Gordon has a tendency to go 'whooo!' I was feeling really down. The minute I walked in, Gordon did that. And it just makes you feel so good because these kids are usually very happy."

It is also important for the joy of giving to be supplemented by other sources of good feelings, especially those that come from being part of a warm, supportive community. When fellow volunteers (or coworkers) become close friends, two things happen. One is that some of the primordial caring that was experienced in the family is carried into the structured roles one plays outside the family, and for this reason, it may be possible to practice the elementary kindness one learned as a child, even though the settings are now different. The other is that one's identity is reshaped by the intimate interaction with these friends, and through this process, more of the person becomes invested in the new roles that he or she plays. People learn that they can trust others and rely on them for help.

Rafe Ramirez offers a rather striking example of finding community through volunteer work. An only child, he lives with his parents in a trailer located about ten miles from the town in which he attends high school. Other than the family's three dogs, Rafe has few companions. Even the nearest neighbors are a mile away. What coaching soccer has given to him is a surrogate family. The head coach who enlisted him has become as close to him as his own father. The boys he coaches are like little brothers. They look up to him and listen to what he tells them. After practice and on weekends Rafe sometimes hangs out with the other volunteer coaches his own age. When asked what he has most enjoyed about coaching, he brushes off the question by saying he just has fun with it. But after further reflection, especially about the long hours and how little time he has for himself, he acknowledges that one of the most rewarding parts of the work has been getting to know the parents. They talk to him about how their son or daughter is doing, comment on the games, and say hello if they happen to see him on the street. It makes him feel anchored, like a legitimate member of the community. Referring to the coaches and parents he has gotten to know during the past three years, he says, "They're always there for me. Whenever I need some help with something, they're always there, giving a helping hand."[14]

There is reason to worry, of course, that the quest for good feelings is being emphasized too much in volunteer and community service programs. If people are being encouraged to help others simply as a technique for boosting their own quotients of good feelings, the spirit of altruism, of service, and of being truly concerned about the needs of others is likely to be compromised. It is perhaps reassuring, therefore, that most of the young people we talked to insisted that they experienced good feelings after the fact but that the desire for such feelings had not been the reason they decided to volunteer in the first place.

Our considerations of caring in relation to the demands of institutional life also help us understand that there is a genuine need for good feelings in our society. In most of our institutions, we are constantly told we should do things better; we are taught to compete; we hear criticisms everywhere; and we internalize that criticism. So it is nice to do something that elicits a smile and an appreciative word from someone else. Sid Gerson, for instance, confesses, "I find myself criticizing myself for so many things, perhaps for a word I said or didn't say, for a thing I did or didn't do, for a way I wrote something. I'm ultra-critical of myself. That leads to a lot of my downfalls. If I'm writing an essay in class, I'll be so concerned with everything I say, with how I present whatever I'm writing about that I will spend so much time thinking and so little time writing. I don't like that at all." For him, then, it was just nice to spend time on Sundays talking with his elderly friend who appreciated his being there and who did not criticize him. It was also nice, eventually, to receive awards from the Fund for New Jersey and from Senator Bill Bradley for his service work.

The following dialogue regarding Jim Grayson is revealing, too. He is a perfectionist who likes to make As and do well in sports and be known as a helpful person as well. But he easily becomes depressed, and he realizes it has to do with wanting to come in first on things. But Jim also hints at more diffuse sources of anxiety, and he talks about invidious comparisons between himself and a brother who seems to have more drive than he does.

Q: Do you get depressed sometimes?

A: Occasionally.

Q: Why?

A: The worst part about it is I don't always know why. I know that I shouldn't eat much chocolate, because I know that does it to me. I found that out. But I don't really know why. Some different things will get to me.

Q: What things depress you?

A: I don't even know exactly. I really don't. I don't know all the time what is de pressing me. I hate coming in behind, really.

Q: Behind in what?

A: Anything. Like you start losing in all these different things. Losing, for the lack of a better word, losing stinks.

Q: You mean losing in sports, or what?

A: Losing in just about anything. I mean, sometimes it's all right.

Q: Losing's one thing, but getting behind is another. What kinds of things would you be behind in?

A: See, I don't really know.

Q: Schoolwork?

A: No, I stay pretty much ahead there. I'm a procrastinator. I don't like that so much. All too often I'll say, 'Well, I'll do it later.' And usually I'll get it done. I wish I could say— like my brother's great at it. He goes, 'I'll sit down, I'll do this now.' My brother just has like this drive, and he just does it.

Although it is easy to attribute such feelings to personalities or to adolescent hormones, they also are a product of the institutional fabric of contemporary life. Institutional goals are purposefully vague, making it difficult to know whether a person is doing the right things to achieve them. In principle, rewards are based on how well we perform, but there is always enough slippage in the ways in which rewards are allocated that individuals are unsure what to do and left feeling that more should have been done. Moreover, it is in the nature of complex institutions, as I have suggested, to create insufficient selves—people who play specialized and fragmented roles rather than those who have a strong and well-integrated sense of who they are. This, too, makes it hard for us to give ourselves good messages.

The good feelings we receive from making a tangible contribution to another person's life are thus quite rewarding. Listen to what Nikki Unger says about the volunteer work she has been doing with children: "It made me feel good. I always worry. I'm a very sensitive person, and I always worry—in a bad sense—when somebody thinks bad or good of me. But I know I have been successful in creating something for these children." She suffers from precisely the kinds of uncertainties I have just mentioned. She says, for instance, that her biggest fear is "messing up" and not achieving some of the goals that have been set before her. As a role player who knows she will have to fill a specialized niche in society, she worries whether she is pursuing the right goals and whether she will be able to fill this niche adequately and in a way that is personally gratifying. Her volunteer work thus gives her good feelings because it boosts her confidence. It is a trial balloon, so to speak, that reduces her anxieties about the future. "It made me feel like, yeah, this is something I want to do. Look, I was already able to do something, and maybe I can continue and do what I want to do and be successful."

The good feelings that come from volunteer work are, nevertheless, tempered in most cases by bad feelings that derive from the same source. Young people may also feel sad or depressed as a result of their volunteering. After discussing how pleasing it is to experience a "helper high," for example, Jason McKendrick went on to observe, "Then you start to feel bad because we are coming back to the suburbs. We're going back to our houses, and we're going to go get our food and stuff like that. You start to realize how great your life is compared to some people, and you start to think about it a lot—a lot." Tucker Aims has been coming to terms with grief lately, too. By working with other young people, he has come to realize that some of them die, which has made him think harder about his own life. Sina Mesnar made a similar observation. Getting to know homeless people, he says, has made him more aware of "just how precarious our lives are."

Sherry Hicks has been affected more than most teenagers have. She says it really depresses her to think about young people dying before they have a chance to make a difference in the world. She is not fantasizing: Nine of her friends have died in the past year. Jackie White is another student who has been affected more than most. "I've lost a lot of my innocence," she says. "I've heard torture stories since I was nine years old, and really nothing surprises me any more. Nothing shocks me per se. But occasionally my anger just comes out."

These negative, painful, sorrowful feelings cannot, of course, be avoided. They raise our level of awareness about the role of institutions in our lives, by showing us that institutions are inevitably limited. We will die. We may experience illness or loneliness or poverty. And even if we do not, we know that many others will. Thus, these experiences bolster our resolve to strengthen our institutions and to fill in the gaps with personal deeds of kindness. As Rachel Farb notes, "I just realize the need to be ready for whatever life brings my way."

10

Careers of Service: The Preservation of Caring

> People not only lose faith in their talents and their dreams or values; some simply tire of them.
>
> Edward Hoagland, *Heart's Desire*

How does volunteering influence the future? Does it encourage young people to think more imaginatively about opportunities for service? Or after a brief courtship with their talents and their dreams, do they simply tire of them?

Kindness can become a part of the routine behavior that occupies our attention in the adult world only if we can imagine how to be kind in these roles. We have to imagine ourselves visiting a sick coworker in the hospital, for example, before we are ever likely to do it. We have to imagine that we could actually save someone's life by giving him or her cardiopulmonary resuscitation—or imagine that we could take part in a protest march, do lobbying on behalf of the environment, or work as a teacher or a nurse.

Young people are the proverbial dreamers, the idealists who imagine living in a better world. Yet as we have seen, they are also intensely realistic. They know that caring for the needy can be hard work and that the "helper highs" that make one feel good may be temporary. They also know that caring requires personal strength, knowledge, and learning specialized skills—and that only so much time is available, much of which must be spent making good grades, getting into the right college, preparing for a career, and pursuing that career. The question remains, then: Does volunteering spark their imagination? And if it does, what kinds of service can they imagine?

Jason McKendrick drives home the importance of asking these questions. Watching him feed the homeless at Pearl's Kitchen, we might imagine him continuing to care for the needy in this capacity for the next ten or twenty years. But we know he probably will not. He will go away to college, become preoccupied with his courses, perhaps embark on a career that requires graduate work or an internship, and gradually take on responsibilities, such as buying a house or supporting his family, that leave him little time to be concerned about the homeless. Reflecting on his future, he says, in fact, that he isn't likely to spend much time helping others because "I need to establish my own ground first." He adds: "I do this stuff on my extra time, and I make time for it because I love to do it. But I can't see myself like totally working for other people. I believe that I am a person, too, so I have to work on myself too." But what does this mean? Is Jason McKendrick unlikely to be kind in any of the other roles he plays? Or is his volunteering at Pearl's giving him ideas about other ways in which to be kind?

I suggest that volunteering does, indeed, spark the imagination of young people, encouraging them to think more broadly about ways to be kind in the years ahead. We can see this even in survey evidence, according to which young people who are currently involved in volunteering are significantly more likely than other young people to say they can imagine themselves doing other kinds of service.[1] But we must also listen closely to what young people say about these possibilities. We must not think that doing one kind of volunteer work—even quite intensely—necessarily broadens young people's horizons to include all kinds of service or that they will be inspired to devote themselves full time to help the needy or to solve social problems. Young people learn quickly to select the kinds of services they can perform, and they pick up implicit messages about how to care that may not have been intended by those who guide their volunteer experiences. At most, their horizons are broadened in small ways. To understand this broadening, we must consider what they say about various kinds of hypothetical service, as both volunteers and possible careers.

Playing Limited Roles

Probably the most fundamental lesson young people learn from doing volunteer work is that one can show kindness by playing limited roles. In contrast with the parental love that young people either experience or want to experience, they learn that it is possible to care without caring unconditionally or without making a long-term, twenty-four-hour-a-day commitment. They can care for the homeless by being there one evening a week. They can help handicapped students without knowing very much about their personal lives. They can even step out of their roles, driving the extra mile to give away a sweatsuit, but only on designated occasions.

It is clear from the ways in which young people talk about other, imaginary kinds of caring that they learn well the lesson of playing limited roles. For example, when asked whether she could imagine herself working with the homeless, a young woman who tutors at her high school confessed, "I could imagine myself doing that, but not on a regular basis. I don't think I could be around that all the time. Just because that's like a depressing environment, and stuff like that turns me off. Being in unhappy places turns me off." Similarly, a young man who also tutors said he wished he could imagine himself working with the handicapped because he knows they could use his help, but he admits he isn't likely to become involved "because I would probably—I would probably throw up!"[2]

Another way in which young people convey their conviction that caring should be offered on a limited basis is in their comments about how best to enlist others in service activities. Although it is not uncommon to hear arguments about good feelings and some of the other benefits we considered in the last chapter, the most prominent theme is emphasizing that caring won't take much of one's time. Consider how Rafe Ramirez says he would enlist people to help at a local soup kitchen. "Show the people that it's not going to take much of their time; it won't hurt them if they give this one Saturday or whatever out of the many Saturdays that they have. It's not that big of a deal. Show them that it's not that much time that they're donating. You've got plenty of time. It's only one day. That's the way I look at it. It's one day. Why not? You have no reason not to. It's not going to cramp your lifestyle in any way. It's one Saturday. You've got plenty of them. Whatever you wanted to do that Saturday, postpone it till the next Saturday. You've got plenty of time."

It is also clear that one of the reasons for playing limited roles is that one must develop specialized skills. We heard this repeatedly as young people talked about administering cardiopulmonary resuscitation (CPR). Many of them recognized that it would be valuable to be able to help someone in this way. For example, one student exclaimed, "If I knew CPR, I don't even think I would think about it. You can save a life!" And this desire to help seemed to be quite prevalent: In the survey, for instance, 68 percent of all teens said they could imagine themselves giving mouth-to-mouth resuscitation. But judging from the more extensive remarks of young people we talked to personally, many were reluctant to say they would try to help in this way because they did not have the specialized training they thought they needed. For example, Rafe Ramirez says he could not imagine himself giving someone mouth-to-mouth resuscitation because he had not taken a course in CPR. He fears he would probably wind up doing more harm than good because he is not qualified. The value of specialized skills was also evident from the comments of those who had received training in CPR. For instance, Jim Grayson, the young man who serves as a volunteer counselor at scout camp, says he could imagine giving CPR because "I earned the certification badge and worked on Rescue Annie for a while—she's the dummy, you blow in her face." A young woman who volunteered for Red Cross made a similar comment: "Yes, I can imagine doing that, because I've been trained doing CPR and basic first aid. I can see myself, I've practiced on a dummy, and if I ever saw anybody go down I would be willing to help, because I know the skill."

Administering CPR was not the only kind of caring that young people responded to in terms of the need for specialized skills. Many of them said they could imagine tutoring, for example, because they knew a particular body of knowledge—math, English, history—and felt they could help others learn it. Some felt that they could volunteer in areas of health care because they knew things about pregnancy, contraception, or AIDS. Others felt they could not serve as a volunteer in a number of areas because they did not have the requisite skills. For instance, young people were about evenly divided as to imagining themselves cleaning up a polluted beach (46 percent in the survey said they could imagine doing this), and those who responded favorably did so because it seemed like a nontechnical task, whereas those who responded negatively often stressed the need for special expertise. As one student explained, "I wouldn't have the skills to do a lot of the things that the people were doing. A lot of times when they go out there, they're specialized people that are cleaning these beaches up and the animals and stuff."

Besides the need for specialized skills, young people also learn that playing a limited role requires a certain level of self-confidence. Not much may be needed because, as we have seen, institutions do so much for us that we can get by most of the time being fairly weak. Young people learn, however, that in the course of doing volunteer work, their self-confidence increases. Thus, they feel more confident in imagining themselves doing other kinds of service work as well. They feel this way not because they already have the appropriate skills but because they can imagine that playing the role will help them develop the necessary skills. Megan Wyse, for example, emphasizes the confidence that she has gained from being involved in a few volunteer activities: "I think you have to be kind of confident to do something like that. I have a lot of friends that are afraid, just afraid to go out to a shelter, afraid to go to the bad neighborhoods, afraid to be exposed to those sorts of things."

Part of the implicit logic of playing a limited role is that one thing will lead to another. Young people describe their motives by telling stories emphasizing strings of events. As they imagine other kinds of service, it helps them to be able to think that such strings will continue to be present.

Jackie White illustrates this point when she explains that her interests are currently changing. Her work in El Salvador sensitized her to problems of oppression and injustice, but now that the peace accord has been signed in El Salvador, she feels it is time to move on to other things. In the process, her interests in equality, human rights, and social justice are leading her step by step. For the past several months, she has been applying these ideas to issues focusing on gender. She organized a discussion group among the students at her high school and also something called International Women's Day that sponsors workshops on issues of gender equality. She says she is thinking about turning next to organizing something similar for multicultural awareness.

Playing limited roles is legitimate because one can thus be realistic about one's own needs and interests. One of the most important needs of potential caregivers is simply feeling safe. Several young people registered this concern in talking about why they would feel uncomfortable administering mouth-to-mouth resuscitation. Tanika Lane, for example, confessed, "If they were going to die, I would, but if you just ask me that right now, I would say no. Putting my mouth on somebody else's, I just don't like that." Personal safety was also an important consideration to many of the young people we talked to about helping the homeless or working at soup kitchens. Although 64 percent of teens nationally said they would be willing to do this, those who had never tried it were often candid in expressing their fears when we talked with them personally. As one young man admitted, "I'd be too fearful for what might happen to me."

Another need that most volunteers want to fulfill is their desire to feel appreciated. Many of the young people we talked to (75 percent in the national survey) said they could imagine helping with the Special Olympics for this reason. As one student explained, "I love kids. Handicapped or not, I love kids. A Saturday is one day, and that's not a lot for me to give up. A sports event for handicapped kids, they're going to go and they're going to have a really great time. I might as well help out. I might as well be a part of that. I love kids, and I love happy kids more." Rafe Ramirez made a similar observation: "It's fun because you see them, and that really makes them happy to be doing things like that. I can see myself doing that."

In addition, playing a limited role means that one is able to choose, just as one chooses courses, churches, sneakers, or friends. "What interests me?" is an essential question. A young woman who had devoted many hours to helping the homeless, for example, admitted that she could not imagine herself cleaning a beach. "I'm just not a very environmental kind of person," she explained.

Another student who had never worked with the homeless ventured that she probably could do that because "I enjoy doing things like that." A lot of other things, she said, simply didn't interest her. Still another student showed how interests and limited roles go hand in hand. Asked whether she could see herself lobbying on behalf of some cause, she said she could if it were just for a day now and then, but beyond that, she said, "No, I think it would really bore me if I had to do it every single day. That's my problem. I get bored very easily. I have a very short attention span."

For teachers, clergy, and other administrators who may be interested in motivating young people to participate in community service programs, one of the clearest implications of these comments is that service projects must be limited in terms of commitment, and they must be oriented toward the real worlds in which young people already live. As we have seen, few teenagers spend more than an hour a week doing volunteer work, and most serve through their schools or some other community organization in which they are already involved. These activities do help young people to imagine that they can serve in other ways, but mostly these are activities that extend naturally from service already performed.

National Service

The feeling that one should be able to offer care in limited ways and at relatively little cost to oneself is a major consideration whenever young people are asked to think about national service. We consider the pros and cons of various community service programs more fully in Chapter 11; here we shall just say that young people have mixed feelings about national service—or any other full-time program of service—simply because they want to limit the amount of time they devote to caring activities.

In surveys, young people are divided between those who largely favor the idea of national service and those who do not. Gallup surveys conducted over the past fifteen years, for example, find that between 47 percent and 62 percent of teenagers favor "requiring all young men to give one year of service to the nation," and between 38 percent and 56 percent say they favor such service for young women.[3] The Independent Sector survey of teenagers showed that 44 percent could imagine spending a year doing community service after high school or college.

Those with whom we talked favored national service mainly because it would offer a way of paying for college. A young woman who was in the midst of deciding on colleges put the matter clearly when she responded, "Well, if that idea was implemented now, it would make college a lot easier for me. It's certainly another opportunity to raise money for college. I think it would be a good way to teach people the value of service without forcing it. I like the idea, personally. But I think, as opposed to it being a sheer year of service, it could be more a culmination of hours of service or the big picture as opposed to saying, 'You go work in such and such area for a year.'"

When asked whether they themselves would participate in a national service program, however, most of the young people we talked to admitted they would not. The most common reason was that they needed to spend their time doing things that would develop the other roles they wished to play—especially their careers. For example, Rafe Ramirez said he would not be willing to spend a year of his life doing community service because he could not see "taking that much time in a lump sum away from myself to do other things." He added, "I just can't see myself giving that much." A young woman who expressed similar doubts admitted, "I guess I'm a greedy person. I want so much for myself as far as like monetary things go that I don't think I could do that."

Even students who appeared to be motivated more by altruism than by selfish interests were reluctant to contemplate spending a year doing community service. They recognized that they could help clean parks, refurbish old houses, or perform other useful tasks. They had, however, learned that the best way to serve others was by truly developing specialized skills. As a young man who aspired to serve others by becoming an orthodonist remarked, "The course my life is following right now doesn't make it possible for me to spend a year doing community service because I need to get through school, college, possibly medical school, and get established in a career. I'll be able to help humanity a lot better once I have done those things."

From Caring to Social Protest

Much of what I have said about limited roles applies equally well to social protest—trying to make the world better by participating in marches or reform movements or working in other ways for social justice or to combat oppression—as to the more ameliorative ways of helping people or working with the needy that we have been considering. Social protest can also be a limited engagement taking only a few hours a week. Indeed, it may not even require as much emotional investment in the needs of other people, especially if it consists mostly of administrative work or tasks such as writing letters or making posters. There is another dimension to social protest, however, that forces many young people to consider it differently from other acts of kindness.

This is the desire to get along, to be liked, and to be tolerant and accepting of other people. These qualities help us adapt to and to play roles in complex situations. Rafe Ramirez, for example, explains that he is "not really big on protests" because he believes that one should not be critical of the way other people live or try to change their minds. "I'm more of a 'you want to believe it, believe it' person," he says. "I'll believe what I want to believe, but don't tell me what to believe. If you want to believe that, that's fine. I'm not going to say anything to you. And if I want to believe what I want to believe, it's OK as long as you don't say anything to me. Just let bygones be bygones. But I wouldn't protest. It would have to be a real extreme case for me to be that into it. I just don't see myself out there on the picket line." Another student who was quite interested in social problems said simply that she objected to protests because they were, in her view, "extremism."

Jason McKendrick adds another consideration in thinking about social protests. He says he is willing to speak out about problems of social justice because he feels compelled to be true to his own convictions: "I believe what I believe." But he also admits he would never do anything on behalf of these convictions that would get him arrested. "If it's disruptive to society, I'm not going to do it," he states flatly. The same sentiment was echoed by a student who admitted, "When it becomes unlawful and causes destruction or enough to have yourself thrown in jail, I don't see there's any point in it."

Another problem with social protest is that young people fear it will require too much of them, particularly if it puts them in jeopardy with the law. Stepping outside the law is perceived to be a major hurdle by many middle-class youth. To break the law means to be placed in a different world, to be at personal risk, and to be in danger of compromising some of the opportunities they want to keep open for themselves. Thus, young people say they admire someone like Gandhi or Dr. Martin Luther King Jr. for being willing to protest against injustice but are unsure whether they themselves have the personal courage to follow their example. As one student explained, "I don't know if I'm strong enough for a jail situation. If it was a one-day thing where I was bailed out immediately, that's one thing. But if I was going to be doing time for a period of time, I don't know if I'm strong enough to handle that form of incarceration." Another said simply, "No, I wouldn't want to have a record."

Just because young people are reluctant to engage in social protests does not mean, of course, that they are unaware of the need to work for political change. As we shall see in the next chapter, many young people have been inspired by their volunteer work to recognize more clearly the role of government. For volunteer activities to stimulate an interest in social protest, though, there needs to be some direct exposure to people who have engaged in protest. Such persons can then serve as role models and can help explain when and under what conditions protest might be appropriate.

The best example among the teenagers we talked to was provided by Chandra Lyons, whom we met briefly in Chapter 3. She recalls skipping school one day with the other members of her social action club to participate in a protest march for a man who had been sentenced to death for a crime for which he was possibly being framed. "His name was Mumia Abu Jamal. We tried to be responsible about it and tell the teachers we were going to do something because we believed in it, and we would not be in school the next day. We ended up having to do a forum on it, on the death penalty, and on his case. It happened on the spur of the moment. We were in the diner and one of our friends from another school said, 'Oh, we're going to a protest tomorrow on this guy.' It was something I was familiar with. David Schwartz, this guy, he seems to come up a lot. He's a lawyer, and he's been working on the case of Omar, who happens to be the boyfriend of the woman who got me set up at the Community Center, and he too has been framed and is on death row and has been doing a lot of work out there. I knew this wasn't just a hoax, and that it had happened that a whole bunch of people who were active in the black community had been framed and were put away just because they were raising their voice. So we went down there and walked in the freezing weather for him shouting 'Free Mumia!'" Having had this experience, Chandra says she would be much more likely to engage in a protest again. She feels she could do so responsibly and without engaging in the dangerous or extremist behavior that other teenagers associate with protests.

The Importance of Information

If we used one word to describe what is most likely to encourage young people to take part in volunteer service in the future, it would be information. It would be easy to dismiss the need for information as self-evident. Yet it was the one thing that came through time and time again as young people talked with us about what they could—or could not—imagine doing in the future to be of service to their communities.

Partly, information means, as we have seen, the need for specialized knowledge to perform certain kinds of service. Many of the young people who knew how to administer CPR had learned it in conjunction with previous volunteer service, such as scouting or working for the Red Cross. Many other kinds of specialized knowledge were learned in the same way. Jason McKendrick, for example, knew all about working with community organizations to get the help needed to keep the van running regularly to Pearl's Kitchen. Amy Stone learned the same things in organizing her AIDS rally. What she knew about AIDS was also a body of knowledge that she felt compelled to use in subsequent volunteer efforts.

When they have the requisite information, young people are less fearful of new situations. Sid Gerson presented an example of this function of information when asked how he would feel about working with AIDS patients: "I'm not frightened of those with AIDS," he says. "I've been well informed about the transmission of the virus. If I take the necessary precautions, I see that I will not be at risk. Therefore, helping them will not put me in such a dangerous position, assuming that I'm following the precautions. Yes, I can see myself doing such a thing."

Information also means personal contacts. These are important because young people recognize that involvement doesn't just happen; it depends on one thing leading to another. This, in fact, is one of the clearest ways in which volunteering opens new horizons: It does so by exposing teenagers to other young people—and to older adults—who give them new ideas about opportunities for service.

Jill Daugherty offered the following example when explaining why she could imagine herself working with AIDS patients: "Because a friend of ours works in Washington, D.C., and he runs an AIDS clinic. Next year, I'm going to be in community service at my school, and I'm going to work with a program called MANA. You go and you feed AIDS patients who can't get out of their homes anymore and who are dying. We have a lot of friends who aren't HIV positive, but who are gay and who have loved many people who have died. I'd like to work for rights for AIDS patients." Another illustration was given by a young man who acknowledged that full-time community service was on his mind because of a fellow volunteer (a year older) who was seriously considering joining the Peace Corps. "I've talked to a guy, and the guy tried to talk me into it. We had talked about joining the Peace Corps after college or something general like that." A similar example was given by a young woman who had gone to a citizenship forum in Washington, D.C., with her Girl Scout troop. As a result of this experience, she said she could envision herself doing volunteer work as a lobbyist. Many of the examples we discussed earlier in talking about role models fit this pattern as well.

At the most fundamental level, information is needed because kindness in the real world does, indeed, consist of playing specialized roles. We recognize that doing volunteer work depends on shopping, shopping for just the right ways in which to serve. And like other kinds of shopping, we rely on information from friends, newspapers, television, advertisers, and other large organizations to tell us what our options are.

Of all the students we talked to, Zia Hillier probably best showed this penchant for shopping. Over the past two years, we recall, she had been involved in at least fifteen different volunteer activities. As she reflected on her experiences, she said she became involved in so many just as a way to see which ones she would enjoy most. In the process, she was able to be of help in a number of ways, yet she also found herself becoming bored and dropping out. For her, like so many other young people, it was important to have plenty of information to spark her imagination and to keep volunteering interesting. She knew she could never be like Mother Teresa, devoting her entire life to the poor. As Zia reflected on her own future, she knew she would want to spend a couple of hours a day figure skating and that it would take a lot of time to do well at Harvard. But volunteer work was something she could still do because she was plugged into an information system that allowed her to serve in limited ways.

In all these ways, information provides a bridge between simply wanting to be helpful and actually putting that desire into practice. Having been extensively involved in volunteer work for a number of years, Jackie White admitted that she still found it difficult to "translate idealism into daily life." She said it was easier in many cases to be concerned about social problems when they were far away than when they were staring her in the face. Yet the main result of her volunteer work was to force her to think about all sorts of other needs and to decide which ones might be most compatible with her particular talents. "I've thought a lot about doing anti-AIDS work, doing AIDS education and maybe condom distribution," she says. She has also thought about legislative work she could do on behalf of the homeless, and she has considered ways in which she could work to help people stay off drugs and alcohol. She wants to avoid tokenism and prefers activities that use the political skills she learned while working for peace in Central America. Volunteering has been a way of keeping her options open and also of reminding her that she can actually make a difference by focusing on a few activities at a time.

As this example also demonstrates, however, information consists of new knowledge about ourselves and our identity. We learn not only how to scout out the environment for opportunities to serve but also how to reflect on our own capacities to serve. When we volunteer, we learn to be helpful and kind. Volunteering demonstrates, as we have seen in previous chapters, that a person can make a small difference in someone else's life—and perhaps even help make the world a better place. One is thus able to carry this identity into new situations and, indeed, to seek out new situations in which to be helpful and kind. More than anything else, this change in personal identity is what it takes to pursue kindness in new situations.[4]

Experimenting with Careers

The need for information—about opportunities and about oneself—is also the key to understanding how volunteering influences young people's ideas about careers. Being motivated to pursue a career in the helping professions is perhaps one of the most powerful ways in which volunteer work can shape the future. Subsequent involvement in volunteer work itself may consist of no more than a few hours a week, whereas a career will constitute a much greater investment of time and energy. There are many examples, in fact, of young people trying something out as volunteers, finding they enjoy it, and then seeking out a career in which they can repeat their experiences. Judging from what young people themselves say about their experiences, however, the more likely sequence is that they already have several options in mind, seek out volunteer work as a way of exploring these options, and then use the information gained in guiding their subsequent thinking. Volunteering is thus important as a source of new information.

Ginny O'Brien shows how volunteering can help supply information about possible careers. She lives in one of those communities you zip right through, probably on your way to the mall, not even knowing it is there. Surrounded by trees, cut off from through-traffic by small streets and cul-de-sacs, it sits there, a quiet monument to the 1950s. That was when families with small children started escaping to the burbs, flocking to the modest Cape Cods and bungalows that developers were throwing up by the hundreds. It was where Ginny's grandparents came when her father was a boy and where her family has lived ever since. A senior now, she is looking forward to escaping, to going away for college, and to spending her life somewhere else. But she also knows how much this community has become a part of her.

Sitting cross-legged on her bed, she looks, talks, and dresses like any typical teenager, if there is such a thing. That is, she is her own person, wearing an outfit of her own creation—dark stockings, flannel shorts, paisley shirt, turtleneck, and blazer—that sets her off from everyone else. Her room, dominated by a four-drawer filing cabinet overflowing with papers and books, is distinctively hers as well. It exudes the same hectic pace and busy engagement with life that comes through in her speech. She plays the clarinet, goes canoeing and hiking when it's nice out, goes shopping when it's not, sings in the choir, runs around with her friends, and makes As and Bs in most of her subjects except calculus, which continues to defy all her efforts.

When Ginny was in the ninth grade, it occurred to her one day that it would be great to become a doctor. She had been in the hospital a couple of times and was impressed with what doctors did. Then again, it occurred to her that it might not be so much fun being one. Like most everyone she knew, she was ambivalent. "I decided that if I wanted to really be a doctor, I should see now what it was like and see whether I really want to dedicate eight years of my life to training for this." Her father had been a volunteer on the local rescue squad for as long as she could remember. The thought of volunteering had never appealed to her; in fact, she had always resented it when her father was away instead of being there with the family. But she realized that it would be a way to see whether medicine really interested her. So she talked her dad into letting her join as soon as she was sixteen.

Ginny joined a 120-hour training program to become an emergency medical technician, or EMT, the kind of person who makes runs with the rescue squad. She says she just wanted to see if she could handle "the blood and guts of it." The first time, she got busy with other things and dropped out, but the second time around she finished the course. She was a probationer for a while and then received her full EMT certification. Because she is still a minor, Ginny is not allowed to do a number of things, such as drive, work with AIDS victims, or go on a call by herself. But for the past year she has been able to participate as a regular member of the team. She puts in five to ten hours a week, depending on the number of calls. The work consists of responding whenever someone needs the rescue squad, administering basic first aid to the victims and keeping them quiet. She also spends time each month updating her certification, attending team meetings, and helping with fund-raisers.

The area that Ginny's squad covers is only about a mile on each side, but she has seen virtually every kind of person in the past year: the elderly, people with mental disabilities, physically handicapped veterans, the homeless, little children who have been hurt in accidents, women abused by their husbands and boyfriends, and drug and alcohol overdoses. One of the calls she remembers most clearly came in about seven o'clock one evening. "It was a summer evening," she recalls. "It was a local house, maybe three or four blocks away from here. The little girl had fallen off her bed and hurt her spleen. We took her to the hospital. She was in a tremendous amount of pain. She was really miserable. She had also gotten several lacerations on her face."

The little girl needed to be taken to the pediatric trauma unit at a larger hospital in a neighboring community, so the squad was asked to wait until she was ready. Ginny remembers that they asked her to help during the suturing. "I stabilized her and held her in a papoose board—it wraps the child in it to keep them secure and from ripping out things—I was comforting her and I started singing a Raffi song, which is a little children's song called 'Down By the Bay.' I started singing to her and the doctor recognized the song. And he started singing too. And we're singing this song, and she got so caught up in the song that she forgot about the pain for a few minutes.

"When she was on the way to the pediatric trauma unit, I continued singing to her. I gave her a teddy bear and blew up a balloon out of a glove. I made her a rabbit out of the glove. She was certainly not comfortable, but she forgot about her pain for a little while. And I knew that she was going to have a lot more pain when they took her in to be operated on. But we got a nice letter a couple days later saying the little girl remembered the funny person in the back of the ambulance who kept singing to her and wouldn't let her go to sleep, because we didn't want her to go to sleep so that we could evaluate her status. I like that because it was significant to me. And I knew that I was making a significant difference to her. There wasn't much we could do medically at that point. But I was helping her to feel better. So I was glad about that."

Not all of Ginny's experiences have been this pleasant. She has seen people in far worse agony, and she has seen people die. Nevertheless, she feels that what she is doing is well worth her time. One of her most memorable experiences, in fact, was with a man who died in her arms. He was an older man who was dying of emphysema. Ginny recounts: "He told me that his family no longer cared for him and he was basically stranded at a nursing home. It really shook me up. He asked for the last rites. He was very Catholic. But there was no priest in the rig or available at that time. I prayed with him on the way to the hospital. He grabbed my hand and he kind of gave it a tight squeeze and said, 'Thank you. No one has ever prayed for me before.' Whether I was mixing religion and public work, I don't know. But I know that I was there for him, and that made a big difference for me. There was nothing else we could do, but I was there for him. And he died knowing that someone else cared for him."

Ginny still is not sure whether she wants to become a doctor. She might go into physical therapy. She is also attracted to teaching. One thing she is sure of, however, is that she likes working with people. Her volunteer work has taught her that. "I really enjoy the people contact," she explains. "It's frustrating for me sometimes to see things and know that either I could do it better or that I don't have the medical resources at that point to do something, to make a difference. But I like the hands-on aspect of it anyway, just knowing that I'm there for the person."

Overall, at least judging from the survey, young people like Ginny O'Brien are not unusual. Of all those who had volunteered, 64 percent said they had benefited by learning about new career options, and 54 percent had developed some new career goals. Fully one-quarter said these had been among the most important of all the benefits they had derived from their volunteering.

People-Oriented Careers

If young people use volunteer work to gain information about possible careers, what careers—or career values—do they then come to favor? Our survey results demonstrate that volunteers do not simply register a higher-than-average interest in all the helping professions, nor are volunteers' career values fundamentally different from nonvolunteers'. In many ways, teenagers who do volunteer work have the same kinds of aspirations as do other young people—an important fact that deserves further consideration, but there are some significant differences. For example, young people who have spent a lot of time volunteering are more likely than other young people to maintain that it is essential to have opportunities in their career to help other people. The former are also more likely to say this about having a chance to work with the needy.[5] It is even more apparent when listening to them talk that many young people find their interests in working with other people reinforced by their volunteer experiences.

Megan Wyse is going to Barnard College next year and plans to major in psychology or social work. She explains her interests this way: "I love working with kids. I feel like they're at a stage of their life where I can make a difference and can affect the rest of their lives. Psychology, because the human mind just interests me, the way the mind works and the way the emotions work." Saying that she wants to make people happy, she adds: "You have to be content with yourself and you have to be psychologically sound to really be able to deal with society, to be happy, and to live a happy life. I think that's really the core of everything, because you can have close to nothing, but if you're happy with yourself and can deal with your own problems, then you're much safer than someone who's rich and who can't deal with anything." Asked how her volunteer work has shaped her goals, she explains, "I think I understand human mentality better, and I'm basically pretty good at working with people, and I can relate to children well." Having had a chance to develop these talents, she feels more confident that she will do well in her career.

In Sid Gerson's case, the Sunday afternoons he sat talking with his ninety-year-old pen pal in the nursing home awakened his interest in learning more about people. In fact, he says the most important consequence of this experience is his current plan to major in anthropology. "I was so interested in learning about things from other generations. I said, Where can I find this type of information? It's very simple. If I take anthropology courses at a school, I'll be learning about other generations. I'll also be learning about other cultures. So I suppose it gave me a little direction as far as education is concerned, post–high school education."

Others also acknowledged that their caring experiences had been instrumental in directing them toward people-oriented careers. Sherry Hicks, for example, remembers that when she was little, all she thought about was money. "I didn't care what I did. All I wanted was money. So when I was in sixth grade, I heard this lady speak about engineering. I found out they made a whole lot of money, so I decided I was going to go into engineering because I was good in math and science. I took all the courses. Like my freshman and sophomore year I took some of the college courses and national tests in engineering. I did well on them, well enough to get into any engineering program I wanted.

"But after I started volunteering, I started realizing that money doesn't matter. I mean, I've never really had money. I think that's the main reason I wanted money. Then I realized that even people that have money, a lot of them have so much they don't know what to do with it, or they've lost touch with who they are. I just figured that if I help someone in my life, then that would be more important than having money. So I decided to go into education, and this year, because of all the governmental things I did, like Girls' State and Close-Up, I decided that I want to major in education and political science."

Asked why she has these interests, Sherry responded: "I don't think it's the basketball players and the singers and the actresses that are the real backbone—the real heroes—of society. I think it's the people like teachers that work, even though they know they're going to get paid less, because they care. I think it's the government officials who will work, even if they didn't get paid for it. I think those are the people that make the biggest changes in the community and that are there because they want to help other people, not there just because they want to make money."

As these examples suggest, volunteering reinforces aspirations for people-oriented careers in a number of ways. One is it suggests alternatives when a person begins to question the desirability—or possibility—of getting rich as a primary goal in life. Another is that volunteering provides an opportunity to prove that someone can indeed work effectively with other people. Still another is that a person can see ways in which the world can actually be made a better place to live—either from being with adult role models who are making a difference or from becoming directly involved himself or herself.

This last possibility is exemplified by Nikki Unger. Her volunteer work with children reaffirmed her conviction that becoming a social worker is something she can do and that it is a worthwhile career. "I was very encouraged in thinking that maybe this is something I really can do," she explains. "I always planned on it, but it was always kind of like a dream-type thing. I never thought I wouldn't do it. But now I'm more sure that I can make a difference and that I don't have to say it's just one person I'm making a difference to. You can make a difference with a lot of people. There are a lot of kids who need people. There is a big need, I think, for social workers. And kids are just always so needy, no matter what's going on in their lives. I felt great that I could be successful and that I could make a difference and that I would be needed."

Not everyone, of course, is influenced to enter a career oriented toward helping people. Jason McKendrick, for instance, says he wants to go into business or restaurant management—at least something where he can use his skills and that will give him a lot of freedom. He figures he is more likely to help people on the side, on his own time, than through his work. "I've always considered it something that I just wanted to do," he says. "I want to give up my own time for it, but not include it in my career. I want to establish my life and then work with others and help other people."

Choosing to volunteer on the side adds flexibility. A person can, again, find limited ways in which to serve. Part of the reason that some people choose this option is that full-time helping does not suit their talents and interests. But there is another reason as well. The thing that worries young people most about moving into full-time careers—even ones that involve working with people—is that they will feel increasingly tied down. This feeling is worth emphasizing because it reflects one of the tensions that arise from learning how to care by participating in volunteer work.

We can understand this tension by considering again the primordial caring that young people experience in childhood. This kind of caring is so encompassing that young people seldom talk about it as a burden. They do not, for example, regret that their parents loved them so completely. When they do volunteer work, however, they learn that there is a new kind of caring—one from which they can more easily extricate themselves. If they get bored working at Pearl's Kitchen, they can simply stop volunteering, or they can turn their attention to some other cause. When young people think about careers of service, however, they realize that they will have less freedom.

Rafe Ramirez reflects this concern as he talks about one of his career options. "Teaching," he observes, "is a 9-to-5 job, and you're kind of not as flexible, and I'd feel tied down. I've been going to school for so long. Twelve years of school, going through college, which is more school, and then getting out and going back to school the whole time, I kind of think that's one reason why I wouldn't want to become a teacher. It would kind of be like it's getting monotonous. After so many years, I think it would be getting monotonous, and I'd want a change of scenery."

Nikki Unger voiced a similar concern: "I've heard that a lot of social workers get burned out. It's a lot to deal with. It's so many hours, and it's a lot to give consistently day after day for long periods of time. There might be times when I would have to step back and hold back a bit."

There is, then, even an element of realism in gauging one's own capacity to help others over sustained periods. Volunteering not only teaches young people to help; it also instructs them to take into account their limits. They know that it is rewarding to serve in small doses but also to retain their personal freedom, so they worry about becoming tied down.

Having It All

The principal way in which young people reconcile themselves to the desire to serve others in their careers, or through volunteer work, and their need to do what they want to do is to assume that they can simply have it all. They are realistic in one sense: They know they want to live in the real world, sharing the same values and doing the same things as everyone else. But as we saw in considering their views of Mother Teresa, they do not want to be saints. In another sense, however, they do not look reality squarely in the face. They assume too easily that they can do everything, pursuing their own interests and serving others, all without having to make any compromises.

For example, Patti Evans wants to be a teacher, possibly working with handicapped students, but she also admits, "I don't want to have to worry about money. If I have kids, I don't want to have to worry that I can't support them or get them everything that they want." Tucker Aims wants to do all he can to support environmentalism, but he sees no contradiction between this and maintaining the luxurious lifestyle to which he has been accustomed: "I want to live in the nicest house I can get and have the most luxuries I can afford."

Most of the others we talked to said they would be willing to sacrifice their time to help others, but not their lifestyle. They still want the creature comforts that their parents have. A few admit that they may not be as successful as their parents in amassing goods, but even these few want to own a house, drive a decent automobile, have children, enjoy themselves in their spare time—and still devote a portion of their time to helping the needy.

Megan Wyse talks at some length about her aspirations. She says she wants to be comfortable and is willing to do without certain things to which others aspire. For example, she thinks she can be happy going to the park instead of taking expensive trips and is willing to live in a condominium rather than owning a house. Yet she also says she wants to have enough money to give her children the same opportunities she has had, especially a good education and a chance to be happy. Mostly, she just wants to have a normal middle-class life, not being so obsessed with wealth that she becomes greedy, but not being poor, either.

Jackie White is more idealistic than most of the young people with whom we spoke. Having traveled so often in Central America, she realizes that Americans live in extravagant comfort. She wishes she could settle for less, but she also knows how hard it is to escape material desires. She says she would like to have just the basics—a place to live, a car to drive, some possessions. But then she confesses, "Maybe I'd rather have halfway between the basics and, you know—more."

In most cases, young people insisted that they wanted to be comfortable, even though they might work at something devoted to the common good. Rafe Ramirez, for instance, says that he will probably wind up teaching, despite his reservations about feeling tied down, and that he wants to make enough money to live comfortably and relax. Scott Hastings says he doesn't expect to be rich, but he does want enough money to pay the mortgage and support a family. Rachel Farb hopes to continue working with handicapped children but wants to go into business, not because of the money, but for the sense of power. She says being able to tell people what to do is exciting and adventuresome, "like swimming across a big lake with people after you." Pamela Benson imagines herself having a nice place all her own: "I just want a nice co-op like my mother has, but just for me. I want a nice car. Not an exceptional car, but I don't want to drive around in a little shit box." Another student had an elaborate picture of the future in mind: "I'd have a brass bed, and I'd have flowers in my room, and pretty, bright colors in my room. For the children's rooms I'll let them decide what they want, but I'd get them a canopy bed and a water bed. My kitchen, it would have a glass table. And I'd have an entertainment center for our guests. I'd have a guest room. My house is going to be three stories, and it's going to have a deck outside on the back. It's going to be pretty." Other young people mentioned their desires for a good car, a nice place to live, a stereo, and enough money to relax and take trips. They admitted they were ambivalent because they also wanted to help others but figured they could do so without making sacrifices in their lifestyle.

It is easy to feel cynical about remarks such as these. We know how readily people forget their good intentions. When the crunch comes from having too little time to do everything, we work harder to meet the monthly mortgage payment and work less hard at the shelter for homeless children. Thinking broadly about caring in our society, it is also easy to feel that kindness is being abused— when the director of a community agency insists on living in a nice home in the suburbs or when volunteers at the soup kitchen drive up in their BMWs. We wonder how deeply committed they are to serving others. And we wonder the same thing when we hear young people talk about their community service. We hear them expressing an interest in careers in the professions and in attending expensive colleges, and we wonder whether their volunteer work will continue or whether it will end as soon as they have filed their college applications.

We can feel that kindness is being abused in all these ways. But we must be vigilant, asking ourselves how deep our own commitments to helping others are. We must also recognize that this is the type of kindness that we are in the business of communicating to our young people. They do not grow up with expectations of becoming saints or heroes. Our schools and community agencies do not transform them from being children to being saints and heroes, either. Instead, volunteering and community service projects teach young people to be kind in ordinary ways, to play roles, to be good citizens, to make a difference in small ways, and to practice kindness amidst the complexities of everyday life. This is the sort of kindness our society can bear—and the sort of kindness it needs.

The Service Economy

A concluding thought: Not all of the youths whose lives have been influenced by caring activities will want or be able to go into service-oriented jobs. Some will develop other interests, and others will find the pressures of finding a decent job leading them into careers in engineering or manufacturing or construction. The evidence is clear, however, that caring activities reinforce young people's interest in service-oriented careers.

According to the survey, the number of hours spent volunteering is positively associated with wanting to be a teacher, to do social work, and to go to law school (among both males and females), and, among females, with wanting to do religious work. Moreover, the more time that young people spend volunteering, the less likely they are to want a career in business or to express interest in working with computers. This is not to say that volunteering necessarily causes these orientations. But these findings do imply that volunteering at least reinforces the likelihood of pursuing service-oriented careers.[6] The wider, long-term implications of this impact on the American economy, therefore, require careful consideration.

On the one hand, the labor force has already become overwhelming oriented toward service occupations. By 1975, 62 percent of employed Americans were working in "service-producing" industries, and by 1990, this figure had risen to 69 percent.[7] Moreover, the projections for the early part of the twenty-first century indicate that the fastest-growing occupations will be in human services, such as home health aides, medical assistants, psychologists, travel agents, and corrections officers. Of the ten occupations projected to grow most rapidly, eight are in human services.[8]

Not everything that the Bureau of Labor Statistics counts as service should be considered a caring activity, of course. Young people, for example, are more likely to talk about entering such helping professions as teaching, nursing, or social work, whereas the government figures include advertising, automobile repair, and zoo management among service industries. Nevertheless, it is clear that the American economy has shifted decisively away from such activities as mining, construction, and the manufacture of durable goods toward occupations in which dealing and communicating with people and identifying and trying to meet their needs are paramount.

On the other hand, much concern is now being expressed about the economy in relation to its foreign competitors. Policymakers worry about training in mathematics and science and fear that the technical capacity in industries such as computing and advanced electronics will shift increasingly to other countries. Some analysts wonder whether the national security can be preserved if all capacity to produce manufactured goods is lost, and others voice concerns about the country's capacity to sustain domestic markets for consumer goods as more and more of the population is employed in lower-paying service occupations.

In the past, the leading nations of the world have carved out distinctive specialties in the larger world economy. At one time, for example, Spain and Portugal dominated the world trade in precious metals; at another time, Dutch textiles reigned supreme, and later the Dutch economy shifted increasingly toward banking and financial services and away from trade. As a large country rich in natural resources, the United States has historically been able to withstand the pressures leading toward too narrow a role in the world economy. Agriculture, steel, lumber, aircraft, electronics, and computers all have been mainstays of the American economy. But that pattern may be changing.

It may be that an ethic of caring will lead the United States to become the world's specialist in service industries. Already the United States supplies much of the rest of the world with some kinds of services, such as teaching at the baccalaureate and graduate levels and supplying health care requiring high levels of specialization. The number of religious workers both at home and abroad is also quite high. As more and more of the population ages or lives on entitlements, service workers will also be employed increasingly in nursing homes, retirement communities, and in public welfare agencies. Yet it is also clear that there are limits to the ability to pay for such services, especially from public funds. There also are limits to the extent to which the United States can remain a strong economy simply by focusing on human services. If only to retain control of our national security, we will want to protect our capacity to build airplanes and high-speed computers. We will also need to employ people in jobs that have little obvious connection with helping the needy or even with showing kindness directly to other people—jobs such as repairing roads, monitoring financial transactions, cultivating crops, assembling automobiles, and writing books.

If elementary kindness is to be part of our society, it must be a trait that can be performed in all these roles, not only in the helping professions. Volunteering is an essential part of the training that young people must receive to live in such a society, because it demonstrates that one can work—at any kind of job—and still do good deeds for the community on the side. But volunteering should also demonstrate that one can be kind in the midst of other duties as well. Kindness, in this sense, means adding the personal touch, going beyond the call of duty, and thinking creatively about the larger problems that one's work may help resolve. Kindness also means combating the indifference and personal insufficiency created by institutions.

Volunteering can nourish elementary kindness, therefore, by making us more attentive to the needs around us and in the wider world. It can teach us how to be kind in limited ways and also help us keep our horizons open. Even if we do not become heroes or saints, we can think more imaginatively about the good that ordinary people can do. As one young man, speaking about the volunteer work he had been doing, concluded, "Maybe I dream bigger because of it."

11
Thinking About the Future

Are America's young people being encouraged to "dream bigger" as they do volunteer work and are drawn into community service projects? Or are they simply being kept off the street, away from the mall, and being used to perform tasks that nobody else wants to do?

These are hard questions. But we must confront them and, one hopes, in a way that will encourage young people to benefit from their volunteer experiences and that will help teachers, clergy, and leaders of community agencies to enrich these experiences.

I have developed an argument in the preceding chapters—based on both national data and detailed qualitative interviews with young people—that contradicts much of the conventional wisdom about caring and volunteering.

Kindness is, I suggested at the outset, a social problem (Chapter 2) because there often is not enough of it. We need more people who are concerned and willing to devote time to helping the needy and to working in other ways for the common good. But kindness is also a problem because it is so easily misunderstood and abused. We do encourage a great deal of volunteering in our society, but it is not always clear how much kindness goes with this volunteering. We can think of notable examples in which kindness has been abused not only by its recipients but also by its donors. We can also think of many worrisome tendencies in American culture—selfishness and materialism, among others—that should make us wonder whether many of us really understand what it means to be kindhearted.

Typically, this sort of reasoning has led observers to deplore the lack of caring in our society and to call for greater efforts to teach people how to be kind. I contended, however, that most people already know how to be kind (Chapter 3). They experienced it as children from their parents or some other caregiver—an "other mother," for example. Most of us, therefore, embark on adolescence with a primordial understanding of kindness that emphasizes caring for personal needs, warmth and intimacy, trust, a whole-person orientation, and a relationship that is not contingent on particular circumstances or roles.

The rub comes, I suggested, when we grow up, move away from home psychologically and then physically, and discover that nothing else is like what we experienced at home. We know that being cared for feels nice, but we also quickly find out that much of the world is competitive and self-interested rather than focused on our needs, that it deals in arm's-length transactions rather than cultivating warmth and intimacy, and that we relate to one another in specialized ways rather than as whole beings. What we need, therefore, is to learn a new meaning of caring and kindness, a meaning that works in the complex world away from home.

I argued that in our society one of the principal tasks of volunteering is to communicate new meanings of caring and kindness. Most of us begin to learn new meanings when we come into contact for the first time with people outside our family who are in need and when we interact with role models and friends in other settings. Volunteering, however, is a special place in which to gain a more mature understanding of kindness. It puts us in situations in which we are expected to be of service to others, and it forces us to think about what we are doing. But we also discover that we must unlearn some of our primordial understandings of caring.

Volunteers—and leaders of volunteer programs—can be more effective by recognizing, first, that they are indeed communicating new meanings of kindness. Thus it becomes important to consider specifically how the tasks being performed differ from ones those may occur naturally in the family or among friends, and it is imperative for times of reflection and guides to be available.

I suggested that most of us already have frameworks that give us reasons to be concerned about the needs of others and that these frameworks— humanitarianism, the pursuit of happiness, reciprocity, self-realization, and, in many cases, ideas about serving God—can generally be found in experiences in childhood and in lessons we learned early from our role models (Chapters 4 and 5). One of the first items for reflection is thus to become more fully aware of these frameworks and to see how they apply to needs in the larger world. We also need to tell stories, as they are our ways of understanding why we are doing what we are doing—our motives. We need to have ways of explaining our volunteer activities.

The stories we learn to tell are not ones we invent from scratch but are woven together from the scripts we are exposed to in volunteer contexts. If we do volunteer work as teenagers at all, most of us do so through projects at school, in our churches or synagogues, or in other community agencies, such as the scouts, the Red Cross, soup kitchens, and neighborhood centers (Chapter 6).

As we adopt the language of these organizations, we learn to talk (and to think) about kindness and caring in new ways. The main thing we learn is that kindness is no longer just a primordial attribute of our personhood but that it can also be thought of as an aspect of the specific roles we play in institutions. We learn, for instance, to think of kindness in terms of helping people with particular needs, of doing what we can in small ways and for limited times, of fitting in and complementing the work of others who also are trying to help, of seeking out certain roles (among the many available) that happen to suit our interests, of developing some specialized knowledge or skills, and of being orderly and efficient in what we do. In the process, we see that it is possible to be kind in new ways and in settings that are quite different from those of our families or our peer groups.

Many of us, however, are likely to feel torn by these new messages about caring. They are, after all, quite different from the ones with which we grew up. They do not seem to be very caring at all sometimes because they do not focus much on high ideals, altruism, or virtue or on cultivating deep emotional ties with those for whom we care. This is why it is easy for us to worry that kindness is being abused. Suddenly, it seems that there is too much self-interest in our kindness and that we are playing bit parts rather than being the main character. Again, volunteers and volunteer leaders need to be aware of these concerns and face them squarely.

I also pointed out that another reason we tell stories is that they help us resolve (or contain) some of these tensions (Chapter 7). For instance, we tell stories about the one person who said thank you or the one person who clearly benefited, and these stories calm our doubts at other times when we think we are making no difference at all. We also observe—and tell stories about—role models who show us that it is possible to play specialized roles but also to step out of these roles, to add a personal touch, and to go beyond the call of duty. This is another reason, then, for providing ample time to reflect and to tell stories, rather than focusing simply on accomplishing tasks.

I then suggested that comparisons between young men and young women are helpful for gaining a better grasp of what happens in the process of relearning what it means to care (Chapter 8). An important part of this transition is the balance between our sense of self and the specific roles we play. We saw that young women are more likely to refer to themselves when they talk about their caring activities and to link these references with the specific circumstances under which caring takes place, whereas young men are more likely to talk in terms of roles, to see the occupants of roles as interchangeable parts, and to use abstract or general language that emphasizes this interchangeability. Neither style of language is necessarily preferable, but it is important for volunteer leaders to recognize that the differences exist. Volunteers can also see in these languages that ways must be found of investing oneself in one's roles and of differentiating the two as well.

Extending these observations, I argued that one of the peculiar features of our society is that we are often encouraged to be weak as individual persons rather than strong (Chapter 9). So many of the traits that have traditionally been considered virtuous, I believe, have become part of our institutions that we often do not have to function as particularly powerful people to get the job done. This is why we can be kind and still not feel especially virtuous. And it is why we need to recognize the work of social institutions rather than thinking that individual volunteers are the solution to all our problems. The main implication of this perspective, I argued, is that volunteering still builds character, but in ways that we may easily dismiss.

In listening closely to what young people said about their volunteer experiences, we learned that these experiences did not turn them into heroes or saints or make them feel strong enough to do everything by themselves. Instead, personal strength consists of learning to take responsibility, developing new skills, gaining the confidence to speak out and to make choices, and discovering one's own interests and talents. If volunteer agencies succeed in teaching these kinds of traits, they then have contributed to building personal character in an important way.

We also considered what young people say about the possibilities of being kind as they enter adulthood and begin pursuing careers (Chapter 10). Volunteering sparked their imaginations and established contacts that will help them explore new careers or new ways of volunteering. I emphasized, however, that young people are also realistic in many ways, recognizing that they still want the comforts of ordinary life, that they are unwilling to sacrific very much to help others, that they may be able to pursue service-oriented careers, and that they may be able to serve the common good by devoting a few hours now and then to community service.

Where does that leave us? Probably with the feeling that kindness is rather flat, and that has been my intention. Kindness is, after all, elementary, and by cultivating it in small ways and in ordinary circumstances, we can carry it with us even in the midst of institutions that encourage us to be indifferent and to simply do our jobs. If we can learn to think of kindness in this way, we can more readily put it into practice than if we insist on viewing it as an attribute of the gods. Volunteer agencies, I think, do us a service not only in helping people but also in helping us understand kindness in new ways. These agencies can do their jobs even better by making sure that these understandings are communicated, especially to young people.

Having said this, I now want to move to the meanings of kindness that seem still to be neglected. Volunteering helps us by making our understandings of kindness more realistic, and it also contributes when it enlarges our dreams. We learn to be caring in small ways, but we also need to be inspired and to recognize that our small kindnesses matter because they are symbols of higher ideals. We therefore need to consider hope and transformation and then to return, finally, to a sober assessment of the limits of volunteering.

Hope for the Future

Volunteering has always been a symbol of hope. When we think of people going out of their way to help others, we feel more optimistic about the future. We may still recognize that the world is faced with immense problems—evident just from watching the evening news. But the presence of caring people restores our faith in humanity.

Some of this is a pipe dream. A few people, even with the dedication of Mother Teresa, will not save us. But the fact that ordinary people can demonstrate kindness in ordinary ways should also be a symbol of hope. Indeed, many of the young people we talked to were optimistic about the future for precisely this reason.

Nikki Unger, for instance, expressed her optimism in this way: "I think that anybody can make a difference just by voicing their support or their opposition to different issues. Like one voice maybe will affect one other voice and that one other voice will affect another voice, and soon there are a whole bunch of voices. I think that's what leads to something being solved, when you've got a whole bunch of people pushing for something. Just like Mother Teresa helps just by spreading the message around so that different people know, and then there are more people behind the cause. The bigger the group, the more effective you're going to be in some instances. And in other instances, an individual can do an awful lot. It all starts with individuals."

As this comment illustrates, one reason that young people think it is realistic to be hopeful about the future is that they have learned that volunteering turns small deeds into large contributions by bringing together the efforts of many people. Jim Grayson made this point in observing that "if you've got a large enough group, I don't think any problem is too big. It may be too big for one person. Then you just get two or three. If it's too big for them, you just get more."

Another young man used the metaphor of a rope to make a similar point: "Social problems are too big for one person, but if I'm going to volunteer, and he's going to volunteer, and you're going to volunteer, and the guy across the street is going to volunteer, we're all only one person. You've got to look at it like it's a rope, and every person is an individual strand, and every day it gets stronger."

The other reason that young people who have done volunteer work say they are hopeful is that they can cite specific examples of people who are making a difference. The most dramatic instance of a young person seeing volunteers make a difference was Jackie White. Her volunteer work in El Salvador was not at all typical of other young people, but she is convinced that ordinary people like herself made it possible for fundamental change to take place in El Salvador. "Being in El Salvador this past October was really important to me," she explains, "because we did get to see a lot of the changes. As soon as we arrived in the country, we noticed that a lot of propaganda posters condemning the FMLN were gone from the highways and that the helicopters were gone. There were also fewer soldiers on the street. While a lot of it was symbolic and a lot of things still had to happen, we could see the changes. People were talking about things in public that you wouldn't dream of a year ago. It was a completely different country. The FMLN had opened its party office in some of the major cities, and its flag was flying free. Offices—that used to look through peepholes before they let people in to protect themselves—now had banners telling people where they were."

Jackie could also see how much things had changed in the countryside. "I realized that the young people were back in the communities. Previously when you'd go to a community in El Salvador all you'd see is children, middle-age women and old people, because most of the men and most of the young people were gone fighting—usually with the FMLN, sometimes with the army, or they had fled. Both armies were in encampments, and the FMLN's encampments were practically in the communities because that's where their base had been throughout the war. But now their families were back in the communities, so you'd see young people sitting around on the porches and talking and everything, whereas before they were off in the mountains fighting."

All this made Jackie hopeful because she could see that things were indeed getting better. Her most memorable experience came a few months later, however, when she returned to San Salvador for an international conference. "I realized that the music they were playing in the hotel was by one of the official bands of the FMLN whose membership actually was killed in the 1989 offensive. Their music is very revolutionary. They talk about freedom and winning peace. I was just astounded. It was particularly meaningful because I've always listened to that music in this country, and it's been something that's really brought me closer to El Salvador. It was symbolic to me. El Salvador is a totally changed society!"

Hope springs, then, not from some eternal source but from people's becoming actively involved. Most of the young people we interviewed felt that they themselves, through their volunteer work now and in the future, could make at least a small difference toward overcoming pressing social issues. As one student explained: "I think I could help with the problems that need education, such as the environment and AIDS. I volunteer now, and I probably will always try whenever I'm in the situation that I can. Just take the teacher. A first-grade teacher who starts talking about the environment with his/her kids in class has made a difference with those twenty-five kids that are in his/her class. These kids will go home and say, 'Mom, why aren't you recycling that?' Being a day camp counselor we taught the kids how to recycle. They were excited, and they went home. They told their parents what they learned that day. That the aluminum goes in this box, and the paper goes in another one."

Personal Transformation

Apart from the hope that may infuse thinking about wider social problems, volunteering sometimes makes a profound impact on the lives of individual volunteers. We need to remember this impact and to understand how it connects with more traditional meanings of caring, especially as we acknowledge that the more usual result of volunteering is to make more gradual changes in the views of young people and to temper their dreams with realism.

Of the young people we talked to, many felt that they had become stronger, and some could even point to eye-opening experiences that made a memorable difference in their outlook on life. Among middle-class teenagers, these experiences often consisted of realizing, perhaps for the first time, that others were less fortunate than themselves or, in other cases, of escaping the boring sameness of daily life and discovering that they could become passionately involved in something. Young people like Jason McKendrick and Megan Wyse illustrate this kind of experience. But there was another, more dramatic kind of transformation as well—more often evident among young people from less advantaged backgrounds. In some cases, these were life-saving transformations.

T. J. Hawke was always daddy's little girl—a tomboy, actually, who preferred blue jeans to dresses, played softball, and went camping with her dad. There was just one problem: Daddy was an alcoholic. When he was drunk, he'd beat her up, and then he'd drink some more.

When T. J. was in the sixth grade, things started going from bad to worse. Her mother, a nurse's aide, decided to go back to school to become a registered nurse. On the outside, everything looked great. Soon there would be more money. What Daddy made repairing automobiles had never been much. Mommy was such a caring person, always going off to help one of the neighbors. She was active at church, serving on the altar guild, and now her father was attending too, helping in the kitchen during potluck dinners and on bingo nights.

Mommy was the Girl Scout leader, the one who took her places, helped with her homework, and comforted her when Daddy got mad. As T. J. entered adolescence, she started to identify more and more with her mother. But Mommy wasn't as available now that she was going to classes at night. And Daddy was acting strange. Drinking more than ever. He seemed threatened by the idea of her mother's getting more education and making more money.

T. J.'s sixth-grade teacher noticed that she was becoming increasingly withdrawn. Always shy, she was the sort of girl who sat in the corner and read books instead of mixing with the other children. One day a letter came from the local Red Cross chapter asking for a student to participate in a training class for volunteers. The teacher chose T. J., thinking it might help with whatever was bothering her. Reluctantly, T. J. went. What she found was a new family that eventually saved her life.

She recalls that first meeting: "It was really interesting because even the first time there I felt a sense of belonging. Like I fit in. They didn't judge me." She liked the way people were working together, and she liked the variety of people she met. Something drew her to come back, and she did, not often but enough to stay involved. She went to meetings occasionally and to workshops. Gradually, somewhere around the ninth grade, she realized this was something she really enjoyed and decided to make a stronger commitment.

With one other girl, who became her best friend, T. J. started volunteering regularly at the Red Cross. She learned to help at the blood bank, showing donors how to fill out forms and working in the canteen that provided snacks afterward. She took a class in cardiopulmonary resuscitation, and she went along on Red Cross training programs at elementary schools. A couple of times, when the Red Cross put on parties for sick children, she dressed up like a clown and helped with the entertainment. That year and the next she put in about two hundred hours.

What kept T. J. involved were the close friendships she developed with the other volunteers. Her friend Stacy and three other students from other high schools became a surrogate family. T. J. says the summer leadership camps she attended were especially meaningful to her. They taught her skills and a better understanding of herself, and they gave her an opportunity to deepen her friendships. Speaking about her group of five, she says, "We have a bond that will never end. We come from different backgrounds. We're different people. But we built a friendship on something that was mutual. The Red Cross brought us together and made us a group."

It was important to T. J. to have this group because things were gradually deteriorating at home. When her father started sleeping with her mother's best friend, her mother divorced him. T. J. was glad when her father moved out, declaring she never wanted to see him or speak to him again. At least the beatings would stop. She became emotionally more dependent on her mother, even though her mother was busy working and preoccupied with a new boyfriend.

T. J.'s extended family was also falling apart. Half Cherokee, she had always been proud of her heritage. Her mother's siblings mingled with her father's siblings. The aunts and uncles and cousins saw a lot of one another, but the divorce caused everyone to choose sides. Family members wouldn't speak to one another anymore. But having responsibilities at the Red Cross gave T. J. something else to think about.

The way it saved her life was toward the end of her junior year. Her mother moved into her boyfriend's townhouse, taking her thirteen-year-old sister with her. They left T. J. living alone in the rundown two-bedroom house that had always been home, ostensibly for insurance purposes and so she could be close to school. All the furniture was gone except for T. J.'s bed and her dresser. She felt abandoned and became increasingly depressed. Thoughts of suicide started clamoring in her mind. As the weeks went by, they became louder and louder until the day her mother went off to get married.

That night T. J. thought for sure she was going to kill herself. She tried to call her mother but didn't know where she was. Her sister, who had been sent to stay with an uncle, knew only that her mother was going to be away for a week honeymooning. It was Stacy, her friend from the Red Cross, who came through for her. After a long session on the telephone, Stacy convinced T. J. she shouldn't be alone. Stacy and her mother picked her up and took her to their house to spend the night.

That was where the police found T. J. the next day. They tracked her down to tell her that her sister had been raped, by her uncle. This was the crushing blow; it destroyed T. J.'s last vestige of faith in humanity. In retrospect, she knows she would have killed herself if she had been alone. But she was at Stacy's, and Stacy's mother got her a therapist to talk to. Even more than that, Stacy herself knew her and knew what she needed.

A year has passed since then. A few months later the house was sold, and T. J. rented a room from another woman she'd met at the Red Cross. She still puts in several hours a week as a blood donor assistant. Now that she has more experience, she is the one who organizes parties for sick children, and she puts on the programs at elementary schools herself. She is the president of a Red Cross club she started at her high school. She also runs the youth group at her church and is active in a student organization to combat alcoholism. She has been honored by several local organizations, and just last week she received a phone call from the White House saying she had been chosen to receive a Presidential Youth Service Award.

T. J. will graduate in a few weeks. She knows she will keep in touch with Stacy and her other friends from the Red Cross wherever they are in the coming years. She is also training a group of ninth graders to take her place. She wants them to discover what she has learned from volunteering. As she put it, "Even though you may be different, you're just as good as anybody else, and you can use those differences to be a leader, to help others, whether you're scared or not, and no matter what anybody else thinks of you."

I do not mean to suggest that experiences such as this are typical, but they are not uncommon, either. They can be found in the lives of other teenagers with whom we spoke—the young woman who ran away from home and discovered how to care by living in a shelter for homeless teens or the young man who learned from his uncle how to volunteer after his mother shot and killed his father. Although such episodes should not be taken as the norm, they should nevertheless be a part of the story, because they remind us that caring has long stood for the possibility of personal transformation.

That possibility is most evident in the religious understandings that have been the prime sources of teaching about caring throughout most of our history. The Greek word *agape*, which means selfless or unconditional love, lies at the core of these understandings. In Christianity, *agape* is an attribute of God, but it can be imitated by humans if their will is divinely transformed. Indeed, *agape* is linked doubly with personal transformation—as its source (in divine love) and as its consequences (in human behavior).[1]

At the end of the twentieth century, we may be less sure that the will can be so fundamentally transformed, as has often been argued in religious teachings of the past. Yet there is ample evidence that we still think of caring as having transformative powers.[2] We speak of romantic love's having the power to sweep us away, and we tell stories of volunteers' gaining a new outlook on life from serving others. Caring is, in this sense, like the music Jackie White heard in San Salvador that day: It is symbolic of change, new life, hope.

Required Community Service

Because of all its potential benefits, community service is now being encouraged—and even required—on an unprecedented scale. From the school house to the White House, leaders are implementing programs that will give young people the option of volunteering, providing incentives for doing so, and, in some cases, mandating service as part of their education. At the local level, schools have begun to require or encourage community service by offering elective options as part of the formal curriculum and by emphasizing its value for college applications.

According to the survey, 55 percent of American teenagers are in schools that encourage community service, and 8 percent attend schools that require for graduation a certain number of hours of community service. But the survey also showed that students view community service requirements with mixed feelings. Only half say that requiring community service is a good idea; nearly one-third (30 percent) say that community service is not as good if you have to do it; and a majority (56 percent) say that they feel better about community service when they do it voluntarily.[3] The young people we talked to were also ambivalent about many of these initiatives, and their ambivalence reflected some of the ideals that we have just been considering.

The main argument in favor of community service requirements (or incentives) is that such programs expose people to the joys of giving who would not otherwise become involved and that, once exposed, these people will continue to volunteer. Rafe Ramirez, for instance, argued, "If you required it a little bit, for a little while, some people would realize it's not so bad, and then they would want to volunteer."

Although Rafe recognized some of the problems, he figured the benefits would be greater. "If you don't have to volunteer, some people have no interest in volunteering and they just sit back and say, oh, I don't have to, so I won't. But then once they do it, they might get an interest in it, and say, all right, I'll help." Another student supported the idea of required community service for a similar reason. "It would be a good thing," he observed, "because a lot of teenagers would find out that they like it; they've probably never tried it before. They never do it, because they don't know if they like it or not, or they're afraid."

Opposition to community service was greatest when young people thought it might be imposed on them. Doing so flew in the face, as they saw it, of how the real world should function. Service can, I have tried to suggest, be understood in many different ways, so it is conceivable that required service could be considered legitimate. As we have seen, young people learn to think of caring as a specialized, limited role that they can choose to accept, much as they might choose to buy a new pair of sneakers. Passing a law that makes community service obligatory or including it as part of a requirement for graduation, therefore, runs counter to this basic understanding.

The following remarks from Patti Evans contain several of these arguments. When asked what she thought about having a law that would require everyone to do volunteer work, she remarked: "Well, the funny thing is, we're just learning about the Constitution and saying that the law can't really tell people what to do without their consent. I don't think that a lot of people are willing to give up time to help the needy. And I think that would just cause a lot of outrage from the people that aren't willing to do that. It would end up putting the people that are needy on the spot. And they wouldn't want the help from people that have to do it. And it wouldn't make you feel as good when you're doing it, when you're helping, if you know that you have to do that. If I know that I don't have to do something, then it makes me want to do it more."

For obligatory community service to be considered legitimate, it would probably be necessary for schools and community leaders to challenge the prevailing assumptions in contemporary volunteer settings about choice, roles, and interests. It seems doubtful that these assumptions could be challenged very effectively because they correspond, as we have seen, to the ways in which we are trained to think about social roles and institutions more generally. One way of challenging these assumptions, however, might be to emphasize civic responsibility more explicitly. The young people we talked to who had the clearest sense of civic responsibility were, in fact, somewhat more inclined to view community service requirements favorably than were other young people.[4]

The idea of schools' requiring community service elicited some of the same reservations as did the idea of passing a law forcing all young people to volunteer. The students we talked to did see value in thinking about ways of gathering more personpower and exposing more young people to the needs of others, but they doubted that on the whole, requirements would be beneficial. T. J. Hawke, for example, thought that requiring students to participate as helpers at a soup kitchen would take away the actual caring that goes on in such places: "A lot of those people wouldn't want to be there. They wouldn't be nice to the people that were coming in, and part of the soup kitchen thought is not only for a good meal, it's for a kind word and a kind hand also." Another student observed the idea might make sense in the abstract but contended that it would not work at his school: "In some high schools, I guess, but not at my high school because there are a lot of them like this. Those kids would feel so controlled. They'd hate it."[5]

Further evidence is provided by the survey. Although it is implausible to think that community service requirements are the only thing influencing how much or how little students value volunteering, it is plausible that such requirements should make some difference. Thus, we find in the survey that students who attend schools that require community service are actually somewhat more likely to value volunteering than are students who attend other schools. However, the greatest differences are not in requiring community service but in encouraging it.[6] Thus, if one of the main goals of community service is to instill the idea of volunteering as a worthy activity, voluntary and elective ways of encouraging service would probably be as effective as service requirements.

A creative solution was suggested by Ginny O'Brien as a result of her own high school experience, including having participated recently in a debate on the issue. She thought a requirement might be more palatable if students were at least given a wide variety of ways in which to fulfill the requirement. "I talked this over with my school principal," she recalled, "because we had thought about running a community service requirement. My way about it was that community service be a requirement to the extent that it's tied in with vocational training. That everybody was required in some respect, but in something they were interested in. So if someone wanted to be a biologist, they could serve in a lab, or they could serve doing research on the beach. Or if someone was interested in nursing, they could work in a hospital. Or if they were going to be a secretary, they could type for the United Way. So it could be tied into an educational aspect and be considered vocational training, but also teach them the value of service."

If students were given options, Ginny felt, they would express greater enthusiasm for what they were doing. Otherwise, their reluctance might destroy even their relationships with the people they were supposed to be helping. For example, if everyone were required to spend time helping at a soup kitchen, something would, in Ginny's view, be lost: "You'd be getting a lot of people who didn't want to do it. It would change the meaning of the activity for the people who did. It would change the atmosphere. I think it would also be detrimental to the visitors to the soup kitchen, the people who are using the soup kitchen, because they'd sense that atmosphere. It would be more regimental and less an act of giving. More of a 'here-in-your-face,' sort of atmosphere."

It also is important that many of the young people we interviewed were opposed to paying people for community service. But this idea created less concern than did mandating service by law, perhaps because young people recognize that pay in some form is part of most adult roles. They objected, however, because they also thought of caring as something that one does as an added feature of one's ordinary roles and as behavior that springs from the broader frameworks for understanding caring that one learns in childhood.

To pay for community service would therefore move volunteering entirely into the arena of a job and destroy its capacity to link people with a primordial sense of caring. One young man put it this way: "Something would definitely be lost, because then they wouldn't be working for that peace, that happiness. They wouldn't be working to help someone. They'd be working to help themselves." Another student elaborated: "I think something would be lost. Volunteering shows that you want to be there, and that you're giving of yourself to do something kind for others. If you're paid to be there, then what's the point behind it? The whole thought behind those things is because they're nonprofit organizations for people who need the help. If you have to pay somebody to be there, then anything with nonprofit, it's going to go down the drain. All those thoughts of the Good Samaritan and the caring people are going to go away. People are going to be out there thinking every time they do something they're going to have to get paid to do it, and they don't ever have to do any helpful work anymore."

Many of the young people we spoke with favored a program of national service, as we saw in the last chapter, because such a program might be able to help them pay for college.[7] Those who opposed national service, however, recognized that this was essentially a way of paying young people to do community service, rather than eliciting it voluntarily. Patti Evans, for instance, objected to national service on grounds that it would "turn volunteer work into money, bribing almost. It would just change it. It wouldn't be because people would want to do it. It would be because they would be getting money, and I do think that would be like a bribe to get more volunteers." Tanika Lane thought it would be nice to get free tuition, but she also expressed reservations: "I think something would be lost—compassion. They wouldn't put love into it. They'd say, 'I'm just doing this because I'm getting paid, and after I get paid, I'm getting out of here.' If they volunteered, though, there would be compassion, caring, or love." Jason McKendrick was more pragmatic. He thought national service could work, but he also worried whether it would really foster caring: "You'd also have to consider what this was doing to people's motives. You're going to find people doing it just to get that scholarship and once they get into college, they're going to stop."[8]

What comments like these underscore is not that national service programs or community service requirements are necessarily bad but that they must be considered not only in terms of financial costs and benefits but also in relation to how they may alter the meaning of caring and volunteering. Community leaders must remember that volunteerism has been attractive because it is voluntary. Freedom of choice is a fundamental norm in American culture. One of the important lessons we learn about caring as we move into volunteer settings is that we can choose the ways in which we will care—selecting roles in terms of our interests and balancing them with other commitments. This is a norm that needs to be preserved.[9]

Another assumption that we hold dear is the view that what we do should be pleasurable—at some level—and that we are more likely to perform well if we are engaged in activities that make us happy. Young people worry, rightly I believe, that forced service or volunteering for pay will diminish the likelihood of experiencing the joy of giving.[10] Moreover, we have seen repeatedly that caring requires interpretation—frameworks and stories—to make it meaningful. Whether caring is part of a national service program or part of a volunteer program initiated by the schools, therefore, ample attention must be given to the deeper symbolic meanings of caring.

The Limits of Volunteering

Critics of volunteering insist that even if it is not being abused—and even if people are doing good things—there is a danger of its becoming a panacea. Mention almost any social problem, draw in a few volunteers to perform some token good deeds, and then forget about it. This is the American way, according to the critics. So what are the limits of volunteering? And are young people who volunteer aware of these limitations?

One of the limits of volunteering surfaced in the last chapter when we were considering careers. At most, people may devote a few hours a week to volunteering, whereas they are likely to spend the majority of their waking hours at work. Some of the young people we talked to insisted, for this reason, that the meaning of caring be broadened to include the ways in which they might contribute to the common good through their jobs. A young man expressed this conviction clearly: "Volunteers can play a big role, but there comes a point where everybody needs to look out for being financially secure and looking out for their own future, their family's future, whatever, and you can't be a volunteer forever. You've got to live off something."

Another limitation of volunteering that many young people seemed to recognize is that some forms of suffering can be ameliorated, but never eliminated, by good deeds alone. A dying person, for instance, can be made more comfortable in the process, but eventually that person—and all of us—will die. In other cases, the extent to which something can be done to eliminate suffering is more open to debate. For example, some argue that hunger can be eliminated from the world, and others say there will always be hungry people. The message, however, is to do what one can but not to despair if problems remain.

Homelessness was one issue that quite a few young people had thought about in this way. Listen to how Patti Evans balances the limits of what volunteers can do with the need for them to do something: "Some people choose not to try and get themselves out of these situations, and other people are just laid off. I think that if you got a lot of the homeless people working and back on their feet and if there were more jobs available, there would definitely not be so many homeless people as there are. A lot of people are uneducated, are on the streets and can't get a job. If they have to be on the streets, I think that people should try and make their lives comfortable by soup kitchens and homeless shelters."

Another limitation of volunteering is that charitable efforts may, ironically, perpetuate some of the very problems they are intended to alleviate. In New York City, for example, public funding for low-income housing has become even more scarce because much of it is channeled into shelters for the homeless, which are more expensive. A typical low-income family, for example, may receive $250 in rent subsidies as long as they have a place to live but have as much as $3,200 a month spent on them if they lose their housing and have to move into a shelter. Although much of the problem is a maze of red tape that prevents funds from going to housing instead of shelters, experts also say that homeless advocates, charities, and other nonprofit agencies—a veritable "homeless industry"—may be a contributing factor.[11]

Few of the young people we talked to felt that they were helping perpetuate problems by participating in volunteer programs. But they did worry, as we saw in discussing Pearl's Kitchen, about whether their efforts were truly beneficial, and they did recognize that many problems would not be solved. Speaking broadly about social problems, Megan Wyse, for instance, observed: "I think there won't be an end to these problems, but you can definitely help reduce problems like homelessness, and drugs and alcohol. There will always be poor people and there will always be some people using drugs, but I think that people themselves can really reduce the problems."

The other limitation that young people mentioned frequently in our interviews was the need to devote other resources to solving social problems, rather than relying entirely on free labor power. Alcoholism and drug abuse provided an interesting illustration of this point because many young people had experienced these problems among their friends and had worked as volunteers to combat them.

These young people also recognized that there were systemic problems that needed to be addressed in other ways. One young woman, for example, said it would help to have a sin tax and to use the proceeds for rehabilitation and educational programs. But, she adds, "I think there are also deep sociological roots for substance abuse and that we should be working to eliminate those, such as child abuse, such as poverty, such as lack of education, lack of support, lack of love, lack of cohesive family structures."

Homelessness was also an issue that young people thought needed a combination of approaches. Listen to what Jackie White says about it: "I don't think it's just going to go away. Nothing's going to just go away. I think that in some cases just rebuilding houses and making houses and jobs and social programs available to people might be enough for some people, for families. In other cases where alcohol and drugs and more despair is involved, for those people, I guess, rehab and trying to bring people back in and trying to enable them to live a decent life in some way is needed. And also, right now, just working to keep housing affordable, to make jobs available, to make education available. I think one of the key things is just trying to eliminate the various stages of poverty and trying to bring all the poorer sectors back into society."

Another student summarized the dominant view with this remark: "People have to be willing to help the government with the drug problem, homelessness, and AIDS. So it kind of works together. The government has to help people, but the people have to help the government."

A view such as this can be repeated almost without thinking because it is so often included in textbooks and classroom discussions. Yet it is often volunteer work that drives the point home. Zia Hillier provided one of the best examples. Explaining why she thinks it would be useful to pursue a career in politics, she recalled a specific episode: "It was a homeless person I befriended. It was really sad because I went to the head of the Opportunities Commission in the state to see if I could try to set up housing for him, because it was getting chilly. They were saying there's a two-year wait. So I thought at least I could put him on a waiting list. But it's like if you don't have a place of residency they won't mail anything to you. They couldn't do it through me. All this bureaucracy that you go through. If you don't have one thing, then you can't get another, but you can't get that thing if you don't have the other thing in the first place." She realizes government must be involved but adds: "It has a lot of faults, too. I'd like to help change it!"

Compassionate Social Polities

These considerations bring us, finally, to the point that can be emphasized best by saving it until last: Elementary kindness means more than simply finding small ways in the midst of everyday life to help a few needy people or to be considerate and conscientious in doing one's job; it also means supporting compassionate social policies. Some of the young volunteers we talked to were completely blind to this dimension of kindness. They helped at the soup kitchen and then passed the buck to others who they thought knew more about politics than they did. But others—the majority in fact—recognized that the problems that concerned them as volunteers were also problems that demanded attention at the level of public policy.

The point is not that volunteering should make people more liberal, more conservative, or more supportive of any one point of view. Volunteering is, as observers have always argued, consistent with democracy and with the preservation of a pluralistic society. In theory at least, volunteering makes people more aware of community issues and empowers them to do something about these issues.[12] Not only is it something in which people of all racial and ethnic groups, faiths, and lifestyles are able to participate, but it also does not reinforce particular political creeds or partisan views of what constitutes the most compassionate public policies.

Even though many young people are motivated by humanitarian concerns to volunteer, these orientations thus do not crystallize around certain liberal positions on social policies. Teen volunteers are quite divided on such issues as the death penalty, abortion, and assistance to the poor, just as all teenagers are, and their opinions on a broad national scale seem not to be affected dramatically in one direction or another by particular types of volunteering or by level of involvement.[13] The volunteers with whom we talked were not equally concerned about all social issues, either, nor did they agree on what the most compassionate policy might be. But they did underscore the importance of extending concerns about elementary kindness to the public arena.

Preserving rain forests is an example. This is one issue that young people believe needs to be addressed with good policies as well as by volunteers. One student explained her views in this way: "I think that a whole group of individuals can have an influence, but I think a lot of times it also takes the government. These construction companies are not going to listen to just a group of people. It's going to take the government to stop them."

Speaking about environmental issues more generally, another student remarked: "I think that mass consciousness raising on a societal level is really critical and really effective." She said she felt this way because much of the problem concerned individual behavior. But she thought that the American economic system also encouraged self-interested behavior and that it would take government programs to alter it. Mass transit, she said, was an example of how government can work to create structures that help protect the environment.

AIDS was another issue that the young people we talked to considered ripe for compassionate social policies. Nikki Unger, for instance, commented that helping AIDS patients must include paying the bill for government-sponsored research. Admitting that AIDS is "very depressing and scary for my generation," another young woman remarked that she is hopeful because there is evidence that people are willing to work for a cure but also to support programs aimed at prevention and education.

From our interviews, we found many instances in which young people had been stimulated to think harder about social policies as a result of their volunteer experiences. As I have suggested, however, volunteering does not generate different attitudes simply as a result of one's experiences. Interpretation is required. If community service is performed simply because it is required or because it will look good on college applications, it is unlikely to encourage support of compassionate social policies. For that to happen, volunteering must be viewed in a way that emphasizes the value of caring, and it must encourage young people to think of themselves as caring persons.

The survey evidence made this point clearly. Teenagers were asked about support for policies to help the homeless find housing, to protect the environment, and to resolve the AIDS problem. We combined their responses to these items to form an index of support for social programs and found that support for these programs was not enhanced by volunteering for a certain number of hours, by simply having worked on a community service project in the past year, by having raised funds, or even by sporadically performing acts of compassion, such as giving money to a beggar on the street. What did make a difference was having good reasons for being kind and compassionate. Indeed, all four of the general frameworks—humanitarianism, happiness, reciprocity, and self-realization—that we considered earlier were positively associated with support for social programs. The instrumental reasons, however, were not.

Moreover, among volunteers themselves, the specific reason for becoming involved that made the most difference was feeling compassion. Those who gave this as an important reason were significantly more likely to favor social programs, whereas those who emphasized enjoying themselves, exploring their strengths, having benefited themselves, or enhancing their résumé were not more likely to favor social programs. In addition, those who said they learned to be helpful and kind were more likely to favor these policies. Indeed, this benefit was more strongly associated with favoring them than were any of the other benefits. For compassionate social policies to gain support as a result of youthful volunteer experiences, therefore, the leaders of volunteer programs need to give young people good reasons for being kind and to maintain and reinforce these reasons as part of the volunteer experience. This, more than the amount of time spent or the type of activity, will reinforce broader ameliorative policies.[14]

In the final analysis, then, there is ample reason for hope—especially if volunteering conveys understandings of the importance of caring itself and if it reinforces concern for compassionate social policies as well as kindness in everyday life. Indeed, the words and the lives of young people themselves are the most tangible reasons to be hopeful about the future of our society. Jackie White probably said it best: "I never lose hope. There's potential for things to happen in this country that are exciting. We need to keep working at changing people's attitudes, enabling people to live a decent life, and trying to undo the hate that makes people harm others. If more people do that, there's definitely hope!"

Appendix A
Methodology

The research on which this volume is based was designed in conjunction with the national survey of volunteering and giving among American teenagers conducted by Independent Sector in 1992. The aim of this part of the research was to probe more deeply into teenage volunteers' understandings of volunteering. To that end, we devised semistructured questions that gave the respondents opportunities to talk in their own words about their experiences and understandings. Because the survey provided representative data and a basis for statistical generalizations, we interviewed in depth selected respondents to talk about particular kinds of volunteer experiences.

Selecting the Respondents

A primary consideration in selecting the respondents was to achieve diversity in the kinds of caring activities represented. We made it a practice not to select respondents performing the same kind of activities for the same organization, except one instance, in order to obtain the differing perspectives of three students who worked together on a project feeding the homeless.

Our respondents were collectively involved in a wide range of caring activities: feeding the homeless, working with AIDS victims, working with inner-city youths, tutoring the blind, volunteering in nursing homes and hospitals, working on emergency medical teams, helping the physically and mentally handicapped, supporting the elderly, serving on church or synagogue boards, raising Seeing Eye dogs, coaching community soccer teams, organizing environmental programs, and working on human rights and social justice issues, to name just a few. Most of our respondents were, or had been, involved in other caring or volunteer activities as well. Thus, the wider range of activities represented includes scouting, sex education, rape counseling, racial awareness, women's advocacy, painting and construction projects, caring for runaways, grief counseling, Special Olympics, drug abuse and alcoholism prevention, flood and hurricane relief, community cleanup projects, fund-raising drives, lobbying, and tutoring.

We also tried to maximize the diversity of our respondents in other ways, by making it a policy not to select more than two respondents from any one high school. We included respondents from public, private nonsectarian, and private sectarian high schools and from schools with fewer than one hundred students to ones with more than fifteen hundred students. A majority of our respondents were in the eleventh or twelfth grade, because they were more likely at this age to have been involved in volunteer activities, but some were in the ninth or tenth grade, and a few were in the seventh or eighth grade. They were identified through a deliberately wide network of contacts and referrals as well, including high school guidance counselors and teachers, pastors and rabbis, scout masters, other community agencies, national volunteer and youth organizations, and young people themselves.

In regard to social class, our respondents are young people from the wealthiest, the poorest, and virtually every background in between. Some of them, for example, live in mansions; others live in welfare housing; and the majority live in modest to comfortable single-family dwellings and apartments. Their parents' occupations (most of their mothers and fathers both held jobs outside the home) ranged from vice-presidents of large companies to assembly-line workers, from physicians and lawyers to the unemployed, and from engineering to teaching to real estate to personnel management to day care. In racial composition, our respondents reflect the larger U.S. population, the majority white, but a substantial minority African American or Latino and several Native American. In respect to religion, they include mainline and evangelical Protestants from more than a dozen denominations, Roman Catholics, Jews, Muslims, atheists, agnostics, and a number with mixed religious affiliations or with no religious inclination at all.

We also sought geographic diversity. Because our budget for travel was limited, we conducted more of our interviews in the Middle Atlantic region (between New York and Philadelphia) than in other parts of the country. We were, however, able to do interviewing in other regions of the country as well, except for the West Coast. Thus our interviews are scattered across sixteen states: New York, New Jersey, Pennsylvania, Delaware, Maryland, Virginia, Kentucky, North Carolina, Tennessee, Alabama, Mississippi, Ohio, Indiana, Missouri, Michigan, and Wisconsin. Our respondents also are diverse with respect to the type of community in which they live, including the inner city, older transitional neighborhoods in cities, suburbs, and small towns.

The Interviews

With only a few exceptions, each interview was conducted in the respondent's home, often in his or her own room in order to ensure privacy (the exceptions were students that we interviewed at school or a community agency or church). All the interviews were conducted by the same person, a professional interviewer who had worked in high school settings and whose experiences as a mother of high school–age young people gave her the background necessary to ask appropriate follow-up questions, for example, about music, clubs, and other activities.

Although I designed the interview schedule and conducted several preliminary interviews, I did not do the interviewing myself, for several reasons: Past experience has shown that a female interviewer is best for reducing possible gender biases, especially when the primary researcher is male. Past experience has also demonstrated that respondents generally speak more freely when the interviewer can disclaim final responsibility for the questions and can be assumed not to know the intention behind particular questions. An additional consideration was that the extensive travel and set-up time for the project required someone who could devote his or her entire schedule to the interviewing for a period of approximately six months.

The interviews lasted more than two hours on average, with several running to four or five hours. Each interview was tape-recorded, professionally transcribed, and independently verified for verbatim accuracy. Each interview produced approximately one hundred pages of transcript.

The interviews tried to obtain a full description of the respondent's principal volunteer activity in which he or she was currently involved and a record of other volunteer and helping activities, both formal and informal and in the present and the past. Another section of the interview was devoted to family background, parents, and experiences of caring, trauma, and other significant childhood events. A third section focused on other current activities, including sports, music, leisure activities, academic performance, and favorite subjects and teachers. A fourth section dealt with beliefs and attitudes toward self, religion, politics, and society.

The final section was made up of questions about the future, ranging from projected college and career plans, to future volunteer work, to social problems and issues of social concern. The questions were open-ended, and the respondents were encouraged to tell stories and to talk at length in order to express themselves in their own words. The interview had a semistructured format: Each respondent was asked all the main questions as written, and each was asked most of the probes as written, with additional probes or questions introduced at the interviewer's initiative, to follow or clarify important subjects. The interview guide is reproduced in Appendix B.

Data Analysis

Because the qualitative data are not drawn from a representative sample, I present verbatim quotations and summaries rather than quantitative results. When generalizations are drawn from the qualitative data (such as when comparing young men and young women), we did tally the responses wherever possible. Most of the broader generalizations, however, are supported by the national survey.

Unless otherwise indicated, all figures in the text and the notes are from the 1992 survey of a nationally representative sample of American youth aged twelve through seventeen. As stated in the Preface, I was a member of the committee that designed this survey and was free to include many questions based on my previous research with adults.

A copy of the interview schedule used for that survey and a summary of the main results are available in Virginia A. Hodgkinson and Murray S. Weitzman, Volunteering and Giving Among Teenagers 12 to 17 Years of Age: Findings from a National Survey (Washington, D.C.: Independent Sector, 1828 L Street N.W., 1992). A copy of the raw data from that survey was made available to me.

With the help of my research assistant Timothy Clydesdale, we then developed an SPSS system file of these data. All the results presented here are from our own analysis of these data. In some instances, the percentages reported here differ by one or two points from those presented in the Independent Sector report. These discrepancies are caused by different weighting schemes, and some erroneous responses were deleted in the course of cleaning the data.

Because the Independent Sector data are available to interested readers, both in the report just mentioned and on disk, I have presented summaries of the results and indicated what questions were used in drawing results, rather than attempting to include all percentages and other statistical tests in the text or the notes.

Other quantitative results discussed in the text are drawn from my own analysis of several other nationally representative surveys, including a survey dealing with volunteering and caring among adults that I designed and conducted in 1989, a survey concerning self-esteem for which I served as a consultant in 1981, and several surveys of giving and volunteering among adults conducted by Independent Sector.

Appendix B
Interview Guide

As you know, this is part of a study being conducted at Princeton University of young people who are involved in volunteer activities. We want you to answer in as much detail as possible, to tell us stories about your experiences, not just answer yes or no. There is no right or wrong; it's just what's in your head. Some of the questions may seem repetitive. Stop anytime. Stick in answers from questions before. I won't say much.

1. *First, just for my records, how old are you?*
2. *And what year are you in school? What school do you go to?*

I. The first set of questions deals with your current (or most recent) volunteer work.

3. *Tell me what sort of volunteer work you're doing (just assume I know nothing about it). In other words, tell me about the program and what you specifically are doing. [Frame in the past tense if the activity is recent rather than current.]*

4. *How long have you been doing this?*

5. *And about how often—or how many hours a week—do you spend?*

6. *[Unless clear] What sorts of people do you try to help?*

7. *Tell me a story that would illustrate some particular experience (here, with this) that has been especially significant or moving to you? Why was this significant to you?*

8. *Tell me, now, in as much detail as you can, how and why you got involved in this—in other words, what motivated you? [Ask the question this way, and wait for the person to tell the story as fully as possible; then probe for*

more detail if necessary.] If fun, why? If you like it, why? If you like helping them, why?

9. *Were there any other reasons why you became involved?*

10. *What have you liked the most about it?*

11. *For each thing liked: Why was that something you especially liked?*

12. *What would you say your most memorable experience has been (with this volunteer activity)? [Probe for a story.] Why was this memorable?*

13. *What have you liked the least about it?*

14. *For each thing disliked: Why didn't you like that?*

15. *What have you gotten from doing this?*

16. *People often say they get good feelings from helping people. Can you describe the sorts of feelings you've gotten?*

17. *Can you think of some specific time when you really felt good or satisfied from this activity? (If so, please describe.)*

18. *Has the way you feel about yourself changed in any way as a result of this activity? (For example, do you have more self-esteem, or hasn't that changed?)*

19. *Do you think you've grown stronger as a person? How? In what way? Can you give me an example?*

20. *Do you expect to be doing this sort of volunteer work for a while longer, or not?*

21. *Have you made any friends as part of this work—people you will probably keep in touch with? If yes: Are these friends fellow volunteers, or are they some of the people you were trying to help?*

22. *Apart from this particular experience, are you part of any group that you meet regularly with and get support from? (formal or church youth group) If yes: What sort of group is it? (Who's helping you?) Can you tell me about the things you do together?*

23. *Have you received any awards or recognition for your volunteer work?*

24. *What is it about your school (church, scouts) that has encouraged you to be a volunteer? Why has this been helpful? (or not helpful?)*

25. *Are you doing any other volunteer activities right now? [For each probe—what you like about it, don't like about it.]*

II. The next set of questions is about your background.

26. *First, I need to know a little about your parents. [Do mother and father separately.] Can you tell me what your mother [father] does for a living?*

27. *Have they always done this, or did they work at something else before?*

28. *And you live (lived) with both your parents? [If parents are separated or divorced, find out how long ago that happened.]*

29. *Do your parents do any sort of volunteer work? [Do each separately.] If yes: Tell me what sort it is. How long have they been doing this?*

30. *When you were younger, did they do any volunteer work? If yes: What did they do?*

31. *Would you describe your mother as a "caring" person—the kind who cares about people and tries to help them? Why or why not? Can you give me an example?*

32. *How about your father? Would you describe him as a caring person? Why or why not? Can you give me an example?*

33. *For either your mother or your father, can you think of some time when you were really impressed that they cared for someone (outside your immediate family)? Tell me about it. [Probe for some pivotal event that may stand out in their memory.]*

34. *What about you? Did you grow up feeling your parents really cared for you? What would be an example?*

35. *Were there times when you felt your parents did* not *care for you? What would be an example of that?*

36. *On the whole, do you feel close, or sort of distant, from your parents? [Probe for both mother and father.] Can you put in your own words what you mean by close or distant?*

37. *Can you remember anything specific your parents tried to teach you about being kind to people or being concerned about the needy?*

38. *What was your reaction when they tried to teach you this?*

39. *Did anything traumatic happen to you when you were growing up, like moving, being sick and in the hospital and people caring for you, having an accident, a relative or a friend die? Something that might have happened either to you or somebody you cared about? How did that affect you?*

40. *As far as you can remember, what was the first time you were really struck by seeing people in poverty? Tell me about it. How did that affect you? What was your reaction?*

41. *Has there been any other time, growing up, when you have really seen people who were very poor?*

42. *Other than your parents, have you known anyone who really showed what it means to be caring and compassionate? Who? [Probe for teachers,*

friends, other relatives.] What would an example be of how this person showed caring?

43. Has there ever been a time when you needed to be cared for, like you were sick, or lonely, or losing somebody you cared about? If yes: What happened? Who cared for you?

44. Did you attend religious services while you were growing up? If yes: How often? What kind?

45. Do you attend religious services now? If yes: How often? What kind? Why do (don't) you attend?

46. Do you remember ever reading or hearing the story of the Good Samaritan? If yes: If you had to tell it in your own words, how would you tell it?

47. Can you remember ever seeing some event that reminded you of the Good Samaritan?

48. Was there ever a time, growing up, when you thought you'd like to go into a career where you could help people? What sort of career was it? Did you keep thinking about that career, or did your ideas change? If so, why?

49. What was the first time you ever did any sort of volunteer work? Tell me what you did.

50. Why did you become involved with this (first time) volunteer activity? What motivated you? (Anything else?)

51. What did you especially like about it? What didn't you like about it?

52. What other volunteer work, if any, have you done in the past? (For each, tell what you liked and what you disliked about it.) Why did you drop out?

53. I'm going to read off a list of things, and if you've ever done any of them, I'd like you to tell me a little about it. (Tell me a description or story about each one you were involved in.) (a) Gone door to door to raise money for something. (b) Made signs or handed out leaflets to protest something. (c) Done some service project at your school. (d) Worked on some kind of community service project. (e) Helped out with something at your church/synagogue. (f) Tried to help someone who was having a tough time in his or her personal life. (g) Voluntarily done something just to help out around the house.

54. Tell me a little about some of your other interests—things you like to do in your spare time. [Probe fully for music, sports, friends, hobbies.] (boyfriend, girlfriend)

55. Have you ever been really engrossed with something—like sports, or a famous athlete, or a musical group?

56. How about schoolwork—what classes or subjects do you enjoy the most? Why do you think you enjoy these particular subjects?

57. *Have you ever had a teacher/sponsor you particularly liked or admired? (If sponsor, ask for a teacher.) Who? Why?*

58. *Is there any other (adult) role model who has particularly influenced you? Who do you admire the most? Why?*

59. *What sorts of grades do you get? (Or did get in high school?)*

60. *What is your hardest subject?*

61. *What is your best subject?*

62. *What would you say is your favorite TV show?*

63. *Have you had any part-time jobs? Doing what?*

III. Next I have some questions about your attitudes and beliefs.

64. *First of all, we hear a lot about individualism these days. Would you describe yourself as an individualist, or not? Why or why not? What does the word* individualist *mean to you?*

65. *Are you the type of person who needs a lot of space, or do you prefer to have a lot of people around?*

66. *Do you like to be independent, or do you like to depend on other people?*

67. *More generally now, what sorts of things do you like best about yourself?*

68. *What things don't you like about yourself?*

69. *Do you get depressed sometimes? ("down" OK) Why or why not? What things depress you? How often do you get depressed?*

70. *On political issues, would you say you are mostly a conservative or mostly a liberal? Give me an example of what you mean by liberal or conservative?*

71. *Are religious beliefs important to you? Why or why not?*

72. *What do you believe religiously? (Anything else)*

73. *Do you do anything from day to day that might be considered religious—like read the Bible, read religious things, attend a religious group? (like church youth group, Young Life) If so, what?*

74. *Do you believe there is a God? If yes or maybe: What do you think God is like? What do you think God expects of you?*

75. *Do you pray? If yes: How often do you pray? What do you pray about? Are your prayers answered?*

76. *How about Jesus—does Jesus have meaning for you? If so, what?*

77. *In comparison with your parents, would you say you are more religious or less religious than they are? In what way?*

78. *How about your grandparents? Are (were) any of them especially religious? In what way?*

79. *Do you think religion helps make people more caring, or doesn't it make much difference? Why do you think that?*

80. *Coming back to the issue of caring and volunteering for a moment—Do you consider yourself an especially caring person or not? Why or why not?*

81. *Have you ever been embarrassed—like feeling people might laugh at you because you did volunteer work? If yes: Give me an example.*

82. *Do people (peers) look up to you because of your volunteer work?*

83. *Do most of your friends do volunteer work, or not? If no: Do any of your close friends do volunteer work?*

84. *Do people you know ever get teased because of some issue they believe in, like saving the whales, or not eating grapes, or being in Peace Club, or something like that? Give me an example.*

85. *From what you know about our society (in general), do you think most people really care about the needy, or are they mostly looking out for themselves? Why do you say this?*

86. *Let me read you another short list of activities, and for each one, I'd like you to tell me two things: Can you imagine yourself doing this? And second, why can you, or can't you, imagine doing it? [Keep reminding respondent to say whether he or she could realistically imagine doing these things, and then probe to see what it is about the respondent or the activity that makes him or her feel each one is or is not a possibility—especially feelings, fears, being repulsed, having other commitments, and so forth.] Be realistic. Don't tell me what you think I want to hear. (a) Giving mouth-to-mouth resuscitation to someone who has stopped breathing. (b) Helping at a soup kitchen for the homeless in an inner-city ghetto. (c) Cleaning sludge off a beach or riverbank after an oil spill. (d) Spending a year of your life before the age of twenty-five doing community service work. (e) Feeding handicapped persons who could not feed themselves. (f) Helping take care of AIDS patients. (g) Volunteering a Saturday to help at an athletic event for handicapped children. (h) Tutoring a student in your community who was having trouble reading. (i) Getting thrown in jail for taking part in a protest march. (j) Helping a group in Washington lobby for clean air.*

87. *Have you ever read or seen anything about Mother Teresa—the woman who works with the poor in Calcutta? If yes: What do you think of her? Why?*

Would you like to be like her? Why or why not? What about her can't you relate to? Why not? Are there any lessons to be learned from her? What?

88. *Have you ever read about anyone else who inspired you to be a caring person?*

89. *Lots of young people say helping the needy is one of their values, but then many of them don't put this value into practice—why do you think this is?*

90. *People who think helping the needy is a good thing sometimes have trouble saying why it is a good thing—Why do you think it is?*

91. *To put it a different way, what do you think the best reason is for trying to be a kind and compassionate person?*

92. *Do you think everyone should try to be kind and compassionate, or is it OK if some people aren't?*

93. *Let's think about a concrete example. Suppose some people are trying to get volunteers to help on Saturdays at a soup kitchen to feed the poor. What do you think they should do?*

94. *Suppose there was a law that said every teenager in the country has to give so many hours a month to helping the poor—Would that be a good thing? How would you feel about it?*

95. *What if your school required every student to work one Saturday at a soup kitchen—Would that be better than just trying to get volunteers?*

96. *Would it still be the same if students were paid to help at the soup kitchen, or would something be lost? Explain.*

97. *Do you think you would be more likely to volunteer yourself if the program were run through a school or through a church or synagogue? Why?*

98. *How do you feel about famous singers and athletes doing benefits to help the poor—Does that inspire you to try to help too, or doesn't it work that way?*

99. *There's some talk about a national service program that would let young people get college loans more easily if they did a couple years of volunteer service. What do you think of that idea? Why do you think that?*

IV. The final section now: These are some questions about the future—yours and the society we live in.

100. *First, what sort of life would you like to be leading ten years from now? [Probe for details about marriage, kids, type of residence, material things, leisure activities.]*

101. *What sort of career are you most interested in? [Take time on this one to make sure you understand the level of education, the kind or organization, and the specific kind of work the person has in mind.] Choice of college and/or major.*

102. *What attracts you to this sort of career?*

103. *For each thing mentioned: And why is that important to you?*

104. *If you didn't follow that career, what would be some of your other choices for a career?*

105. *What things are most important to you in deciding on a career? How about money, is that important? How about being able to do something well? How do your own talents connect with the sort of career you have in mind? Do you want to do something that gives you a lot of freedom? (whatever it means to you—flexibility of schedule, decisions)*

106. *Has your volunteer work influenced your ideas about a career very much? If yes: In what ways?*

107. *What experiences, do you think, have influenced your career ideas the most?*

108. *Do you think your career will make it possible for you to help people? In what ways?*

109. *How might the pressures of your career make it harder for you to help people?*

110. *For you personally, do you think you'll be doing more to help people through your job or through some kind of volunteer work?*

111. *Do you think it will be possible for you to live comfortably and still help people? [Probe to see what "comfortably" means, that is, having lots of material possessions.]*

112. *Do you think you would be willing to sacrifice something in order to be of more help to people? If yes: What would you be willing to give up? [Probe for things like not being quite as successful at work, not having as many material possessions, and giving up some free time.]*

113. *Some people who say they want to help people when they're teenagers seem to lose sight of that goal by the time they become established in their careers. What do you think they could do to prevent that from happening?*

114. *Do you think doing volunteer work would help?*

115. *As you think about the future of our whole world, do you feel fairly optimistic or fairly pessimistic? Why?*

116. *Here's one last list of things. Tell me first if it's something you've thought about very much, and then if you have, what you think can be done*

about it, whether you feel it is a serious and important problem, and whether it is hopeless, will just sort of go away, or will take some kind of serious effort. (a) The problem of AIDS. (b) The problem of homelessness. (c) Environmental problems, like pollution and the greenhouse effect. (d) The drug and alcohol problem. (e) The problem of war and nuclear arms.

117. *Do you personally see any ways that you are going to be able to help solve some of these problems?*

118. *Are these mostly problems the government will have to solve, or can individual citizens make a difference? What difference can individual citizens make?*

119. *Do you think volunteers can play much of a role with problems like this, or are the problems too big?*

120. *Finally, just a few more bookkeeping things:*

> *You are (male/female).*
> *And you live (where).*
> *Your religious preference is?*
> *The highest grade your father completed in school?*
> *The highest grade your mother completed in school?*
> *You have how many brothers and sisters? Older or younger?*
> *Today's date is?*

121. *Is there anything you'd like to add in your own words? [Probe also to see what the person thought of the interview.]*

122. *Can you recommend anyone else that I might talk to?*

After tape is turned off: Ask whether it would be all right to telephone if any follow-up questions need to be asked. If yes, write down name and phone number.

Notes

Chapter 1

1. Specific examples are described in *Community Service Bibliography* (Los Angeles: Constitutional Rights Foundation, 1993); Shirley Sagawa and Samuel Halperin, eds., *Visions of Service* (Washington, D.C.: National Women's Law Center and American Youth Policy Forum, 1993); *Student Community Service Program: National Directory* (Washington, D.C.: Action, 1993); *What You Can Do for Your Country* (Washington, D.C.: Commission on National and Community Service, 1993); *Youth as Resources: A Program and a Perspective* (Washington, D.C.: National Crime Prevention Council, 1993).

2. See Alasdair MacIntyre, *After Virtue: A Study in Moral Theory*, 2nd ed. (Notre Dame, Ind.: University of Notre Dame Press, 1984); Jeffrey Stout, *Ethics After Babel: The Languages of Morals and Their Discontents* (Boston: Beacon Press, 1988); Robert B. Louden, *Morality and Moral Theory: A Reappraisal and Reaffirmation* (New York: Oxford University Press, 1992).

3. Recent scholarly contributions include Alan Wolfe, *Whose Keeper? Social Science and Moral Obligation* (Berkeley and Los Angeles: University of California Press, 1989); Philip Selznick, *The Moral Commonwealth: Social Theory and the Promise of Community* (Berkeley and Los Angeles: University of California Press, 1992); James Q. Wilson, *The Moral Sense* (New York: Free Press, 1993); Robert Wuthnow, *Meaning and Moral Order: Explorations in Cultural Analysis* (Berkeley and Los Angeles: University of California Press, 1987).

4. William J. Bennett, ed., *The Book of Virtues* (New York: Knopf, 1994); William J. Bennett, "Getting Used to Decadence: The Spirit of Democracy in Modern America," in *Heritage Foundation Reports*, December 7, 1993; Michael Lerner, *Jewish Renewal* (New York: Putnam, 1994). Also on Michael Lerner, see Lee Moriwaki, "Adding Values to Schools," *Seattle Times*, February 5, 1994, p. 1; Jeremy Rifkin, "The Clinton Dilemma," *Tikkun*, May 1993, pp. 14–16; Amitai Etzioni, *The Spirit of Community: Rights, Responsibilities, and the Communitarian Agenda* (New York: Crown, 1993); Robert N. Bellah, Richard Madsen, William M. Sullivan, Ann Swidler, and Steven M. Tipton, *The Good Society* (New York: Knopf, 1991).

5. See my book *Acts of Compassion: Caring for Others and Helping Ourselves* (Princeton, N.J.: Princeton University Press, 1991).

Chapter 2

1. In the national survey I conducted in 1989 for my book *Acts of Compassion*, when I asked, "On the whole, do you think people in our country are genuinely concerned about helping the needy, or are they mostly concerned about their own activities and interests?" 67 percent answered that people were self-interested, and 25 percent thought that they were concerned about others. When this same question was asked in 1992 in the Gallup Organization for Independent Sector's national survey of youth aged twelve to seventeen, 70 percent responded, "Concerned about their own activities and interests," and 11 percent said, "Concerned about helping the needy" (in both studies the remainder answered, "Both" or "Don't know").

2. Unless otherwise indicated, the results reported in this and subsequent chapters for teenagers are from the 1992 national survey of young people aged twelve to seventeen conducted by the Gallup Organization for Independent Sector. The figures are from my own analysis of the raw survey data; further details about the survey are presented in Appendix A, "Methods." Copies of the raw data and published reports summarizing the data, as well as comparable data from adults, are available from Independent Sector, 1828 L Street, N.W., Washington, D.C. 20036.

3. U.S. Bureau of the Census, *Statistical Abstract of the United States: 1992* (112th ed.) (Washington, D.C.: U.S. Government Printing Office, 1992), p. xiii.

4. Ibid., p. 57.

5. Ibid., p. 84.

6. Ibid., p. 87.

7. S. K. Henshaw and J. Van Vort, eds., *Abortion Services in the United States, 1988* (New York: Alan Guttmacher Institute, 1992).

8. *Statistical Abstract*, p. 84.

9. Ibid., p. 186.

10. Ibid., p. 157.

11. In the teen survey, 84 percent reported that "making the world a better place" is a very important or absolutely essential goal for their lives; only 55 percent said this about "giving time through volunteer work to charitable and religious or community organizations, or other charitable institutions or causes." In regard to other goals and values that compete for time, energy, and attention, 94 percent stated that "achieving success in your work or career" was very important or absolutely essential; 89 percent said this about "having fun and enjoyment in life"; 76 percent stated it about "being able to have a nice home, furnishings and clothes; and 61 percent said they valued "making a lot of money" this much. There is also cause for concern when the values associated with current volunteer efforts are examined. One hope is that caring for others can be a deterrent to the materialism that appears so widespread in our society. Yet volunteers are no less likely than nonvolunteers are to say that having a nice home, furnishings, and clothes is one of the top goals in life. When teens were asked how important "being able to have a nice home, furnishings and clothes" was to them as a personal goal, 29 percent of those who had done volunteer work in the past year stated that this was "absolutely essential," compared with 27 percent of those who had done no volunteer work. When we add those who said that this was "very important" to them, the respective figures are 75 and 78 percent.

12. These figures are from the 1992 Independent Sector surveys of adults and teenagers.

13. *Statistical Abstract*, p. 374.

14. Details about this survey are presented in my book *Acts of Compassion: Caring for Others and Helping Ourselves* (Princeton, N.J.: Princeton University Press, 1991).

15. Ibid.

Chapter 3

1. Aristotle, *The Politics*, bk. I, chap. 1.

2. Thomas LeClair, "The Language Must Not Sweat": A Conversation with Toni Morrison," in *Toni Morrison: Critical Perspectives Past and Present*, ed. Henry Louis Gates Jr. and K. A. Appiah (New York: Amistad, 1993), p. 371.

3. The high school years are good ones for capturing the transition from experiences of caring within the family to the challenges of knowing how to offer care and service in the wider world. But we should not assume that this transition is therefore primarily a problem in human development. The young people who participated in the study were, of course, undergoing development. Some were more mature than others. Many of them talked about what they had learned and how they had changed as a result of their volunteer activities. Their experiences cannot, however, be easily placed on a developmental continuum. These young people were not so much making a transition from one world to another as living in two worlds, the world of their childhood homes and the world of their involvement at school and in the community. They will continue to do so, just as we all do. This is what interests me about their lives, not the developmental stage they happen to exemplify. All of us continue to feel the tension between our sense of caring and our commitments in the wider world. We do so because we thrive on informal and personalized caring and because we also live in a world of institutions that requires us to play specialized roles, to differentiate our relationships and the parts of our lives, to relate to strangers, and to obey impersonal norms.

4. Jean-Jacques Rousseau, *The Social Contract*, ed. Lester G. Crocker (New York: Washington Square Press, 1967 [1762]), p. 8.

5. Jean-Jacques Rousseau, *Discourse on the Origin of Inequality* (New York: Washington Square Press, 1967 [1755]), p. 203.

6. Ibid., p. 203.

7. See, for example, C. D. Batson and J. Coke, "Empathy: A Source of Altruistic Motivation for Helping," in *Altruism and Helping Behavior: Social, Personality, and Developmental Perspectives*, ed. J. P. Rushton and R. Sorrentino (Hillsdale, N.J.: Erlbaum, 1991), pp. 167–87.

8. James Q. Wilson, *The Moral Sense* (New York: Free Press, 1993), p. 54. His discussion mentions both the Milgram shock-treatment experiments and the studies of Nazi soldiers as examples of human willingness to go along with mistreatment in order to win approval.

9. The idea that nurturing relationships in childhood and adolescence are the groundwork for broader commitments to service and caring fits readily with the sizable literature on developmental psychology that focuses on attachment. This is reviewed in John Bowlby, *Attachment and Loss*, 2nd ed. (New York: Basic Books, 1982); and in Mary Ainsworth, *Patterns of Attachment* (Hillsdale, N.J.: Erlbaum, 1978). According to the literature, infants and young children who develop strong, nurturing attachments

to their mothers (or other caregivers) are healthier physically and emotionally, more secure, better able to adapt to new situations and to enter them with an attitude of trust, and better able to achieve other developmental tasks as they mature. Although little attention, if any, has been paid to the effects of early attachments on later caregiving behavior, one would seem to facilitate the other. Most of the research has, however, concentrated on attachment only in infancy and younger childhood. Much less is known about the effects of such continuing attachments in later adolescence and young adulthood.

10. These figures are from my analysis of a survey I helped design, called the Gallup Self-Esteem Survey, conducted among a nationally representative sample in 1982. In it, nearly two-thirds of the adult respondents stated that they felt "very close" to their mothers (63 percent) and about half (47 percent) said this about their fathers. The figures reported in the text apply to those respondents who said they felt either "not very close" or "not at all close." Other surveys also suggest that teenagers generally feel they get along well with their parents. In one survey, fewer than one in twenty claimed not to get along well with his or her parents. See Robert Bezilla, *America's Youth in the 1990s* (Princeton, N.J.: George H. Gallup International Institute, 1993), p. 35. In response to "How well would you say you get along with your parents?" 52 percent said very well, 44 percent said fairly well, and 4 percent said not well at all.

11. It is difficult to discern from surveys exactly what caring means, but the fact that it is valued by virtually everyone is apparent: Among teenagers nationally, for example, 90 percent say that "having a warm relationship with others" is very important or absolutely essential to them, and 79 percent say this about "having a sense of belonging."

12. Among teenagers nationally, the average amount of time devoted to volunteering within the past month was 7.8 hours for those who said they had received a great deal of satisfaction from their family within the past year, 6.1 hours for those who had received some satisfaction, and 4.0 hours for those who had experienced little or no satisfaction from their families. Teenagers who have been close to their families also value "a sense of belonging" more than others do, and this, too, is associated with higher rates of volunteering. The role of family is also indicated by the fact that 50 percent of those who derive a great deal of satisfaction from their family also value giving time to volunteering, compared with only 26 percent of those who receive some satisfaction from their family.

13. Among teenagers nationally, the average amount of time spent volunteering within the past month by those who said they had received kindness from someone other than their parents while they were growing up was 7.7 hours, compared with 3.5 hours by those who had not experienced such kindness.

14. One might suppose that receiving care in the family makes more of a difference or is limited to those who are especially in need themselves. Some past research has shown some effects from having experienced a crisis oneself and later caring for others. According to the current data, however, neither having been seriously ill nor having had a close friend or relative become seriously ill or die was significantly related to valuing giving time to helping the needy.

15. Teenagers who reported that both their parents did volunteer work put in an average of 11.8 hours per month on volunteer work themselves, compared with only 4.6 hours for those from homes in which neither parent volunteered. The effects of one or the other parent's volunteering are considered in Chapter 7. It is important not to attribute causality entirely to parental volunteering in this relationship, because many of

the young people we interviewed in depth said that their parents had started volunteering after they themselves had become volunteers.

16. Those teenagers who said they had seen a family member helping others outside the family had volunteered an average 7.8 hours in the past month, compared with 5.6 hours for those who had not seen this. Within each subgroup, the percentages who maintained that volunteering was very important as a personal goal were as follows: 48 percent for those who had a family member help others while they were growing up, 37 percent for those who did not, 57 percent for those whose parents both did volunteer work, 47 percent for those who had one parent do volunteer work, 40 percent for those who had neither parent do volunteer work, 49 percent for who saw someone other than a family member helping others, and 37 percent for those who did not see this.

17. Giorgio Agamben, *The Coming Community*, trans. Michael Hardt (Minneapolis: University of Minnesota Press, 1993), p. 68.

18. According to the teen survey, by age twelve, 41 percent said they had seen people in extreme poverty; by age seventeen, this proportion had increased to 55 percent. Only 7 percent of all teenagers reported that they themselves grew up in poverty.

19. Gillian Roberts, *Philly Stakes* (New York: Ballantine Books, 1990), p. 4.

20. One young man, for example, remembers driving through the inner city for the first time and seeing people who were really poor. He says he wished he could win the lottery so he could help them, but his main response was just to become more appreciative of what he had and not to take things for granted.

21. On balance, young people who are exposed to extreme poverty appear to interpret the situation in a way that is conducive to becoming involved as volunteers. At least the survey showed that those who said they had seen extreme poverty while they were growing up put in more hours a month (8.7 on average) than those who had not seen extreme poverty (5.9 on average). Some of the difference, of course, may be due to young people's seeing poverty as a result of early involvement in volunteer activities.

22. Nationally, 56 percent of all twelve-year-olds said they had done volunteer work when they were younger (by age seventeen, this proportion increases only to 62 percent). The teen survey shows that twelve- and thirteen-year-olds are about as likely to be involved currently in volunteer activities as are sixteen- and seventeen-year-olds. However, there is a maturation process at work during these years. Older teens are involved in a wider range of activities than younger teens are, including political organizations, foundations, and international programs. They are more likely to be involved in more than one organization, less likely to volunteer through school programs, and more likely to seek out their own ways of volunteering and to do volunteer work on their own; and they devote significantly more hours per month to their volunteering.

Thirty percent of sixteen- and seventeen-year-olds have volunteered alone or informally during the past year, compared with 22 percent of twelve- and thirteen-year-olds. The former are more likely than the latter to have volunteered for more than one organization in the areas of health, human services, environment, and their informal activities. On average, the former (counting only those who volunteer at all in specific areas) spend sixteen hours a month on health projects, compared with three hours for the latter; fifteen hours for the former, compared with seven for the latter, on education projects; and eleven hours for the former, compared with six for the latter, on human service projects.

23. The importance of knowing that the recipient appreciates what you do is evident in a number of cases. For example, Patti Evans had to serve as a "volunteer" in a nursing

home for the elderly in order to be confirmed at her church. At first she resented having to do it but then found that she enjoyed meeting the people and that they really appreciated what she did for them. "You know, some of them are crabby, but it's only because they're lonely. I really liked putting a smile on their face. When they saw me they would smile."

24. Among twelve-year-olds, 52 percent say they have done door-to-door fund-raising (nearly the same percentage as those who say they have done any kind of volunteer work), and this percentage is the same among seventeen-year-olds. The fact that the percentage does not increase with age, even though other kinds of volunteer work become more common, is perhaps another indication that fund-raising is a negative experience for many young people.

25. A young woman who had volunteered for a political campaign when she was in the seventh grade provides another example of a negative experience: "You want respect. Usually you get that. In political work I've learned you don't. If you're a peon, you're treated like a peon. I despise door-to-door campaigning, and I hate phone banks. This year I worked on the Bill Clinton campaign, not that long. I just hated the impersonality of it."

26. Something else we observed is worthy of note. Some of the teenagers we talked to had become most actively involved as sophomores and juniors and then were less active as seniors. This was not a pattern that we could document in the survey because the data on involvement were not as detailed as the material we collected in the qualitative interviews. There, we observed that some of the more active volunteers had done little in junior high, or perhaps little even in the ninth grade, but that once they started, they became involved in several activities. Then, by the middle of their senior year, they started to cut back.

Several possibilities could explain this pattern. One, to which several students themselves referred, was that a willing volunteer suddenly became a target for requests from more and more organizations. Having made themselves available once, they became vulnerable to friends, teachers, pastors, and others who wanted to enlist their help.

Another, perhaps more cynical possibility, is that they became involved about the time they started thinking of college applications and then ceased volunteering during their senior year when they had in fact been admitted to the college of their choice. If this were the reason, none of the students we talked to at least was willing to admit it. Their level of involvement as sophomores and juniors—in many cases, even to the point of damaging their academic performance—also seems excessive if admission to college was all they had in mind.

The more likely possibility is consistent with the broader transition I have described in this chapter. What happens, I think, is that some young people grow up with a fairly undifferentiated notion of caring, regarding themselves as persons who should and do indeed try to be helpful. Having that generalized commitment to helping, they thus find it difficult to refuse when opportunities to volunteer arose. They simply became involved in everything because these all were chances to care for others. As their understanding of caring began to change, however, and particularly as they come to associate caring with more specialized interests, they started to pull back. Indeed, some of them described their period of overinvolvement as a kind of search during which they were attempting to find their particular interests. Others noted that pulling back allowed them to concentrate more on those activities that fit their own interests best or that allowed them to develop specialized skills. The trajectory of involvement, overinvolvement, and cutting back, then, appears to be further confirmation that the process of learning how to care is actually one of *relearning* what it means to care, shifting from a diffuse, primordial understanding to one that is more specialized and more amenable to the ways in which volunteer activity is currently organized.

27. Besides volunteering, young people sometimes learned that caring must be partial and specialized, by helping their friends informally and discovering that the problems required professional intervention or organized services. One young man provided two examples: "This boy named Robbie, he was gonna kill hisself. He said that he was having problems at home and stuff. I tried to talk to him, but it didn't do no good. So when he told me that, I told his social worker at school, and I call that saving a life right there. So then they got him some counseling. Then this girl that lived on the South Side, last summer I saved her from out the water from drowning. She was right there by me, I was swimming. I thought she was just playing. So then I picked her up and I swim to the edge, and I laid her on the edge, and I told the lifeguard to come here. He started pushing on her chest and gave mouth-to-mouth resuscitation. She was seriously drowning. Throw-up was coming out of her mouth. That was the nasty part about it."

Chapter 4

1. The continuing interest in Joan of Arc is evident in several recent interpretive studies: See Anne Llewellyn Barstow, *Joan of Arc: Heretic, Mystic, Shaman* (Lewiston, N.Y.: Edwin Mellen Press, 1986); Marina Warner, *Joan of Arc: The Image of Female Heroism* (New York: Knopf, 1981); Frances Gies, *Joan of Arc: The Legend and the Reality* (New York: Harper & Row, 1981).

2. Mark Twain, "Saint Joan of Arc," in *The Complete Essays of Mark Twain*, ed. Charles Neider (Garden City, N.Y.: Doubleday, 1963 [1904]), p. 323.

3. Robert N. Bellah, Richard Madsen, William M. Sullivan, Ann Swidler, and Steven M. Tipton, *Habits of the Heart: Individualism and Commitment in American Life* (Berkeley and Los Angeles: University of California Press, 1985), p. 334.

4. The high degree of consistency between importance attached to "I feel compassion toward people in need" and "I feel it is important to help others" is evident in the gamma of .75.

5. On the importance of a humanitarian outlook among rescuers during World War II, see Kristen R. Monroe, Michael C. Barton, and Ute Klingemann, "Altruism and the Theory of Rational Action: Rescuers of Jews in Nazi Europe," *Ethics* 101 (1990): 103–22.

6. Another example of the emphasis on equality in humanitarianism comes from a teenager in Alabama who said about the poor: "I don't think we should really look down on them just because they are needy. A lot of people have the tendency to sort of look down on them because they are needy. They are poor. They're not like us. I think they have just as much of a right to be able to bear themselves as anyone. It's not to show other people that you care, you do this, you do that, but the thing that's important is the people that you actually help. You help them through some type of difficult situation or something. That makes them feel good. That makes them feel like somebody does care about them."

7. In the teen survey, 90 percent agree that "I feel a moral duty to help people who suffer," but only 28 percent agree strongly; among volunteers, the proportion is about 10 percent higher than among nonvolunteers. Thus there is a widespread sense that alleviating suffering is an activity that carries moral authority, yet for many in our society,

this sense is vague or not felt acutely or personally. The humanitarian frame—namely, feeling compassion—is strongly and positively associated with agreeing strongly with this statement about moral duty; the other frames—happiness, reciprocity, and self-realization—are also positively associated with it, but much less powerfully. (Using gamma as a measure of association, the figures for the relationship between the moral duty item and the compassion, enjoyment, reciprocity, and personal strength items are .55, .27, .20, and .29.)

8. An emphasis on natural human rights was one of the reasons that some young people regard humanitarianism as a moral duty. For example: "I think it is because I think everyone has certain rights, like the natural law. Everyone should be able to eat, and everyone should be able to grow up without being afraid of your parents, and grow up with a roof. I just think there are things that if everyone tried, it would be possible to everyone to have that. Even if it's not a roof, like if you're in Africa, I just think it's possible, and it's fair and right for everyone to be kind of on the same plane, not totally just left behind somewhere. I think it's the job of the people that are on the boat to put the life buoys out for the people that are out, that have fallen off." Others grounded humanitarianism in religious arguments, as seen in Chapter 4.

9. The moral authority of the humanitarian frame is tempered by the fact that most people also believe it is their right to pursue their own goals first. Among those who strongly agree with the moral duty item, 68 percent also agree that "we all have the right to concern ourselves with our own goals first and foremost, rather than with the problems of other people." The two items do not have a statistically significant association, meaning that one varies independently of the other.

10. Based on national responses in the teen survey to a question aimed at finding out whether the respondents were oriented toward a humanitarian framework (saying that just wanting to give of oneself is a major reason to be kind and caring), it appears that although this framework is widely available in the culture, it is also reinforced by the following: previously being exposed to caring activities of all kinds, being helped by others, seeing family members helping others, having both parents volunteer, receiving kindness from nonparents, and seeing nonfamily members helping others. A humanitarian framework also is more common among females and students from professional and managerial backgrounds (as opposed to skilled, semiskilled, clerical, or labor backgrounds) and among better students.

11. From the teen survey we learned that the pursuit of happiness is a nearly universal framework among young volunteers. Ninety percent reported that thinking they would enjoy the work was at least a somewhat important reason for their volunteering, and 89 percent said that enjoyment was a very important goal in their life. In addition, these teens believed that happiness generated search behavior, that is, finding the volunteer activity that offered the most enjoyment and that fit with one's ideas of having a good time. Thus, people who have done volunteer work in community agencies are slightly but significantly more likely than other volunteers are to say that enjoyment was a significant reason for their activity (41 versus 34 percent), whereas those who did it in an educational setting, perhaps their own school, were slightly less likely to mention this as an important reason (36 versus 41 percent). Happiness as a reason for caring was not related to parental occupation—another indication of its universality across different social segments—and it was not related to having done volunteer work when younger or seeing family members helping others or parents volunteering.

12. The belief that one's happiness is contingent on the happiness of others is an important link between this framework and putting care into practice. One young woman explained her belief in this way: "I don't think a person can be really happy unless they think that people around them are really happy, too. People may wish that they could live with themselves, but you're still influenced by everything that's around you. Just like unconsciously, if there's a person next to you that hasn't eaten for three days, and is passing out because of it, even if you try to ignore that, there's going to be a part of you that knows that it's there, and knows that you're not doing something about it. So you're never going to be able to be happy unless you try to do something for the person next to you, just because it'll always be there. Not only does every person have a right to be able to eat and able to smile, but you can't be the best that you can be unless you think you're doing the best that you can do."

13. In the teen survey (based on saying that feeling good is a major reason to be kind), happiness as a framework for caring goes with becoming a stronger person and with wanting to give of oneself, and so it is rooted in some of the same ideas and experiences as the other frameworks are. It is not affected as much by previous volunteer work or by parents' volunteer work, but it is more common among young people who have done some volunteer work and have been helped by others, who have seen family help others, and who have seen nonfamily role models helping others. It also is more common among females, is independent of parents' occupation, and is only weakly related to grades. On the whole, the happiness framework is thus fairly universal across social categories. The survey also shows that it is not related simply to valuing having fun and enjoyment in life but is rooted in a people orientation, that is, valuing being around people and gaining enjoyment from them, for example, warm relationships, a sense of belonging, and respect from others. The happiness framework is also rooted in family relationships that are described as satisfying.

14. Edward O. Wilson, *On Human Nature* (Cambridge, Mass.: Harvard University Press, 1978), p. 156.

15. In the teen survey, previously benefiting was an important reason for volunteering and also was evidence of its relationship to privilege, as it was more likely to be cited by better students (among A students, 30 percent said very important, versus 23 percent among C students). This response was less common among students from semiskilled and laborer backgrounds, and so it goes somewhat with privilege, with having a sense that one has special advantages and should pay others back or pay society back.

16. Two sources of the reciprocity framework are evident in the teen survey, judging from the responses to the item about paying one's debts as a major reason for kindness: One is having incurred specific debts, and the other is an orientation to social reform. The effect of having incurred debts can be seen in the following percentages that reported that repaying is a major reason: all teens, 44 percent; teens who say they benefited previously from their volunteer experience, 65 percent; teens who were helped by a nurse, 61 percent; and teens who were helped by nobody, 39 percent. The idealism of social reform is evident in those who value making the world a better place (among those who said this was essential to them, 51 percent said that paying one's debts is a major reason for kindness, compared with 37 percent who said that it was only somewhat important and 17 percent who said that it was not important); similar patterns pertain to questions about wanting to change the world.

17. A young woman who was quite poor herself also emphasized that she felt a need to give to those less fortunate than herself: "Because I'm a lot more fortunate than a lot of other people, and if I guess in some ways if you believe in the things that God had taught, if you have more, then you give somebody else a little bit more. You do unto others as you would want them to do unto you, and if they were in your position, and you were in their position, I would want them to try to help me so I want to try to help them as much as possible."

18. For a more extended discussion of the concept of serial reciprocity, see Michael P. Moody, "Pass It On: Serial Reciprocity in Theory and Practice," working paper, Department of Sociology, Princeton University, 1993.

19. In the teen survey, the answers to whether "helping makes me a stronger person" is a major reason to be kind indicate that the self-realization framework is also originates, much as the pursuit of happiness framework does, in previous exposure to helping behavior, but not as strongly. It also appears to be more evident among better and more achievement-oriented students and to be associated with already having a sense of personal efficacy.

20. In regard to the four main indicator questions in the teen survey for the four frames discussed in the chapter, 85 percent chose at least one as a major reason to be kind, showing that the frames are, in combination, nearly universal, and only 19 percent limited themselves to only one, meaning that 66 percent chose at least two, 44 percent chose at least three, and 20 percent chose all four. Moreover, the effect of multiple reasons on doing and valuing caring is generally positive; that is, the more reasons one has, the more likely one is to care. For example, 65 percent of those with four reasons say that giving time is very important, versus 32 percent with no reasons and 33 percent with only 1 reason. Or 43 percent with four reasons say that it is a moral duty to alleviate suffering, compared with 7 percent with no reasons and 22 percent with only one reason. Another indication of the fact that these four motive frames go together but do not overlap completely is that the gammas among them range from .41 to .70 and average .52.

21. Five percent reported that no reason was very important; 6 percent, only one reason; 89 percent, two or more reasons; 82 percent, three or more reasons; 66 percent, five or more reasons; and 28 percent, ten or more reasons.

22. Some indication of the relative distinctness of these frameworks is evident in the survey. Among those teens who stated that feeling compassionate toward the needy was a very important reason for their volunteering, for example, fewer than half (47 percent) said that expecting enjoyment was also a very important reason; only about one-third (37 percent) said that exploring their personal strengths was this important; and even fewer (29 percent) reported that they were involved because they had previously benefited. The gamma statistics for these relationships (respectively, .35, .26, and .23) also show that the various frameworks are associated only moderately.

23. The instrumental reasons for caring—the kind that Rafe Ramirez criticizes—are evident among a minority of young people. For example, among teenagers nationally who had done any volunteer work in the past year, 28 percent said, "Volunteering can help me get my foot in the door at a place where I would like to work"; 29 percent said, "I can make new contacts that might help my future career"; 28 percent said, "Volunteer experience will look good on my résumé"; and 25 percent said, "Volunteering helps me deal with some of my own problems." Also, 31 percent admitted that "being kind and considerate helps me get what I want in life" was a major reason for caring.

One thing that the survey casts doubt on, however, is the idea that volunteering is done mostly by high academic achievers as a way of enhancing their résumés for the colleges of their choice. At least if this is what is going on, the better students are cleverly hiding this fact, and the mediocre students are more willing to admit it. Among mostly A students, only 14 percent stated that they volunteered because it would look good on their résumé, compared with 26 percent of B students, and 34 percent of students with grades of C or below.

24. Clifford Geertz, *The Interpretation of Cultures* (New York, Basic Books, 1973), p. 5.

Chapter 5

1. Gallup surveys of thirteen- to seventeen-year-olds report that 95 percent believe in God or a universal spirit, 93 percent believe that God loves them, 29 percent believe that they have personally experienced the presence of God, 42 percent pray alone frequently, 36 percent read the Bible weekly, 39 percent consider their own religious beliefs very important, and 25 percent believe that religion can answer today's problems. See Robert Bezilla, *America's Youth in the 1990s* (Princeton, N.J.: George H. Gallup International Institute, 1993), p. 153.

2. The figure on citizenship is 73 percent. See Robert Bezilla, *Religion in America, 1992–1993* (Princeton, N.J.: Princeton Religion Research Center, 1993), p. 66. Forty-four percent stated that religious faith is a very important personal quality; 70 percent cited hard work; 87 percent listed self-respect; and 65 percent mentioned independence. See Robert Bezilla, *America's Youth, 1977–1988* (Princeton, N.J.: George H. Gallup International Institute, 1988), p. 133.

3. The respective figures are 40 percent and 23 percent.

4. Bezilla, *America's Youth, 1977–1988*, pp. 136-37. Five percent say that religion is not at all important, and 15 percent, that it is not too important; 49 percent say that it is less important than it is to their parents; 26 percent say that it is more important; and 24 percent say that it is about the same.

5. For twelve- and seventeen-year-olds, respectively, the percentages for each indicator of religious commitment are church membership, 62 and 47 percent; weekly attendance, 54 and 38 percent; never attend, 10 and 20 percent; a great deal of satisfaction from religion, 39 and 27 percent; little or no satisfaction from religion, 14 and 22 percent; conservative, 20 and 21 percent; moderate, 64 and 47 percent; and liberal, 16 and 32 percent.

6. "My religious or spiritual concerns led me to volunteer" was selected as a very important reason for volunteering by 32 percent of all teens, by 40 percent of those who are members of a church or synagogue, and by 42 percent of those who attend religious services every week. The percentages among weekly attenders who said that other reasons are very important were, for gaining new skills, 45 percent; for expecting to enjoy the work, 42 percent; and for wanting to feel needed, 42 percent. In addition, 47 percent said that volunteering is important to others whom they respect (that is, they chose this as a very important reason), suggesting that the social ethos of churches may be as important, if not more so, as a stimulus to volunteering as is the specific content of religious teachings.

7. The percentages in each subgroup saying that volunteering is very important as a personal goal are as follows: church members, 52 percent, and nonmembers, 36 percent;

mother a church member, 50 percent, and nonmember, 38 percent; father a church member, 49 percent, and nonmember, 33 percent; religious conservative, 57 percent, moderate, 44 percent, and liberal, 42 percent; attend religious services weekly, 53 percent, two or three times a month, 43 percent, one to three times a year, 41 percent, and do not attend, 28 percent; a great deal of satisfaction from religion or spirituality, 65 percent, a fair amount, 41 percent, some, 39 percent, and little, 24 percent.

8. When the effects of attendance and satisfaction are examined jointly, it is satisfaction, rather than attendance, that has the greater influence on volunteering. Thus those who receive a great deal of satisfaction from their religion or spirituality are just as likely to value volunteering even if they seldom or never attend religious services as if they attend every week. And those who experience this level of satisfaction but never attend services are far more likely to value volunteering than are those who attend every week but receive little satisfaction from it. These results are from a three-way cross-tabulation of valuing volunteering by religious attendance and religious satisfaction. The percentages reporting that volunteering was very important to them varied only between 63 and 60 percent by levels of church attendance for those who received a great deal of satisfaction from their religion or spirituality, between 43 and 37 percent for those with a fair amount of satisfaction, between 43 and 35 percent for those with some satisfaction, and between 23 and 17 percent for those with little satisfaction. Within each level of attendance, in contrast, the difference between those with a great deal of satisfaction and those with little satisfaction was at least forty percentage points. At the extremes, 60 percent of those who received a great deal of satisfaction but who never attended services said that they valued volunteering, compared with only 23 percent of those who attended services weekly but received little satisfaction from them.

9. This observation is based on comparisons among those who believe that "making a strong commitment to your religion or spiritual life" is absolutely essential, very important, somewhat important, or not very important. For instance, among those who list "absolutely essential" and among those who list "not very important," the percentages that volunteered within the past year in the area of education are 29 and 16, respectively, and the percentages that volunteered in areas of health, environment, or community services are 57 and 41, respectively; the differences for having done religious volunteer work are, of course, stronger (49 and 13 percent).

10. Robert Wuthnow, *Acts of Compassion: Caring for Others and Helping Ourselves* (Princeton, N.J.: Princeton University Press, 1991), chap. 7.

11. These conclusions are drawn from several national surveys and are reported in my book *Sharing the Journey: Support Groups and America's New Quest for Community* (New York: Free Press, 1994), chap. 11.

12. The percentages among conservatives, moderates, and liberals are, respectively, church member, 76, 63, and 36 percent; mother a church member, 74, 64, and 43 percent; father a church member, 57, 43, and 29 percent; siblings church members, 57, 46, and 34 percent; and close friends church members, 57, 50, and 37 percent.

13. On an item in the teen survey that read "I feel a moral duty to help people who suffer," the percentages, by religious orientation, that strongly agreed—from very conservative to very liberal—were, respectively, 43, 30, 27, 24, and 25 percent. If we limit the analysis to those who attend church weekly—thus selecting for true religious liberals, as opposed to secularists—we find even sharper patterns: 45, 32, 27, 21, and 25 percent.

14. Among volunteers who attend church weekly, from very conservative to very liberal, the percentages that say that religious concerns are a very important reason for their involvement are 60, 54, 38, 39, 31, and 22. Since these differences apply to teenagers who attend church, it is evident that other social supports and beliefs must also be contributing factors.

15. William Barrett, *Death of the Soul: From Descartes to the Computer* (New York: Doubleday, 1986), p. 125.

16. Peter L. Berger, *Rumors of Angels: Modern Society and the Rediscovery of the Supernatural* (Garden City, N.Y.: Doubleday, 1969), pp. 65–66: "By signals of transcendence I mean phenomena that are to be found within the domain of our 'natural' reality but that appear to point beyond that reality."

17. Those who volunteered through their churches were also less likely to offer instrumental reasons for their behavior, such as expecting others to help them, making career contacts, developing job possibilities, or using their volunteering to improve their résumé.

Chapter 6

1. I consider the ways in which schools help, hinder, and guide the process of learning how to care, by paying attention to the experiences young people themselves have had in working through their schools. Their views are, of course, biased by their experiences, just as the views of teachers and administrators are biased by theirs. Readers interested in the latter can consult the vast literature about programs that has been written, as it were, from "the top down." Lists and descriptions of national programs can also be found in this literature. Useful as that information is, I think that it is valuable to hear what the young people themselves have to say.

2. Virginia A. Hodgkinson and Murray S. Weitzman, *Volunteering and Giving Among American Teenagers 12 to 17 Years of Age: Findings from a National Survey* (Washington, D.C.: Independent Sector, 1828 L Street, N.W., 1992), p. 13.

3. In the teen survey, those who volunteer through service clubs are more likely than other volunteers are to say they did it simply for the enjoyment, because it would be more fun than their schoolwork and because it might open up job possibilities, but they were less likely than other volunteers were to say they did it because of compassion or simply because they felt it was important to help.

4. Hodgkinson and Weitzman, *Volunteering and Giving*, p. 15. This is my figure, estimated by subtracting the 30 percent of teenagers who volunteer through religious organizations from the 60 percent who do any kind of volunteer work, and then adjusting for the one-quarter or so of the latter who volunteer as part of their extracurricular activities at school.

5. Hodgkinson and Weitzman, *Volunteering and Giving*, p. 15.

6. When talking about joining a mission church in her neighborhood, Sherry Hicks also illustrates the importance of finding a place that seems like home: "At first I just went because my brother kept begging me to go. I always knew that I wanted a religion. I had tried different religions, and I didn't like this religion, or I didn't necessarily agree with everything in this religion. So finally I went to this church, and I don't know what it was, but it just felt like a huge family."

7. According to the teen survey, two-thirds of those who volunteer in religious organizations say that their close friends are church members (the figure is 65 percent, compared with 38 percent for those who do not volunteer in a religious organization).

8. A young man who did volunteer work through his church's youth group offered this illustration of how such participation makes one feel stronger: "I've been in this church since I was born. When we lived here before, we were a member of the church up until I was eight, and we moved to Tennessee and tried to find a church down there for the little time that we were down there. When we came back, we immediately joined this church. I've been a part of this church for so long, and I've been so involved in everything they do, musicals, choir, youth group. I've been so involved in this church, it's just good. It's something Christian that just has built up inside of me. I guess it's just part of my background. I've learned to share. My parents have taught me to share, our religion has taught me to share, my friends have taught me to share. It helps me feel good about myself. It helps build my character in a positive way. I mean there's so many ways to build character in a negative way, I believe now, that to be such a part of the few things that build positive character is important."

9. Because churches consider themselves communities, a mark of caring is to build relationships among people. The mere existence of such relationships is valued whether or not they entail service and fulfill specific needs. A legitimate way in which to talk about one's caring activities, in fact, is to say that one is trying to build relationships. For instance, one student has spent several Saturday mornings in the last few months preparing a brunch for the elderly members of her church. She has been assisted by several other young people. She explains that she does this because the church realized that its size was making it difficult for connections to be created between younger and older people in the congregation. "We felt that we needed to really connect the youth and the older adults," she says, "because they rarely see much of each other at our church, and that it being such a large church there should be a connection. So now the youth have begun to participate, and it's a mission open to the youth at our church."

Chapter 7

1. The contrasting views of organizations are outlined in Walter W. Powell and Paul J. DiMaggio, eds., *The New Institutionalism in Organizational Analysis* (Chicago: University of Chicago Press, 1991), pp. 1–38.

2. I have in mind especially the discussion of Javanese ritual in Clifford Geertz, *The Interpretation of Cultures* (New York: Harper & Row, 1973), chap. 6.

3. The use of "drama" as a way of talking about the constructed character of social reality is, of course, well established in sociology. See, for example, Peter L. Berger, *Invitation to Sociology* (Garden City, N.Y.: Doubleday, 1963), pp. 138–39.

4. When adults are asked to name their "most admired woman," Mother Teresa is almost always one of those mentioned most frequently, seldom falling below second or third place in the past decade. Among teenagers, however, Mother Teresa has never placed in the top ten. Their favorites, like adults', include current and former First Ladies but (unlike adults) generally feature famous actresses, rock singers, talk show hosts, and models. See Robert Bezilla, *America's Youth in the 1990s* (Princeton, N.J.: George H. Gallup International Institute, 1993), p. 162. Mother Teresa ranked second

among adults, behind former First Lady Barbara Bush and ahead of former British prime minister Margaret Thatcher and former First Lady Nancy Reagan. The teens' top choices were actress Julia Roberts, Barbara Bush, singers Paula Abdul and Madonna, and talk show hostess Oprah Winfrey; also in their top ten were singer Janet Jackson and model Christie Brinkley.

5. Among adults who do volunteer work, the story of the Good Samaritan is widely known, especially among churchgoers, and is positively associated with valuing (and doing) volunteer work. See my *Acts of Compassion: Caring for Others and Helping Ourselves* (Princeton, N.J.: Princeton University Press, 1991), chap. 6. Although the teen survey did not ask questions about the Good Samaritan story, my impression from our qualitative interviews is that the story is not as well known among young people as among older adults.

6. This section is an extension of my work on storytelling among adult volunteers: *Christianity in the Twenty-First Century: Reflections on the Challenges Ahead* (New York: Oxford University Press, 1993), pt. 2.

7. Nationally, 65 percent of all teens can think of someone they have known or read about who illustrates what it means to be a compassionate person. The most commonly mentioned are mother (21 percent), a friend (11 percent), Mother Teresa (10 percent), grandparents (8 percent), and parents (7 percent). Other than Mother Teresa, these all are immediate and part of one's nuclear or extended family. After them, the most commonly mentioned examples of compassion are friends, neighbors, and teachers.

8. Although it is not surprising, we should note that the teen survey documents a positive correlation of moderate strength between having had role models outside one's own family who showed care to other people and placing high value on giving time to helping the needy oneself and regarding it as a moral duty to help the disadvantaged. The survey data also show that these effects hold for both young people whose parents have served as models of caring and those whose parents have not served in this way.

9. Tanika Lane uses these words to explain why Oprah Winfrey is her role model: "Because she had a rough childhood. She got raped and everything, but that's not an excuse for her not becoming all that she is now. She also acts, and I like acting. I want to have my own talk show because I love to talk. I love to hear my voice over the radio station or whatever. I just think that Oprah is what I want to be like in the future."

10. As another example, a young man—who identifies the supervisor at the neighborhood center where he volunteers as the most caring person he knows—makes a special point of defining caring in terms of going beyond the call of duty: "The reason I say that is because she is a woman that I've really seen go, like I say, beyond the call of duty. I've seen this woman go in her pocket and give freely, or give her time to help someone who really needed it. I've seen some of the kids in the program who needed food in their home and they're really funded by it, but she says, 'This is just between me and you. I will help you,' and help them. She's gone out of her way for them. Like I said, she's one of those people you can tell that she's not doing it because it's her job, she's doing it because she cares. Because what she was doing is really not required as a part of her job."

11. Another student, describing her French teacher, gives additional insight into why stepping out of role behavior may be helpful: "She's one of the few teachers I know who will listen to you and I feel that I can talk to, but she's always made me feel better about talking to her because she tells me about her problems. I mean, I've heard that there are

policies for teachers not to do that and various reasons, but it's always made it nice for me that she's very emotional, too. And she gets very upset about different things easily, too. I think we're probably a lot alike. When I know what's going on in her life—she's like, oh, my brother-in-law's sick or something, and I know what's going with her, it makes it easier for me to talk to her about like what's bothering me. I like her concern for the school and what goes on in the school, and there are so many things I think are great about her. She has many opinions, and she's always voicing them. I mean, she's not stubborn, but she's got definite ideas about things."

Chapter 8

1. Even national newspapers seem to make stories about chicken soup standard winter reading. See, for example, Florence Fabricant, "Soup That's One Part Chicken, 10 Parts Comfort," *New York Times*, January 23, 1991, p. B5; Victor Cohn, "'Souped Up' Medicine," *Washington Post*, March 27, 1990, p. WH11; Molly O'Neill, "It Cures What Ails," *New York Times Magazine*, February 4, 1990, p. 45.

2. Among these studies, see especially Karen J. Blair, *The Clubwoman as Feminist: True Womanhood Redefined, 1868–1914* (New York: Holmes & Meier, 1980); Ruth Bordin, *Woman and Temperance: The Quest for Power and Liberty, 1873–1900* (Philadelphia: Temple University Press, 1981); Lori D. Ginsberg, "'Moral Suasion Is Moral Balderdash': Women, Politics, and Social Activism in the 1850s," *Journal of American History* 73 (1986): 601–22; Nancy A. Hewitt, *Women's Activism and Social Change: Rochester, New York, 1822–1872* (Ithaca, N.Y.: Cornell University Press, 1984); Carroll Smith-Rosenberg, *Religion and the Rise of the City: The New York City Mission Movement, 1812–1870* (Ithaca, N.Y.: Cornell University Press, 1971).

3. Nancy A. Hewitt, "Varieties of Voluntarism: Class, Ethnicity, and Women's Activism in Tampa," in *Women, Politics and Change*, ed. Louise A. Tilly and Patricia Gurin (New York: Russell Sage Foundation, 1990), p. 80.

4. These figures are from the Self-Esteem Survey to which I have referred several times in previous chapters.

5. Robert Bezilla, *America's Youth in the 1990s* (Princeton, N.J.: George H. Gallup International Institute, 1993), p. 36: When asked, "Would you say you get along better with your mother or your father?" 52 percent said mother, 24 percent said father, 21 percent said both, and 2 percent said neither; 60 percent of females compared with 46 percent of males said mother; and 21 percent of females, compared with 27 percent of males, said father.

6. In the 1991 teen data, 20 percent said both their parents were currently doing volunteer work, whereas 22 percent said only one parent was involved, meaning that the one-parent pattern is actually more common. Overall, 16 percent of teens said only their mother was involved, compared with 6 percent who said only their father was involved. Among white males, the ratio of mother-only to father-only involvement was approximately 1.5; among white females, this father-only involvement was around 4.0. For black females, it was nearly 10.0, compared with 4.0 for black males.

7. The proportions of students who reported that volunteering was very important as a personal goal for each subgroup was 57 percent if both parents had volunteered; 57 percent if only the mother had volunteered; 37 percent if only the father had volunteered; and 40 percent if neither parent had volunteered.

8. In 1975, 51.8 percent of wives whose husband was present in the family and whose youngest child was between the ages of six and thirteen were in the civilian labor force; by 1991, this figure had risen to 72.8 percent. Over the same period, the figures for wives with their husband present and the youngest child between the ages of fourteen and seventeen years rose from 53.5 percent to 75.7 percent. See U.S. Bureau of the Census, *Statistical Abstract of the United States: 1992* (112th ed.) (Washington, D.C.: U.S. Government Printing Office, 1992), p. 388.

9. According to Virginia A. Hodgkinson and Murray S. Weitzman, *Volunteering and Giving Among Teenagers 12 to 17 Years of Age: Findings from a National Survey* (Washington, D.C.: Independent Sector, 1828 L Street, N.W., 1992), pp. 85–95, women who work full time devote an average of 3.8 hours per week to volunteering, compared with an average of 2.8 for women working part time; married women put in 3.1 hours, compared with 2.3 hours for single women and 1.4 for divorced or separated women.

10. *Statistical Abstract*, p. 392.

11. Arlene Kaplan Daniels, *Invisible Careers: Women Civic Leaders from the Volunteer World* (Chicago: University of Chicago Press, 1988).

12. Tucker Aims also says he has been teased about being in the scouts: "No! I remember the little guys who were troop leaders, like when we're out in public, and they'd say, 'All right. You need to wear your Boy Scout uniform to make sure people know who you are and you're supposed to be there.' So me and all my buddies, we'd put on normal clothes under our uniform and as soon as the scout leaders told us what to do and left, we'd take off our uniforms and do it in our normal clothes."

13. A similar comment was made by Tanika Lane: "I've been called stupid, waste of time. If I was you, I wouldn't do that. That's a waste of time, like going after school, going to different interviews, or Teen Haven."

14. It is not, however, evident that young women are necessarily more in need of warm relationships or have a desire to belong more than young men do. In the survey, there were no differences in the extent to which males and females valued warm relationships and a sense of belonging as personal goals. For females and males respectively, the percentages that said "having a sense of belonging" was absolutely essential were 28 and 28 (including those who said very important, 80 and 79), and for "having a warm relationship with others," 46 and 43 (including very important, 92 and 90).

15. The figures were 61 percent and 60 percent, respectively, for females and males in the 1991 Independent Sector survey of teens.

16. In the teen survey, 52 percent of females answered that volunteering was very important as a personal goal, compared with 39 percent of males.

17. Bezilla, *America's Youth in the 1990s*, p. 93. The percentages of women and men currently involved in caring activities were 38 and 29, and those saying their would very likely volunteer were 35 and 13.

18. I refer to results from the Self-Esteem Survey to which I referred in previous chapters. The questions were sufficiently general that sharp differences should not be expected; nevertheless, the differences were statistically significant, and the relationships were moderate in strength. Thirty-eight percent of the women had given time to helping the poor, compared with 31 percent of the men; and on saying that their own efforts to help others were very important to their sense of self-worth, women outranked men by a margin of 54 percent to 41 percent.

19. Hodgkinson and Weitzman, *Giving and Volunteering, 1992*, p. 69. The figures reported are 2.6 hours per week for women and 1.6 hours per week for men. According to

these data, among volunteers only, women put in 5.0 hours per week on average, compared with 3.3 for men.

20. Overall, black men actually average about an hour a month more than black women do, and this is true as well among volunteers only (2.3 hours more on average for males than for females). Most of the difference is that black males are more likely to report moderate amounts of volunteering (for example, 26 percent, compared with 17 percent among black women, volunteer for ten hours a month). A higher proportion of black women than men, however, have volunteered twenty or more hours per month (12 versus 8 percent).

21. These data are from my national survey for my *Acts of Compassion: Caring for Others and Helping Ourselves* (Princeton, N.J.: Princeton University Press, 1991). The percentages for males and females, respectively, for specific activities and values are as follows: lent more than $100 to a relative or friend, 66 and 59 percent; saved someone's life, 21 and 12 percent; given money to a beggar, 55 and 44 percent; stopped to help someone who was having car trouble, 77 and 45 percent; donated time to a volunteer organization, 48 54 percent; cared for someone who was very sick, 48 and 66 percent; gone door to door to raise money for something, 31 and 47 percent; tried to get someone to stop using alcohol or drugs, 50 and 56 percent; helped a relative or friend through a personal crisis, 68 and 74 percent; taken care of an elderly relative in his or her home, 28 and 34 percent; feeling that helping people in need was only fairly important or not very important, 33 and 20 percent; and saying that giving one's time to help others is only fairly important or not very important, 43 and 30 percent.

22. Carol Gilligan, *In a Different Voice: Psychological Theory and Women's Development* (Cambridge, Mass.: Harvard University Press, 1982).

23. Wuthnow, *Acts of Compassion*, chap. 9.

24. See Carol Gilligan, Janie Victoria Ward, and Jill McLean Taylor, eds., *Mapping the Moral Domain: A Contribution of Women's Thinking to Psychological Theory and Education* (Cambridge, Mass.: Harvard University Press, 1988).

25. The text of Jill Daugherty's experience is interesting to read in full: "I remember in seventh grade being really mad that there were people that didn't have things that I had. That didn't have like a home or that were ill and that I was healthy. I remember getting really, really mad, and my mom said, Well, why don't you just do something? That's when I went to do different things with the church, so that helped me out a lot. My neighbor, who lives around the corner, is an older man, and he lives alone. His wife has died or is in a nursing home, I think. He has this old, decrepit dog. He's just a very decrepit-looking person. It would bother me because he walked hunched over. He would walk around, and I'd say, 'Mom, I don't like it. I just don't like it. I don't like it.' I threw a temper tantrum, I think. I think I was just very mad that he was in this home all alone. None of our neighbors would go over and see him, and no one would go over and do anything for him. It was right before Christmas and we were making cookies, and Mom said, 'Why don't you take him over some cookies?' I was in sixth grade, and I also thought he was a demon or something. I was scared of him—the old person that's just going to eat you up if you go into his house. I was scared. So, I went over, and I said, 'Merry Christmas!' I gave him some cookies. He thanked me and stuff. His name is Mr. Lange. So I see him walking by. He walks his dog every day, every morning and every night, every morning, every night. He walked it through the storm, everything. He's really neat. So I see him now, and I say hi. We stop and we talk. I think that was the first

time I got just really mad. I don't know what it was that made me mad about it, but it just didn't sit right with me for some reason."

26. Among males, 71 percent agreed (17 percent strongly), compared with 66 percent among females (16 percent strongly); 29 percent of males disagreed, as did 34 percent of females. The responses to this question also reinforce the conclusions drawn from our interviews with volunteers, insofar as teenagers who have recently been active in volunteer work do not differ significantly from those who have not been involved.

27. The one exception to this pattern was among black males, for whom the two items were negatively associated (a gamma of -.26). Among white males, white females, and black females, the items were not significantly associated.

28. Deborah Tannen, *You Just Don't Understand: Women and Men in Conversation* (New York: Ballantine Books, 1990), p. 25.

29. The respective percentages of women and men who said that each reason was very important were as follows: "I feel compassion toward people in need," 69 and 49 percent; "Volunteering makes me feel needed," 48 and 34 percent; and "I thought I would enjoy doing the work," 46 and 32 percent.

30. In my 1989 survey, I found that 57 percent of women, compared with 44 percent of men, said they received a great deal of personal fulfillment from "doing things for people."

31. In my 1989 survey, I found that 48 percent of women, compared with 36 percent of men, listed "I want to give of myself for the benefit of others" as a major reason to be kind and caring. In contrast, women were slightly more likely than men to reject (that is, to say it was not a reason) the statement "Being kind and considerate helps me get what I want in life" (41 and 35 percent, respectively).

32. These results are unpublished figures from my 1989 *Acts of Compassion* survey. The figures for men and women, respectively, are "Being very likely to help if the person works for a competitor," 16 and 19 percent; "Being at least fairly likely if the person works for a competitor," 53 and 53 percent; "Being very likely if the person grew up in the same neighborhood," 39 and 42 percent (78 and 82 percent, at least fairly likely); "If the person is willing to pay, at least fairly likely," 37 and 31 percent; "If the person could be useful, at least fairly likely," 62 and 52 percent (24 and 19 percent for very likely); and "Having experienced the same problem, being very likely," 43 and 51 percent.

33. Mary Field Belenky, Blythe McVicker Clinchy, Nancy Rule Goldberger, and Jill Mattuck Tarule, *Women's Ways of Knowing: The Development of Self, Voice, and Mind* (New York: Basic Books, 1986), pp. 52–86.

34. See the material on narrative and sociobiography in support groups in my book *Sharing the Journey: Support Groups and America's New Quest for Community* (New York: Free Press, 1994), chap. 10.

Chapter 9

1. The answer to the question about what kinds of social arrangements create strong people, unfortunately, is confounded by the fact that we live in a society that credits itself with valuing the individual person, indeed, that encourages what is commonly referred to as *rugged individualism*. It would thus seem that the best clue to figuring out what kind of social conditions produce strong people is in our own society. But this argument

also implies that our own society should be exceptionally high in virtue (at least if virtue is indeed associated with being a strong person).

Even if we think this to be the case, it would be wise to back off momentarily from that assumption. A better approach would be to ask what kind of society needs strong people—in the sense of either needing people to be strong in order for them to survive or needing strong people to carry out the ordinary tasks of any viable society. We should also recognize that no society is unitary; that is, some societies may need a few people to be strong and others to be weak, whereas other societies may need everyone to be strong. For some of the literature arguing that contemporary social conditions require strong people, see Reinhard Bendix, *Nation-building and Citizenship*, rev. ed. (Berkeley and Los Angeles: University of California Press, 1977); and George M. Thomas, John W. Meyer, Francisco O. Ramirez, and John Boli, *Institutional Structure: Constituting State, Society, and the Individual* (Beverly Hills: Sage, 1987). Other studies of contemporary American culture also emphasize individualism but can be interpreted in a way that questions whether an individual person is strong or weak. See, for example, Christopher Lasch, *The Culture of Narcissism: American Life in an Age of Diminishing Expectations* (New York: Norton, 1978); and Robert N. Bellah, Richard Madsen, William M. Sullivan, Ann Swidler, and Steven M. Tipton, *Habits of the Heart: Individualism and Commitment in American Life* (Berkeley and Los Angeles: University of California Press, 1985).

2. Although my argument is intended only as a bare outline, there is one loose end that needs to be secured. This is the fact that power always has a representational quality. That is, the power or virtue conferred by society on an individual person symbolizes something about that society's actual or desired social arrangements. For example, the honor conferred on a prize-winning scientist represents the broader role of science and technology in society. An amulet or a totem in a primitive society symbolizes the common ancestry and unity of the clan that worships that amulet or totem. Recognizing this representational aspect of power allows us to move beyond the somewhat mechanical nature of an argument that links individual power too directly with the presence or absence of institutional resources. Even societies with powerful institutions may single out a few people to credit with extreme virtue as a way of representing what is valued in those institutions (prize-winning scientists again being a good example).

The same is true, incidentally, in settings with weak institutions. For example, the few rugged individualists of the American frontier do not necessarily mean that all pioneers were considered strong or virtuous. For our immediate purposes, the representational quality of power means that we must be careful in how we try to understand those people who have been singled out by their communities as exemplars of kindness. Some of the ways in which kindness is understood in the wider culture are likely to be reflected in the views and images of these exemplars. If they are regarded as efficient, self-interested caregivers, for example, that may be an indication of the value associated with efficiency and self-interest in American life. Exemplars, however, sometimes play a different role. They exaggerate virtue to such a degree that it cannot—and need not—be attained by others. The adulation accorded Mother Teresa, for instance, may mean that kindness is valued in our society but that it is beyond the reach of ordinary people.

3. When considering the transfer of virtue from people to institutions, we also should recognize the implications of institutional diversity. Institutions have become not only more powerful but also more specialized. Furthermore, the contemporary person is not protected by a large number of them: the military, banks, restaurants, schools, and so

on. If virtue has now been transferred to institutions, the implication of this diversity is that virtue itself has become more diverse, in two respects.

First, particular virtues are likely to be associated more with some institutions than with others: for example, courage with the military, faith with the church. In addition, the same virtues are likely to be defined differently in various institutional settings. What is courageous about the military is probably different from what is courageous about the social welfare system. Thus standards for evaluating virtue are likely to depend on their particular institutional contexts. For the individual person, courage may still be regarded as a desirable attribute, but it may be harder to recognize it in some settings than in others and, indeed, be unclear whether it should be present in all situations.

4. The incipient erosion of moral authority is also evident in Amy Stone's views of religion. She attended church every week while she was growing up and still attends at least twice a month. She went to Sunday school and was an active participant in youth group. Even now, she says her prayers every night before going to bed, and she believes in Jesus as the son of God and as her personal savior. She regards Jesus as a model of caring and tries to be like him. In all these ways, she is deeply involved in Christianity.

Indeed, Amy was one of the most involved of all the teenagers we interviewed. Yet she does not regard Christianity as a universal truth that implies binding moral obligations. She relativizes it by saying that people who happen to have been raised as Christians should try to defend it and follow its rules but that others need not believe it. She does not extract principles of virtue from it that may be universal to all religions; in fact, Christianity does not enter her discussion very often as a reason to be kind and caring. Instead, she allows other language from the wider culture to influence how she talks about Christianity. For example, when discussing the Good Samaritan, she suggests that the main point to be learned is that helping others will "always pay off."

5. William H. Gass, "Exile," in *Best American Essays, 1992*, ed. Susan Sontag (New York: Ticknor & Fields, 1992), p. 123.

6. Another student echoed these sentiments about striking a balance between self and community: "I would describe myself as someone who believes that the individual is very important but that you can't just be an individual in this world. You must learn how to relate with others and really recognize the community we live in and that it is a community."

7. Jackie White, who works with the Central American political organization, also offers a revealing perspective on the strains that may develop between being a volunteer and fitting into ordinary teenage roles: "I don't know if any of it is bad, but one thing is that it's hard to be a quote, unquote, 'normal teenager.' It was particularly an issue earlier on in high school and junior high, because a lot of my friendships were not in school, because a lot of my social life and work and life involvement has not been centered around school or around people in school. Just practically, that was an issue. It's been hard. And also because I never quite feel very bonded in some ways to the teenager experience. I mean, to an extent I feel that, but in a lot of ways I feel like I don't fit in."

8. The teen survey supports the claim that young people who spend more time volunteering come to feel that they are better or stronger persons. One would assume that the more time that young people spent volunteering, the more likely they would be to say they had experienced various benefits, but this was not always the case. Consider

learning how to get along with and relate to others. Half the teens who had volunteered more than twenty hours in the past month said this had been a very important benefit. But so did half of those who had volunteered at least once but had done nothing within the past month. Apparently, most benefits are rather easily obtained; that is, they come from volunteering even once, not from how much one continues to volunteer. Thus it is important to know whether any benefits become more important (experienced more often or valued by more of those who experience them) as the level of volunteer work increases. There are a few, such as new skills, especially leadership skills. This makes sense, because people are generally not put into leadership positions until they have worked actively at something over a period of time. The other two are more interesting: One is learning respect for others, especially gaining a greater understanding of different kinds of people. The other is a sense of being a better person. (Of the eighteen benefit items in the survey, the five associated positively with greater numbers of hours volunteering at a statistically significant level and that showed differences of at least ten percentage points between those putting in no hours and those putting in at least twenty hours were learning to respect others, learning new skills, being a better person, understanding people different from oneself, and developing leadership skills.)

9. Albert Camus, *The Stranger* (New York: Vintage Books, 1989 [1942]).

10. Christina Garcia, *Dreaming in Cuban* (New York: Ballantine Books, 1992), p. 184.

11. When asked how much personal satisfaction they get, the percentages of all teen respondents who said they receive either a great deal or a fair amount of satisfaction from each of the following was schoolwork, 70 percent; doing things for others, 83 percent; religion or spirituality, 58 percent; leisure activities, 84 percent; being good to yourself, 86 percent; and one's family, 94 percent. Among those who said they received a great deal of satisfaction from doing things for others, 50 percent received this much satisfaction from at least three of the other five sources, and only 14 percent said they received a great deal of satisfaction from no other source.

12. On a ten-point scale, where 10 was defined as "feeling as good as you can possibly feel," the mean score for each of the following was as follows: got an A on a hard test, 9.4 points; got $500 for your birthday, 9.2 points; got concert tickets for your favorite group, 8.6 points; got a thank-you call from a friend you had helped, 8.6 points; gave a dollar to a beggar, 7.6 points; had spent an hour helping a handicapped child play ball, 8.3 points; helped clean up the park as part of a school project, 7.5 points; just returned from a week in Mexico helping the poor, 7.7 points; and cleaned the bathroom as a surprise for your mother, 7.0 points. As evidence of the relationship between these items and volunteering, those students who had volunteered at least twenty hours in the past month (compared with those who had volunteered none) averaged 8.2 versus 7.5 on feelings from helping the poor, and 8.7 versus 8.1 on helping a handicapped child.

13. For teens who had ever done volunteer work, the percentages that said that each of the following had been a very important benefit from the experience were as follows: "I learned how to get along with and relate to others," 46 percent; "I learned to be helpful and kind," 52 percent; "I learned how to relate to children," 43 percent; "I learned to respect others," 58 percent; "I learned new skills," 44 percent; "I explored or learned about career options," 24 percent; "I did better in school/my grades improved," 21 percent; "I'm more aware about programs in my community," 26 percent; "I learned how to help solve community problems," 20 percent; "I've developed new career goals," 23

percent; "I gained satisfaction from helping others," 54 percent; "I'm a better person now," 40 percent; "I'm more patient with others," 39 percent; "I understand more about good citizenship," 37 percent; "I understand more about how government works," 14 percent; "I learned to understand people who are different from me," 42 percent; "I developed leadership skills," 40 percent; and "I understand more about how voluntary organizations work," 31 percent.

14. Scott Hastings also emphasized community: "Most of the kids in my school don't really care about you, like as a person. They care at lunchtime if they don't have any lunch money; they care if you have money and if you're going to give it to them. But the people in 4-H, it's a smaller group so you get to know them better. You really get to know them really well. They care about what you do and how you feel and stuff like that, so that's just good."

Chapter 10

1. In the teen survey, the overall percentages that could imagine themselves doing each of the following activities were as follows: giving mouth-to-mouth resuscitation to someone who had stopped breathing, 71 percent; helping at a soup kitchen for the homeless, 67 percent; cleaning sludge off a riverbank beach after an oil spill, 47 percent; spending a year of one's life right after high school doing paid community service work, 46 percent; visiting an elderly person in one's community who had no relatives and was all alone, 86 percent; feeding a handicapped person, 70 percent; tutoring a student who was having trouble reading, 82 percent; helping take care of AIDS patients, 50 percent; helping the poor in another part of the world, 56 percent; working in a clinic for drug addicts, 51 percent; helping with a school program to warn students about drugs and alcohol, 80 percent; and helping with an athletic event for handicapped students, 77.

The factors that heighten the willingness to contemplate such activities are the following: proximity to one's own community or circle of acquaintances, a lack of "squeamishness triggers," and a relative absence of danger. Thus students are more willing to warn other students about drugs or do tutoring than to go work with the poor in another part of the world or even to clean sludge at the beach; they also are more likely to imagine tutoring or visiting the elderly than feeding a handicapped person. Working with AIDS patients or drug addicts appears to create the greatest fears. Those who have been most involved in volunteering are more likely to say they can imagine all these activities than are those who have not been involved.

The greatest differences, however, are for activities in which volunteers may have already been involved, such as working at a soup kitchen, or for activities that create fears in other students, such as working with AIDS patients. Students who had spent twenty or more hours volunteering in the past month were fifteen percentage points more likely to say they would give mouth-to-mouth resuscitation than were students who had done no volunteering in the past month. Other items that showed similar differences were helping at a soup kitchen, cleaning a beach, feeding a handicapped person, caring for AIDS patients, working with drug addicts, and helping with the Special Olympics.

Volunteering was also associated with imagining a wider range of caring activities; thus 56 percent of those who had put in twenty or more hours could imagine doing at least nine of the twelve activities, compared with 37 percent of those who had not volunteered. At the other end, 41 percent of the nonvolunteers could imagine doing six or fewer of the activities, compared with 17 percent of the twenty-plus volunteers.

2. Not in my backyard—NIMBY—is another way in which people learn to limit their kindness. They may be willing to pay taxes to house criminals but not to have a prison in their neighborhood. Among the young people we talked to who had been extensively involved in volunteer work, only a few invoked the NIMBY problem, asserting that social problems should be kept out of their immediate neighborhood. But they were quite localistic in saying that they would not be likely to become involved with a problem unless it affected their neighborhood.

This reasoning came up occasionally when talking with young people about environmental issues. Even though they recognized that these issues are connected globally through the interdependencies built into the ecosystem itself, they were unlikely to state that they would become involved unless their own community were affected. Asked if he would lobby for clean air, for example, a young man from a rural area remarked, "I can't see myself doing that. I've never been anyplace where there isn't clean air. Out here there is more air than you can think of, and if the people don't want the smog in the cities, they can move out. There's plenty of room out here."

3. Robert Bezilla, *America's Youth in the 1990s* (Princeton, N.J.: George H. Gallup International Institute, 1993), p. 96.

4. In the teen survey, saying that one learned to be helpful and kind is a critical factor in altering one's views of helping behavior in the future. It increases the likelihood of saying that one would help out in all of the ways listed. And for a majority of these activities, it made a more significant difference than did more programmatic benefits, such as learning how voluntary organizations work or becoming more aware of community programs. Specifically, the degree of association between saying one had learned to be helpful and kind and other items, as indicated by gamma was as follows: can imagine giving CPR, .21; working in a soup kitchen, .29; cleaning a beach, .15; spending a year doing community service, .27; working with the elderly, .29; feeding the handicapped, .31; tutoring, .40; working with AIDS patients, .24; working with the poor, .24; working with drug addicts, .17; helping with antidrug campaigns, .28; and helping with the Special Olympics, .41 (eight of twelve associations were stronger for saying that one had learned to be helpful and kind than for saying that one had become more aware of community programs as a result of one's volunteering).

5. Because gender is a large factor in career values, I report the following results from the teenage survey separately for young women and young men. Among female students who had volunteered at least twenty hours in the past month, 40 percent said it was essential in their careers to have an opportunity to help people (compared with 26 percent of those who had not volunteered in the past month); among male students, the respective figures were 29 and 20 percent. On having a chance to work with the needy, the respective figures for women were 25 and 18, and for men, 21 and 15. There were no differences among females and males between volunteers and nonvolunteers in the proportions that valued other career attributes, such as a high salary, a flexible schedule, or freedom from pressure.

6. Although it is likely that some students are propelled into volunteering in the first place because of an interest in a career such as teaching or social work, an interest in these occupations is still positively associated with number of hours actually spent volunteering, controlling for earlier involvement in volunteering. Saying one learned to be

helpful and kind as a result of one's volunteer work also heightened the career value that students placed on having opportunities to help others and working with the needy, and it was associated with higher levels of interest in nursing, teaching, social work, religious work, medicine, and working with the elderly or handicapped. The gamma statistics for the association between saying that one learned to be helpful and kind and each of the following were (NS means not significant): wanting an opportunity to help others, .44; working with the needy, .39; high salary, NS; flexible schedule, NS; use talents, .27; freedom from pressure, .13; intellectually challenging, .29; maintain high morals, .36; contribute to learning, .30; occupations favored: nursing, .23; paramedic, .18; teaching, .23; social work, .31; religious work, .35; working with the elderly or handicapped, .39; medicine, .20; business, NS; computers, NS; engineering, NS; and media, NS.

7. U.S. Bureau of the Census, *Statistical Abstract of the United States: 1992* (112th ed.) (Washington, D.C.: U.S. Government Printing Office, 1992), p. 397.

8. These are home health aides, personal and home care aides, medical assistants, human service workers, medical secretaries, psychologists, travel agents, and corrections officers; the other two are systems analysts and computer scientists, and radiological technologists and technicians (*Statistical Abstract*, p. 380).

Chapter 11

1. I traced the connections between ideas about altruism and notions of social and personal transformation more fully in my "Altruism and Sociological Theory," *Social Service Review*, September 1993, pp. 344–58.

2. Sina Mesnar offered this example: "As an individual learns, he develops himself more. All the prejudices, biases are swept away, and the person becomes enlightened. He understands the situation around him. He just simply doesn't see it on the surface. He can delve further into it. Try to find the root of the problem. If this person can do this, it can influence other people that it's an absolute and keep on going. It spreads." Chandra Lyons commented: "I refuse to be pessimistic, because I think if you don't have vision for something to be better, it will not happen. I think we must look for light in the world because without light you won't be able to see, and then you won't be able to envision anything and then it will all die."

And Jim Grayson said: "No matter how often you look around and you see corrupt people or people that are bad, and some people start saying, 'Well, see that, all people are bad, or people are all bad.' You can still say, 'No, there are good people on this earth who still love other people, even though they don't necessarily love you back.'"

3. "Requiring community service is a good idea" evokes agreement from 50 percent of all students, from 54 percent of volunteers, and from 62 percent of students in schools with service requirements. "It's OK as long as people benefit from it" evokes agreement from 45 percent overall, and "I feel better when I do something voluntarily" gains agreement from 56 percent (58 percent in schools with service requirements and 67 percent of volunteers). In addition, 30 percent said, "It's not as good if you 'have to' do it," and 9 percent said, "Being required to do community service would make me angry."

4. Strings can be attached to volunteer programs to strengthen the linkages between caring and civic responsibility. For example, a program in Boston that has run success-

fully for six years and was chosen as a model for other national service programs requires volunteers (who mostly do fix-up work in poor neighborhoods) to register to vote, obtain a library card, and complete a short course on preparing their tax returns. See Al Santoli, "We're on a Mission," *Parade*, July 18, 1993, pp. 18–19.

5. The following finding from the teen survey cast some doubt on the utility of community service requirements: Schools that encourage community service have a significantly higher level of involvement in volunteer activities among their students than do schools that do not encourage community service (9.6 versus 4.7 hours per month on average); schools that require community service are only marginally better than those that do not and are not as good as those that encourage it (8.6 versus 7.7 hours).

6. Among those who said their school required community service, 56 percent felt that volunteering was very important as a personal goal; among those who said their school encouraged community service, this figure was 52 percent; and among those whose schools did not encourage community service, it was 38 percent.

7. A young man from a low-income family expressed his support for the idea of national service in this way: "I think it's great. I would definitely volunteer a couple years just to get money to go to college. I think that it would be great, and a lot of people would use that opportunity."

8. Megan Wyse also offered an interesting commentary on national service: "I have mixed feelings about it, because then people are doing it for the wrong reasons, and they'll start looking at it differently and maybe resenting it a bit. I think it's needed, so I think that's a good idea because it will be used as an incentive for people to work and do volunteer service that's needed, and that's a good idea because it's getting the job done. And it's for higher education anyway, so the means are good, and the ends are good. I just think it gives volunteer work a whole different meaning, where it's almost a job and that you're getting money, which I think takes a lot out of doing volunteer service."

9. Jill Daugherty illustrates this point in talking about community service: "I agree with it and I disagree with it. I agree with it because I think it teaches values, but then again that may not be the value people want instilled in their children. Making community service a graduation requirement or something along those lines: I think I disagree with that. If you do it because you want to do it, I think you're doing it because you want to do it, and it makes it more valuable and more and more genuine. But if you're doing it just because you know you have to do it to graduate—I have friends who have to do it to graduate from their private schools, and they do it. They put down anything they can to get the hours. They don't do it with the feeling that they have to do it. They don't put the time in that really is expected, I don't think. I know that next year I'm doing community service at school. That's not a graduation requirement, but if I don't get in all the hours, that's OK. I know that the hours I put in will be well spent."

10. Nikki Unger opposes required community service in these grounds: "People who are forced into doing something they don't want to are rarely going to be helpful because people can see through when you're being forced to do something and you're not there out of your own accord. It's like reading a required book. You could like it if it weren't required, but as soon as it's required, it takes kind of the joy out of it. You should do something out of the goodness of your heart. That's what you get satisfaction from. When you're forced to do it, you don't get any satisfaction because you're like, well, I'm not doing anything special."

11. Celia W. Dugger, "Homeless Shelters Drain Money from Housing, Experts Say," *New York Times*, July 26, 1993, p. B1.

12. The role of empowerment was evident in the teen survey. Volunteering is associated with feeling that it is in one's power to make a difference in society. This feeling is then associated with saying that volunteer efforts can make an important difference in improving the society. Then instead of focusing only on volunteer efforts, people say in effect that if volunteering can help, so can a lot of other things. These other things include, in particular, charitable and community efforts, such as strengthening local neighborhoods, sponsoring community service programs, and getting corporations more involved in helping activities. But they also include policies such as raising taxes to sponsor social welfare programs, stimulating economic growth, working harder, and deemphasizing money. Believing that volunteer efforts are a good thing also goes with favoring social policies aimed at addressing AIDS, helping the homeless, and protecting the environment. Favoring volunteer efforts, in contrast, is not conducive to favoring policies aimed at maintaining high standards of living, promoting economic growth, and keeping taxes low. It neither encourages nor discourages support for these. For each of the following, the gammas for believing that volunteer efforts will help a lot were spending tax dollars on social welfare, .37; corporations doing more, .61; the rich giving more money, .36; requiring community service, .61; economic growth, .31; greater emphasis on local neighborhoods, .45; less emphasis on money, .31; and working harder, .38. For specific policies, helping with AIDS, .26; helping the homeless, .34; protecting the environment, .25; maintaining a high standard of living, .07; promoting economic growth, NS (not significant); and keeping taxes low, NS.

13. Overall, the percentages expressing strong agreement, agreement, disagreement, and strong disagreement to the death penalty are 30, 32, 20, and 18; to the right to abortion, 34, 23, 16, and 28; and to more assistance for the poor, 56, 37, 5, and 2.

14. The gammas for the relationships between the index of social program support (created by adding up "very important" responses to each of the three specific policy questions) and each of the following were hours volunteered per month, NS (not significant); gave at least twenty hours of time last month, NS; did fund-raising, NS; did a community service project, NS; gave money to a beggar, NS. General reasons for being kind: want to give of myself, .25; makes me a stronger person, .21; feel good about it, .29; pay my debts, .24; helps me get what I want, NS; specific reasons for volunteering, enjoyment, NS; felt compassion, .24; wanted to help, .28; explore my strengths, .12; previously benefited, NS; enhance résumé, NS. Benefits from volunteering: learned to be helpful, .28; became a better person, .20; good citizenship, .25; learned how voluntary organizations work, .21; career contacts, NS; job opportunities, NS; and leadership skills, NS.

Index